Anthony Burgess was born in Manchester in 1917. He graduated at the University of Manchester and after six years' service in the Army worked as an Instructor for the Central Advisory Council for Forces Education, as a lecturer in Phonetics and as a grammar school master. Between 1954 and 1960 he was stationed in Malaya and Brunei as an education officer in the Colonial Service. His first novel was published in 1956 and he became a full-time writer in 1960.

His interest in linguistics and music (he has composed works for orchestra and other media) have influenced his writing and criticism; among his books are *Inside Mr Enderby*, *Enderby Outside*, *Shakespeare*, *A Clockwork Orange*, *Nothing Like The Sun* and *The Malayan Trilogy*. His latest novel is *Napoleon Symphony*.

Anthony Burgess

Language
Made Plain
Revised Edition

Fontana/Collins

First published in 1964 by the English Universities
Press Ltd.
Revised edition first published in Fontana 1975
Copyright © Anthony Burgess 1964, 1975

Printed in Great Britain for William Collins Sons
and Co Ltd Glasgow by
Richard Clay (The Chaucer Press) Ltd, Bungay,
Suffolk

To Liana

Preface to the Second Edition

Over ten years have gone by since I wrote this book, and the world of language study has changed, as has the bigger world that encloses it. Names like Khrushchev, John F. Kennedy, Lyndon Johnson had a more than historical meaning in 1963. Where these appeared in the text, as 'topical' names to be analysed phonemically or transliterated, they for the most part appear no more, though Khrushchev is too phonemically interesting a name to discard. In Great Britain there has been a change in coinage, as also of television series, and I have accordingly made appropriate adjustments.

In universities the study of language had developed at a great rate. Transformational grammar had hardly been heard of when I drafted this book, and Chomsky was no celebrity. I have written a new and very elementary chapter on Saussure, the Prague School, and Chomsky himself, but I have not attempted to reorientate the section on phonetics, though I know that many teachers would now prefer the approach of phonemic opposition – defining a speech-sound, that is, in terms of a differential duality. My chief aim is unchanged – to persuade the ordinary reader to be interested in those aspects of language which are closest to his own needs, especially the need of finding a painless way into the learning of foreign tongues.

I am persuaded, chiefly by correspondents and meetings with college students both in the United Kingdom and the United States, that the book has been useful on the elementary level I have always had in mind. Scholars have grumbled about rash generalisations and, I think, a classroom tone of excessive breeziness. But two notable scholars did me the honour of ending their two-volume historical survey of non-scientific writing about English with the chapter I entitle *Words*. Caxton as the beginning, Burgess at the end.

I have corrected all the errors I could find. Some derived from my own carelessness or stupidity, and I do not doubt that there are still traces of these not totally liquidable human qualities. As a writer grows older he becomes more and more nauseated at the lengthening trail of tastelessness and dumbness he leaves behind him. Fortunately I have been able to do something with this book: with my twenty-nine other books I have to leave things as they are. *É peccato.*

Rome, 1975   A. B.

Preface to the First Edition

This is an introduction to the study of language and of languages. It is intended for anyone who is interested in finding out something of the mechanics and psychology of the most basic of all social functions, but my own (sometimes warring) twin vocations led me to conceive of two special kinds of audience. I am a professional novelist and critic – by which I mean that I make my living by writing works of fiction and writing about works of fiction – and so my trade is with words. I have a feeling that many other people whose trade is with words are not sufficiently concerned with finding out what words are. They are happy to join words together but not, in my view, interested in analysing their sounds, forms, and meanings. I want to try to stimulate an interest in the basic elements of which literature is made.

I address myself also, as a former teacher (both in England and abroad), to teachers of languages who feel that every pupil, in whatever kind of post-primary school, should have some basic awareness of the total linguistic process and not just a knowledge of particular languages. Indeed, I feel that no student can ever gain an intelligent knowledge of his own language, or of an imposed or elected foreign one, without knowing something of the way in which language in general works. I believe that many teachers agree with me. The second part of this book attempts to relate the learning of particular languages to the general linguistic theory that is outlined in the first part.

In many ways, this book is a primer for amateurs by an amateur. It does not dig deep, and it is far from scholarly But it does contain the essentials, the irreducible minimum of information about language which any person who writes, reads, listens to the radio, or watches television needs to possess. We are told nowadays that, whatever our specialisation, we cannot regard ourselves as literate unless we know something of atomic physics, power politics, jurisprudence, communications, and public economics and finance. But before all these comes society, and before society comes language.

This book attempts to be objective, sceptical even, but a certain social bias is implied. The world is shrinking, supra-national communities are being painfully forged, we are all travelling more. We need to know the most efficient ways of learning other people's languages. In another sphere, we are being set upon by the most deadly propaganda machines the world has ever known, made to submit to all kinds of linguistic pressures. Let us at least try to understand what is going on.

A. B.

Contents

PART ONE
Language in General

Chapter 1

Signals in the Dark

1

Words (their meaning, spelling, pronunciation); the way foreigners talk (foreigners being everybody except us) – these frequently arouse strong feelings but very rarely much curiosity. Language tends to generate heat rather than a desire for light; the very word can be an accusation (Mr Waldo, in Dylan Thomas's *Under Milk Wood*, is guilty of, among other crimes, 'using language'). The correspondence columns of daily newspapers carry periodic wrangles about niceties of English usage, often ill-informed, sometimes fatuous. The country was once divided over the plural of 'mongoose'. I have seen grown men fighting with broken bottles (VJ Day in Gibraltar) over whether 'donkey' meant the same things as 'ass'. In the days when British currency possessed an eighth part of a pound, I knew a family which split over the correct verbal rendering of 2*s* 6*d*. Some said it was two and sixpence, others that it was half a crown. One man who said it could be both was shunned by both factions. In quarrels about words, people seem unwilling to see reason. Mercury, the rogue-god who presides over language, renders them blind to dictionaries and to experts. There is a general conviction that language is not a matter for experts. We all know all about language because we all use language. No similar conclusion is drawn from the fact that we all use kidneys, nerves, and intestines.

A language is a system of communication used within a particular social group. Inevitably, the emotions created by group loyalty get in the way of objective judgements about language. When we think we are making such a judgement, we are often merely making a statement about our prejudices. It is highly instructive to examine these occasionally. I myself have very powerful prejudices about what I call Americanisms. I see red whenever I read a certain popular woman columnist in a certain popular daily paper. I wait with a kind of fascinated horror for

her to use the locution 'I guess', as in 'I guess he really loves you
after all' or 'I guess you'd better get yourself a new boy-friend'.
I see in this form the essence of Americanism, a threat to the
British Way of Life. But this is obviously nonsense, and I know it.
I know that 'I guess' is at least as old as Chaucer, pure British
English, something sent over in the *Mayflower*. But, like most of
us, I do not really like submitting to reason; I much prefer blind
prejudice. And so I stoutly condemn 'I guess' as an American
importation and its use by a British writer as a betrayal of the
traditions of my national group.

Such condemnation can seem virtuous, because patriotism –
which means loyalty to the national group – is a noble word.
While virtue burns in the mind, adrenalin courses round the
body and makes us feel good. Reason never has this exhilarating
chemical effect. And so patriotic euphoria justifies our contempt
of foreign languages and makes us unwilling to learn them
properly. Chinese is still regarded in the West as a huge joke –
despite what T. S. Eliot calls its 'great intellectual dignity' – and
radio comedians can even raise a snigger by speaking mock-
Chinese of the 'Hoo Flung Dung' variety. Russian is, of course,
nothing more than a deep vodka-rich rumble bristling with
'vitch' and 'ski'. As for German – that is an ugly language,
aggressively guttural. We rarely admit that it seems ugly because
of two painful wars, that it is all a matter of association. Sometimes our automatic sneers at foreign languages are mitigated by
pleasant memories – warm holidays abroad, trips to the opera.
Italian can then seem beautiful, full of blue skies, *vino*, sexy
tenors. Trippers to Paris, on the other hand, furtively visiting the
Folies Bergère, project their own guilt on to the French language
and see it as 'naughty', even 'immoral'.

Within the national group, our prejudices tend to be very
mixed and, because they operate mainly on an unconscious level,
not easily recognizable. We can be natives of great cities and still
find a town dialect less pleasant than a country one. And yet,
hearing prettiness and quaintness in a Dorset or Devon twang, we
can also despise it, because we associate it with rural stupidity or
backwardness. The ugly tones of Manchester or Birmingham will,
because of their great civic associations, be at the same time somehow admirable. The whole business of ugliness and beauty works
strangely. A BBC announcer says 'pay day'; a Cockney says 'pie
die'. The former is thought to be beautiful, the latter ugly, and

yet the announcer can use the Cockney sounds in a statement like 'Eat that pie and you die' without anybody's face turning sour. In fact, terms like 'ugly' and 'beautiful' cannot really apply to languages at all. Poets can make beautiful patterns out of words, but there are no standards we can use to formulate aesthetic judgements on the words themselves. We all have our pet hates and loves among words, but these always have to be referred to associations. A person who dislikes beetroot as a vegetable is not likely to love 'beetroot' as a word. A poet who, in childhood, had a panful of hot stewed prunes spilled on him is, if he is a rather stupid poet, quite capable of writing 'And death, terrible as prunes'. We have to watch associations carefully, remembering that language is a public, not a private, medium, and that questions of word-hatred and word-love had best be tackled very coldly and rationally.

We are normally quick to observe regional variations in the use of the national language, but we feel less strongly about these than we do about class divisions in speech. If we speak with a Lancashire accent,[1] we will often be good-humoured and only slightly derisive when we hear the accent of Wolverhampton or Tyneside. Sometimes we will even express a strong admiration of alien forms of English – the speech of the Scottish Highlands, for instance, or Canadian as opposed to American. But we feel very differently about English speech when it seems to be a badge or banner of class. The dialect known variously as the Queen's English or BBC English or Standard English was, originally, a pure regional form – so-called East Midland English, with no claim to any special intrinsic merit. But it was spoken in an area that was, and still is, socially and economically pre-eminent – the area which contains London, Oxford, and Cambridge. Thus it gained a special glamour as the language of the Court and the language of learning. It has ever since – often falsely – been associated with wealth, position, and education – the supra-regional dialect of the masters, while the regional dialects remain the property of the men. In certain industrial areas it can still excite resentment, despite the fact that it no longer necessarily goes along with power or privilege. Out-of-work actors can speak it, so can underpaid schoolmasters; tycoons, proud of their rise to the top from humble origins, will

[1] An *accent* is a set of sounds peculiar to a region, as opposed to a *dialect*, which covers, in addition to peculiarities of sound, peculiarities of grammar and vocabulary.

often cling to their under-privileged mother-dialect, or a slight modification of it. It is difficult for many inhabitants of a class-ridden country like Great Britain to see virtue in Standard English or even to accept that it is possible to learn it, as one learns any foreign language. Its virtue lies in its neutrality, its lack of purely local associations, its transparency, its suitability for intellectual discourses or dispassionate Government pronouncements. It is cold, tending to wit rather than humour, the airy as opposed to the earthy.

There is room for regional dialects and room for the Queen's English. The place for the regional dialect is the region in which it was born; it is right for the public bar, the football field, the village dance. Queen's English is for the BBC talk on Existentialism, the cocktail party, the interview for a better job. What is dangerous is the tendency among 'natural' speakers of the Queen's English (those brought up on it from the cradle) to despise those who cannot or will not speak it themselves. The reason for this contempt is clear. The man or woman who is limited to regional speech appears to lack experience of the great world – smart restaurants, art galleries, concerts, polite talk. We are always ready to look down on people: it is an abiding pleasure, a poultice for our own sore sense of inferiority. We must think of the supra-regional advantages of the Queen's English – its universal intelligibility, its neutrality – rather than its class associations.

Snobbishness as regards speech appears when least expected, often disguised as something quite different. To return to my popular daily newspaper (which I read with the same painful pleasure as I find in the probing of a bad tooth) – this consistently uses the term 'mum' in its articles and news-items; not 'mum' meaning 'silent' but 'mum' meaning 'mother'. I dislike the word intensely, though reason tells me that, as it is a short word, it is useful for headlines (compare 'wed' for 'marry' and 'bid' for 'attempt'). Also, it is a term full of warm human connotations, highly suitable for a journal that prides itself on its warm human appeal. Yet I experience considerable revulsion when I read the following: 'PRINCESS MARGARET TO BE A MUM' or 'MUM SEES BABY DROWN'. I try to justify this feeling by saying that 'mother' is full of associations of great dignity, while 'mum' is limited and vulgar. Yet I doubt if this explanation is really valid. The revulsion is too violent. I suspect the great demon of snobbishness; a diabolic voice whispers: 'This is a working-class word. It reeks of the clothes-horse in the kitchen, bread-and-dripping by the fire. Despise it.'

Before we can study language scientifically we must strangle our group prejudices; we must explode a great number of hoary fallacies, themselves derived from emotional attitudes. As no language is either beautiful or ugly, so no language is intrinsically either superior or inferior to another. The fact that English has become a world auxiliary is no evidence that it is a *better* language than Basque or Finnish; its spread is the result of an historical accident which is based on a fact of geography. Languages are developed in social groups, and each group develops the language it needs. If certain primitive jungle folk have no word for 'snow' and cannot count beyond two (sometimes we can't ourselves: *uni*lateral, *bi*lateral, *multi*lateral), they are not in the least inconvenienced: they have what they want; when they want more they will get it. And, while it is perhaps just to hold a concept of 'primitive communities', it is probably dangerous to talk about 'primitive languages'. In point of richness of grammar and luxuriance of vocabulary, the languages of certain 'backward' peoples like the Eskimos are highly sophisticated.

No man, however learned or powerful, can exert control over a language, despite the 'Newspeak' of George Orwell's *Nineteen Eighty-Four*. Languages change, and we cannot stop them from changing nor, once we are reconciled to their changing, can we determine the modes in which they shall change. It is not even possible to legislate for a language, to say what is right and what is wrong. If it is wrong to say 'you was', then the educated men of the eighteenth century were wrong. If sluts drop their aitches, then Queen Elizabeth I was a slut. What we regard as errors are often merely survivals from an earlier form of the language. And so with seemingly eccentric usages. Characters in William Faulkner's novels of the American South say 'hit' for 'it'; Lancashire dialect speakers say 'it' for 'its' (so did Shakespeare: 'Come to it grandam and it grandam shall give it a plum'). These are good Anglo-Saxon. They may not be in use in Standard English, but it is hard to see how they can be 'wrong'.

And so we must avoid making quick judgements, laying down the law, nursing prejudices, sneering, waving jingoistic flags, bringing a spirit of petty parochialism to the great world of human language. Languages are made by the people for the people, and people must use language as their needs dictate. No academy has the monopoly of 'correctness'; no dictator knows best. If we want to understand the phenomenon of language – and it is an astonishing one – we must approach it in humility, letting what-should-be wait upon what-is.

Our ignorance about the fundamentals of language is not solely derived from wilful prejudice, natural inertia, or national apathy. Most of our school teaching of language is amateurish and incompetent: many a sixth-form boy can read Racine with ease but have difficulty in asking a gendarme the way to the Metro. Foreign tongues are taught after a fashion, but language itself – its nature, function, psychology, physiology, history – totally neglected. Our English grammar books are shamefully out-of-date: inaccuracies of definition and ineptitudes of terminology are perpetuated; pointless exercises are set; nobody seems to care to look for the true facts of English structure. Our teaching of foreign pronunciation is a farce. More than all this, the tyranny of the printed or written word prevails. We still tend to think that language is more significant when it is seen than when it is heard. We forget that language is primarily sounds, and that sounds existed long before visual signs were invented.

Thus, many people still believe that there are only five vowel sounds because there are only five vowel letters. Some teachers are convinced that 'Austrian armies awfully arrayed' shows an analogous phonetic pattern to 'Boldly by batteries besieged Belgrade'. The gimmick-form 'Rock 'n' Roll' is considered perverse when it is merely phonetic. A writer as sensitive to sound as J. B. Priestley can describe the speech peculiarity of one of his characters (in *Angel Pavement*) as follows: 'He softened all the sibilants, putting an "h" behind every "s".' Ivor Brown writes about 'Shakespeare's instinctive feeling for the letter "r"'; time and time again he was to play on its emotional vibration, especially when linked with the letter "o".' Later he speaks of the 'letter's potency'. This is pure Egyptian superstition. The unwitting high priest of this cult of 'letters' was Arthur Rimbaud, who wrote a famous sonnet on the Vowels; but Rimbaud was really concerned with the significance of the vowel letters in alchemy, not in language at all.

One feels strongly that practitioners of literature should at least show an interest in the raw material of their art. Very few do. That awareness of the nature of sound which opens Nabokov's *Lolita* is something rare in modern fiction: 'Lolita, light of my life, fire of my loins. My sin, my soul. Lo-lee-ta: the tip of the tongue making a trip of three steps down the palate to tap, at three, on the teeth. Lo. Lee. Ta.' Nabokov recognizes that the two 'l's of the name are different. It is no accident that this analytic acuteness of ear should be found in one of the most subtle and musical prose-writers of our time.

As the world shrinks and the need for every educated man and woman to know foreign languages grows more urgent, we have to devise techniques for learning them quickly and accurately. Our best beginning is an examination of the nature of language itself. There is no reason why this should be regarded as an expert study: we need no special equipment; a laboratory is set on our shoulders. Apart from the utility of such a study, there should be in everyone a natural curiosity about the most fundamental of all social activities, a curiosity which our systems of education have done nothing to foster and everything to dull. It would be too much to say that all this is a matter of life and death; but a verse from the Book of Judges indicates that occasionally it can be. Let this stand as our epigraph:

'Then said they unto him, Say now Shibboleth: and he said Sibboleth: for he could not frame to pronounce it right. Then they took him, and slew him at the passages of Jordan.'

2

No society, whether human or animal, can exist without communication. Thoughts, desires, appetites, orders – these have to be conveyed from one brain to another, and they can rarely be conveyed directly. Only with telepathy do we find mind speaking straight to mind, without the intermediacy of signs, and this technique is still strange enough to seem a music-hall trick or a property of science fiction. The vast majority of sentient beings – men, women, cats, dogs, bees, horses – have to rely on signals, symbols of what we think and feel and want, and these signals can assume a vast variety of forms. There is, indeed, hardly any limit to the material devices we can use to express what is in our minds: we can wave our hands, screw up our faces, shrug our shoulders, write poems, write on walls, carve signs out of stone or wood, mould signs with clay or butter, scrawl sky-signs with an aircraft, semaphore, heliograph, telephone, run a pirate radio transmitter, stick pins in dolls. A dog will scratch at a door if it wants to be let in; a cat will mew for milk; a hostess will ring a bell for the course to be changed; a pub-customer will rap with a coin for service; a wolf will whistle; the people in the flat upstairs will bang with a stick if our party is too noisy. One can fill pages with such examples, bringing in the language of flowers and the signalling devices of honey-bees, but one will always end up with human speech as the most subtle, comprehensive, and exact system of communication we possess.

And yet even this, which seems self-evident, will be questioned by experts in other fields of communication. The musical composer will contend that his art can go deeper and wider than words. We are moved by music in ways that words cannot describe, and such emotion can drive us to action – war, murder, love, religion. There is obviously a sort of communication in music which digs down to unconscious levels of the mind, hardly as yet understood, and this special communication of art is one of man's most incredible activities. We cannot deny the width of appeal that music possesses: the man in Stoke-on-Trent may not be able to read Pushkin, but Tchaikovsky can move him to tears; Benjamin Britten speaks louder than W. H. Auden. But speech has a more general usefulness, and art – whether it be music, poetry, painting, drama, or ballet – makes up only a small part of the total life of a society. Without speech, and the various notations of speech, human society would not be possible at all.

Having lauded one sign-system in particular, let us return to signs in general. These can take two main forms which, as with most opposed things, can shade gently into each other: they can be *conventional* or they can be *iconic*. 'Iconic' derives from the Greek word for an image, and it is supposed that most primitive human signs try to present a universally recognisable image of the thought or desire which the signaller wishes to communicate. Thus, if we are in a foreign country and cannot speak the language, we can show hunger by going through the motions of putting something into our mouths and then pretending to chew. This is iconic. The phrase 'I'm hungry' is only understood by those who know English: a convention long established is that these sounds stand for this particular human need, and the convention has to be specially learned. An intelligent cat, like the Siamese I once had, will show that it wants milk by licking an empty saucer. This seems to be a piece of iconic signalling: the sign is an image of the fulfilment of a need. What can we say of the sign often used in ballet or mime to indicate love – the hands over the heart? Is this conventional or iconic? In a sense it over-laps both categories, for, though we no longer believe that the heart as a physical organ is the seat of love, yet we accept for the moment that the old crude anatomy of the passions is correct: within a conventional acceptance the sign then becomes iconic. And so with the transfixed heart of the Valentine. But if choreo-graphers decide between themselves that a slap on the thigh shall indicate love, then that is a purely arbitrary symbol, a pure piece of conventional signalling.

The conventional and the iconic appear in all the arts, though the terms 'representational' and 'non-representational' are better known. Painting and sculpture are expected to be iconic: we are disappointed if we do not get, in however distorted a manner, a recognisable image of a person or thing. Music is nearly always a language of conventional signs (whose 'meaning' perhaps only the unconscious mind can recognize), but with composers like Richard Strauss there is a strong iconic urge. In Strauss's symphonic poem *Don Quixote* we can hear horns imitating the bleating of sheep; a wind machine gives us pure wind. The same instrument appears in Vaughan Williams's *Sinfonia Antartica* to represent the howling of Antarctic gales. This kind of iconic composing is rare and it is frequently condemned for its alleged crudity, but no composer faced with setting the words 'He ascended into Heaven' is likely to make his vocal line move downwards.

Human speech is essentially a system of conventional signs, though theorists like Max Müller once held that all language sprang out of a desire to imitate natural phenomena (this was called the 'Bow-wow' theory). There are, in all languages, many words which attempt an image of the things they represent, just as the child's word 'quack-quack', meaning 'duck', is an image of the duck's characteristic noise. 'Splash' sounds like water, 'frou-frou' sounds like the rustle of skirts. 'Pop' is right for the bursting of a balloon, and 'boom', however feebly, suggests a bomb going off. Even with purely visual images, it is possible to find a certain appositeness in the forms of words, though often only the linguist can explain the appositeness. Take 'moon', for instance. Latin and its derivatives, as well as Russian, have a *lun*-form, and Malay has *bulan*. It is the u-sound which is descriptive: the lips have to imitate a moon-shape in order to give the right quality to the tongue-sound; the back of the tongue is raised high, very close to the palate (which Malay, incidentally, calls the 'sky' of the mouth), and this seems to suggest that the moon is something high up. A word like 'little' seems apt, for the i-sound is made by narrowing the passage between the front of the tongue and the palate, suggesting that only something very little could creep through. To give the impression of even greater littleness, the form 'leetle' is sometimes roguishly used: the ee-sound is even higher than the i-sound, making the space between tongue and palate only big enough for something microscopic to crawl through; with 'teeny-weeny' we are on the borders of invisibility.

But this class of iconic words is so small as to be virtually negligible. In any case, some very important words – the structural words like 'of', 'if', 'when', 'so' – can never have had a corresponding image in the outside world. Language is arbitrary, conventional, and has been so from the beginning; only the poet can invent a Golden Age of iconic language. The device of onomatopoeia – sound imitating sense – is beloved of lyric poets like Keats ('The murmurous haunt of flies on summer eves') and Tennyson ('The moan of doves in immemorial elms'), but there are severe limits to what it can do. It is what it *tries* to do that is important, and 'conventional language striving to be iconic' might be added to the already innumerable definitions of poetry.

But one cannot doubt that the earliest attempts to represent words by visual signs were iconic. Chinese symbols still show, in varying degrees of clarity, ancient attempts to *draw* the referent of the word (that is, the thing in the outside world which the word represents), and, when this direct representation failed, to use metaphor for rendering the abstract concrete. And so with Egyptian picture-writing, which is full of recognisable lions, gods, snakes, birds, water-pots. Our own alphabet (as we shall see in a later chapter) is ultimately derived from hieroglyphics, but all picture elements have long disappeared: the essence of the alphabetic method is its conventionality. Only in the letter O, which seems to come from an Egyptian drawing of an eye, do we find anything approaching an iconic purpose: the letter represents the shape of the mouth when pronouncing the o-sound; here is the 'moon' business in reverse.

An alphabet is a series of signs representing signs. The sounds I make when saying 'man' stand for something in the outside world; the letters which make up MAN stand for those sounds.

Thus, with a visual system of representation, we are two removes from reality. We are three removes from reality when we use a system like Braille or Morse: the dots and dashes or embossed symbols stand for alphabetic letters; the alphabetic letters stand for sounds; the sounds stand for what exists in the mind or in the outside world. It is as well to stay as close to reality as possible; that is why the study of language is a study of sounds and what sounds can do.

3

Why and how and when did man start using those sounds which we call human language? We can only guess. The Garden-of-Eden picture of Adam solemnly and deliberately naming everything is misleading: it assumes, like the myth of Genesis itself, a sudden act of creation after an infinite silence. Primitive man may have communicated with visual signs before he developed into a talker, but there is no reason to suppose that his meaningful movements of hands, face, and body were accompanied by silence; he was probably very far from being a mere dumb gesticulator, a sort of silent Tarzan film. I imagine early human society as full of noise – babblings and lallings and gurglings, diversified with grunts and howls – though such noise might be a mere by-product of tongue and lip movements corresponding to the movements of bodily gesture. It is helpful to think of the present relationship of speech and gesture in reverse. We all use nods, shrugs, arm-movements, smiles, frowns, to help out speech; perhaps primitive man used sound to help out gesture. When sound became genuine speech it had probably already shown its potential usefulness through the pleasure-principle: speech is pleasant in itself, as children know; the exercise of the vocal organs can give delight without expressing meaning. Speech might also be an invaluable means of establishing and maintaining social contact in the event of the speaker being cut off from his fellows. Bodily gesture has a very limited visual range: trees, stones, whole forests, whole hills may get in the way of it; darkness will render it quite useless. Speech is magical: it is powerful though invisible; it is light in darkness.

Let us examine these two espects of speech – speech as a medium of pleasure; speech as a medium of contact when tactile or visual signals cannot operate. The first – the sheer joy or even elation in the use of speech – is not merely a cradle pleasure to be outgrown; it is the basis of song and poetry. Most literary artists are tempted sometimes to concentrate on word-pattern for its own sake rather than word-pattern as a signal of meaning. The words of a poem come first; the meaning later, even not at all. 'Take care of the sounds, and the sense will take care of itself.' Surrealism has a fair ancestry. The nonsense-poem, the hey-nonny-no lyric, the pleasures of double-talk, the delight in strange or invented words: condemnation of these by no-nonsense, say-what-you-mean-sir Gradgrinds misses one very important, though non-utilitarian, point about language. All art springs from delight in raw material; to play with the raw material of literature is a natural pleasure linking us with a remote era that had speech but no language, but was perhaps finding language through delight in speech.

The second aspect of speech is social rather than aesthetic, though it also has little to do with 'meaning' as we understand that term. Speech is still a means of establishing or maintaining contact with other members of society; it serves the pure social instinct of wanting to feel oneself part of a group. Malinowski, the anthropologist, used the term *phatic communion* to describe this kind of speech activity. (The Greek root of 'phatic' means 'show; indicate'.) Talk about the weather rarely indicates much real interest in the weather: it is just something to say, a means of making contact of showing friendliness. Phrases like 'Roll on Death, and let's have a go at the angels', 'Never mind, lads, it'll soon be Christmas', 'Put another pea in the pot and hang the expense', 'Ah, well, as one door shuts another door closes' – these may seem pointless, feeble, silly, but, as any serviceman knows, they are the warm and comfortable stuff of human companionship. (Incidentally, they belong to strong-rooted regional speech more than to deracinated Standard English.) Speech to promote human warmth: that is as good a definition as any of the phatic aspect of language. For good or ill, we are social creatures and cannot bear to be cut off too long from our fellows, even if we have nothing really to say to them. We can feel strongly for primitive man in the dark; for all our science, we have not really overcome our fear of it or, when human contact is lost, our sense of devastating loneliness in it. If we are walking, late and alone, on a dark country road, and we hear another human being approaching, we are instinctively drawn to the uttering of a few friendly meaningless words. Primitive man, separated from his fellows in the big incomprehensible blackness, must have chattered incessantly to keep contact alive.

Phatic communion, like pleasure in language for its own sake, has a great deal to do with the making of literature (which, after all, may be regarded primarily as a non-informative medium of human contact). The babbling and bubbling of Elizabethan stage-clowns goes along with the puns and the Euphuisms; the garrulousness of pamphleteers like Nashe and Greene is more phatic than meaningful. The products of our Golden Age of literature seem the natural expression of life in a small, warm, compact, very human society – that of Shakespeare's London. What was once the heart of culture no longer produces culture; it merely markets it. It is a huge depersonalised abstraction, no longer a society at all. Literature, as cities grow, becomes increasingly an expression of loneliness and exile – a cry in the dark, whistling in the dark.

Out of the babbling and chattering of primitive man, something like language as we know it was eventually to crystallise. We tend to think of the making of language as deliberately architectural – blueprint grammar, a dictionary-load of bricks. This is partly because of the Genesis myth and partly because of the way in which we learn foreign languages: we start off with a silence, then we try to fill the silence by learning words. We think, in fact, of the conscious creation of a structure out of verbal atoms: our unit is the smallest possible verbal form. But the unit of primitive man would be much more like a phrase, a clause, a total statement. He would learn to associate a segment of the flow of speech with a particular experience to be described or expressed. When we see a sunrise, we instinctively analyse into particles: sun, east, sky, red, gold, rising. Primitive man would see the process as a single experience, indivisible. The analytical faculty comes very late in the evolution of mankind. The isolation of the word, the breaking down of language into the stuff of grammars and dictionaries, belongs to the last few centuries. The Romans are, comparatively speaking, our near neighbours in time, but they lacked the analytical equipment to dissect their language as Hillard and Botting and Kennedy have dissected it. Before the stoic grammarians invented the classificatory system on which our own is based, they had to accept the complex of Latin as it was.

Primitive language, then, must not be thought of as a sort of pidgin – 'him house belong me' – with words like painful little barks all separated out. 'They will be loved' is the English for the Latin *amabuntur*. The English way (and English is a progressive, self-simplifying language) is to analyse a complex experience into irreducible particles: four words to the one of the Latin. Old Western languages – like Greek and Latin – are *synthetic*: they build up long words and do everything with inflexions or endings. We all remember *mensa, mensa, mensam, mensae, mensae, mensa* – the various inflexions of the singular form of the Latin word for a table. Modern languages tend to be *analytic*. We have an unchanging singular form 'table', and we express relationships by means of additional words: 'to a table', 'with a table', and so on. The oldest languages of all must have been highly synthetic – verb-forms and noun-forms of great length.

We have seen that language satisfies man in two ways – it can be pleasant in itself; it can be a device for social contact. But we would all accept that the really important purpose of language – the *use* of language – is to convey wishes, thoughts, and feelings from one person to another, or from a person to a group, or from a group to a person, or from a group to a group. Our highly complex modern societies depend on the precise functioning of such communication. But, as science and technology develop, it becomes more and more evident that language is not precise enough. Mathematicians and engineers rely on signals capable of cold, single, unambiguous meanings; words tend to ambiguity and vagueness – in every serious discussion much time has to be spent in re-defining common terms like 'love', 'justice', 'freedom'. Language has, in fact, many of the qualities possessed by human beings themselves – it tends to be emotional when pure reason is required, it tends to be unsure of what it means, it tends to change form, meaning, and pronunciation. It is slippery, elusive, hard to fix, define, delimit.

So, when we talk about a language – English, French, Russian, Sanskrit – we refer to a process rather than to a thing. English consists of its future as well as its past and present, and when we discuss any English word we are talking of things not yet known. A language consists of potentialities whose nature we can only guess at, though its genetic qualities help to determine its development. But, if we try to grasp the flow of the language at that nonexistent point called 'now', we are still in the dark as to its boundaries, and we cannot be sure of its content. How many words are there in English? We cannot say. It is not enough to

point to the number of words in a dictionary, because no dictionary – however large – can pretend to be complete, nor can a
dictionary take in all the various derivatives of a word. Fresh
words are being made every day; borrowing from other languages
goes on incessantly. If, in my own home, my family uses invented
words like *shlerp*, *focklepoff*, and *arpworthy*, we are entitled to
regard these as part of English (they certainly belong to no other
language, and yet they are recognisable linguistic forms) just as
chortle, *brillig*, and *abnihilise* belong to English. It is best to
regard the language as a growing corpus of words and structures
which nobody can know entirely but upon which anybody can
draw at any time – a sort of unlimited bank account. It is not
just the sum total of what has been spoken and written; it is also
what *can* be spoken and written. It is actual and potential. In
another sense, it is a code, always ready for individual acts of
encoding.

The difficulty in linguistic study is a difficulty of balance. We
have the language itself; we have the *idiolect*, or sum-total of any
one person's linguistic actions and linguistic potential; we have
the single speech-act. The general pulls one way and the particular
another; the potential and the actual are hard to juggle with;
language is seen as a warm and living thing and also as an
abstraction. We must keep our heads, remembering W. B. Yeats's
words: 'I made it out of a mouthful of air.' He was referring to the
creation of a poem; we refer to language, in which an infinitude
of poems awaits realisation. Let us forget our big words and vast
potentials and start with a mouthful of air.

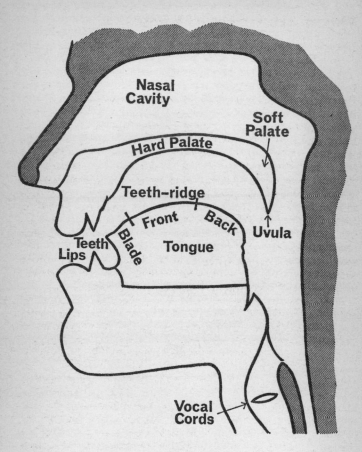

THE ORGANS OF SPEECH

Chapter 2

The Instruments of Speech

1

Phonetics, 'the science of speech,' was glamourised in Shaw's *Pygmalion,* and was later super-glamourised by Lerner and Loew in *My Fair Lady.* Since Professor Higgins, phoneticians have seemed the most human of all scientists, and their weird way of writing down sounds ('That ain't proper writing,' says Eliza Doolittle) more intriguing than forbidding. But, since Shaw wrote the play which was designed to show what important people speech-specialists are, Phonetics has become more than a matter of wandering streets with a notebook: it has drawn on the helper-sciences of electronics and statistics and erected massive laboratories. In this chapter, and the two that follow, we shall nevertheless content ourselves with the laboratory that our speech-mechanism provides, 'a mouthful of air', and a few special phonetic symbols. Our purpose is, after all, a very humble one: we merely want to understand the *elements* of speech.

Before we go any further, we have to distinguish two separate kinds of speech-study. The first is *Phonetics,* which examines speech-sounds without direct reference to how these are used in language. It is interested in the mechanics and acoustics of speech, and it rejoices in the endless variety of sounds that are possible to the human mouth. The other study is called *Phonology,* or *Phonemics,* and it relates speech-sounds directly to their linguistic function. Let us make all this clear with an example. Pronounce the words 'cool', 'kill', and 'keel'. You would agree, I think, that they all begin with a k-sound. (Ignore the spelling. If we have 'k' before 'o', 'u', or 'a', we represent the k-sound with a 'c'. This is a mere spelling convention.) Pronounce the words again; pronounce them several times. You will discover that the three k-sounds are not exactly alike. They are all recognisably k-sounds, but for 'cool' the k-sound is made a little further back in the mouth than for the k-sounds of the other two words. And the k-sound in 'keel' is a little nearer the teeth than is the k-sound in 'kill'. It seems, then, that there is a general class of k-sound and that this can be divided into species. The general class, the k-family, is called a *phoneme*, and the types of k-sound within the family are called *allophones*. Experiment with other groups of words, like 'tar', 'ten', and 'tea', and you will find the same principle applying. The three t-sounds are different from each other, but they all belong to the same t-family: they are allophones of the t-phoneme.

The phonologist, the man who is concerned with phonemes, is not greatly concerned with the sub-division of the phoneme into allophones. To him, the phoneme is the speech-unit. He knows that it is not possible to pronounce the k-sound of 'cool' in 'kill' or 'keel'; he knows that if we pronounce the l-sound at the end of 'cool' in place of the l-sound at the beginning of 'look' we are not going to alter the meaning of the word. The two l-sounds are different, as you can verify for yourself: they are allophones of the l-phoneme. But the difference is not a significant one: it makes no *semantic* alteration ('semantic' is the word we use when we are talking about 'meaning') in the utterance. But to the phonetician, these divisions of the phoneme are of great interest: the atomisation of 'k' or 'l' or 't' into its allophonic constituents is the primal joy of the phonetician. Every single possible human sound falls within his province; his primary concern is not the linguistic function – the 'meaning' – of these sounds.

In studying speech-sounds either phonetically or phonologically, we have to equip ourselves with a precise means of notating them: we need a special alphabet, though the phonetician needs a bigger one (one with more letters) than the phonologist. The need for a special alphabet is made clear when we consider the limitations of our ordinary everyday one – the alphabet which is capable of using the same letter for the different o-sounds of 'not', 'note', 'woman', and 'women'. The difficulties we would encounter if we had to rely on the ordinary Roman alphabet for a study of the English vowel-sounds are best seen in the following sentence. This contains all the English vowel-sounds. Pronounce it in a mechanical, zombie-like way, giving every word the same importance, the same stress. For 'AND', though, use the slack sound used for the apostrophe before the 'n' in 'Rock 'n' Roll'.

WHO WOULD KNOW AUGHT OF ART MUST LEARN, ACT, AND
 1   2   3   4   5 6   7   8   9 10

THEN TAKE HIS EASE.
11 12 13 14

Isolate the vowel-sounds, and we have the following:

O	OU	OW	AU	O	A	U	EA	A	A	E	A-E	I	EA
1	2	3	4	5	6	7	8	9	10	11	12	13	14

This is at once seen to be hopelessly inadequate. That is why we use the symbols of the International Phonetic Association (the International Phonetic Alphabet or IPA), which is accepted and understood wherever language scholars meet. Symbols of the IPA[1] will, in this book, be placed between oblique lines, so that the above vowel-sounds are notated as follows:

/uː/	/ʊ/	/oʊ/	/ɔː/	/ɒ/	/ɑː/	/ʌ/	/ɜː/	/æ/	/ə/
1	2	3	4	5	6	7	8	9	10

/ɛ/	/eɪ/	/ɪ/	/iː/
11	12	13	14

Note that Nos. 1, 4, 6, 8, 14 consist of a letter followed by a colon (ː). This colon indicates that the vowel-sound is long: it actually takes longer to pronounce No. 1 than No. 2, longer to pronounce No. 4 than No. 5. Note also that Nos. 3 and 12 do not consist of single letters but of two letters. These are *diphthongs* or double sounds: they represent a journey made by the tongue from the position for the first vowel towards the position for the second vowel. English is very rich in diphthongs:

FEAR	THE	POOR	OUTSIDE	THE	DOOR.	BEWARE	OF
1		2	3	4		5	6

POWER;	AVOID	DESIRE.
7	8	9

/ɪə/	/ʊə/	/aʊ/	/aɪ/	/ɔə/	/ɛə/
1	2	3	4	5	6

/aʊə/	/ɔɪ/	/aɪə/
7	8	9

Note that Nos. 7 and 9 of this group are *triphthongs* or three-fold sounds: the journey made by the tongue to encompass the diphthong /aɪ/ or /aʊ/ has an extra lap added, and this ends up in the middle of the mouth with the slack neutral vowel /ə/ (the

[1] The symbols used in this book belong to the *narrow* notational system of the International Phonetic Alphabet. For a comparison between this and the *broad* system, see Appendix One. The narrow system has more symbols and hence is more accurate than the broad.

vowel of the second syllable of 'father', 'mother', 'sister', 'brother'.).

There is no need to plunge into learning the symbols of the IPA. We shall meet them singly and without fuss in the course of our survey of speech-sounds. It is enough, for the moment, to recognise their usefulness.

2

We come now to the organs of speech. Speech-sounds are made out of out-breathed air. This air is moulded into different shapes, obstructed and then released, or allowed to escape to the outer atmosphere under pressure. In other words, the air from our lungs is modified by the various organs that lie in the throat and mouth. We can take it as a near-invariable rule that speech is made from out-breathed air, though certain African languages use an in-breathed ('imploded') sound – /m/ or /n/ – at the beginning of some words. In the name 'Mboya' we start off with an in-breathed /m/.

In the upper part of the windpipe lies the *larynx* (or Adam's apple), which contains and protects the *vocal cords*. The vocal cords resemble a pair of lips. Stretched across the larynx, from front to back, they are tough pieces of membrane capable of coming together and then separating again. The space between them is called the *glottis* (the Greek word for 'voice'), but it is really the cords themselves that constitute the voice. Air makes them vibrate, and this vibration is the rich musical sound we hear in song. The vibration of the vocal cords is not enough in itself to provide richness, any more than a violin string removed from the violin-body can give as much more than a thin screech. Voice requires resonators, like any musical instrument, and resonance is given by the chest, the throat, the mouth-cavity and nose-cavity, and the sinuses. These hollows of various sizes magnify the fundamental sound produced by the voice.

We can, then, bring the vocal cords together (it is a process we can learn to do consciously) in the same way that we can bring our lips together. The out-breathed air coming from the lungs forces its way through the two membranes and makes them vibrate. This vibration goes on when we pronounce a vowel-sound or when we articulate a consonant such as /b/, /d/, /m/, /z/. (These phonetic symbols have the same value as in the ordinary alphabet.) These sounds, made with the vocal cords brought together and vibrating away with the impact of air from the lungs, are called *voiced* sounds, that is, sounds made with the voice. There would not be much speech without the voice (for a start, there would be no vowels), and we have some notion of what it is like to have no voice when we are suffering from laryngitis. When the vocal cords are diseased and have to be removed, there are two ways of creating a substitute: one can learn to send up 'voiced' air from the stomach (this is true ventriloquism or 'belly-talk') or one can be equipped with an artificial larynx. But these medical aspects of speech really lie outside our province.

When the vocal cords are apart from each other – like parted lips – the air is allowed to come up through the windpipe without meeting any obstruction in the larynx. This gives us pure *breath*, which we hear in the English aspirate /h/. When we utter sounds like /p/, /t/, /k/, /f/, /s/, the vocal cords are wide apart, unvibrated by the air from the lungs, and we call these sounds *unvoiced* sounds. If one alternates sounds like /s/ and /z/ very rapidly, one is making the vocal cords open and shut athletically. You can tell the difference between an unvoiced sound and a voiced sound by covering your ears with your hands when you speak. If you can feel a vibration, then the sound is voiced. The vibration of the vocal cords has communicated itself to the bones of your head.

Another thing that the vocal cords can do is to come together tightly, presenting a shut double-door to the air that is clamouring to come up from below. This is known as *closed glottis*. When the vocal cords suddenly separate, the air – formerly compressed underneath – rushes out in an explosion of some violence. This effect is known as a *glottal stop* (really, of course, it is a stop followed by a release) and it is far more common in language than people realise. There is no letter for it in the ordinary Roman alphabet, and this blinds (or deafens) most of us to its existence. We can hear it in the Cockney 'Wha' a lo' of li'l bo'les' ('What a lot of little bottles') or in the Scotsman's 'Sa'urday'. The IPA represents it as a question mark without a dot, thus: /ʔ/.

The other vocal organs are visible in a mirror or even capable of being touched. Some are movable, as the vocal cords are; others stay still. Let us look at the movables first. Open your mouth to a mirror, and you will see a small fleshy organ hanging at the back: this is the *uvula* (Latin for 'little grape'). It is, as it were, a tail light attached to the *soft palate* or *velum*, and the soft palate is capable of moving down to meet the back of the tongue

or up away from it. It is a door connecting the mouth with the
nose cavity or *nasal pharynx*, and it determines whether the air
breathed out from the lungs shall escape by the mouth or by the
nostrils. If the soft palate moves up, then there is a space between
the uvula and the back of the tongue, and the air can come into
the mouth and then go out between the lips into the great world
outside. Most of the sounds we make are made with this mouth-
air. But if the soft palate moves down, so that it rests on the back
of the tongue, then the air cannot come into the mouth from the
windpipe: it meets a closed door. All it can do is to move into the
nose cavity or nasal pharynx, and then make its exit through the
nostrils. The sounds /m/, /n/, and /ŋ/ (the last sound is the 'ng' of
'sing') are made by allowing the air to come out via the nose (by
courtesy of the soft palate) and are hence called *nasal* sounds.
Vowels can be nasalised as well, and the French language has a
plentiful supply of nasalised vowels. In very casual English
speech nasalisation of a vowel takes the place of a following /n/.
I knew a man who habitually entered a pub with the one word
/pɑ̃ː/ . . . (The little sign called a *tilde* that appears over the /ɑː/
signifies nasalization.) This meant 'Pint'. Over the years this man
had simplified the word in the following stages: (1) /paɪnt/ (2)
/paɪn/ (3) /pɑ̃ɪ̃/ (4) /pɑ̃ː/. Children with adenoid growths – spongy
matter obstructing the passage of air into the nasal pharynx –
cannot pronounce nasal sounds and so are unable to say the
following very clearly: 'Do not be afraid, I am only the sandman,
and with my bag of golden sand I bring sleep to everyone.' What
we get instead is something like 'Do dot be afraid, I ab odly the
sadbad, ad with by bag of golded sad I brig sleep to everywud'.
When we have a bad cold – mucus clogging the nasal pharynx –
we have the same sort of difficulty. For some reason this is
popularly called 'speaking through one's nose', which is precisely
what it is not.

The most lively of the movable speech-organs is the tongue,
and, as we shall see, it is by far the most important of them all:
indeed 'tongue' is a synonym for 'language' in many languages or
tongues, and 'language' itself derives from the Latin word for a
tongue. We can, for convenience, divide this very meaty organ
into three parts – the *blade*, including the *tip*; the *front*; the *back*.
When the tongue is lying at rest, the blade is opposite the ridge
of the upper teeth, the front is opposite the hard palate (or roof
of the mouth), the back is opposite the soft palate. These three

parts of the tongue govern, as far as speech is concerned, these three corresponding parts of the mouth. The remaining movable organs are the lips, which are the first speech-instruments we learn to use as babies (apart, of course, from the vocal cords, which we make lusty use of as soon as we are born). Our first words are 'baba', 'papa', 'mama', all based on lip-sounds.

The fixed organs are the *hard palate*, that concave, rocky, rather ticklish, dome of the mouth; the *teeth*; the *teeth-ridge* or *alveolus* – that convex part of the roof of the mouth which lies immediately behind the roots of the teeth.

These, then, are the agents which mould, bully, and coax our 'mouthful of air' into speech.

3

Almost from the very beginning of recorded human language, it seems to have been recognised that there are two complementary elements in the total body of speech-sounds – vowels and consonants. The ancient Hebrews found the consonants earthy and the vowels heavenly, and they never allowed the latter to come down to earth and be represented alphabetically. There is no doubt something gross and brash and materialistic about consonants: they are noises made by banging things together, rubbing, hissing, buzzing. Vowels, on the other hand, are pure music – woodwind to the consonantal percussion – and, because they are produced by the creation of spaces between the tongue and the hard or soft palate, and these spaces are not measured scientifically but arrived at by a sort of guesswork, they tend to be indefinite and changeable. The history of the sound-changes of any language is mainly a history of its vowels.

Again, our difficulty in learning a foreign language is chiefly a vowel-difficulty. The problems offered by the initial and middle consonants of the name Khrushchev are soon overcome. You make the kh-sound /x/ by retching briefly; you practise on 'smashed china' for the shch-sound (щ in the Russian alphabet; /ʃtʃ/ in the IPA). But to make the u-sound (/y/) in French *lune* or German *über* requires a complete reorientation of vowel-habits: we have, to put it technically, to change our phonemic thinking. In our brief survey of speech-sounds, we can dispose of consonants quickly and gaily enough; vowels are a different matter. Consonants first, then.

TABLE OF CONSONANTS AND SEMI-VOWELS

	Plosive		Fricative		Nasal		Lateral		Trilled		Semi-Vowel	
	U.	V.	U.	V.	U.	V.	U.	V.	U.	V.	U.	V.
Bilabial	p	b	φ	β	—	m	— ·	—	—	—	ʍ	w
Labio-dental	—	—	f	v	—	ɱ[1]	—	—	—	—	—	—
Linguo-dental	—	—	θ	ð	—	—	—	—	—	—	—	—
Dental and Alveolar	t	d	s —	z {ɿ ɹ}	—	n	ɬ	{l ɫ}	—	r r	—	—
Palatal	—	—	ʃ	ʒ	—	ɲ	(l)[2] —	(l)[2] λ	—	—	ɥ	j
Velar	k	g	x	γ	—	ŋ	—	(ɫ)[2]	—	R	—	—
Glottal	ʔ	—	—	—	—	—	—	—	—	—	—	—

The above table does not give every possible consonant and semi-vowel—merely the chief ones.

U. = Unvoiced.   V. = Voiced.

[1] A nasal sometimes used after /v/ in words like ' even ', ' Stephen ', etc.
[2] Secondary articulation (viz., what the rest of the tongue is doing while the tongue tip is on the teeth-ridge).

Chapter 3

Bangs, Hisses, and Buzzes

1
Plosives

One way of making a consonant is to play a rather sadistic trick on the air that comes up from our lungs. We can hold it back, preventing it from reaching the world outside, and then, when it thinks it is imprisoned for ever, suddenly release it. The release is so sudden and unexpected that it is accompanied by a rather violent noise – an explosion. And so consonants of this kind are called *plosives*; sometimes, because of their trick of stopping the air coming out of the mouth, they are called *stop consonants*.

If we close our lips tightly, imprisoning air in the mouth, then suddenly open the lips, we get the plosive consonant /p/. If we do the same thing with our vocal cords vibrating, we get the plosive consonant /b/. Remembering that the word *bilabial* means 'involving the use of both lips', we can give these two phonemes their scientific names:

/p/ – unvoiced bilabial plosive
/b/ – voiced bilabial plosive

For the plosives /t/ and /d/, the stopping of the air is made by pressing the tongue-tip against the teeth-ridge or alveolus. Again, the vocal cords are open and hence not vibrating for the first phoneme of the pair; for the second there is vibration or voice:

/t/ – unvoiced alveolar plosive
/d/ – voiced alveolar plosive

The use of the tongue against the alveolus is perhaps more characteristic of English than of other languages. French, Italian, Malay, for instance, prefer to bring the tongue-tip on to the teeth themselves rather than on the teeth-ridge above. The Irish, when uttering a word like 'true' (/t/ followed by a trilled /r/), make the /t/ so very much on the teeth that, in novels and stories, their pronunciation is often rendered as 'thrue'. This difference between what we may call the English /t/ phoneme and the non-English /t/ phoneme is something to listen for on the radio, twirling the dial with a purely phonetic purpose. A transistor set can be a very useful portable speech laboratory.

Our third pair of plosives is made by stopping the air from the lungs with the back of the tongue pressed against the soft palate or velum; the sounds made on release of the air are

/k/ – unvoiced velar plosive
/g/ – voiced velar plosive

There are certain subtleties and refinements involved in both the stop and the release. Sometimes we content ourselves with the stop and ignore the release. This always happens when two plosives follow each other, as in 'licked' (/kt/) or 'stopped' (/pt/) or a phrase like 'bad boy' (/db/) or 'good girl' (/dg/): with each pair of stops, only the second is released. It is eccentric to say 'badder boy' or 'gooder girl' in the belief that you are giving the consonants their 'full value'. The average man often knows better than the elocution teacher. In some languages there is never any release. The stop consonants of Malay (they cannot be called plosives, for they do not explode) merely stop the air and then let it die, as in words like *sĕdap*, *balek*, *sĕbab*, *kulit*. The effect to the British ear is something like that of the glottal stop.

Unvoiced plosives in English are often very breathy – *aspirated*, in fact, so that (and this is especially true of Lancashire speech) we hear a definite /h/ following the /p/ in a word like 'pal' or 'pale'. One of my Lancashire friends, who talked of going to a pub to drink some pale ale with his pal Percy, expended a lot of breath in the process. This perhaps gave him a thirst. In speaking most Continental languages, we have to tame this British forcefulness and make our plosives glide straight on to the following vowel without any breathiness.

In some forms of English, particularly American, /t/ in the middle of a word is changed to something approaching /d/ – a sort of partially voiced /t/, represented as /ţ/. You will hear this in words like 'water' and 'Saturday'. Sometimes the change is more radical, so that /t/ is transformed into a weak /r/ and we hear something like 'warer' or 'Sarurday'. The process is respectable enough ('porridge' was once 'pottage', from French *potage*), though it is not normally associated with Queen's English. It is not a symptom of laziness but a result of *assimilation*: the vowels that flank the /t/ are, of course, voiced sounds, and they try to make the /t/ assimilate some of their voiced quality. When they turn the /t/ into /r/ they are making it assume some of the non-percussive quality which is the characteristic of a vowel: the /r/ is, in fact, so weak as to seem to stand on the border-line of vowel and consonant.

Children often confuse plosives: they say 'tum' for 'come', though they are no longer as savagely punished for it as Ernest was in Samuel Butler's *The Way of All Flesh*. They also say 'bockle' for 'bottle'. This confusion can be seen in such a word as 'apricot', whose older (Shakespearean) form is 'apricock', derived from the Arabic *al-precoq*, itself derived from the Latin *praecox*.

2
Nasals

The three voiced plosives /b/, /d/, /g/ are, of course, made with mouth-air. When they are sounded through the nose (by courtesy of the soft palate, which drops to allow this to happen) we get the three common nasal sounds /m/, /n/, /ŋ/ – this latter symbol standing for the 'ng' in 'sing'. These nasals can be pronounced sharply, like plosives, in such forms as the child's 'mamamama-mama', but they can also take on the continuous quality of a vowel, as in the expression of content (a warm fire, a sofa, a box of chocolates) which can be written as 'mmm'. /ŋ/ never appears at the beginning of a word in any of the major Western languages, though Eastern languages are happy to use it initially (Malay – *ngada*, *ngap*, *ngĕri*) and Chinese has it as a word complete in itself – *Ng*. In the English of Chaucer's time it was always followed by /g/, as it still is in the North, where 'singing' is pronounced 'singgingg'. Even in the South, teachers seem to encourage children who say 'singin' ', 'goin' ', 'talkin' ' to think that they are 'dropping their g's' and to replace /n/ by /ŋg/. This shows the primacy of spelling over pronunciation: because people see two letters in the ordinary spelling 'ng' they think there are really two sounds there. It is curious that the Cockney's 'singin' and dancin' ' is considered vulgar while the County's 'huntin', shootin' and fishin' ' is regarded as genteel. Anyway, so-called 'g-dropping' is merely the substitution of one nasal (/n/) for another (/ŋ/), and its ancestry is most respectable.

When a plosive appears before a nasal an interesting pheno-menon takes place. Say 'kitten', 'garden', 'shopman', 'button', and you will find that you are, as it were, exploding the /t/, /d/, or /p/ through your nose. The tongue or lips remain in the position for the plosive and the soft palate drops to let the air rush out through the nose for the nasal consonant that follows. Some people pronounce 'mutton' and 'garden' more or less as they are spelt, insisting on a vowel between the plosive (/t/ or /d/) and the nasal (/n/). This is finicking elocution-teacher stuff: it is best to cut down work to a minimum and let the soft palate change over from plosive to nasal without any intervening vowel. This process is known as *faucal plosion* (the fauces is the narrow passage between the soft palate and the base of the tongue).

We have already referred briefly to nasalisation and noted that one of the great phonetic characteristics of French is its tendency to nasalise vowels. This nasalisation is the result of dropping nasal consonants but allowing a nasal ghost to haunt what is left of the word. In *un*, for instance, the final *n* has long disappeared from the pronunciation, but the *u* remembers it and, as a kind of memorial tribute, nasalises itself. French is fond of dropping final sounds, but, while it is ready to forget completely the final /t/ in *restaurant*, it is always faithful to the departed nasal: the final *a* comes straight out of the nostrils.

3
Fricatives

Certain consonants are made by 'rubbing' the air-stream between two vocal organs that have been brought very close together: the root of *fricative* is the same as that of 'friction'. The effect is the same as that of gas escaping through a tiny aperture: we are aware of pressure, we are aware of duration. Fricative consonants can be continued as long as the breath lasts, and hence they are acoustically very different from plosives, which are instantaneous, gone with the wind. Let us start with the lips.

By rubbing air between the nearly closed lips we are able to make two sounds which are no longer officially English phonemes, though they are to be found in other languages. The unvoiced lip fricative is, to the English ear, like a combination of /p/, /f/, and /h/. It was a common sound in ancient Greek, and the IPA uses the old Greek letter to represent it: /ø/ (phi). The Romans heard it as an aspirated /p/ and so Latinised Greek words which contained it as *philosophia*, *Phoebe*, and so on. We, who use the Roman alphabet, continue the custom and the very name of our present study begins with an aspirated /p/ which has become pure /f/: Phonetics. The voiced lip fricative is represented by a kind of beta-letter: /β/. It is the sound we hear when the modern Greeks utter the name of their hero Byron (to the English ear it seems like 'Vyron') and when the Spaniards say the *v* in *vaso*.

It seems likely that the voiced bilabial fricative (/β/) existed for a long time in colloquial English, especially that of lower-class Londoners, and that it was used indifferently where we would now use /v/ and /w/. To Charles Dickens, a great novelist who worked before descriptive linguistics had come into existence, it appeared that the two Wellers, *père et fils*, said /v/ when they meant /w/ and /w/ when they meant /v/. It seems unlikely that Mr Weller said, 'Be wery careful o' vidders all your life,' but probable that he said, 'Be /β/ery careful o' /β/idders . . .' And so, when Sam, asked whether he spelt his name with a 'V' or a 'W', replied, 'That depends upon the taste and fancy of the speller,' he was as good as saying that the English alphabet had no letter for the bilabial fricative /β/. Certainly, both /v/ and /w/ seem only recently to have come to the enjoyment of clear identities, though many foreigners regard them still as unnatural sounds. /v/ has no place in either Chinese or Malay; the bilabial fricative is as common in the speech of English-speaking Orientals as it was in the speech of nineteenth-century London. /w/ puzzles some Continentals.

More familiar than the two bilabial fricatives are the *labiodental fricatives*, sounds made by pressing the upper teeth on the lower lip and allowing the air to filter through the tooth-gaps. These two phonemes are:

/f/ – unvoiced labio-dental fricative
/v/ – voiced labio-dental fricative

The latter sound has to be taught to Oriental students of English. The directions are simple: bite the lower lip and sing at the same time. Two fricatives that may be regarded as typically English (though they once existed in all Germanic languages and are found still in Icelandic) are those made by placing the tongue-tip between the teeth and (*a*) blowing for the unvoiced fricative; (*b*) singing for the voiced fricative. The unvoiced sound is the 'th' of 'thin', 'thick', 'eighth', 'path' and the voiced sound is the 'th' of 'then', 'that', 'those', 'them'. We use only the one digraph (two letters) to represent the two different phonemes in the ordinary alphabet; this is highly confusing. In the IPA we use the Greek letter $/\theta/$ for the unvoiced sound, the Anglo-Saxon (and Icelandic) letter $/\eth/$ for the voiced sound, thus:

$/\theta/$ – unvoiced linguo-dental fricative, as in 'thin'
$/\eth/$ – voiced linguo-dental fricative, as in 'then'

The voiced linguo-dental fricative is found in Welsh disguised as *dd* (*gorwedd; cerdded*); an approach to it is made in some Spanish words, such as *madre*, where the *d* is articulated almost on the points of the upper teeth. Castilian Spanish (*not* South American) has $/\theta/$, represented, before *i* or *e*, by *c*, as in the name Cervantes, or else by *z*, as in *lapiz* or *luz*. Yet the two phonemes are regarded by many foreigners as typically English eccentricities, and the pretence goes on in many a classroom abroad that they are hard to learn.

English-speaking children and members of the Edwardian aristocracy traditionally have difficulty with these two phonemes: inability to say them is called *thetatismus*, but the cause of this is usually less mechanical than acoustic. To many ears they sound like allophones of /f/ and /v/ respectively, and this is particularly true of speech in the East End of London, where they tend to ask the riddle 'How many fevvers on a frush's froat?' and get the answer 'Five fousand free hundred and firty-free'. Yet such speakers do not lack the mechanical equipment to make the two sounds: they have teeth, they have tongues. It is a matter of their not finding $/\theta/$ and $/\eth/$ significant or 'phonemic'.

A pair of fricatives made by putting the tongue-tip on the alveolus and rubbing the air-stream between gives us a near-universal hiss (/s/) and buzz (/z/) – the unvoiced and voiced alveolar fricatives. Spanish possesses the letter 'z' but not the phoneme /z/; German avoids /s/ whenever it can, pronouncing words like *Sohn* and *Sommer* with a /z/. English has a healthy distribution of both phonemes, but British English hates representing /z/ phonetically, even where usage allows this. Many people consider spellings like 'civilized' uncivilised; they agree with Shakespeare that 'whoreson zed' is an 'unnecessary letter'. This is a pity. The spellings 'cloze' and 'close' would distinguish two different words; 'boyz' and 'girlz' would be helpful to English-learning foreigners.

Let us now give the point of the tongue a rest and place the *front* of the tongue on the hard palate (a piece of meat on an inverted butcher's slab) and squeeze the air-stream between. This gives us our two palatal consonants – the sound in 'fish', 'shell', 'passion', which is unvoiced; the sound in 'pleasure', 'leisure', French *je*, *jamais*, which is voiced:

/ʃ/ – unvoiced palatal fricative ('sh')
/ʒ/ – voiced palatal fricative ('zh')

These two sounds are often substituted by drunks for the corresponding alveolar fricatives /s/ and /z/. ('Yesh, that'sh absholutely true, conshtable. I wazh jusht shnatching a little shnoozhe in the front sheat.') This is because less delicacy of control is required to articulate with the front of the tongue than with the tip of the tongue, and drunkenness does not admit of much delicacy.

/ʃ/ is common enough in English, but /ʒ/ is very rare and never found at the beginning of a word (except in *Doctor Zhivago* – a very British film). Two far more common phonemes consist of combinations of these two sounds with plosive consonants, thus: /tʃ/; /dʒ/. The first one is heard in words like 'chicken', 'cheat', 'catch', 'bitch', 'fetch' and 'kitchen'; the second one appears as 'j' in words like 'joke', 'John', 'jam', 'jelly', as 'g' in 'gentle', 'gin', 'pigeon', and as 'dge' in words like 'dodge', 'wedge', 'gadget'.

This combination of a plosive with a fricative is a feature of English well worth examining. The plosive, instead of terminating in an explosion, allows the two articulating organs to separate gradually, so that we hear a near-by fricative. /tʃ/ and /dʒ/ are not the only examples of this; we have also /tθ/ in 'eighth', /dθ/ in 'width', /ts/ in 'bets', /dz/ in 'beds'. The form (plosive ending in a fricative) is known as an *affricate*. The only two affricates we associate with the beginning, as well as the middle and end, of an English word are /tʃ/ and /dʒ/, but various regional forms of English substitute /ts/ for /t/ in words like 'too', 'ten', 'tell'. (I have just seen a television commercial in which a young housewife praises a detergent. Her last words are 'Keeps my hands pretty, /ts/oo.') /dz/ sometimes appears instead of /d/. I have heard 'Drop /dz/ead'. The 'Z' in German words like '*Zeche*', '*Zeug*', '*Ziel*' is a /ts/. In German words that have the same origin as certain English words this /ts/ is equivalent to English /s/ (*Zelle*= 'cell') or English /t/ (*zu*='to' or 'too').

We move to the soft palate and the back of the tongue for our last fricatives. If the back of the tongue rubs against the soft palate (or velum), without any vibration of the vocal cords, then we have the fricative heard in German or Welsh *Bach* or Scottish *loch*. The Greeks had a letter for this sound (χ), and we remember this when we represent it phonetically as /x/. The 'X' of our abbreviation 'Xmas' commemorates the Greek spelling of Christ's name (Χρίστος). The 'ch' which the Romans used to represent the Greek velar fricative ('chorus', 'chaos') shows that they thought the sound to be a sort of aspirated /k/. This sound is not so outlandish: all the Celtic languages have it and most of the Germanic ones. Arabic and Malay use it as well as Russian and Spanish. The voiced version of the velar fricative is less common. It is a gargling noise found in Arabic and, with some German speakers, at the end of words like *Pfennig, Honig, Leipzig*. Here is the IPA symbol for it: /g/.

/x/ – unvoiced velar fricative
/ɣ/ – voiced velar fricative

4
Different Kinds of L

The consonants we have glanced at so far are fairly straight-forward in the way they are articulated and the way they jet out the air from mouth or nose. The L-sound is rather more mysterious. Primarily, it is made by stopping mouth-air with the tip of the tongue against the teeth-ridge and allowing the air to sneak out along one or both sides of the tongue. For this reason, /l/ is called a *lateral* consonant. Sometimes, because the air-stream can be divided into two separate side-currents, it is also called a *divided* consonant.

The /l/ phoneme in English has two distinct allophones. (I had better qualify this statement at once by saying *British* English.) The /l/ we hear before vowels or after consonants has a thin, clear quality, suggesting somehow the resonance of the vowel /iː/ in 'see'. Listen to it: 'light'; 'long'; 'lean'; 'flight'; 'cling'; 'clean'. It is usually called 'clear L', and it is the /l/ we hear in every possible position in French, Italian, Spanish, German words. But there is another kind of /l/ – the one we hear in 'tell'; 'ale'; 'fall'; 'milk'; 'talc'; 'film': in other words, the /l/ that comes after a vowel and before a consonant. This is called 'dark L'. What makes them sound different?

Here we have to use some heavy technical language. In the first place, let us write them down in the symbols provided by the IPA. /l/ is the phoneme; |l| is the allophone known as 'clear L'; |ł| is the allophone known as 'dark L'. (Note that we use vertical lines to enclose allophonic symbols.) Both have a *primary* articulation of tongue-tip against teeth-ridge; but they also have a *secondary* articulation, and this is what makes them sound different. With |l|, the front of the tongue is raised towards the hard palate: 'clear L' is a *palatalised* sound. With |ł|, the back of the tongue is raised towards the soft palate: 'dark L' is a *velarised* sound.

Most dialects of British English (Tyneside is one exception that springs to mind) use both the clear and dark varieties. American English tends to use only 'dark L', which gives transatlantic speech one of its special peculiarities. When we are learning most foreign languages, it is safe to assume that the 'clear' variety of /l/ is in use wherever the letter 'l' appears. What makes French *ville* different from English 'veal' is partly the length of the vowel, but chiefly the quality of the l-sound ('clear' in French, 'dark' in English). We can represent the French word as /vil/, the English word as /viːł/.

'Dark L' sometimes becomes so dark in English that it changes into a vowel. I have heard Cockneys pronounce /mɪłk/ as /mɪok/. With some words, the 'dark L' becomes the semi-vowel /w/, so that 'eels' is pronounced not as /iːłz/ but as /ɪwz/. Sometimes the 'dark L' grows so obscure that it disappears entirely. This has happened in Queen's English in words like 'walk', 'talk', 'palm', 'calm'.

Both 'clear' and 'dark' L are *voiced* sounds: the vocal cords vibrate steadily while they are being uttered. Welsh has the distinction of possessing an *unvoiced* l-sound, one of the distinguishing badges of the language; Welsh spells this sound consistently as *ll*. It is found in such common names as Llanelly, Llewelyn, Llandudno, and the near-rude place-name that Dylan Thomas invented – Llareggyb. It is an insult to a noble language to ignore this special Welsh phoneme and treat it as an allophone of the English /l/. Unvoiced L, which the IPA represents as /l̥/, is an easy enough sound to learn. Put your tongue in the position for 'clear L' and blow instead of singing. Or, in other words, aspirate your /l/. There is no need to take special lessons in Cardiff or Ynys Ddu.

5

Different Kinds of R

It is proper to consider the various r-sounds immediately after examining /l/ and its sister/ļ/. The fates of 'l' and 'r' have often been closely linked in the history of language. Western people expect the Chinese to say 'flied lice' for 'fried rice' (some, but not all, do). The Malay word for 'English' is *Inggĕris.* Insulting prison-camp Japanese would say 'broody' for 'bloody'. 'Glamour' is derived from the Middle English 'gramarye', meaning nothing more glamorous than 'grammar'. 'Flagellation' comes from Latin *flagellum*, which is a diminutive of *flagrum* ('a whip'). *Blanco* ('white') in Spanish is *branco* in Portuguese. It would seem that both L and R have something of the indefinite quality of a vowel and, where they do not change into vowels, they are sometimes willing to change into each other.

That the English r-sound is generally ready to change from caterpillar-consonant to vowel-butterfly is shown in a very great number of words: 'here', 'there', 'father', 'park', 'shirt' are just a few. The 'r', in a final or near-final position in English, can turn into a 'slack' vowel-sound like /ə/ or /ɜː/ ('here' = /hɪə/; 'shirt' = /ʃɜ·t/) or a lengthener of the preceding vowel (/park/ has become /pɑ·k/). (Note that a long vowel is only half-long – a single dot instead of a full colon – before an unvoiced consonant.) The English r-sound is, in fact, a very weak fricative, so weak that it can hardly stand upright and is, indeed, an upside-down symbol in the IPA: /ɹ/. This is the usual sound we hear at the beginning of English words like 'right', 'rose', 'wrong' in most parts of the country. The point of the tongue curls up a little and engages the hard palate.

The Americans and Irish have not allowed the r-sound in words like 'hard', 'girl', 'mother' and the rest to disappear completely. They make the tongue-tip curl up considerably – a kind of back-twisting movement which is called *retroflex* – and this gives us the obscure sound we represent as /r/. But, in a great deal of American pronunciation, we get the impression that the tongue is curling up without engaging the palate, and that the vowel that comes before the 'r' in words like 'are', 'dark', and so on is pronounced merely with the tongue in a retroflex position. An Englishman will say /pɜːļ/ for 'pearl', but an American is likely to say either /pɜːɹļ/ or /pɜ·ļ/, the dot in the latter transcription signifying that the tongue is curled up or 'retroflex' while the vowel is being uttered. Our two kinds of r-sound so far, then, may be tabulated as follows:

/ɹ/ – fricative 'r'
/ʐ/ – retroflex or 'inverted' fricative 'r'

One may note before passing on to further types of r-sound that it is traditional for babies and members of the aristocracy in old-type films or stories to have difficulty in pronouncing 'r' and to substitute for it either /w/ – as in a 'wed, wed wose' – or the bilabial fricative /β/. This is regarded, somewhat belatedly, as a sign of the decadence of the British aristocracy. But it is generally true that few native English speakers can manage the 'real r-sound' which is trilled or rolled. This is the vigorous sound /r/ we find in Scottish speech, made by repeatedly and rapidly tapping the tongue-tip against the hard palate or alveolus. It is used by Scots in every possible word-position: 'girl' = /gɛrɫ/ (/ɛ/ as in /gɛt/ = 'get') or /gʌrl/ (/ʌ/ as in /bʌt/ = 'but'); 'right' = /rait/; 'for' = /fɔr/, and so on.

Speakers of English south of the border do, in fact, manage an r-sound with a single tap of the tongue on the teeth-ridge when 'r' comes between two voiced sounds. Listen to the r-sound you make in 'quarrel' or 'quarry'. It is not fricative; it has a ghost of the quality of the Scots trill /r/. We need a special sign for it: /ɾ/.

There is another kind of r-sound which we have to learn if we want to speak French well. This is the 'grasséyé "r" ' or uvular 'r', made by rolling the uvula against the back of the tongue. It is represented as follows – /R/. We hear this also in Northumberland and Durham: listen to any native singer of the song 'Blaydon Races'. A similar kind of r-sound is produced when there is merely a narrowing of the space between tongue-back and uvula and a uvula fricative 'r' is produced: /ʁ/.

These 'un-English' types of r-sound may be listed as follows:

/r/ – rolled or trill 'r'
/ɾ/ – one-tap or semi-rolled 'r'
/R/ – uvular rolled 'r'
/ʁ/ – uvular fricative 'r'

6
Semi-Vowels
A vowel-sound, as we shall soon see, is made by leaving a space between the tongue and the palate (hard or soft), and then

allowing air to pass through the space; at the same time, of course, the vocal cords are vibrating. But the quality of a vowel-sound is partly determined by what the lips are doing at the same time. For /u/, for instance (the vowel in 'soon', 'fool', 'true'), the lips pout, kiss-wise. If we pronounce /u/ vigorously, prolonging the sound, and then suddenly leave off, there will often be an 'after-sound' produced by the lips themselves – the sound /w/ as in 'well', 'wit', 'one'. This is not quite a consonant and not quite a vowel: it is convenient to think of it as a *semi-vowel*. It is a voiced sound, but there is an unvoiced version of it which we represent by 'wh' in ordinary English spelling – 'why', 'when', 'what', 'which' – but by an inverted 'w' in the IPA: /ʍ/.

We have already seen, in our section on the bilabial fricative, how speakers of foreign languages tend to distrust English /w/ and even consider that it does not exist. Some Welsh speakers have this same notion and give us ''oman' for 'woman' (this is at least as old as Shakespeare). But English itself has occasionally thrown away its /ʍ/ in words like 'who' and its derivatives 'whom' and 'whose' (/hu:/; /hu:m/; /hu:z/). It is as though, when the vowel /u/ appears immediately after /w/, the mouth decides that there is no need for mockeries like unvoiced semi-vowels which are a mere ghost of /u/. But the reverse process has taken place with the word 'one' (/wʌn/). The voiced semi-vowel /w/ seems to be there to remind us that the historically earlier vowel in 'one' (/o/) was one that required lip-work.

If we pronounce the vowel /i/ (as in 'see') with great vigour, there is a tendency for the front of the tongue to hit the palate for an instant at the end, producing the 'after-sound' we hear in its own right as the first sound of 'yes', 'yet', 'yoke', 'yacht'. It seems rather unreasonable to us that the IPA should use /j/ to represent this sound, but it will seem just to the Germans, whose word for 'yes' is *ja*. Besides, as we shall see, /y/ is needed for another job. This palatal semi-vowel is voiced, but it has an unvoiced companion /ç/ – the sound at the beginning of 'huge', 'humour', 'Hugh', and at the end of German *ich*, *mich*, *dich*. It can be thought of as /j/ with /h/ sounding at the same time.

The four semi-vowels can be listed as follows:
/w/ – voiced bilabial semi-vowel
/ʍ/ – unvoiced bilabial semi-vowel

/j/ – voiced palatal semi-vowel
/ç/ – unvoiced palatal semi-vowel

7

Palatalisation

We have completed our survey of the most important consonants and semi-vowels. There are, of course, others – some of them outlandish, some common – which are best considered in other contexts (some of the clicks of African languages, for instance; a particular semi-vowel in French which requires prior knowledge of the corresponding vowel-sound). Before we move on to the flutes and lutes of speech, leaving the noises behind, we ought to note an interesting phonetic phenomenon which is perhaps less common in English than in the languages of Europe – *palatalisation*. It happens sometimes that a sound associated with, say, the teeth-ridge is, as it were, dragged further into the mouth to be articulated on the hard palate. We have seen how a drunken English-speaker will palatalise 'seat' to 'sheat' and 'please' to 'pleazhe' (in other words, /s/ becomes /ʃ/ and /z/ becomes /ʒ/). In the Latin languages this palatalisation process works on the nasal /n/ and the lateral consonant /l/. The palatal nasal /ɲ/ sounds to English ears like /nj/, the sound of 'canyon'. French and Italian write it as 'gn' (*agneau; agnello* – both meaning 'lamb'); Spanish has 'ñ' (*la uña* – 'the finger-nail') and Portuguese uses 'nh' (that Spanish word appears as *a unha*). The palatalisation of /l/ used to exist in French words like *Versailles* and *fille*, but now only the semi-vowel /j/ quality remains there. But palatalised /l/ continues in Italian ('gl' as in *megliore*), Spanish ('ll' as in *llena*), and Portuguese ('lh' as in *galhina*). Represented as /ʎ/ in the IPA, it strikes the English ear as an /l/ followed rapidly by /j/ – as in 'million' pronounced quickly.

The Russian language is mad about palatalisation. It will palatalise everything, and frequently does. Thus, international words like 'telephone' and 'telegram' appear (I am using the Roman alphabet for greater clarity) as *tyelyefon* and *tyelyegrama*. The word for 'no' smites some ears as very like a sneer – *nyet*. What will strike the uninstructed, in fact, as a bristle of /j/-sounds is nothing more than the Russian tendency to bring everything to the region of the mouth where /j/ (as in 'yes', remember) is made. The big secret of learning Russian pronunciation lies high in that rocky dome called the hard palate. But more of this later.

Chapter 4

Flutes and Lutes

1
Front Vowels

We all know what vowels sound like. We must now learn what they *feel* like and even *look* like. Sleepless nights can profitably be beguiled by going through the gamut of English vowels (as in 'Who would know aught of art must learn, act, and then take his ease') – silently, if need be: five-finger exercises on a dummy piano. One finger at least can be used for checking the tongue-positions and finding out what the lips are doing; the first thing that this exploring finger will discover is that, in the making of vowel-sounds, the tip or point of the tongue is not used. In practising vowel sounds, the tongue-tip can be tucked behind the bottom teeth and forgotten. We are concerned with the front of the tongue (which, at rest, faces the hard palate), the back of the tongue (which, when lying quietly, faces the soft palate), and the middle or central bit which lies between front and back. Vowels, of course, are *voiced* ('vowel' comes ultimately from the Latin *vocalis*, which speaks for itself). First we shall find out what vowels can be made when the front of the tongue is raised towards, or pulled away from, the hard palate.

Here is a sentence: 'Tea is *thé* in French.' This can be represented in phonetic script as:

$$/\text{ti: ɪz te ɪn frɛnʃ.}/$$

There are, you will note, four vowels: /i/; /ɪ/; /e/; /ɛ/. The vowel /e/ is not found on its own in Queen's English, only in the diphthong /eɪ/ ('way', 'hay', 'day'). It is common enough in other languages and in various English dialects. Let us, for a reason that will be clear very shortly, concentrate on the three vowels /i/; /e/; /ɛ/, ignoring /ɪ/ for the time being. Say /i/ several times and you will discover that the front of the tongue is raised almost to the limit; if it were to be raised any more it would touch the hard palate and the resultant sound would not be a vowel /i/ but the fricative /j/. So /i/ is our high front vowel or *close front vowel*: you cannot have a higher tongue-position, the tongue cannot be closer to the palate without losing the vowel altogether. This is a 'smiling' vowel: it is the vowel in 'cheese' – word beloved of photographers. The lips are spread.

If now the front of the tongue is lowered a little (and the jaw lowered with it, so that the mouth opens slightly) we get the *half-close front vowel* /e/ (the sound in French *thé*). If the tongue is

Fig. 1.

further lowered (and the jaw with it) we have the vowel in 'French' or 'men' or 'debt' – the *half-open front vowel* /ɛ/. Say this trio of vowels over and over again: /i/; /e/; /ɛ/; /i/; /e/; /ɛ/ – ad nauseam. Note the rate of jaw-dropping, tongue-lowering, mouth-opening.

We have three front vowels, then: (1) close; (2) half-close; (3) half-open. To complete the sequence, we need a *fully-open* vowel. This will be the a-sound in the French word *café*, the German sound in *Mann*, the Lancashire and Yorkshire vowel in 'man', 'cat', 'fat', 'fan' and so on. It is *not* the a-sound in the Queen's English pronunciation of those words, though it does appear as the opening sound of the dipthong /aɪ/ in 'fine', 'wine', 'die'. /a/, then, is our *open front vowel*.

In pronouncing these four – /i/; /e/; /ɛ/; /a/ – take careful note of the way in which the tongue is lowered from the hard palate. The distance between the vowel /i/ and the vowel /e/ is the same as the distance between the vowel /e/ and the vowel /ɛ/. And the tongue travels the same distance from /ɛ/ to /a/ as from /e/ to /ɛ/. When you get up in the morning or, intrigued by your darkling studies, switch the light on and look into a mirror, you will be able to see that the jaw drops, the mouth opens in equal stages. But the movement downwards of the front of the tongue is not precisely vertical: it is oblique and may be presented diagrammatically as in Fig. 1 (page 51).

2
Back Vowels

Let us now try to make a similar sequence of four vowels at the back of the mouth, raising the back of the tongue towards, and then away from, the soft palate. We can start with the vowel /u/ – a good clear 'moon-croon-June-tune' sound made with the tongue well back and the lips rounded as for a kiss (the vowel is, and no

Fig. 2.

wonder, associated with romance). Prolong it, as a child does when it sees the sweet it likes: 'Oooooooooo.' The sound is normally long in English words, appearing as /uː/. Now let us open the lips slightly, allowing the back of the tongue to drop from this high or *close* position to a *half-close* stage. The sound we now get, if the lips remain rounded, is /o/ – a pure round o-sound which no longer exists in the Queen's English, though French has it in, for instance, *eau ,beau, peau*. Pop-singers use the phoneme /o/ consistently, whether they are British or American, when pronouncing words like 'no'. Let the mouth open further, with the lips still round, and the *half-open* position of the tongue gives the sound of 'for', 'saw', 'bought', 'caught', 'laud', 'cord' – /ɔ/, normally a long sound (/ɔː/) in English. Finally, if we spread the lips (no more rounding) and utter the sound the doctor asks us to make when he wants to examine our throats, we have the most *open* back vowel of them all – /ɑ/, the sound which appears long (/ɑː/) in English words like 'tar', 'bar', 'car', and so on. Recite the whole sequence many times – /u/; /o/; /ɔ/; /ɑ/ – noting the stages of tongue-dropping and mouth-opening. The fall of the back of the tongue is genuinely vertical, so that we may show these vowel-stages as in Fig. 2.

3
A Vowel Chart
We have now plotted the tongue-positions for eight vowels – four of them made with the front of the tongue, four of them made with the back of the tongue. We are now in a position to construct a very useful chart, a diagram which represents, in a very square conventional form, the mouth-area in which the tongue operates in order to make vowel-sounds. It is an area guarded by eight vowels which correspond roughly to the cardinal points of a compass; these vowels are thus called *Cardinal Vowels* (see Fig. 3).

On this chart I have placed certain other vowel-sounds,

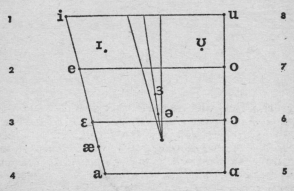

Fig. 3.

common in English. /ɪ/ made a brief functional appearance in our sentence 'Tea is *thé* in French'. It is, in fact, the vowel of 'is', 'in' 'it', 'civil', 'civility' (in this last word it appears four times). We could not discuss it when dealing with front vowels, for it is not strictly speaking a front vowel at all: the front of the tongue moves in just a little towards the centre of the mouth. Pronounce the word 'easy' over and over again, and you will be aware of how the front of the tongue moves not merely down but back. Contrast this with the French word *cité* (/site/) and you will feel the difference.

The sound /ʊ/ is the sound you use in 'full', 'bull', 'could', 'wood', 'stood'. It stands in the same relationship to the back vowels as /ɪ/ to the front vowels: it is advanced a little towards the centre. Lurking in the centre of the diagram (Fig. 3) you will see two spiders, sounds made with the middle of the tongue, both very common in English. /ɜ/ is found long in ' word', 'bird', 'sir', 'fur' (/wɜːd/; /bɜːd/; /sɜː/; /fɜː/). Like all long vowels in English, it loses some of its length when it appears before an unvoiced consonant, as in 'skirt', 'shirt', 'work', 'earth' (/skɜːt/; /ʃɜːt/; /wɜːk/; /ɜːθ/).

We need no statistician to tell us that its companion /ə/, which is short, is the commonest sound in English, though the fact that it has no letter in the ordinary alphabet disguises this. It is the 'slack' sound that comes in the second syllable of 'father', 'mother', 'sister', 'brother', 'dinner', 'supper', and in the first syllable of ' apart', 'address' (except in American), 'canoe', 'conundrum'. It is the indefinite article 'a' in 'a boy', 'a girl', 'a love affair'. It is the tongue at rest in the middle of the mouth, it is colourless and lazy-sounding. The foreigner's clue to the learning of natural-sounding English is found here.

The remaining symbol which I have placed on the chart which is Fig. 3 is /æ/ – a letter we use in 'Caesar' with the value of /iː/ but which, in the IPA, stands for the a-sound in Queen's English 'man', 'can', 'sat', 'mad'. It is hard for many English-speaking people to learn, as it does not appear in any of the Northern dialects (which prefer something like Cardinal Vowel No. 4: see Fig. 3, lower left-hand corner). We can see from our chart how to learn it. It is a matter of making the front of the tongue assume a position half-way between Cardinal Vowels Nos. 3 and 4. Or, to put it another way, one must make the tongue move sufficiently south from the /ɛ/ of 'men', 'then', 'den' to a sound which will seem right to the 'natural' speaker of Queen's English. There then remains practice with sentences like 'That bad man has grabbed Jack's black hat and Sam's cap'.

So far, in discussing these English vowels, I have been evading an issue. We can take it that the eight Cardinal Vowels represent fixed positions of the tongue, so that /i/ is falsely represented as a phoneme if the /i/ we are studying is Cardinal Vowel No. 1. It is an allophone of the /i/-phoneme – |i| – with an unvarying position: the tongue is as high as possible and as far forward as possible. The other three corners of the vowel chart – |a|; |u|; |ɑ| – represent similar extreme tongue positions (for |ɑ|, for instance, the mouth is as wide open and the tongue as retracted as possible).

So far so good. But in placing /ɪ/, /ʊ/, /æ/, and the rest in fixed positions on the chart I am committing an absurdity. These cannot have fixed positions: the tongue position of each of them varies from speaker to speaker and, in any individual speaker's set of vowel-sounds, from word to word and from position to position in any given word. Take /ɪ/, for example. It appears five times in the word 'incivility' (/ɪnsɪvɪlɪtɪ/). Each |ɪ| is subtly different from every other |ɪ|. There are here, in one word, five allophones of the /ɪ/-phoneme. What, in fact, I have done on the vowel chart is to set down certain of my own allophones for these non-cardinal vowels. Your own may be very different.

Here comes a difficult question. At what point does the range of tongue-positions available for, say, the phoneme /i/ meet the range of tongue-positions available for, say, the phoneme /e/? If I start right at the very top, with my tongue in the position for Cardinal Vowel No. 1, and then move the tongue imperceptibly down, still producing types of /i/ – theoretically an unlimited number of them – I must sooner or later move to a different phonemic area. This, at least, is true in theory. But practice works differently, and we soon find ourselves at the very heart of the phonemic mystery. For to an Englishman 'peat' (/piːt/) is manifestly a different word from 'pit' (/pɪt/) – in other words, /i/ is clearly not the same phoneme as /ɪ/. But to a Frenchman or a Malay it will appear differently: to him /i/ and /ɪ/ will seem to belong to the same family: in other words, they will sound like allophones and not like phonemes.

It is because it is difficult to ascribe barriers or frontiers to phonemes that so much confusion exists in the world of vowel-sounds. The Northern Englishman, as much as the Chinese,

Indian, or French student of English, will be convinced that the Queen's English a-sound in 'man' is really a form (i.e. an allophone) of the e-sound in 'men'. Foreign students may work for weeks, even months, on minimal pairs (that is, pairs of words in which the difference between the members of the pair is a difference of one sound) and still be unaware of any significant (i.e. phonemic) difference:

leak	lick		dead	dad
seat	sit		said	sad
feet	fit		fed	fad
week	wick		lend	land
greed	grid		pedal	paddle

The recognition of phonemes, the allotment of boundaries to phonemic areas – this is not a mechanical matter but a psychological one. We all carry mental images of vowel-sounds, and these images can persist whatever the tongue is doing. Thus, an Englishman will say /fɪt/, a Frenchman /fit/, and a Scotsman /fet/ or even /fɛt/, but all will hold the same mental image of the word 'fit'. Because of this extreme fluidity of vowels, the lack of physical obstacles to the wandering tongue, languages tend to change. We shall, in a later chapter, see how drastic these changes can be.

4
More Cardinals

Go back to Fig. 3 and recite the eight basic vowels again. You will note that for No. 1 (the sound in 'see') the lips are spread, for No. 2 (the sound in French *thé*) the lips are spread, and there is the same spreading for No. 3 (the sound in 'men') and for No. 4 (the sound in the Lancashire pronunciation of 'man'). In other words, these four front vowels are all enunciated with the lips spread – the mouth all set for smiling or grinning and, in the case of No. 4, even for laughing ('hahahahaha'). When we move to No. 5 – the back vowel we make for the doctor and pronounce long in 'bar', 'father', 'ma' – we find that the mouth is as wide and as square as a letter-box slit: the lip-spreading is extreme. Nos. 1, 2, 3, 4, and 5, then, are vowel-sounds made with the lips spread. Let us digest that.

After digestion, turn to the remaining vowel-sounds which are numbered on the chart: No. 8 (as in 'moon'), No. 7 (as in French *beau* or even the o-sound of English 'obey' when this word is spoken quickly), No. 6 (as in 'saw'). All of these are pronounced with the lips rounded: for No. 8 they pout; for No. 7 they express slight surprise; for No. 6 they show disappointment or pity. Now we must equip ourselves with a conjurer's baton and effect certain remarkable transformations.

Pronounce No. 1 with the lip-rounding of No. 8. It is best to do this by holding on to a long /i/ and then pouting as for /u/. The resultant sound is not an English one, but it will be familiar. It is the sound we hear in the French *lune*, or in the German *Münze* – a *rounded close front vowel* represented in the IPA as /y/.

Pronounce No. 2 with the lip-rounding of No. 7. This is more difficult. The lips should show a pure 'o', while the tongue holds the /e/ of *thé*, *café*; this is the sound to be heard in the French *bleu*, *deux*, and in German *hören*, *möglich*. It appears in Danish as ø, and the IPA has borrowed this symbol: /ø/.

Pronounce No. 3 with the lip-rounding of No. 6. This, again, is difficult: it will take some time for the image of the sound to fix itself in the mind. The lips will try to say /ɔ/ in 'saw' (keep the vowel short) while the tongue is in the position for the /ɛ/ in 'men'. This is represented as /œ/ – a symbol derived from French. Indeed, this is the sound you hear in the French words *œuf*, *œuvre*, *neuf*, *heure*. In *un* it is nasalised (/œ̃/).

There is one more piece of lip-rounding to do, and this is not on the remaining front vowel No. 4 (|a|) – a sound which from now is, poor thing, ignored in this context – but on No. 5 (|ɑ|). Here there cannot be any borrowing of lip-rounding from a back vowel, for |ɑ| is itself, of course, a back vowel. What we do is to bring lip-rounding from nowhere, saying a short |ɑ| while our lips form a great circle. This gives us the short vowel in 'not', 'clod', 'want' (in their British pronunciation, that is: the Americans do not use the sound) and a new phonetic symbol |ɒ|.

Having brought over lip-rounding from No. 8 to its opposite number No. 1, and from Nos. 7 and 6 to their respective opposites Nos. 2 and 3, we must practice a little more magic. This time we bring over *lip-spreading* from No. 1 to No. 8, from No. 2 to No. 7, and from No. 3 to No. 6: we are letting the front vowels work on the back vowels for a change.

If we say No. 8 (|u|) with lips spread (as for No. 1) we get a sound not normally heard in the polite version of any language. It is the 'boo-hoo' vowel we use when we are crying. Say /u/ as in 'moon', prolonging the sound; consciously spread the lips .Ponder on the resultant vowel /ɯ/. You will have heard it used in vulgar speech, where the speaker does not trouble to round his lips for statements like 'You sued him for a new blue suit'. It is not up to us to condemn this vowel. I came near to condemnation, however, when a recent television programme on the Moon used this vowel /ɯ/consistently. It had the effect of making the moon seem flat and square.

If we say No. 7 (|o|) with the lip-spreading appropriate for No. 2 (|e|) we get a strange vowel represented as |ɤ|. This, again, is not to be found in polite English speech except for the word 'good'. This is normally pronounced /gʊd/, but some speakers drop the vowel to /ɤ/, producing something between 'good' and 'gud'. A television commercial talks about '/gɤd/ chocolates'. The vowel, in this context, often seems to have sinister overtones. But it deceives many Southern listeners to Lancashire speech. Lancashire English is commonly supposed to interchange the /ʊ/ of 'put' with the /ʌ/ of 'butter', so that 'mother' is believed to be pronounced /mʊðə/ and 'push' is believed to be pronounced /pʌʃ/. In actual fact, neither sound is really used at all. Instead, /ɤ/ stands equally for the vowel in 'mother' and the vowel in 'push'. (Compare this with the bilabial fricative of Sam Weller's speech, discussed in the previous chapter.) It would be profitable to take a sentence and compare the Queen's English (or Southern) and Lancashire pronunciations of the relevant words:

'Don't *rush* upon your *mother*, *utter* threats or even *mutter*,

If she *puts* no *sugar* in your *cup* or on your bread no *butter*.'

Queen's English: /rʌʃ/; /mʌðə/; /ʌtə/; /mʌtə/; /pʊts/; /ʃʊgə/; /kʌp/; /bʌtə/.

Lancashire English: /ɹɤʃ/; /mɤðə/; /ɤtə/; /mɤtə/; /pɤts/; /ʃɤgə/; /kɤp/; /bɤtə/.

The perceptive reader may now guess as to what the next (and last) of these vowels must be. If we pronounce the /ɔ/ of 'awe', 'caught', 'lord' as a short vowel without lip-rounding (in other words, lending the lip-spreading of No. 3 to the tongue-position of No. 6) we have, in fact, this very 'mother' vowel /ʌ/. Or, rather, we have a cardinal vowel |ʌ| which is an allophone of the total /ʌ/-phoneme. It is a wide phoneme, admitting many variants.

Let us now place these seven new vowels on a chart. Our last chart (Fig. 3) showed the *Primary Cardinal Vowels*; this new one will show the *Secondary* ones:

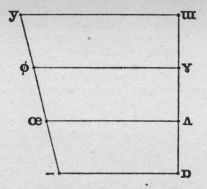

Fig. 4.

Note: We have seen that there are certain semi-vowels which correspond to phonemes we can place on the Primary Cardinal Vowel Chart. Thus, /j/ is a kind of /i/ carried to extremes – the tongue touching the palate instead of merely being close to it – and /w/ is the lip-rounding of /u/ rendered as an audible smack. With one of the Secondary Cardinal Vowels – |y| – we can make a semi-vowel that appears in certain French words. By saying /j/ with the lip-rounding of /y/ we get the semi-vowel /ɥ/ – the sound represented by *u* in words like French *muet, huit, lui*.

5

Centralization

One characteristic of very careful English speech – the speech of the trained 'elocutionist' – is the tendency to make all front vowels as far front in the mouth as possible and all back vowels as far back as possible – in other words, to emphasise the essential 'frontness' or 'backness' of these phonemes. But everyday speech is not so particular: the tongue does not dart forward or push back quite so energetically as in 'trained' speech, and both front and back vowels approach the middle of the mouth, the central zone where /ɜ/ and /ə/ are made. To represent these centralised vowels we can use the existing phonetic symbols with dots placed over them or a wiggly line (as for 'dark L') drawn through them. Thus, 'boot' or 'blue' pronounced by a Cockney will be made nearer the middle of the mouth than the back, and the pronunciation can be rendered as /büːt/ or /blüː/. Even with cultivated speakers, forms like 'due' and 'you' show centralisation, owing to the influence of the palatal /j/; thus we have /djüː/ and /jüː/. A centralised /ɪ/, as in much Australian speech, can be shown as /ǐ/ or /ɨ/. All these centralised forms are, as far as English is concerned, allophones of the primal front or back phoneme. But the Russian letter ы represents a genuine central phoneme – /ɨ/ – in which the tongue tries to say the /ɨ/ of 'sit', but as far back as possible.

6
Diphthongs

For some languages, especially English, a battery of pure vowels – that is, vowels made with a firm and unwavering tongue-position – is not enough. Sometimes the tongue will start at one vowel-position and then move in the direction of another: whether it actually reaches the second vowel-position is not important, for the journey counts more than the arrival. This sort of tongue-journey gives us the sound known as a *diphthong*, and the phonetic representation shows both the starting-point and the proposed destination. A good example is the personal pronoun 'I', which is a diphthong starting from /a/ (anywhere in the bottom left-hand corner of the chart in Fig. 3) and moving towards /ɪ/. The phonetic symbol is /aɪ/. Here is a list of English diphthongs:

(a) Diphthongs moving towards /ɪ/:

/eɪ/ – as in 'way', 'hay', 'eight'
/aɪ/ – as in 'die', 'high', 'cry'
/ɔɪ/ – as in 'toy', 'foil', 'noise'

(b) Diphthongs moving towards /ə/:
/ɪə/ – as in 'ear', 'beer', 'mere'
/ɛə/ – as in 'air', 'bare', 'scarce'
/ɔə/ – as in 'oar', 'bore', 'coarse'
/ʊə/ – as in 'poor', 'sure', 'tour'

(c) Diphthongs moving towards /ʊ/:
/aʊ/ – as in 'cow', 'house', 'loud'
/oʊ/ – as in 'no', 'know', 'toe', 'bone'

(d) Triphthongs – the two /a-/ diphthongs followed by /ə/:
/aɪə/ – as in 'ire', 'fire', 'liar'
/aʊə/ – as in 'power', 'flour', 'shower'

Note that these English diphthongs and triphthongs have as their final element either a fully central sound (/ə/) or a sound approaching the centre – /ɪ/ or /ʊ/. We can make a diphthong chart as in Fig. 5 (the diphthongs on it are, please remember, the ones I myself make). A vast number of variants is possible. For instance, we hear /eɪ/ as /ɛɪ/ or even /æɪ/ in quite cultivated speech, while /oʊ/ can be anything from /ɣʊ/ to /əʊ/. In learning foreign languages we may try to impose our own diphthongal habits on a very different sound-system, but we can avoid this if we remember that English is nearly unique in possessing the

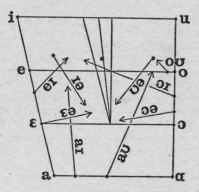

Fig. 5.

central and near-central vowels which form the second elements of our diphthongs. Moreover, what sound like diphthongs in such languages as Italian are more often two vowels, fully enunciated, following each other rapidly, as in /ai/. And the German diphthongs of *klein* (/klain/) and *Haus* (/haus/) tend to reach (or very nearly) a second element which is fully forward (/i/) or fully back (/u/). The English language dearly loves the middle of the mouth.

We are now in a position to make a fairly comprehensive list of vowel-sounds:

Phonetic Symbol	Sample Word(s)	Tongue Position	State of Lips
(a) /i/	sea; *si*	Close front	Spread
/ɪ/	sit; will	Less close, less front	Spread

Phonetic Symbol	Sample Word(s)	Tongue Position	State of Lips
/e/	*thé; café*	Half-close, fully front	Spread
/ɛ/	men; *père*	Half-open, fully front	Spread
/æ/	man; cat	More open, fully front	Spread
/a/	man: cat (Lancs.)	Fully open, fully front	Spread
/ɜ/	word; girl	Central	Spread
/ə/	the; 'a' in allow	Central	Spread
/ɑ/	car; father	Open back	Spread
/ɒ/	not; god	Open back	Rounded
/ɔ/	for; law	Half-open back	Rounded
/o/	*eau; beau*	Half-close back	Rounded
/ʊ/	put; pull	More close, less back	Rounded
/u/	blue; *tout*	Close, fully back	Rounded
(b) /y/	lune; *Führer*	Close front	Rounded
/ø/	*bleu; böse*	Half-close front	Rounded
/œ/	*cœur; œuf*	Half-open front	Rounded
/ɯ/	'Boo-hoo'	Close back	Spread
/ɤ/	Lancashire version of 'u' in 'but'	Half-close back	Spread
/ʌ/	mother; but (Queen's English)	Half-open, back or slightly centralized	Spread

Chapter 5

Sounds in Action

1

So far we have been discussing the sounds of language in a void, dissecting and probing as on some cold pathologist's slab. To talk of /p/ or /b/ or /i/ or /u/ is to talk of an abstraction – something taken out of the warm current of speech. Now we must put the sounds back in again and see how they behave in company with other sounds. We want to examine, not bare phonemes, but words, phrases, babble and gabble.

We have already referred, in passing, to that attribute of vowel-sounds which is called *length*. Some phonemes take longer to say than others: /siːd/ takes about twice as long as /siˑt/; /siˑt/ takes about twice as long as /sɪt/. Length of vowel varies from dialect to dialect in English. An Englishman will, for instance, accept /mæn/ as the normal native pronunciation of 'man'; he will regard /mæːn/ as 'transatlantic'. And indeed there is an American tendency to 'drawl' or lengthen vowels which is in marked contrast to the so-called 'clipped' British habit. But even within the limits of an *idiolect* – one person's mode of speech – there will be shortenings or lengthenings of vowel-sounds according to context. For instance, if I say 'Give it to her' – stressing the 'Give', as though the person addressed is holding the thing back – the vowel of 'her' will be short (/ɜ/). If now I stress the 'her' ('Give it to *her*, not to him'), the vowel will take on full length (/ɜː/). And so, in 'Where has she *been*?', the /i/ of 'been' appears long (/iː/). In 'She's been to *London*', /i/ is quite short. 'I asked you what you heard, not what you saw' gives us the last word with a fully long /ɔː/. 'I saw nothing at all of the film' has a 'saw' with a quite short /ɔ/.

Still, we tend to think of certain vowels in English as *naturally* long: /iː/ as in 'see'; /uː/ as in 'you'; /ɔː/ as in 'paw'; /ɑː/ as in 'far'. We think of a shortening of these as a kind of perversion of their essential quality, just as we regard a lengthening of /æ/ to /æː/ or

/ɪ/ to /iː/ as a deformation of those sounds. And so, with the notion of a *long* vowel in our mental ears, we have difficulty in mastering the short /i/ and /u/ of languages like Spanish. Italian lengthens vowels before double consonants, so that *bello* sounds like *beeeeello* to some ears. We have to learn when to lengthen and when to keep short.

Length is allophonic, not phonemic: 'seed' can be pronounced as /siːd/ or as /sid/ and still be recognisably the same word. But an Englishman hearing a Frenchman pronounce 'peace' as /pis/ instead of /piːs/ may be unsure what vowel the Frenchman *intends* – whether /ɪ/ (which will transform a word of noble connotations to a rough lavatory one) or the right phoneme /iː/. Length is a vowel-attribute to be carefully watched.

Another important attribute in languages of Germanic origin – important, that is, from the viewpoint of meaning – is that known as *stress*. It is also vital in Slavonic tongues like Russian, but it has less to do with the Romance languages – French, Italian, Spanish, and the rest. Every English word has – if it possess more than one syllable – its own characteristic stress, and stress (indicated by the sign /ˈ/ before the syllable concerned) can sometimes determine meaning, besides affecting the quality of the phonemes which make up the word. Thus, 'increase' as /ˈɪnkriːs/ is a noun denoting 'addition or enlargement', whereas 'increase' as /ɪnˈkriːs/ is a verb meaning 'to enlarge, to add to'. 'Compact' can appear as /kəmˈpækt/ – an adjective meaning 'firmly united or joined together'; it can also be /ˈkɒmpækt/ – a noun with various meanings, one of which is 'a lady's portable vanity-box'. So also 'conduct' is a verb as /kənˈdʌkt/ and a noun as /ˈkɒndʌkt/.

This lexical differentiation, as we may call it, makes the stress of a number of English words very important, but the shifting of stress may – without actually altering meaning – bring about profound phonemic changes. The 'correct' pronunciation of 'controversy' has the stress on the first syllable, while a pronunciation that has gained wide currency (and hence cannot really be judged 'wrong') has the stress on the second syllable. Compare the two: (1) /ˈkɒntrəvɜːsɪ/; (2) /kənˈtrɒvəsɪ/. The two vowel-sequences are quite different. So are they in 'purport' as a noun – /ˈpɜːpət/ – and 'purport' as a verb – /pəˈpɔːt/.

Stress is heavy in English words and heavier still in Russian, nor, in either language, does ordinary spelling give any indication as to where emphasis should be thrown. That is why it is a relief to go back to the unemphatic flow of French after tussling with the capricious hammer-strokes of the language of Dostoevsky and Solzhenitsyn – lexically, stress means little in French and little in Italian; the mild stresses of Spanish are always regular and so take care of themselves: in fact, the daughters of Latin are not at all as one would expect – tempestuous and fist-banging. Greek, whose only daughter is modern Greek, was no more concerned about stress than Latin seems to have been – not, anyway, to judge from the stress-variability of the following Greek derivatives in English:

photograph – /ˈfoʊtəɡrɑːf/ (or -/ɡræf/)
photographic – /ˈfoʊtəˈɡræfɪk/
photographer – /fəˈtɒɡrəfə/

Stress has an important part to play in those meaningful groups of words we call sentences or phrases. We have to use a new set of signs to show emphatic syllables and weak syllables here – a kind of Morse (dash for stress; dot for no-stress):

■ • • ■ • ■ •
Where do you think you're going ?

But as soon as we start considering the rhythms of whole statements we are inevitably led to that other attribute of speech – intonation, speech-melody, the rise and fall of the voice. This is a huge subject we can only touch on briefly here. Certainly, the tunes of English are subtly important, conveying not only meaning but social attitudes. Take the following, for example:

I expect you'll want a wash   I expect you'll want a wash

The first seems inoffensive enough – an offer of ablution facilities to a guest who has just arrived off a long journey. The second implies several things: the speaker is not very willing to give anything (even water, soap, and the use of a towel); yet at the same time there is a faint suggestion that the person addressed is habitually dirty, not just travel-stained.

On the level of pure lexical meaning, intonation can turn a statement into a question:

He's going now   He's going now ?

The intonation patterns of other languages can be learned by listening: foreign radio stations supply as much as one needs for an elementary image. At least, this is so with European languages. When one comes to a *tonal* language like Chinese one faces very large difficulties indeed. What we may call (though the time has not yet come to define the term accurately) the *words* of Chinese are all formed in the same way: they are monosyllables, either closed (consonant at the end) or open (vowel at the end). Thus, the sentence 'A teapot is used for making tea and a kettle for boiling water' is rendered as:

Ch'a hu shih p'ao ch'a yung ti, shui hu shih shao shui yung ti.

(This is in the national Chinese dialect known as *Kuo-yü*.) If you consider the limited number of phonemes that are available to the human mouth, you will see that there are not enough different monosyllables available to make all the words that a complex civilization needs in its language. Consider how we would fare if English were made up solely of monosyllables, if all sentences were like 'My friend John says that it is high time you went to the Bank to get some cash to pay him what you owe him'. Already we have a fair number of monosyllables which have the same sound but different meanings – like 'know'/'no'; 'way'/'weigh'; 'I'/'aye'/'eye'. Consider how many of these *homophones*, as they are called, there must be in Chinese. The sentence *Ma ma ma ma ma* can mean 'Has mother scolded the horse?' This is no joke.

In order, then, to differentiate between monosyllables made up of the same sounds but carrying different meanings, Chinese makes use of *tones*. In *Kuo-yü* (the National Language) there are five, though the fifth is falling into disuse. These are:

1. *Shang P'ing Shêng* – a sharp falling tone.
2. *Hsia P'ing Shêng* – a curt upper rising tone.
3. *Shang Shêng* – a long rising tone 'broken in the middle'.
4. *Ch'ü Shêng* – a 'departing tone' – a falling-away melody.
5. *Ju Shêng* – an abrupt intonation which shortens the vowel.

In learning a sentence like *Mên k'ou yu jên* ('There is someone at the door') we have to learn the tone which helps give each word its meaning, thus: *Mên* 2; *k'ou* 3; *yu* 3; *jên* 2. The difficulties involved in tackling a tonal language are great but not insuperable. No language is all that difficult if we learn to understand its idiosyncracies. Chinese is fascinating.

2

A point I made above is that it is possible to learn the intonations and stress-system of a language by listening – so long as one listens long enough and attentively enough. But it is not so easy to learn the phonemes of a foreign language by listening – despite the claims of certain gramophone record companies. Children, if they are young enough, can pick up foreign sounds accurately: it is instructive, in Malaya, to listen to the perfect mastery of Chinese tones evinced by British children with Chinese amahs. Rare mimics – and all mimics are rare – can grasp a foreign sound-system almost instinctively: one thinks of Peter Sellers in England, Danny Kaye in America. But the great majority of language-learning adults cannot imitate sounds with any approach to exactness: told to try /y/ in French *lune*, they will say something like /i/ or something like /u/, but never the compromise sound that is the right one. To ask most adults to imitate the sounds they hear is like asking a non-pianist to listen to a Bach fugue on the radio and then sit down at the keyboard and rattle the music off. Only a knowledge of phonetics can show us the way through foreign mysteries.

I must emphasise that by 'a knowledge of phonetics' I do not mean merely a knowledge of the International Phonetic Alphabet. The symbols, despite what many teachers seem to think, have no validity in themselves: they are merely signals relating to actions of the vocal organs. But, if I have put in some time on tongue-raising and lip-spreading, I will know what exactly the symbol /i/ can mean when I meet it in a dictionary. It is important, incidentally, that any foreign-language dictionary we buy should be big enough and scholarly enough to give pronunciation in the symbols of the IPA. It is a waste of money to buy some match-box sized amateurish lexicon which gives 'approximate' pronunciations in a variant of ordinary English orthography – like *kaffay* for *café*, or *bam-bee-noh* for *bambino*. The French–English dictionary I possess cost rather more than a bottle of gin, but it is worth spending money on a professional performance. I look up the word *homme* and find, before the definition, the phonetic rendering /ɔm/. I know that the first of these two symbols stands for a *short* sound in the region of Cardinal Vowel No. 6 (Fig. 3). If I take something like the /ɔ/ in 'fought' (/fɔːt/), only very much shortened, so that it takes almost no time to utter, I am in the correct phonemic area. /m/ causes no difficulty. I want to say, not just *homme* ('man'), but 'a man' – *un homme*. I look up *un* and find /œ̃/. Here I have a phoneme in the region of Secondary Cardinal Vowel No. 3. I revise the technique for saying it – a form of /ɛ/ with the lip-rounding appropriate to /ɔ/, snorted through the nose – and I practise saying it.

But learning to pronounce *un homme* correctly is not just a matter of getting two words right: add one word to another word, and the answer is not two words – it is a new entity, a phrase. So now I have to note that, though the dictionary gives *un* as /œ̃/, something special happens when *un* appears before a vowel – in this case, the /ɔ/ of *homme*. The *n* of *un* – normally silent – acts as a link between the two vowels (/œ̃/ and /ɔ/) and is pronounced. /œ̃/ + /ɔm/ = /œ̃nɔm/.

The problems that English speakers of French encounter when trying to differentiate between *femme* ('woman') and *faim* ('hunger') are overcome if a little phonetic thought is taken. The dictionary gives the following pronunciations: *Faim* – /fɛ̃/; *femme* – /fam/. The second word is straightforward: the /f/ and /m/ are found in the English sound-system as well as the French; the /a/ is lower than the /æ/ in 'man', the jaw drops more for it. As for /fɛ̃/ – we know that /ɛ/ is somewhere near Cardinal Vowel 3 (Fig. 3) and that it is nasalised, snorted through the nostrils. To fix the difference between the two words we must now practise a whole phrase – *La femme a faim* ('The woman is hungry'): /la fam a fɛ̃/. The difficulty of distinguishing between the pronunciations of the two words can be overcome in a very short time. Phonetics is the key.

If we can use phonetics for breaking down foreign words in this manner, we ought also to use our knowledge of how sounds are made, and how sounds can be scientifically notated, to study the allophonic differences within the English language – what for example makes an Australian pronunciation of 'No' different from that of an American or Queen's English version of it. Experiment is required: the tongue has to travel about, searching, and the ear keep on the alert. The diphthong /oʊ/ (in 'no', 'go') is very variable as far as the first element /o/ is concerned, but the second element usually remains pretty stable. Thus, British English is capable of /ɜʊ/, /əʊ/, even (though this is extreme) /eʊ/: what gives the diphthong its 'oh' character is the second element – the tongue reaching towards /ʊ/. But it seems certain that no user of a diphthong in words like 'show', 'though' allows the first element to drop as low as, say, the /ɑ/ of 'car' (pronounced short) or the /a/ of French *café*. To do so would be to risk producing a diphthong proper only to words like 'now', 'house' – a sort of /aʊ/. This limits the area in which the tongue can search for a first element in Australian 'no'. Try /ɜʊ/; try /əʊ/; try /øʊ/, even. It is clear that none of these will do – they are altogether too 'Pommie' or U.K. English. The untutored ear fancies that Australian 'no' is something like 'now'. But /aʊ/, as we have seen, is not an accurate rendering. Move the back of the tongue higher; try /ʌʊ/. That seems more like it – a diphthong starting off with the vowel of 'up'. Try /ɣʊ/: that seems *very* much more like it.

How about American 'no'? Experiments will probably end up with something like /ɔʊ/. How about the 'no' of Welshmen? Listen carefully. There seems to be no second element there; the sound does not seem to be a diphthong at all. It is a half-open vowel, not far from Cardinal Vowel No. 6 (Fig. 3) – something like a very round /ɔ/.

Dialectology is the name we give to the study of the make-up of the regional variants of a language. To travel England with the Cardinal Vowel Charts clear in one's head, a notebook and pencil handy – this can be fascinating. It is more than a mere amusing hobby, however: it is vital, a fingering of the warm pulse of human language.

Chapter 6

Sounds in Space

An alphabet seems the most natural thing in the world to people brought up on ABC bricks, but – if this were not a sober book – I should be betrayed into large enthusiasms about the 'miracle' of its invention, placing it high above television, jet propulsion, and nuclear fission. It is clever enough to be able to record and reproduce by electronic means the sounds our mouths utter, but the conversion of speech into impulses and impulses into speech cannot match the fundamental achievement of converting the temporal into the spatial – for speech works in time, but letters stand in space.

It is doubtful if the Alphabet is much more than 3,000 years old, whereas speech is nearly as old as man. Thus, the dawning of the principle of representing a spoken sound by a written letter has come very late in our history, and it still has not come to a large proportion of mankind – the Chinese, for example. The Alphabet is the last and most efficient device for giving symbolic permanence to the spoken word. Unlike fire and agriculture, it did not come at various times to various races – widely separated in space but undergoing parallel developments. It came once and once only to a race of Semites trading in the Mediterranean lands, and – like many epoch-making discoveries – it came almost in a fit of absent-mindedness.

Before the Alphabet, there were certain rough and cumbersome ways of giving permanence to words, but these had nothing to do with words as temporal events, successions of speech-sounds. The Egyptians, the Mexicans, the Red Indians drew pictures which stood for words – they got behind the word itself and recorded what the word stood for. Picture-writing is our oldest form of setting down signs for the *referents* of language (that is, the things in the outside world that language refers to), and it has always been the least efficient.

The reason for this is, of course, that there are comparatively few aspects of language that lend themselves to adequate pictorialisation. We can draw the sun, the moon, spears, jugs, loaves, stylised men, and horses, but a statement even of so simple a type as 'I lost my wife and five children in the last inter-village war' is hard to set down in pure pictures. The fact is that the *pictograms* (to use the technical term) of the pre-alphabetic civilisations were never really intended to provide a comprehensive writing system: we tend to impose our own needs on societies quite happy without mail-boxes, libraries, and daily newspapers. Pictograms probably only arose as reminders, signs of ownership, commemorative inscriptions. Consider how little urge there would be to make inscriptions at all when there were only stones and chisels as writing implements: if we had to leave the smooth ease of pen-and-ink and typewriter to go back to painful hammering, writing would die out quickly enough.

But the pictogram still retains its usefulness, even in our sophisticated alphabetic societies. It is the most primitive and naïve of all inscriptive techniques, but it can prevent – in international youth hostels – a male from using a female bathroom, and vice versa: the conventional symbol for a male is a two-legged stick-man, that for a female the same, only with a skirt. Zig-zagging lines will represent running water; a bed will show a dormitory. Our traffic signs show a fair variety of pictograms: a cross for a cross-roads, a zed for a bend, a T for a road junction, a schoolboy and schoolgirl for a school (this pictogram used to be an *ideogram* or *logogram* – terms we shall come to in a moment. There was a symbolic torch representing the *idea* of learning; this may have been too complex for many drivers, hence the reversion to a primitive pictogram).

The development of writing is associated with a number of different social functions which, on close examination, are seen to be cognate. The growth of agriculture involves star-gazing and moon-watching – in other words, attempts to establish the limits of the seasons. Also, fertility rituals are performed and gods of fertility are worshipped. A priestly class emerges – elders who have no other work than to perform due ceremonies, predict drought or abundance, intercede with the gods. It is difficult, in these early societies, to separate religion from agriculture: the priest is a magician is an astrologer is an astronomer is a scientist. He guards sacred mysteries; he needs to keep complex records; he compiles the tables of the law. By now simple pictograms are

Fig. 6.—Some Chinese Characters.

by no means enough: we are in the age of secret sophisticated writings, sacred carvings or *hieroglyphics*.

We are, in fact, in priest-ruled Egypt, with its holy men who learn how to predict the rise and fall of the Nile but are inevitably unwilling to share their secrets with others. Their kind of writing seems to use straightforward pictograms – which, theoretically, any plain man can understand, just as any plain motorist can understand traffic signs – but in reality they use a priestly code, communication between the elect, holy and terrible symbols. An Egyptian priest would be a fool to make his system of writing common knowledge; he plays up the mystery of language and enhances his own power; he has a vested interest in codes and acrostics and other means of delimiting a system of communication to a chosen few.

There were various means of creating inscriptive symbols which should transcend the limitations of pictograms. One way was the way of metaphor. The Chinese to this day use a drawing of a man or a field to represent respectively these two words, bringing the symbols together to make the new word 'farmer'. That is easy enough, but how about abstract words, words like, for instance, 'not'? 'Not' in Chinese shows a sort of plant with a line above it: the plant is trying to grow, but the line seems to be stopping it. This is a little poem of negativeness, a metaphor of 'notness'. The Chinese word for 'bright' brings together two symbols – that for the sun and that for the moon: two concrete images suggest a common property, abstracted into the word 'brightness'. That is another way of doing it.

When, in fact, symbols are used to express ideas rather than to represent objects in the external world, we have *ideograms* ('idea drawings') or *logograms* ('word drawings'). With some of these (Chinese 'not' is a good example) it is possible to see vestiges of picture-writing; with many the pictorial origins are obscure and the shapes seem quite arbitrary. Thus, the Arabic numerals seem (except for the first) to relate to nothing pictorial: 2, 3, 4, 5, and the rest are arbitrary characters which have no universal verbal significance (1 is *un* to the French, *ein* to the Germans, *satu* to the Malays) but in all countries carry the same arithmetical meaning. They are true ideograms. The Roman numerals come closer to pictograms, especially when they appear on a clock-face – I, II, III, IIII, V. They are drawings of fingers, except for V which represents the space between index finger and thumb and thus stands for the whole hand. Signs like $+$, $=$, % have clear meanings to everyone, but they do neither a pictorial nor a phonetic job (' $+$ ' does not show the sounds of 'plus'); they are pure ideograms.

The modern Chinese language contrives to get on very well with its ideograms: it produces books on Marxism and nuclear physics; the bulk of the literate are not noticeably clamouring for a Western alphabet. But, occasionally, especially when introducing a foreign word, Chinese becomes suddenly aware of sounds and forgets all about referents: it will transliterate a foreign name like Churchill not by using the ideograms for a church and a hill but by choosing words which carry roughly the same sounds as the English name. This puzzles some readers of Chinese newspapers, for pronunciation varies so widely all over China that it is not possible for the ideograms chosen to convey the same sounds to everybody. I was once in the company of two Chinese who could not understand each other's dialect. They were able to converse only by writing down their words as ideograms. The parallel of monoglot Englishmen and Russians finding common ground in symbols like 159% is an exact one.

As soon as sound-elements are introduced into non-alphabetic writing, as soon as a symbol represents a phonetic rather than a semantic notion, then we are on the way to learning our ABC. The first glimmerings of phonetic writing among the Egyptian priests appear in puns, play on words with the same sound but with different meanings: homophones, in fact. It is easiest to understand this sort of trick if we think of the possibilities of English homophones. Let us imagine that we are in the same position as the Egyptian priests, possessing no alphabet, only pictograms. We have the word 'sun', and 'sun' is easy enough to represent: all that is required is a circle with a few wiggly lines for rays. We also have the word 'son', and 'son' is not so easy to draw: we can, after much trouble, achieve a fair likeness of a young man, but how can we denote relationship? The easiest thing to do is to use our pictogram for 'sun' for 'son', exploiting the homophonic. This will normally be enough, for context should make all clear: 'The father loves his /sʌn/' is not ambiguous. But, to avoid confusion in statements like 'The /sʌn/ sank into the sea', it might be useful to prefix the 'sun' pictogram with a conventional sign denoting human maleness. The image of a man would do. Let us take another example: 'sea' and 'see'. 'Sea' is easily shown as wavy water; if we want the verb 'to see' we can put the image of a human eye in front of it; if we want 'see' in its episcopal sense, how about a simple drawing of a chess-bishop? This way of defining by means of prefixes will give us a whole set of little signs called *radicals*. The eye-radical followed by the drawing of a watch will indicate clearly what verb is meant; the man-radical can give the pictogram of a buoy a completely unambiguous meaning. Radicals exist in Chinese, and the learning of them eases recognition of certain words. When a radical is fused with a pictogram and, over long years, simplified and conventionalized, it becomes difficult to pick out the representational element from the resultant ideogram.

This kind of punning – which, incidentally, must often have been deliberately formed to confuse rather than enlighten – is still very popular in children's-page competitions. The most elaborate type of pun is the multiple or syllabic – 'horsefly' shown as a horse and a fly; 'well-bred' as a well and a loaf; a chair, a man, and a ship to make up 'chairmanship'. One can go to excruciating lengths – as in charades – with 'Socratic' (a sock, a rat, a 'this-sum-is-right' ideogram) or – which deforms the word somewhat, but no matter – a paperclip, a toe, a horse's mane and an ear for 'kleptomania'. These tricks and puzzles fossilise a stage of emergence towards the syllabic sense: one more step and we shall have an alphabet.

Everybody is able to recognize a syllable, even if some difficulty is experienced in defining what a syllable is. The old notion that a syllable was a vowel or a combination of vowel and one or more consonants will not really do. In a word like 'rhythm' there are recognizably two syllables, but the second of them need not have a vowel: /rɪðm̩/. In fact, we use the symbol of a vertical line under a consonant symbol to indicate that that consonant is syllabic. Here are other examples: 'fission' – /fɪʃn̩/; 'nation' – /neɪʃn̩/; 'national' – /næʃn̩l̩/. If we think of a syllable as a sound or group of sounds pronounced in a single impulse, we have a tentative definition that is unsatisfactory but, for the moment, will serve. Everybody can, then, recognise a syllable and can accurately count the number of syllables in a given word, but not many can give the number of *sounds*. 'Civility' has four syllables: everybody will recognise that. The number of sounds will be guessed at from the number of letters and, for once, the guess will be right. But how many sounds are there in the disyllables 'open'; 'fairground';

'butcher'? How many in the trisyllables 'possible'; 'photograph'; 'pertinent'; 'Westminster'? To the person with the minimum of phonological training there should be no difficulty in giving the right answer; to the majority there will come an accession of head-scratching and doubt.

It is no wonder, then, that with the men of a few thousand years ago there should be no urge to dissect words into phonemic units. Syllables, however, were a different matter, and the first breakthrough from a priestly script (hieroglyphics) to a demotic or popular one was easy and natural enough: the old pictograms, in a conventionalised and simplified form, were turned into the materials of *syllabaries*. A syllabary thinks in terms of a single symbol standing for a consonant plus a vowel. It works best with languages like Japanese, where every word can be broken up into syllables each following that easy formula: YO-KO-HA-MA; HI-RO-SHI-MA; MI-KA-DO.

Not that Japanese makes exclusive use of a syllabary. It is a language which early adopted the ideograms of Chinese but finds a syllabary useful when new or foreign words have to be presented. Chinese does not like borrowing from other languages; it prefers to re-formulate a new idea in its own terms, so that 'electricity' is rendered as 'light spirit' and 'gas' as 'coal spirit'. But Japanese will gladly accept English words like 'gas', 'page', 'bus', 'pound', 'dress', and 'typewriter', so long as it can fit them to the native sound-pattern as *gazu, peju, basu, pondo, doresu*, and *tuparaita* respectively. To get these words on to paper it will use a syllabary – either the *Hiragana* or the *Katakana*. In fact, written and printed Japanese makes use of both of these, together with about 1,500 Chinese ideograms.

The *Katakana* syllabary has five symbols corresponding to the five vowel-letters A I U E O. It then has five corresponding to the syllables MA MI MU ME MO, five corresponding to NA NI NU NE NO, five corresponding to SA SI SU SE SO, and so on – the remaining consonants Z P B T D K G Y R H W each possessing five forms according to the vowel – A I U E or O – which is attached to it. This gives $14 \times 5 = 70$ symbols + 5 (vowels on their own) + the solitary closed form (i.e. ending in a consonant) UN = 76. This is about the average number of signs required for a syllabary. Fig. 7 shows the beginning of an article I wrote for a syndicate of Japanese newspapers. In it you will notice the whole consort dancing together – Chinese ideograms, *Hiragana,*

英作家のみたソ連の民衆生活

アンソニー・バージェス

のんびり

【本社特約OCS通信】英国の小説家アンソニー・バージェス氏はこのほどソ連のレニングラードを訪問し、帰英後BBC放送で旅行談を放送した。次に紹介するのはそのときの放送談話大要であるが、いわゆるソ連国民の非能率ぶりとか一筋舌についても作家らしい機知に富んだ解釈を示し多くの示唆をふくんだ観察を行なっている。

〃能率〃は上層部だけのもの？

私はソ連人の能率の悪い点が一番好きである。鉄のように冷たく厳しい社会生活を予想して、私はレニングラードを訪れたのだが、そこで見たのは最もヒューマンな人間べつのことでいえば最も非能率的な人間であった。

といっても非能率的な国民がスプートニクや宇宙飛行士を生み出すはずはないのだが、おそらく能率というものはソ連社会では一番の上層部に浮いている薄いエキスのようなものなのだろう。学校に関西子の少女は「ほかの新聞はもう売り切れました」

る。また英字新聞を買おうと、英国共産党のデイリー＝ワーカー紙しかおいていないのは間違いで、ソ連人が

たとえてみると先生方がみな職員会議に集まっているか最高学級の物理実験に立ち合い、生徒たちは教室で自習をしているようなものもしかしたらこれをウ。

and *Katakana* syllabaries. My own name appears to the right –
just left from the title in its hatched or shaded box. It is read from
top to bottom as A-UN-SO-NI BA-ZI-YE-SU, which is, to
Japanese ears, near enough to *Anthony Burgess*.

In the East, then, one may see all the pre-alphabetic sign-
systems in daily use: the pictogram, the ideogram, and the
syllabary. There, however, there has been no sense of the need to
take that extra step towards a true alphabet. Admittedly, it is a
difficult extra step, and it was only achieved by the Semitic peoples
of the Mediterranean because of an accident – that accident being
the peculiar structure of Semitic languages.

All Semitic languages – Hebrew, Arabic, Phoenician, and the
rest – possess in common a peculiar devotion to consonants. In
fact, a Semite does not think of a Semitic word as being made of
syllables (consonant plus vowel); he thinks of it as being made of
the strong bones of consonants with the vowel sounds floating
above like invisible spirits. Moreover, the vowels of a Hebrew or
Arabic word have little to do with the determination of meaning:
meaning is firmly staked out by the consonants alone. Thus, the
three consonants K-T-B in Arabic possess a root meaning of
'reading', so that *kitab* means 'book', *khatib* means 'mosque
reader', the prefix 'm-' makes *maktaba* – 'bookshop' or *mokhtab* –
'college'. The consonants alone will establish meaning if the
context is clear. In Hebrew the staking-out of three consonants to
create a word gives a characteristic flavour to proper names like
Jacob, Rachel, David, Moloch, and Joseph. Spell the words as
JCB, RCHL, DVD, MLCH, JSPH and the meanings remain clear
– in Hebrew. English is a language which defines meaning as much
with vowels as with consonants, and so DVD is too ambiguous as
it stands: it could be, besides 'David', 'divide' or 'dived'. And
MLCH could be, besides 'Moloch', 'milch', or 'mulch'. Only in
the Semitic languages – rich in consonants but comparatively
poor in vowels – can a group of consonants stand for the whole
word.

We believe that the Phoenician traders of the Mediterranean
were the first to take over simplified Egyptian symbols and use
these to represent consonants. They created a *betagam* instead of
an *alphabet*: a BCD, not an ABC. They were not interested in
finding vowel-letters, because vowel-letters were not necessary in
the writing of Phoenician – a Semitic language. This meant that
they were able to make do with twenty-odd symbols – a tremen-

dous and epoch-making economy. Had they thought – as speakers of non-Semitic languages like English and Japanese must think – in terms of consonant-plus-vowel, they would not have been able to leap beyond a syllabary of seventy-odd symbols, for Mediterranean man was not yet ready for the concept of vowels and

Fig. 8.—Origin and Development of A, M, O, R.

consonants as independent partners in language. But the Phoenicians had the concept of *free consonants*, and this made their discovery of a betagam or BCD possible.

What urged them to create this system of easily learned and handled letters? Not literature, not religion, but trade. They presumably needed to make out their bills and enter their books with some speed: a few quick strokes, and there was a memo or a delivery note or an invoice. Not for them the leisure of hieroglyphics or syllabaries. An Egyptian eye or head, bird or running water must become mere abstract lines or circles – as with the letters of our own alphabet, which ultimately have the same derivation. Whether their letters would be curved or angular must depend on the materials used: our own A and T and K are essentially *chiselled* letters; the curved forms like S and O and U suggest a softer ground, like paper, and the squiggling motions of a reed-pen (see Fig. 8).

In which direction did their letters travel – left to right, right to left, up, down? It varied; it did not seem to be of much con-

Fig. 9. – Some Biblical names in Hebrew script unpointed (i.e. without indication of vowel-sounds). The letter *Aleph* is represented here as meaning either 'A' or ' ''. Actually it has no equivalent in English: it is a 'smooth breathing' – not a vowel at all. In both Hebrew and Arabic script we must read from right to left.

sequence. Our own left-right habit is not based on any law of nature, any more than traffic rules are. When it comes to painting a name on a factory chimney, we are as ready as are the Chinese or Japanese to start at the top and move down. The two great Semitic languages have settled for opening a book at the back and reading from right to left (see Figs. 9 and 10). When I first learned to use Arabic script I feared I would get ink on my sleeve: it soon seemed to me the most natural and the cleanest – as well as the most sensuously satisfying – way of writing imaginable.

The earliest Semitic scripts have survived only fragmentarily, leaving no literature or tables of the law. The Hebrew and Arabic alphabets are very much with us today. The examples given in Figs. 9 and 10 show how important the consonantal letters are. Hebrew script has kept itself strictly to the Hebrew peoples and those few non-Semites who have been Judaised; Arabic script has travelled the world with the Arab traders and missionaries and been imposed on alien races along with Islam; wherever the flag of the star and crescent has been planted, the Arabic alphabet has been planted too – from the Indus to Spain and furthest east of all to the Indies. This has led to various modifications of the alphabet to fit the non-Semitic structure of languages like Spanish and Malay. Malay, for instance, is allowed to use more vowel-signs than would be thought proper in Mecca, though even then it keeps them down to a minimum. Persian (and this comes as a surprise to many) is an Aryan language, belonging to the same family as English and French and Russian, and it has not really taken kindly to the imposition of an alphabet that is nearly all consonants. If the Arabs had conquered England in the Middle Ages (and this might well have happened), English would have had to fit itself into the straitjacket of the Islamic BCD. How some English names take to this treatment is shown in Fig. 10.

So far we have moved from pictograms to ideograms, then to syllabaries, then to a kind of demotic or popular writing which used only consonants. The final stage came when speakers of Aryan tongues (more about what 'Aryan' means in a later chapter) wrestled with a Semitic alphabet and found it wanting. It was the Greeks who introduced vowel-symbols and thus opened up the way to a very exact means of rendering spoken sounds. The vowel-symbols had their origin, like the rest of the alphabet, in old pictograms (see Fig. 8); Greek was content with seven:

α ε η ι υ ω ο

These letters are the so-called 'lower case' forms. The peoples of Italy took the capital or 'upper case' forms of five of these letters (they did not want η and ω) and thus equipped the Roman Empire that was to come, along with its tributaries, with the tradition of the five vowels A, E, I, O, and V.

LIOD NNOK RTHARS

Read from right to left.

SR ATHR KONN DOIL = Sir Arthur Conan Doyle

MOH KOLRSH

SHRLOK HOM

= Sherlock Holme(s)

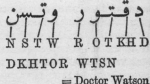

NSTW ROTKHD

DKHTOR WTSN

= Doctor Watson

DRY DNLTOKS

SKOTLND YRD = Scotland Yard

لوور نوروود

Lower Norwood

Fig. 10. — English names taken from a translation of a Sherlock Holmes story into Malay. This is the Arabic alphabet in its *Jawi* (i.e. Eastern) form. Note that there are no capital letters, that fewer vowel signs are used than in the Roman alphabet (they are especially avoided before two consonants), and that what vowel letters there are perform two functions. و is /o/ or /u/ inside a word but /w/ at the beginning of a word; /i/ and /e/ are shown by two inferior dots which also serve initially for /j/. ر, و, ا and د (road) are joined to a preceding letter but never to a following one. Most letters are given a calligraphic flourish at the end of a word.

This question of upper and lower case letters (printers call them by these names because of the positions of the type-boxes that hold them) is too big to go into here. Arabic, we may note, has never had the tradition of small letters and capitals; the International Phonetic Alphabet gets on well enough with just lower case symbols. The original Roman alphabet was all capitals; small letters are a later development associated with a running or 'current' script, for capitals cannot easily be joined to each other. We would probably save much time and money if we followed the Arabic tradition of using small, or lower case, letters only. German insists on a capital initial for every noun; we all insist on capital initials for proper names, the beginning of a sentence, and abbreviations like UNO, NATO, USSR, and the rest. Also, in English, we have the egomania of a capital for the first personal pronoun. Archy, the cockroach that wrote poems on Don Marquis's typewriter, could not use capitals and still became a best-seller; the American poet e. e. cummings, though able to use a shift-key, still preferred lower case letters all the time.

The Roman alphabet spread all over the West, undergoing only slight modifications in the various colonial territories where it was used to write down the local language; the Greek alphabet was introduced into the non-Greek territories of Eastern Europe by more peaceful means than conquest. The present-day Russian alphabet resembles the Greek alphabet very closely; indeed, some letters are identical. St Cyril, a missionary of the ninth century A.D., took the Greek alphabet with him to the Slav territories he wished to convert to Christianity. Inevitably, it underwent modifications owing to the particular needs of Slav, and it became virtually a new alphabet – called, to this day, after the saint: the Cyrillic (in Russian, *Kirillitsa*) alphabet.

The world has now three great alphabets – the Roman, the Cyrillic, and the Arabic. The Roman and Cyrillic, even to the least trained observer, must seem to possess a common origin, but the Arabic looks like neither, nor does it resemble the Hebrew alphabet or the syllabaries of India. Nevertheless, we can assert that all alphabets derive from the original Phoenician invention: the lack of consistency in writing or drawing the symbols, the tendency of each nation to develop its own quirks and create special letters to render its own idiosyncratic sounds – these are possible reasons for the eventual divergence of forms. But if we look closely at, say, the 'L' symbol of Arabic, Greek, Russian,

Коммунистическая партия Советского Союза

ПРАВДА

Орган Центрального Комитета
Коммунистической партии Советского Союза

Fig. 11. – The title-box of the Russian newspaper *PRAVDA*
('*TRUTH*'). Above the name we read *Kommunisticheskaya Partiya
Sovyetskovo Soyuza*. Note the palatalised vowels я (ya) ; e (ye)
and ю (yu). The г of the third word is normally pronounced like the
'g' in 'gas', but in adjectival forms like this it becomes /v/. The phrase
means 'Communist Party of the Soviet Union'. Below the title we read
*Organ Tsyentral'novo Komityeta Kommunisticheskoi Partii Sovyetksovo
Soyuza*. This seems fairly clear : 'Organ of the Central Committee of the
Communist Party of the Soviet Union.' I have used an apostrophe to
represent the Ь in the second word. This symbol is a softener or
palataliser of the preceding vowel. The encircled hero is, of course,
Lenin.

HEADLINES FROM PRAVDA :

Манчестер рукоплещет Ю. Гагарину

Manchester rukopleshchet Yu. Gagarinu :
' Manchester acclaims Yu(ri) Gagarin '

ГАНГСТЕРИЗМ В
ПОЛИТИКЕ США

Gangsterizm v Politikye S.Sh.A.
' Gangsterism in the Politics of the USA '

Hebrew, and the Roman alphabet, we cannot doubt the possession
of common elements – two lines at an angle. The Roman 'S' is a
sort of snake; so is the corresponding Arabic sign. Even the
Arabic 'T' symbol bears a ghostly resemblance to our own. The
feeling that all alphabets are fundamentally one should ease our
task in learning how to use the two great foreign alphabets.

COCA-COLA	STRIPTEASE	FOOTBALL
Кока-кола	στριπτηζ	φυτμπολ
Кока-кола	стриптиз	футбол
كوكاكولا	ستريفتيذ	فوتبول

ASPIRIN	GUINNESS	JAZZ
ασπιριν	Γινιs	διεζ
аспирин	Гиннисс	джэз
اسفيرين	كينيس	بجيذ

* 'International' words in (a) Roman, (b) Greek, (c) Cyrillic (or Russian), (d) Arabic ('Jawi' form) script.

(Note: in Modern Greek β = /β/ ; μπ is used for /b/.)

Fig. 12.

Whether or not we wish to learn the languages that these alphabets enshrine, sheer human curiosity should drive us to find out at least what the letters stand for. And to handle the Arabic alphabet is to be led into a little world of exquisite sensation.

Chapter 7

Adventures of an Alphabet

The languages that have been most satisfied with the Roman alphabet as a set of phonemic signals are, inevitably, those that are derived from the Roman language – Italian, Spanish, Portuguese, French, Rumanian. The Roman alphabet fitted Latin like a glove, and it has fitted the dark-eyed daughters nearly as well, though French – language of dissent – has tended to chafe a little, introducing the gussets of diacritical helpers (acute and grave and circumflex and cedilla). The modern Latin tongues are so clearly agreed as to what the letters of the Roman alphabet signify, that we are able to deduce by comparison what they stood for in Latin: we can almost reproduce the very phonemes that Vergil, Horace, and Catullus juggled with. Thus, the letter 'i' means /i/ in Paris, Madrid, Rome, Lisbon, Bucharest; 'e' means a half-close or half-open front vowel (/e/ or /ɛ/); 'o' means a half-close or half-open back vowel (/o/ or /ɔ/); 'a' can confidently be taken to stand for /a/ and 'u' – except in French – for /u/. It seems unlikely that they could have any widely differing meaning in the parent language. This family sticking-together with the vowels, this loyalty to the imperial mother, is not exactly matched with the consonants. If 'c' means /k/ before 'a' or 'o' or 'u', it does not always mean /s/ before 'i' or 'e'. French opts for the /s/, Italian for /tʃ/, Castilian Spanish (but not provincial or South American) for /θ/. Nor do the Latin daughters agree about rendering the palatal 'n' (/ɲ/). Portuguese has 'nh', Spanish has 'ñ', French and Italian have 'gn'. But, within the particular language, there is usually absolute consistency, so that French and Italian 'gn' *always* mean /ɲ/, Spanish 'g' before 'e' or 'i' *always* means /x/, Spanish 'll' and Portuguese 'lh' *always* stand for /λ/.

But how about the Roman alphabet in England? What has gone wrong here? Why is it that no foreigner can say with any confidence, seeing a new English word in print, what the pronunciation is likely to be? Why is the story of the Frenchman who drowned himself after reading 'Agatha Christie's Mousetrap

Pronounced Success' not really funny? How has it come about that we can spell 'fish' quite logically as 'ghoti' (the 'gh' in 'laugh', the 'o' in 'women', the 'ti' in 'ration')? Why have we diverged so from common Continental agreement about the significance of the Roman letters? That in itself would be tolerable if English spelling were consistent; but English not only fails to agree with French, Spanish, Italian, and the rest – it fails to agree with itself. The only problem of learning English is the problem of spelling. If only English would say that 'xgyjpth' stands for /i/ and 'zfrkhtgg' stands for /u/ and be absolutely consistent about it, then there would be no problem for anyone – native or foreigner. It is the total lack of logic that is infuriating. How did it come about? What can we do about it?

We may as well begin with a piece of Anglo-Saxon or Old English. This ancestor of our present language was, very roughly speaking, used until the Normans settled in England and ferti-lised it with their brand of French. The following will only be intelligible to the lay reader if he is told that it is a translation of the Lord's Prayer; it is very much a foreign language to us now:

Fæder ūre,
þū þe eart on heofonum,
sī þīn nama gehālgod.
Tōbecume þīn rīce.
Gewurþe ðīn willa on eorðan swā swā on heofonum . . .

This is recognisably written with the Roman alphabet, but with certain letters that the Romans never used: the Germanic phonemes /θ/ as in 'thin' and /ð/ as in 'then' required special letters (the second of them, you will note, is used with its original Germanic value in the International Phonetic Alphabet). The letter 'þ' (the Anglo-Saxons called it 'thorn') was eventually to disappear, to be replaced (as was 'ð') by the Frenchified 'th', but it still survives as the first letter of 'þe Olde Englisshe Tea Shoppe'. It has been mistaken for 'Y', but it certainly is not pronounced /j/. Along with these two consonant-letters, the Roman digraph 'æ' (pronounced /ai/ in Latin) is used, representing the compromise sound in the Southern pronunciation of 'man' – a sound that is not quite an 'e' and not quite an 'a'. Above certain vowel-letters appears the diacritic '‾', a symbol of vowel-length, but also a phonemic differentiator. The two phonemes /i/ and /ɪ/ would both appear as forms of the one phoneme /i/ to the Roman ear; consequently, the Roman alphabet has only left the one letter 'i' to represent them both. Anglo-Saxon 'i' stands for 'ee' in 'see' (/iː/); 'i' stands for /ɪ/ ('willa' is the ancestor of our modern 'will'). Already the Roman alphabet is being strained to meet the requirements of a non-Latin language. Add the fact that some unvoiced consonants tend to be voiced in Anglo-Saxon between two vowels, and we find that the 'f' of 'heofonum' (ancestor of modern 'heaven') represents /v/.

Still, in the earliest stage of English, 'a', 'e', 'i', 'o', and 'u' meant roughly what they still mean in the International Phonetic Alphabet and what they always meant in the Latin language. When we read Chaucer, we assume that these five vowels have *French* meanings, because 'ou' – following the new French custom – stands for /u/, and 'u' seems to stand for /y/ in French *lune*. Roughly speaking, in the fourteenth century the following words had something like a Continental pronunciation: 'lady', 'made', 'name' (/a/); 'house', 'flour' (/u/). The spellings of 'see' and 'sea' crystallise a half-close long vowel and a half-open long vowel respectively. Thus, the old pronunciation of 'see' would be /seː/ and that of 'sea' /sɛː/. The doubling of a letter to show length seems reasonable enough; the addition of an 'a' to show that a vowel is open rather than close is more subtle, but still logical. The same thing happens with back vowels. 'Moon' shows a long close o-sound; the pronunciation would be /moːn/. 'Road' has an 'a' after the 'o' to indicate that the 'o' is half-open or /ɔː/ (think of 'a' after a vowel-letter as a 'tongue-down-a-bit' signaller). The long 'i' (/iː/) which the Anglo-Saxons represented as 'i' is increasingly shown through the formula 'i + consonant + e = /iː/', so that words like 'shine', 'fine', 'mine', etc., had, up to the end of the fourteenth century or perhaps later (one cannot be absolutely sure), the sound /iː/ in the middle.

The pronunciation of certain common English words in the medieval period can, then, be shown in relation to the Cardinal Vowel Chart as in Fig. 13. These long vowels use a Continental method of representation, helped out by doubling ('oo' or 'ee') to show length or an added 'a' to show both length and half-open tongue-position. The chart (Fig. 13) looks incomplete because there is no word corresponding to Cardinal Vowel No. 5 (/ɑ/). It must be said that, in the history of spoken English, that particular area of the mouth has been less important to speakers than to doctors. There are grounds for supposing that the use of the so-called long 'a' (aaaaah) has always been limited and often sporadic. It does not exist in American English and, in England itself, it seems to be limited to East Midland English. Neither Chaucer nor Shakespeare knew it; in the eighteenth century, a French word like *vase* has to be pronounced /vɔːz/ because /ɑː/ was not available, and even the place-name 'Gibraltar' came in as /dʒɪˈbrɔːltə/ because a Spanish 'a' was too much like /ɑː/. It seems likely too that the corresponding rounded open back vowel – /ɒ/ as in 'hot' – has never really been popular in England, and

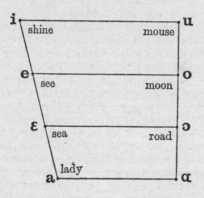

Fig. 13.

that something like /ɔ/ or even /a/ has been preferred. Americans say 'hot' as very nearly /hʌt/; Shakespeare's 'too, too solid flesh' in *Hamlet* may have been more 'sullied' than 'solid'. We can take it that, in most kinds of English up to, say, the end of the eighteenth century, the phoneme /ɑː/ was a pretty wide one, moving back to the borders of the territory of /ɑ/ and doing jobs that we now expect /ɑ/ to do.

So far we have established that the letters 'i', 'e', 'a', 'ou', 'oo', 'oa' for a long time represented 'Continental' vowels in English, that an Italian or Spaniard coming to words like 'see' or 'lady' or 'moon' in Chaucer's time would, giving the vowel letters the same value as in his own language, contrive – with a bit of extra vowel length – an exact English pronunciation. In other words, the Roman alphabet in England was still meaning pretty much what it meant to the rest of Europe. But, and we now remove our hats in the presence of a great mystery, a strange process began to operate in the English long vowels towards the end of the Middle Ages – a process known as a vowel shift.

Long vowels like /iː/ and /eː/ and /uː/ and /oː/ tend to be unstable. The tongue does not really like to hold the same position for a long time (which means, in fact, less than a second at the very longest) and so long vowels in English have always had a touch of the diphthong about them – the tongue has wanted to glide rather than stay still and hold the one long sound. Try pronouncing /iː/ in isolation, making it really long, and you will probably notice that your tongue wavers a little between the position for /i/ and the position for /ɪ/ – in other words, it glides or diphthongises. Now, probably while Henry V was fighting in France, the long /i/ of 'shine' was ceasing to be long /i/; it was becoming unstable, turning into a diphthong, toppling from its high position (see Fig. 13) and moving in the direction of changing to a diphthong like /ai/. What has happened to the /iː/ in 'shine' is that it has dropped with a crash to the bottom of the Cardinal Vowel Chart and become /a/ trying to climb back towards /i/. This is what the diphthong we know in 'shine' (/ʃain/) really is: the tongue trying to recover from its fall from /i/ to /a/ but never succeeding. Here, then, is the reason why 'shine', 'fine', 'tide', 'my' (which is really 'mij' – another way of writing /iː/) have the diphthong /ai/. There has been a change of sound, but the actual spelling still commemorates the pronunciation of the Middle Ages.

Now take another look at Fig. 13. With this vowel shift, 'shine' no longer occupies the /i/ area of the mouth: there is a vacancy. 'See' rises to fill the vacancy. What was /eː/ now becomes /iː/, and words like 'see', 'fee', 'keen', 'reed', 'weed' have the /iː/, pronunciation we use to-day. But this movement upwards of 'ee' leaves a vacancy. 'Sea' rises to fill the vacancy, and the pronunciation is no longer /sɛː/ but /seː/.

Almost to the time of the French Revolution a distinction was made in the pronunciation of 'ee' words and 'ea' words. 'See' was /siː/ but 'sea' was /seː/; 'feet' was /fiˑt/ but 'feat' was /feˑt/. 'Tea' was always /teː/. The distinction is still made in Ireland; indeed, the Irish version of English is a sort of fossilisation of eighteenth-century London speech. (Note again: the vowel shift gave 'speech' as /spiˑtʃ/ but 'speak' as /speˑk/.)

With the rising of 'sea' to the /e/ position, there is again a vacancy. The /aː/ of 'lady' rises to fill the vacancy, so that the Tudor pronunciation of 'lady' was something like /lɛːdɪ/. Since the time of this great vowel shift there has been another, so that, while words like 'see' and 'feed' have kept their /iː/, words like 'sea' and 'read' have risen to join them, and 'see'/'sea'; 'tee'/'tea' and the rest have become homophones. The vacancy left by the rising of /seː/ to /siː/ has been filled by words like 'lady' and 'make', whose /ɛː/ became /eː/. Eventually, /leːdɪ/ and /meˑk/ were diphthongised to /leɪdɪ/ and /meɪk/, and this diphthong is there in most words with 'a + consonant + e' at the present time – 'fade', 'trade', 'cake', 'fate', and so on. Note that some words with 'ea' have lagged behind the others in the upward shift, and so we have 'steak' and 'break' with /eɪ/ in them (/eː/ in Ireland) instead of the expected /iː/ (though some Welshmen pronounce 'steak' as /stiːk/). This explains the fact that 'break' rhymes with 'make' to-day, but in Shakespeare's time rhymed with 'speak'. It also explains some of the foreigner's difficulties in learning English from a book.

The vowel shift that took place with the long front vowels also took place with the long back vowels. The Anglo-Saxon, 'hūs' and 'mūs' were shown in the Middle Ages as 'house' and 'mouse' because, as in French, the letter 'u' was required to represent the front rounded vowel /y/. With the general shift, 'house' ceased to be /huːs/ and dropped to a diphthongal state like 'shine' – /a/ trying to climb back towards the high vowel but not succeeding. And so 'house' was pronounced, and still is, as /haʊs/, though some Scots still prefer /huːs/. The vacancy left by the shift of 'house' to diphthongal status was speedily filled by 'moon'; this ceased to be /moːn/ and became /muːn/ – the pronunciation it has to-day. 'Road' rose to fill the gap left by the rising of the 'moon', and so the old pronunciation /rɔːd/ was changed to /roːd/. Diphthongisation gives us our present pronunciation /roʊd/.

This strange behaviour of the long English vowels at the close of the medieval period has resulted in the 'un-Continental' spelling system we have, or part of it. The instability of vowels is, as we have seen, partly a consequence of their length, and with languages like Spanish and Italian, which tend to specialise in short vowels, we may expect a vowel-letter to mean what it meant to a Roman. With the short vowels of English – such as /ɪ/ in 'bit', /ɛ/ in 'men', /ʊ/ in 'full' – there has been less tendency to change, and so the letter values have been more or less maintained over the centuries. Still, there remains the puzzle of the vowel /ʌ/ in 'mother', 'son', 'sun', the lack of a consistent symbol for it. It has never had a letter of its own, any more than /ə/ has, precisely because it is a comparatively new sound (some dialects of English, such as Lancashire, still do not accept it), sprung into being long after the period of adapting the Roman alphabet to the needs of English. The phoneme /ʊ/ represents the traditional short u-sound, still flourishing in words like 'put', 'pull', 'push', 'full'. It also appears in words like 'foot', 'wool', 'should', where the shortening of a long /u/ also brought a slight lowering and advancing of the tongue (/ʊ/, we remember, is a little lower and a little further forward than /u/). Our modern /ʌ/ is a sound made with spread lips, representing an unrounding of a back vowel like /o/ or /ʊ/. If we think of it as the phoneme that results from pronouncing a short back vowel with lips spread instead of pursed or rounded, then we have a good rough general picture of it.

If the letter 'u' can stand for /ʊ/ as in 'pull', /ʌ/ as in 'cut', and keep its traditional Roman vowel in 'blue', it can also seem to do fantastic things in words like 'bury' and 'busy'. We are reminded here that, like French, English had a rounded high front vowel (as in *lune* or Chaucer's 'vertu') which the Anglo-Saxons, like users of the IPA, represented as 'y'. The unrounding and lowering of this /y/ will easily explain 'busy' as /bɪzɪ/ and 'bury' as /bɛrɪ/. The reader can play the game of deciding why 'what', 'war', 'swan' and similar words have 'a' representing /ɔ/ or /ɒ/. He will find the answer in the semi-vowel /w/ or /ʍ/ preceding the vowel: the lip-rounding associated with these two sounds is transferred to the following vowel. This business of one sound's influence on another, the tendency to assimilate, has much to do with the disparity between the way we pronounce and the way we spell. The normal plural ending '-s' stands for either /s/ or /z/, according to whether the preceding sound is unvoiced or voiced (e.g. 'cats', 'ducks', 'snakes' have /s/, but 'dogs', 'pigs', 'birds' have /z/). This is a trick the foreign student of English has to learn with no real assistance from the *look* of the word.

Consonants have not undergone such violent changes as vowels (especially long vowels) and a consonant letter in English can often be expected to give approximate guidance (in terms of the mother alphabet) to the sound it stands for. Digraphs like 'th' and 'sh' and 'ch' have had to be specially made for English; the last two are consistent, but 'th' gives no indication as to whether a voiced sound or unvoiced sound is meant. Still, a consonant letter normally signals the presence of a consonantal sound, with certain exceptions. The digraph 'gh' is a memorial to a departed /x/ (an unvoiced velar fricative as in 'loch' or 'Bach'). 'Light', 'bright', 'right', and the rest retain an unvoiced semi-vowel (/ç/) in their Scots pronunciation ('It's a braw bricht moonlicht nicht'), but the 'gh' is merely an indicator of diphthongisation (igh = /aɪ/) in Queen's English. In words like 'taught', 'caught', 'bought', it is an indicator of length (/ɔː/), though an unnecessary one, for 'taut' and 'taught' are both pronounced /tɔːt/. In 'laugh' and 'cough' it means /f/, and in 'hiccough', by a mistaken analogy with 'cough', it disguises a /p/.

The English 'r' was once the signaller of a good strong trill, but it now (in Queen's English) stands for a weak fricative before or between vowels. In words like 'fire', 'more', 'there', 'moor', 'beer' it merely stands for the central vowel /ə/. In words like 'girl', 'word' 'hurl' it means that the preceding vowel is /ɜː/. In 'far', 'card', 'cord' it acts as a mere signaller of length (/fɑː/; /kɑːd/; /kɔːd/).

Certain consonants are silent because they act only as visual pointers to the foreign derivation of the word which contains them, as with 'psychology', 'yacht', 'debt' (Latin *debitum*). 'Ch' ceases to mean /tʃ/ when it appears in a word that comes from Greek, like 'chaos' or 'chorus'. But, on the whole, the tricks of English consonantal representation are easily learned.

The reader will now have seen enough of vowel change in English (there is, of course far, far more) to know that English has been a highly changeable language and that the alphabet has been very slow to accommodate itself to change. Our vowel symbols (and some of our consonantal ones) give a picture of how the language used to be pronounced – as much as six or seven hundred years ago. The development of new sounds with no corresponding invention of new symbols also helps to explain our spelling chaos. But there are other factors, too. Seventeenth-century pedants stuck unnecessary letters into words merely to show the origin in Greek or Latin: 'debt' and 'doubt' are fine examples. In Shakespeare's time, and after, there was no agreed system of spelling: you could spell as you pronounced or as you thought you pronounced. In the days of the new literacy this was a godsend to printers. To 'justify' a line (i.e., to fill it out to the right-hand margin) they would add odd unnecessary letters, turning 'dog' to 'dogg' or even 'dogge'. This practice ended during the seventeenth century, partly as a result of the development of the news-sheet during the Civil War, when compositors had no time to make their pages look pretty, with neat margins, and tended to use the same spelling for any given word each time that word appeared. Standardisation of spelling was partly Dr Johnson's achievement (one of so many), hammered home with the bulk of his incredible Dictionary.

We all tend now to spell in the same way; we admit there are such things as 'spelling mistakes' and we are prepared to be penalised for making them. Private letters, however, will often break the rules and breathe that old freedom of the Elizabethan days. I have an educated correspondent who recently spelt 'Sealyham' as 'Celium' and 'coat of arms' as 'court of arms' (the latter shows that she pronounces 'coat' as /kɔːt/; it is a pointer to the fact that she is Welsh). Such 'phonetic' spelling would, if recorded sound did not exist, be a valuable guide to a posterity looking for the facts of twentieth-century pronunciation: we ourselves owe a vast amount of our knowledge of English sound-changes to the letters of the past. Despite the existence of 'public' spelling rules, however, and our general acceptance of standards, we are not happy about English spelling and are always talking of doing something to change it.

Innumerable suggestions have been made, often by people untrained in linguistics and George Bernard Shaw is but one of many who have sponsored – in life or from the grave – a 'rational' spelling scheme for English. Shaw's *Androcles and the Lion* has appeared in improved spelling; a modified phonetic alphabet is already in use in some schools. British units of money and mensuration are, rightly or wrongly, being brought into line with Continental practice; would it be wise to take the plunge and give to the English alphabet something of the consistency possessed by the alphabets of Europe? There are many reasons for being cautious about the taking of such a radical step.

The rationalisation of English spelling means to many people only one thing – spelling English 'phonetically', making each symbol used stand for one sound and one sound only, achieving absolute consistency in our written or printed symbols. Is such consistency possible without losing the semantic identity of the word itself? For, to take a simple example, 'the' is /ðə/ before a consonant and /ði/ before a vowel; sometimes the indefinite article is, in very deliberate American speech, pronounced /eɪ/; most often, though, it is /ə/. The pronunciation of any word will vary according to the emphasis it is given within a certain context. If the word is, to the eye, always to be the same word, an exact phonetic rendering is not really desirable.

Attempts to bring spelling of English words in line with the values of the mother alphabet depend on which pronunciation is to be considered 'correct' or standard. The Queen's English rendering of the diphthong in 'rain' is /eɪ/, and to spell it as 'ei' seems reasonable: Eliza Doolittle's test-piece would then be 'The rein in Spein steiz meinly in the pleinz'. But is it fair to impose this rendering on those elements of the reading population who do not use this diphthong? 'Rain' is a more rational spelling than 'rein' to the Cockney, whose diphthong approaches /aɪ/ or /æɪ/. Northerners say /reːn/ or /rɛːn/. What can be done about eliminating the letter 'r' in words like 'park', 'dark', and so on? There is no corresponding sound in Queen's English, which uses /pɑ·k/ and /dɑ·k/, but a host of other English dialects – including the various forms of American English – use some allophone or other of the /r-/-phoneme. Like Chinese, the written form of English has to serve for a great number of spoken forms, so that 'father' means /fɑːðə/ or /faːðə/ or /fæːðr/ or /fɛːðər/ or /faːvə/, according to class or region. There is a lot to be said for regarding our existing English spelling as part phonetic and part ideographic: we get some idea of the sound of the word, but we chiefly regard the word as a visual shape suggesting a bundle of phonemes which carries an accepted meaning.

Any changes we wish to make in English spelling ought, perhaps, to be limited to the consonants; to legislate for the vowels of the entire English-speaking world is presumptuous, for no standard spoken form of the language can ever be universally imposed. But even if we eliminate 'gh' from 'light' and 'night' we are depriving the Scots of a consonantal pointer; moreoever, we shall have to create a new convention to show that 'i' is pronounced /aɪ/ and not /ɪ/. The allegedly vulgar American 'nite' is sensible enough; but is it worth while taking all this trouble for a mere handful of words containing 'gh'? I would, as I have previously indicated, be glad to see a more consistent use of 'z', creating unambiguous forms like 'boyz', 'birdz', 'scizzorz' (or 'sizzorz'). I should like 'dh' to be used for the voiced form of 'th', so that 'thin' could be set against 'dhen' and 'thought' against 'dhough'. (Incidentally, one would not object to the spelling 'dho' for this latter; unfortunately, nearly all one's proposals for spelling reform are of this small and niggardly order – too insignificant to mean very much in the great disorderly jungle of English orthography.)

There is a very strong argument against a 'phonetic' spelling for those words that derive from Greek and Latin – an argument which consults the foreign learner rather than the native school-child. 'Education', 'situation', 'edifice', and other Romance words are near-identical in spelling to their forms in the modern Romance languages. The learner of English whose native word is *éducation* or *educacion* or *educazione* will hardly see something like 'edyukeishun' as familiar; the existing English spelling, though it may give no clue to pronunciation, is at least intelligible as a written symbol. And even when one considers the proposal to drop the 'k' in 'knife' as altogether reasonable, one is brought up short with the realisation of how much this spelling helps the Frenchman with a *canif* in his pocket.

Should we leave well alone? On the whole, yes. Sort out a few minor irrationalities but leave the great horrible bulk of our spelling untouched: much of it is a link with Europe, all of it is a link with our past. To understand how our spelling comes about is to forgive it. Let us make the fullest possible use of the International Phonetic Alphabet as an auxiliary, both in our English schools and in our classes for foreigners; if we want to show what the phonemes of our language are, here at least is a scientific way of doing it. But let us not exaggerate the difficulties of English spelling; let us merely be more tolerant of innocent transgressions, not always ready to bang a gong like a spelling-bee master. Nobody wants a 'silent' correction of Jane Austen's *Love and Freindship*. A guage works as well as a gauge, and parralell lines still meet at infinity. Academic examiners should have more important things to look for than offences against orthographical rectitude.

It remains to say that some people – including some teachers – have seriously proposed that we solve all our problems of spelling by letting the pronunciation follow the orthography rather than vice versa. I have heard a teacher try to teach the pronunciation of 'cabbage' as 'cab age' because of this mystical belief in the primacy of the visual form. On such people may the gods of language have a cruel revenge. Such a sin is the ultimate one of exalting the shadow above the substance, the appearance over the reality.

Chapter 8

Words

1

For the moment – but only for the moment – it will be safe to assume that we all know what is meant by the word 'word'. I may even consider that my typing fingers know it, defining a word (in a whimsical conceit) as what comes between two spaces. The Greeks saw the word as the minimal unit of speech; to them, too, the atom was the minimal unit of matter. Our own age has learnt to split the atom and also the word. If atoms are divisible into protons, electrons, and neutrons, what are words divisible into?

Words as things uttered split up, as we have already seen, into phonemes, but phonemes do not take *meaning* into account. We do not play on the phonemes of a word as we play on the keys of a piano, content with mere sound; when we utter a word we are concerned with the transmission of meaning. We need an appropriate kind of fission, then – one that is *semantic*, not *phonemic*. Will division into syllables do? Obviously not, for syllables are mechanical and metrical, mere equal ticks of a clock or beats in a bar. If I divide (as for a children's reading primer) the word 'metrical' into 'met-ri-cal', I have learned nothing new about the word: these three syllables are not functional as neutrons, protons, electrons are functional. But if I divide the word as 'metr-; -ic; -al' I have done something rather different. I have indicated that it is made of the root 'metr-', which refers to measurement and is found in 'metronome' and, in a different phonemic disguise, in 'metre', 'kilometre', and the rest; '-ic', which is an adjectival ending found also in 'toxic', 'psychic', etc., but can sometimes indicate a noun, so that 'metric' itself can be used in a phrase like 'Milton's metric' with full noun status; '-al,' which is an unambiguous adjectival ending, as in 'festal', 'vernal', partial'. I have split 'metrical' into three contributory forms which (remembering that Greek *morph-* means 'form') I can call *morphemes*.

Let us now take a collocation of words – a phrase or sentence –
and attempt a more extended analysis. This will do: 'Jack's
father was eating his dinner very quickly.' Here I would suggest
the following fission: (1) 'Jack'; (2) '-'s'; (3) 'father'; (4) 'was';
(5) 'eat'; (6) '-ing'; (7) 'hi-'; (8) '-s'; (9) 'dinner'; (10) 'very';
(11) 'quick'; (12) '-ly' – making a total of twelve morphemes.
'Jack' can exist on its own, but the addition of '-'s' (a morpheme
denoting possession) turns a proper noun into an adjective.
'Father' cannot be reduced to smaller elements, for, though '-er'
is an ending common to four nouns of family relationship,
'fath-' on its own has no more meaning than 'moth-' or 'broth-'
or 'sist-'. 'Eat' can be an infinitive or imperative, but the suffix
'-ing' makes it into a present participle. 'Hi-' signals an aspect of
the singular masculine personal pronoun, but it can have no real
meaning until it is completed by the objective ending '-m' or,
as here, the '-s' denoting possession. 'Dinner' is indivisible, for
'din' on its own belongs to a very different semantic area, and to
use 'din' for 'dinner' (as some facetious people do) or to make a
duplicated child's form 'din-din' is merely to use a truncated
form of a whole word, implying the prior existence of that word.
Finally, 'quick' is an adjective; the morpheme '-ly' turns it into an
adverb.

It will be seen from the above that morphemes fall into two
classes. There are those which cannot stand on their own but
require to be combined with another morpheme before they can
mean anything – like '-'s', '-ing', 'hi-', '-ly'. We can call these
bound forms, or *helper morphemes*. The other morphemes are
those which can stand on their own, conveying a meaning, and
these can be called *free forms* or *semantemes* ('meaning-forms').
'Jack', 'father', 'was', 'eat', 'dinner', 'quick' are of this order:
these are simple free forms, because they cannot be subdivided
into smaller elements. But words like 'Jack's', 'his', 'quickly' *can*
be subdivided, each into either (*a*) a free form + a bound form or
(*b*) two bound forms (like 'hi-' and '-s').

I have used the term 'word' so far without attempting a definition, yet the fact that we have been able to analyse words into
morphemes shows that we are finding no difficulty in recognising
a word. But the time has come for definition, and the great
Bloomfield, who may be regarded as the father of modern linguistic theory, suggested that a word was a 'minimum free form',
meaning a form unlimited as to the number of bound forms or

'helper morphemes' but strictly limited to one free form only. This would make words of 'John' (one free form), 'John's' (one free form and one bound form), 'its' (the same), 'his' (two bound forms adding up to one free form). It would not, however, make words of compounds like 'penknife', 'manhole-cover' or German *Geheimestaatspolizei* ('Secret-state-police' or 'Gestapo'). There would have to be a new term, such as 'word-compound', to cover these and the following fantastic verb coined by Robert Browning:

> 'While treading down rose and ranunculus,
> You Tommy-make-room-for-your-uncle us.'

But these compounds frequently set into what are, at least phonemically, simple entities – 'breakfast' (/brɛkfst/, not 'break fast'); 'cupboard' (/kʌbəd/, not 'cup board'); 'bo's'n', not 'boatswain'. It is difficult to draw the line, and the need for Bloomfield's limited definition is not at all clear: a compound word is still a word, doing a word's job.

Bloomfield also said that a free form could be recognised by its ability to stand as a complete utterance – granted, of course, a context of other words or of pure situation which would make the meaning of the isolated free form quite clear. Thus, we can take words from our sentence 'Jack's father was eating his dinner very quickly' and demonstrate this thesis without too much strain:

> 'Whose is that cap?' '*Jack's.*'
> '*Father!*' (The speaker is calling.)
> 'She *is* pretty, isn't she?' '*Was.*'
> 'What's he doing now?' '*Eating.*'
> 'Whose book will you borrow?' '*His.*'
> 'Why have you come? What do you want?' '*Dinner.*'
> 'Ugly, isn't he?' '*Very.*'
> '*Quickly!*' (The speaker gives an errand-goer a shove.)

The trouble with this is that a breakdown occurs with the indefinite articles 'a' and 'an' and the definite article 'the'. These can only make complete statements in a context of language, not of life: it is the words themselves that are referred to, not – as with the above examples – what the words stand for. Thus, 'What word did you use then?' ' "The".' – 'Do you say "a" or "an" before "hotel"?' ' "An".'

It seems that, if Bloomfield's thesis is to hold so far, we must regard the articles as bound forms, forms incapable of acting on their own – that is to say, not as words at all. Not all languages possess a definite article, but some that do seem unable to regard it as a separate word. Rumania has a newspaper called *Timpul* ('The Times'); the original Latin was *Tempus illud*, but now the remains of the *illud* act as an article glued to the end of the noun. The same glueing of an article to the end of a word is found in Aztec – *tomatl*; *chocolatl*; *Quetzlcoatl*; *Popacatapetl*. Arabic glues its article to the front, as in our own Arabic loan-words 'alchemy', 'algebra', 'alcohol', 'apricot' (*al-praecoq*), in *Al-Sultan*, even in the holy name *Allah*. (Note that the great Alexander appears in Arabic as Al-Iskander; the 'Al' is assumed to be an article and removed to leave 'Iskander' – a common Muslim name.) English itself has timidly played with the glue-pot: 'an adder' should be 'a nadder', 'an apron' was once 'a napron', and 'an orange' ought to be, as in Spanish, 'a norange' (*una naranja*).

So, if the articles – 'the', 'a', ' an' – are bound forms, they cannot be words; yet we say they *are* words: they have space before and behind; they are defined in dictionaries. Evidently something is wrong somewhere. For that matter, something seems to be wrong with the limitation of 'single-word sentences' to bound forms. If a pupil says, 'I came quick,' and the teacher utters the chiding correction ' "-Ly" ', then an error of usage is being corrected: the referent of '-ly' is itself. But if a man says, 'It's been ages since I saw you. I'll just run up to the nursery and take a look at your son,' the proud parents can answer: '-s!' (/zzzzz/), meaning 'We've more than one son now!' In other words, that bound form the plural suffix can refer, not to mere accidence (the correct inflection of a word), but to something in the real, external world – 'more than one son'.

I suggest that we allow the morpheme in its two forms – the morpheme expressing meaning; the morpheme which merely helps to modify meaning or create larger structures – to rest as our scientific unit. The term 'word' cannot have any *significant* denotation: a word is what my typing fingers think it is – a cluster of symbols or even a single symbol separated by space from other clusters or single symbols. The symbols represent phonemes. The words of connected speech do not even have the frame of silence around them: they are all glued together in a single act of communication. But it is convenient to assume that words have real existence and even to create a science of word-study called *lexicology* (not to be confused with *lexicography*, which is the harmless drudgery of dictionary-making). Not delving too deeply into what a word is, we are able to embrace the single phoneme /ə/ (the indefinite article 'a') or /o/ (French for 'water' – *eau*) as easily as the word-monsters of the so-called agglutinative languages: *nakomajn'ytamjun'n'ybolamyk*, for instance, which, according to W. J. Entwistle (*Aspects of Language*, 1953), is the Koryak for 'They're always telling lies to us' (Koryak is spoken in Siberia). It appears to be a good language for telegrams.

2

Get ready for two new fearsome technical terms. Looking at words, we soon become aware that they fall into two rough categories – words that mean something when in isolation, like 'apple', 'gramophone', 'tulip'; words that only possess meaning when combined with other words in phrases or sentences – such as 'it', 'and', 'if', 'or'. These are, of course, analogous to the two types of morpheme that can exist within the word itself, like the free form 'eat' and the bound form '-ing' in 'eating'. So in the statement 'The orange is yellow', we can pick out 'orange' and 'yellow' as words which carry meaning if chalked up singly or written in the sky by sky-writing aircraft. These free forms, because they possess independent meaning, are called *autosemantic* words. 'The' and 'is', on the other hand, mean nothing outside the context of a sentence; they only develop meaning when we make a synthesis of them with words like 'orange' and 'yellow'. We can say that they are *synsemantic*.

But can a word really possess meaning outside a context? Are not perhaps all words really synsemantic? Having read the sentence 'The orange is yellow', you will have a clear enough image of a fruit which is juicy within and yellow without. But if the word 'orange' were suddenly to be written on the sky by an aircraft, would we – without the assistance of other words – really be sure of its meaning? Certain contexts or associations might fix 'orange' as a fruit (oranges are reguarly advertised through various media), but the word might merely mean a colour. In Liverpool, 'ORANGE' painted on a wall might have completely different associations – William of Orange, the Orange Lodges, the Battle of the Boyne – and the citrous element would be expunged by the political. Similarly, 'yellow' without a context hovers between the colour and the adjective meaning 'cowardly'. Indeed, one can think of few words that are genuinely auto-semantic, and these are not necessarily autosemantic in every language. 'Milk' in English is unambiguous enough, but *leche* in Spanish can be an insult, and *susu* in Malay can mean as much the source of the milk as the milk itself. This is as much as to say that no single thing in the non-linguistic world is capable of preserving the word attached to it from vagueness, imprecision, ambiguity.

One may, however, except proper names – words or word-groups signifying some unique natural or human referent: 'the Taj Mahal'; 'William Ewart Gladstone'; '*La Bohème*'; 'the English Channel'; 'Ben Nevis'; 'Brigitte Bardot'; 'Lolita.' Yet these names only strictly come within the field of the lexicologist (and the lexicographer, for that matter) when they start to shed their particular denotation. If a girl is called a 'proper little Lolita', then 'Lolita' is turning into a common noun – a word expressive of a whole class instead of a single fictitious character. Indeed, proper names do not really possess a meaning at all: they are arbitrary signs, mere laundry marks. What does the name 'Theodore' mean? Its *etymology* (etymology deals with word-origin) is Greek, and the Greek words which make up the name mean 'God's gift', but this tells us nothing about the person or persons to whom the name is attached. (Etymology, one may say now, has nothing to do with the meaning of any word. 'Silly' is derived from Anglo-Saxon 'saelig' – 'happy, blessed, holy' – but this etymology does not help us to fix the present-day meaning of the word.) 'Theodore,' then, means all people called Theodore, taking the widest context; taking the narrowest, it means all the people called Theodore whom we happen to know or know about.

The science of meaning is called *Semantics*, and it deals with language at those points where it is closest to the 'real world'. The phonetician and grammarian tend to lock themselves in their laboratories, but the semantic specialist is close to the very roots of thought and action. George Orwell, in his novel *Nineteen Eighty-four*, saw how it might be possible for semantic control of language to change the whole pattern of a society. 'Newspeak' is the official language of Ingsoc ('English Socialism'), and its limitation of the field of possible linguistic expression aims at making heterodox opinion impossible: political rebellion cannot be conceived in the mind, for the semantic elements of dissidence do not exist. If 'bad' means 'opposed to the principles of Ingsoc', and Big Brother is the eternal personification of these principles, then a statement like 'Big Brother is bad' is absurd; it is like saying 'x = not-x'. In the totalitarian societies of our day we have seen how meaning can be delimited to serve the ends of the Party; but even in free societies we are perpetually bombarded by semantic perversions – mainly from politicians and advertisers, whose interests are furthered by the distortion or delimiting of meaning. 'The pacific uses of the H-Bomb' is as absurd as the Orwellian 'War is Peace'; 'peace offensive' is a phrase used glibly and often; 'X is a man's smoke' is a deliberate exploitation of a limited area of connotation; 'It's the ice-cream treat of the TV age' does not really admit of analysis.

Semantics is so big and important a subject that, in the few decades of its acknowledged existence as a science, it has already built up its own vast polyglot library. The book by Ogden and Richards – *The Meaning of Meaning* – states in its title what the basic inquiry of Semantics is; it is an inquiry which may well go on for ever. We all use words; do we know how tentative, complex, and fundamentally dangerous it is to commit even the simplest statement to the air? A friend says to me, 'I like cats'; I say that I understand his meaning. But once I start to analyse I find myself plunging into a world where things seem neither intelligible nor necessary: what is 'I', what is 'like', what is 'cats'? I am drawn into ontology, psychology, physiology, zoology, and I end doubting the existence of everything, including the possibility of language's possessing any sense-potentialities at all.

One thing we can be fairly sure about is that a word – a 'phonemic event' – only exists at all because of some entity that has prior existence in the non-linguistic world. This non-linguistic world may be seen as having two aspects: first, there are the things to which language ultimately refers – 'real' events or objects, which we assume have a life of their own; second, there is an area of mind where the speaker and hearer (or writer and reader) meet to agree on some interpretation of the real event or object. Thus, at one end we have the *word*, at the other we have the *referent*, in the middle we have the *sense*. The referent is perhaps a matter for the philosopher; the word is certainly the linguist's concern; the sense interests everybody, from the logician to the literary critic.

Whether the referent of a word really (in the sense of 'demonstrably') exists is no concern of ours. We may talk about the attributes of God even though some would say that God's existence has not been satisfactorily proved. We may talk about the characters of a novel, knowing that these exist only in a very special sense – certainly not as the Albert Memorial or Red Square exists. A hypothesis may have a mental existence and the ginger-and-white cat that sits by me at this moment of writing may have a physical one: to the user of words they inhabit the same area of reference. Ultimately, of course, even the most abstract idea must go back to something in the world of sense, so that the notion of God may derive from tree-spirits, which themselves are an attempt to explain the outward manifestations of a tree's life. I repeat: this is no concern of our present study, though we cannot help being curious about referents. After all, Dr Johnson said in the preface to his Dictionary: 'I am not yet so lost in lexicography, as to forget that words are the daughters of earth, and that things are the sons of heaven.'

A speaker speaks a word; a hearer hears it. If he understands the word he has stepped into the same area of sense as the speaker. The meaning of a word, then, may be thought of as this common area of meeting. But the sense, it goes without saying, depends on the referent, and the nature of the referent has to be defined by the context. Thus, the 'cat' of 'The cat sat on the mat' is different from the 'cat' of 'Bring back the cat for thugs and rapists'. We cannot say that 'cat' is a single word possessing two distinct meanings; there are two words phonemically identical but semantically different: we call these *homonyms*. The 'cat' of the second sentence refers back etymologically – by the grim fancy of 'cat o' nine tails' – to the cat of the hearthrug, but word-origin can never be invoked, as we have already pointed out, in the examination of meanings.

But what makes words less precise than mathematical symbols is their tendency to suggest meanings other than the ones intended in particular limited contexts. The definition of context is often not enough; many words tremble at various frontiers of sense; ambiguity is a vice of words. Ambiguity comes about not merely through homonymity, but through metaphorical extension (which may or may not lie behind homonymity, as with 'cat'), and through the fact that words attempt two opposing jobs – particularisation and generalisation. 'Cat' will describe a new-born kitten and a fully-grown tiger, so that opposite notions (weakness, strength; tame, wild; tiny, huge) are contained in the same word. 'I love fish' can have opposed meanings; Shakespeare makes Henry V say that he loves France so well that he will not part with a single province of it. It is, indeed, only with the poet or imaginative prose-writer that language functions smoothly. Ambiguity ceases to be a vice; its deliberate exploitation is revelled in. There are layers of meaning, all relevant to the context. Homonyms become deliberate puns – not necessarily comic. Lady Macbeth will *gild* the faces of the grooms with blood, 'for it must seem their *guilt*.' 'Die' in *Romeo and Juliet* means what it says, but also means to experience the sexual orgasm. 'Reasons,' to Falstaff, can be plentiful as blackberries ('reasons' = /reːznz/ = 'raisins'). A scientific age like our own tends to worry about this aspect of language. Some readers of a novel of mine were unhappy about the title, *The Worm and the Ring*: they wanted to know what it really meant. It meant, I told them, sexual incapacity, the failure of a marriage because of the moral weakness of the husband, the lowliness of crawling things and the golden round of heaven, the Wagnerian myth (*Wurm* = dragon). They were dissatisfied: meaning should be mathematical, unambiguous. But this plurality of reference is in the very nature of language, and its management and exploitation is one of the joys of writing.

Words tend not merely to be ambiguous but to be emotional. 'Mother' has a clear dictionary meaning (a *denotation*), but, because of the filial status shared by all men, it is drenched in associations of strong feeling, it has powerful emotional *connotations*. Thus, 'mother' may be attached to a country or a college ('motherland'; *alma mater*) so that appropriate attitudes of loyalty may be induced in citizens or alumni. But the connotations can be wiped out completely in a term like 'mother-of-pearl', which is as cold as 'matrix'. This has much to do with the distribution of emphasis: 'pearl' is the stressed element and the rest of the compound is pronounced weakly: /mʌðərəvˈpɜːl/. The same process was at work in 'This is the BBC Home Service', where the highly emotive 'home' was given less stress than the following word. As ambiguity may be used by advertisers and demagogues to confuse or deceive, so that emotional connotations of words like 'England', 'children', 'duty' can be exploited in wartime oratory or in bad poetry at any time. Words like these are assured of a 'stock response' in the unwary reader; the bad poet lets emotive associations do his work for him.

It follows from what I have said that the learning of foreign languages involves more than the amassing of denotations, the taking in of primary meanings only. *Fille* and *baiser*, which seem to mean 'girl' and 'to kiss' respectively in French, are notoriously dangerous words to use. *Buang ayer* in Malay means literally 'to throw water' but has taken on a particular gross meaning; *bulan* in the same language can mean primarily 'moon' or 'month' but also, by a natural extension, 'menstruation.' One has to watch context all the time. Meaning resides shadowily in the morpheme, less so in the word, less so again in the phrase or sentence or paragraph; but meaning only comes to its fullest flower in the context of an entire way of life.

3

Everything flows, including language, and one of the difficulties we meet with in the study of meaning is the fact that meanings change. There are various reasons for this – some essentially linguistic, others psychological or historical. *Pas* means 'step' in French, and *ne* ... *pas* means 'not' (literally: 'not a step'). Because *pas* is associated with the negative *ne*, it has taken on a negative meaning of its own, as in *Pas moi* – 'not me'. This, the effect of association, is entirely a linguistic cause of semantic change.

But most changes take place because society changes – either in its attitude to life or in its formal institutions. 'Parliament' does not mean for us what it meant in the Middle Ages, because the institution which is the referent of the word has changed radically. Hamlet, talking about actors, refers to the 'humorous man' – not the comedian, but the emotional actor: the old theory of humours (the primary fluids of the body which, according to the proportions of their mixture, determined a man's temperament) has long gone, but left this word behind to take on a different meaning. It is not long since 'atom' meant what it meant to the Greeks – 'what could not further be divided'. The word can no longer mean that, but we retain it. Inertia, conservatism will ensure that a word remains in the vocabulary, but change of meaning will be enforced by the non-conservative elements in man himself.

We cannot examine all types of semantic change here, but we

can note the tendency of words to move from a wider to a narrower range of meaning. For instance, 'fowl' once meant any kind of bird but now only means a chicken; 'hound' was once any kind of dog but its meaning is (except in a jocular sense) now strictly limited; a deer was once 'beast in general'. All these words retain the older meaning in their modern German form: *Vogel; Hund; Tier*. 'Meat,' once any kind of food, is now restricted to what comes from the butcher, though the older sense is fossilised in 'sweetmeat'. The opposite process – expansion of meaning instead of restriction – is rarer; perhaps the change in meaning of 'bird' (which once meant merely a young bird) is due to the limiting of the meaning of 'fowl'.

Sometimes a limitation of meaning will be associated with a sort of value-judgement, so that 'smelly' refers only to a bad smell. We can call this a pejorative change and note some very peculiar examples. Italian, for instance, derives its word for 'bad' – *cattivo* – from the Latin word for a prisoner, *captivus*. A cretin is, etymologically, a Christian. A knave was merely a boy (German *Knabe*). A villain once merely lived on a farm in Roman times; he was to become a serf and, finally, a bad man. This kind of social prejudice is matched by xenophobia or hatred or contempt of the foreign, making the Portuguese for 'word' – *palavra* – into 'palaver'. As the *hoc est corpus* of the Mass has become 'hocus pocus', so Mary Magdalene's weeping has become 'maudlin', and the fairings from St Audrey's fair 'tawdry'. Ameliorative changes – in which the worse becomes the better – are far rarer than pejorative ones: one should note 'nice', though – *nescius* ('ignorant') in Latin, and always unfavourable (it could mean either 'lascivious' or 'trivial') in Shakespeare's time.

It is interesting to see what we do with foreign importations in our own day. The *Blitz of Blitzkrieg* lost its native meaning of 'lightning' and now carries connotations of wanton destruction and massive bravery. 'Beatnik' – a hybrid of American-Jewish origin – meant a member of a group devoted to pacifism and self-denial but it quickly became as contemptuous a term as 'teddy-boy' (itself an example of pejorative change). Conversely, 'spiv' – which had a brief currency just after the war with a cluster of bad meanings – was taken over by the French as an adjective: *trés spiv*, as applied to a garment, meant 'stylish' – a good example of ameliorative change. The Malay word *pĕrang*, meaning 'war', passed into RAF usage with the particularised meaning of an attack, usually a ' wizard' one. Other, more recent, borrowings, like *sputnik*, *espresso*, have kept close to the things originally described; *ombudsman*, like science fiction, provides us with the name before the referent.

English is quick to develop old words to serve new purposes. Often *apocope* is the way (cutting off the body but retaining the head), as in 'pop' ('popular music'), 'trad' ('traditional jazz'). 'Television' quickly became 'telly' – a half-contemptuous, half-affectionate shortening. One of the simplest and most telling of adaptations has been in the field of rocketry, where 'go' is now an adjective meaning 'fully prepared'. The age of brinkmanship and the nymphet is quick to satisfy its semantic needs; it is even looking ahead, in its masochistic way, with the term 'megadeath'. Let us hope its referent stays in the world of real, not meta-phorical, nightmare.

Chapter 9

Sentences

A word in a dictionary is very much like a car in a mammoth motor-show – full of potential but temporarily inactive. To get the car on the road a whole complex of things is required – fuel and a controller at the wheel, direction and traffic-signs. To get a word moving we need the things that come under the heading of *grammar*. Grammar is a technique for describing words in action. It classifies words into parts of speech, lists the changes of form that words can undergo when in contact with other words (*accidence*), examines the placing of the totality of words needed for the expression of thought into a significant order of pattern (*syntax*).

Because grammar looks like a science and yet does not behave like one (words often jump out of their classificatory cages), teachers and textbook-writers have been wary of delving too deeply into it. A lot of out-of-date conceptions lie fossilised in grammar-books, and their makers – who often have stockbroker incomes – do not like to admit this. Nor does the inertia of teachers or the examiner's love of the unambiguous encourage them to revise the thirty-third edition. It is best to let things carry on as they are; let sleeping dogmas lie. The pupil-examinees do not want fresh light on grammar; they merely want to get rid of it.

Grammarians like the one whose funeral Browning describes first made their appearance at the time of the New Learning. They wanted to analyse the linguistic data offered by Greek and Latin (a grammar school is strictly speaking a Latin grammar school); inevitably, when they turned to describe the behaviour of the vernacular they took their classical grammatical apparatus with them. Most of the languages of Europe have, ever since, been analysed as though they *ought* to be the tongue of Homer or Horace. Some grammarians have smacked the bottom of English because it has carelessly lost all its genders and most of its case-endings. This is not cricket, meaning not Latin. Fortunately for them, few European grammarians have ever been called upon to examine a non-Aryan language like Chinese or Tibetan and equip it with a descriptive apparatus. The fact is that English, German, French, and the rest will, to some extent, yield to the categories of Latin because, like Latin, they are Aryan or Indo-European languages. But Japanese and Eskimo, not having had a classical upbringing, refuse to play the game.

The smugness of scholars like John Stuart Mill, who saw in the 'eight parts of speech' fundamental categories of human thought, required, and still requires, the cold douche of contact with an Asiatic language. There is nothing universal about our Western grammatical compartments, and, at best, they are somewhat shoddy and makeshift even when applied to the languages for which they were formulated. There are too many assumptions, too little desire (there never is much where vested interests are involved) to look facts in the face.

One assumption is that every sentence (meaning every complete statement) has to have a subject and a predicate, meaning at least one noun and one verb, as in 'Dad drinks' or 'Mum nags'. Grammarians know that many complete statements (statements made complete by context of situation) do not fulfil this fundamental law. The following are in common use and hence are good English: 'Fire!' – 'Out of it!' – 'Away!' – 'Oh, no!' – 'Go!' – 'Help!' Grammar insists that, in a ghostly sort of way, the parts of speech required to make a full subject-and-predicate form are really there but have been suppressed: they are 'understood'. They re-formulate these utterances as follows: '(There is a) fire!' – '(You get) out of it!' – '(Go) away!' – 'Oh, no, (don't do it/ I'm not having that/I disagree/etc.)' – '(You) go!' – '(Somebody) help (me)!'

The falseness of these assumptions should be self-evident: at no level of the brain does the speaker of the so-called 'elliptical' utterances imagine the 'understood' words. But the grammarian may point to some earlier stage of the language, when the understood forms, now suppressed, were fully expressed. His whole argument falls down when we see that languages have always used the device of a single-word utterance, that the missing forms only exist in the grammarian's mind. We are right to remind him that his job is to examine and analyse the forms of speech in actual use – what is, not what should be.

A further exploding of the Western theory that a verb is an

essential part of a sentence is contrived through an examination of languages like Russian, Chinese, and Malay, which have never possessed the *copula* – the verb 'to be', as in sentences like 'He is a good man'. Malay renders this as '*Dia* (he) *orang* (man) *baik* (good)' and Russian as '*On* (he) – *dobriy* (good) *chelovyek* (man)'. There is no point in the Western grammarian's asserting that 'is' must be understood; how can a word be understood if it does not even exist as a part of speech?

We must, then, revise our views as to what a sentence is, particularly rejecting the subterfuge of 'ellipsis' and the 'understood' subject or predicate. English has never felt any sense of the unnatural in its omission of verbs. Newspaper headlines miss them out consistently and, in doing so, merely seem to be exploiting a natural English tendency – enshrined historically in 'Up, guards, and at 'em' and proverbially in 'Red sky at night, shepherd's delight', 'More haste, less speed', 'The more the merrier', and so on.

To see what categories of speech the grammarian considers important, we ought to make up some typically 'grammar-book' sentences (that is, sentences that do not give the Latinist palpitations) and examine the function of the words therein.

(*a*) THE GIRL IS PRETTY. (SHE IS PRETTY.)

'Girl' is a noun, subject of the verb 'is'. For 'girl' 'she' can be substituted; this makes 'she' a pronoun. 'The' is a bound form which cannot be categorised except as the definite article. Attempts to describe it as an adjective cannot really be justified. 'Pretty' is an adjective (it qualifies the noun if placed close to it; it is predicated of the noun if it comes after 'is') and its behaviour is manifestly different from that of 'the'. 'Girls are pretty' makes sense; 'Girls are the' does not. 'Is' is a verb of a special kind. As, like 'seems' and 'becomes', it cannot express total meaning in itself (unless used theologically or metaphysically), it can be called a *synsemantic verb*. 'Be!' makes no sense, nor does 'Become!' or 'Seem!', but 'Glow!' or 'Go!' or 'Come!' make sense enough: words like the latter can be called *autosemantic verbs*.

(*b*) THIS PRETTY GIRL SHALL BE MY WIFE.
THE GIRL WITH THE FLAXEN HAIR SHALL BE MY WIFE.
THAT GIRL, WHOM I HAVE ADORED EVER SINCE MY EARLY MANHOOD, SHALL BE MY WIFE.

These three sentences are identical in their essential structure – '– Girl shall be my wife'. In the first sentence we see 'this' – a demonstrative adjective, in the third sentence 'that' – again a demonstrative adjective. The phrase 'with the flaxen hair' in the second sentence is doing the same sort of work as 'pretty' in the first. If 'pretty' is an adjective, 'with the flaxen hair' can be called an adjective phrase (or word-group). Phrases of this kind tend to begin with a preposition (a particle expressing relationship between the noun which is subject or object of a verb and the noun which is the core of the phrase):

> THE GIRL with the flaxen hair
> on the bus
> in my dreams
> from East Sussex
> at the house on the corner

In the third sentence, the word-group 'whom I have adored ever since my early manhood' is doing an adjectival job (it is interchangeable with the adjective 'adorable', for example). It is not quite an adjective phrase, for it contains two pure sentence elements – 'I' and 'have adored' (a subject and a verb); we call it an adjective clause. Such clauses begin with a relative pronoun – a word that refers back to a word in the main sentence (in this case, 'girl') and at the same time links this main sentence (in this case, 'That girl shall be my wife') to the adjective clause itself. Here are other examples of adjective clauses:

> THE GIRL whom I see every day on the bus
> who lives next door
> whose mother works in my office
> with whom I play tennis OR
> whom I play tennis with OR
> I play tennis with

This last adjective clause is genuinely elliptical: 'whom' is really understood. This omission of a relative pronoun is rare in other languages.

(c) HE WILL COME TONIGHT.
  HE WILL COME AT ABOUT QUARTER PAST NINE.
  HE WILL COME WHEN THE SUN IS SETTING.

In the first sentence, 'tonight' tells us more about the proposed action expressed in the verb 'will come'. 'Tonight' is therefore an adverb. 'At about quarter past nine' (note the preposition at the beginning) is an adverb phrase. 'When the sun is setting' (or 'As soon as the sun sets' or 'While the sun is going down') contains a subject-predicate combination ('sun/sets'). The introductory word or phrase ('when' or 'while' or 'as soon as') joins the two sentences 'He will come' and 'when/while/as soon as the sun etc.' It is thus a join-word or conjunction, like 'and' or 'but' or 'also'. The adverb 'tonight' and the two adverb-substitutes express time (they answer the question 'When will he come?') but a number of other adverbial notions can be expressed:

MANNER: COME quickly
                    with all haste
                    as if your life depended on it
PLACE: WAIT here
                    by the old mill-stream
                    where the three roads meet
REASON: Why (do) I DO IT?
                                        for kicks
                                        because I like it
CONCESSION: Nevertheless   HE IS UNHAPPY
                        Despite his wealth
                        Although he is rich

We must note that adverbs of manner – 'quickly', 'beautifully' – and adverbs of degree – 'more', 'most', 'rather' – can modify an adjective ('beautifully warm'; 'most kind') or an adverb ('exceptionally badly'; 'rather coldly'). Whether we are right to call them adverbs when they are really adjective-helpers or adverb-helpers is a matter for discussion, especially when a word like 'very' cannot modify a verb.

(d) I like WOMEN don't like me
    I like TO DANCE is to know the poetry of motion
    I like WALKING IN THE FIELDS is good exercise
    I like WHAT YOU DID THEN was uncalled-for.

The forms in capitals can act as object of 'I like' or as subject of what comes after. 'Women' is a noun; 'to dance' is a noun phrase (infinitive form: verb without subject preceded by the preposition 'to'); 'walking' is a verbal noun followed by a phrase which sits on the borderline between an adjective phrase (what sort of

walking?) and an adverb phrase (where is the walking?) The
final noun-substitute is a noun clause: note the subject-predicate
'you/did' preceded by the relative pronoun 'What'.

There is no room here for a fuller account of the parts of speech
we recognize in English sentences. We ought to add that the odd
interpolated forms like 'Of course', 'not likely', 'most emphatically
not', 'with all my heart', as well as plain 'yes' and 'no' can be
called affirmative and negative words and phrases, while expressions like 'Er . . .', 'Well . . .', 'you see . . .' can best be regarded
as punctuation forms which break up the flow of a statement
without contributing much to the meaning. These 'thrown-in'
words and phrases are often assigned to a rag-bag category called
the *Interjection*, created to accommodate otherwise unclassifiable
elements. Some of history's great cries of agony, like 'My Son,
my son!' or 'Light, light!' or Faustus's 'Ah, Mephistophiles . . .'
are, to the strict old-time grammarian, not really analysable as
complete utterances. They have been regarded as mere 'throw-
ins', not sentences at all. So much the worse for the strict old-time
grammarian.

Terms like 'noun', 'adjective', 'verb', and so on are useful
generalising tools which help us to cope with the problems of
learning foreign languages. We can learn a good deal from a
table like this:

Adjective before Noun	*Noun before Adjective*
English	Romance
German	languages (normally)
Russian	Malay
Chinese	Welsh
Romance languages, when adjective is not really precise (*beau bravo*; *ragazzo*; *bonne idée*, etc.)	Polish

There is a disconcerting logic about German which, putting the
adjective before the noun, puts the whole of an adjective phrase
there, too. English has 'buttered bread' but 'bread spread with
butter and strawberry jam'; German has 'with butter and strawberry jam spread bread'. In other words, in speaking German,
one must have the entire content of one's adjective phrase worked
out before the noun which it qualifies makes its appearance.
This to some extent applies also to noun, adjective, and adverb

clauses, for in these the verb is always shunted to the end. A sentence like 'This is the girl with whom I to the cinema went' calls for precise formulation of the clause before utterance, so does 'He told me that I forgiven was'. Note this separation of the subject from the verb, seen at its most idiosyncratic with a compound verb like 'I shall have gone'. This consists of (a) subject 'I'; (b) *finite* (i.e. subject-taking part of verb) 'shall'; (c) infinitive 'have'; (d) past participle 'gone'. In a German noun clause the English order is reversed: 'He told me that by that time I gone have shall' – in other words, giving the formula (a) (d) (c) (b). Similarly, one has 'I think that he it done have must'. One ought to practise such seeming perversions in English before trying them out in German. Even in ordinary sentences, German prefers to have a compound verb curiously split up: 'I have to him spoken'; 'He has it arranged.' This is analogous to out-moded English poetic forms like 'Him have I often seen, with torso bare', where English also takes on the adjective-position of the Romance languages.

There are two aspects of grammar which cause heart-burnings when languages of a conservative type – like German or Russian – or old languages like Latin and Greek have to be learned. These are (a) a rich system of *inflections*, whereby a noun or verb changes its ending according to the job it is doing in the sentence and (b) a complete panoply of *genders*, so that some nouns are masculine, some feminine, others neuter. More progressive languages, like English, have discarded gender and most of the noun inflections, while Italian and Spanish, retaining all the wealth of verb-endings bequeathed by Latin, have simplified the noun and made gender no real problem. Persian, Malay, and Chinese have no gender and no inflections: through studying these languages we learn how much useless luggage the grammar-books of the progressive West have still to carry.

Gender, in fact, is a luxury which contributes nothing to meaning. If I say *le bière* and *la café* I am breaking fundamental French rules but not rendering myself unintelligible. In English, where gender only persists with sea-going craft, it may be a breach of etiquette to call a ship 'it' and not 'she', but no semantic law is transgressed against. It may seem wasteful that English needs 'he' and 'she' essentially only for human beings, while 'it' has to embrace everything else, but English has at least resolved the old confusion between sex and gender, which need not have anything to do with each other at all. In German *das Mädchen* is neuter, though it means 'the young girl', and 'the horse' – *das Pferd* – is also neuter, whether gelded or not. In Russian 'dog' (*sobaka*) is feminine even when male, and Latin *poeta* ('poet') belongs to a feminine declension. It has been suggested that gender had its origins in animism – that primitive attitude to nature which gave everything a soul and saw biological sex as a necessary attribute of the animate. It is more likely that gender is an attempt – at a later stage of human development – to impose order on disorder, to herd a mass of primitive particulars into a few general groups, using the sexual categories – of which 'neuter', which posits the *absence* of sex, is logically one – as the best known and most convenient. Such categories have also been applied to metals, and dies, screws, and templates are still given a 'male' or 'female' appellation. With 'bastard' files the whole sexual business is taken even further.

The only motive for categorising nouns according to gender – which means according to *ending* – is a syntactical one: gender is important only if other words (not nouns) are affected by it. In Latin, *murus* ('wall') is masculine, *porta* ('door') is feminine, and *tectum* ('roof') is neuter. This involves a particular choice when we want to apply the adjective 'good' to these words. *Murus* must be *bonus*, *porta* must be *bona*, *tectum* must be *bonum*. Words are fond of influencing each other in this way. Old English had a full set of genders in nouns and corresponding endings in adjectives; these have only disappeared in Modern English because, with phonological change, the endings that indicated gender have dropped off: *mona* has become 'moon', *ealu* has become 'ale', *sunu* has become 'sun' and so on. In the daughters of Latin the gender principle has declined: the masculine nouns of Latin remain masculine, the feminine have remained feminine, but the Latin neuters have been adopted by the masculine gender: thus, *tectum* has become *le toit* in French, *il tetto* in Italian, *el techo* in Spanish.

The definite article in the modern Romance (or Latin) languages is derived from the Latin demonstratives *ille* and *illa* – the masculine and feminine forms respectively for 'that' (the English 'the' has a similar derivation from the Anglo-Saxon demonstrative). All of them agree on *la* for the feminine article; *le, il, el* represent different decisions as to what to make out of *ille*. The indefinite article (*un/une*; *un/una*) has been made out of the Latin numerical adjective *unus -a -um*, meaning 'one'. Gender, then, determines the choice of a word for 'the'. (In German we have three to choose from – *der/die/das*.) It also tells us – as in Latin – what adjectival ending to choose – simple enough in the Romance tongues but difficult in German, where the adjectival ending will vary according to whether the definite or indefinite article (as well as other genuine demonstratives) or no article at all comes before. In Russian, the verb-ending in the past tense depends on the gender of the subject – as though English had 'John slept' but 'Mary slepta'.

Gender-learning is a nuisance to us because of our complete emancipation from it in our own language. It does not matter to us when we are reading a foreign language, so long as that language has a clearly defined word-order, so that we know which adjective qualifies which noun. But in Latin, where word-order is fluid, especially in poetry, agreement between noun and adjective may be our only way of making sense out of a passage. In learning to speak enough of a modern foreign language to find our way about, we need not take gender too seriously if it causes us genuine distress. There are some varieties of German where *der*, *die*, *das* are blurred and slurred into a sort of omnibus *de* and adjectival endings are similarly indistinct. Even if our genders are all wrong – and this applies to any language – we can still be understood, for in modern languages gender is not *functional* – it is a mere decorative survival of any earlier stage of the language. For a language teacher to spend his first lessons concentrating on gender with a class that cannot see the use of it – this is near-criminal.

Accidence is mainly concerned with examining patterns of word-endings as they appear in that total meaningful structure we call a sentence. Nouns in Latin are very fully 'inflected': a noun will vary its ending according to its relationship with other words. *Mensa* is a 'table' (the English 'mess' in its military sense is ultimately derived from it), but only if it is the subject of a verb: *Mensa* is here. For the rest, I kick the *mensam*, admire the colour (of the) *mensae*, give a good polish (to the) *mensae*, take a leg from the *mensā*. There can be many *mensae* in a shop, and we can admire all these *mensas*. The colours (of the) *mensarum* can be admirable, and we would like to walk off with all the *mensis*. This seems complicated and confusing, but it is only a matter of using a glued-on ending instead of a free preposition. If English glued its prepositions on to the end of 'table', instead of having them in front of the word, we would have something like this:

Singular		Plural
table	*Nominative*	tables
table	*Accusative*	tables
tableof	*Genitive*	tablesof
tableto	*Dative*	tablesto
tableby,	*Ablative*	tablesby,
tablewith, or		tableswith, or
tablefrom		tablesfrom

The noun in English used to have a whole set of such *cases*, and modern German still uses them. Here is the word for 'day' in Anglo-Saxon and German (masculine in both languages):

ANGLO-SAXON

	Nom.	*Acc.*	*Gen.*	*Dat.*
Singular	daeg	daeg	daeges	daege
Plural	dagas	dagas	daga	dagum

GERMAN

Singular	Tag	Tag	Tages	Tage
Plural	Tage	Tage	Tage	Tagen
	Nom.	*Acc.*	*Gen.*	*Dat.*

The genitive singular survives in English, always acceptable for nouns denoting living things – like 'John's', 'boy's', 'girl's', 'dog's' – though ''s' strictly turns a noun into an adjective (the apostrophe, incidentally, manifestly commemorates a departed 'e', though Elizabethan etymologists saw there a truncated form of 'his'). We are not too happy about expressions like 'the apple's core', 'the door's handle', 'the box's lid', though one cannot say that they are 'wrong'. By a simple act of extension, an 's' sign of possession is also used in plurals: 'women's'; 'men's'; 'mothers''; 'boys''.

The Romance languages have dropped all noun inflections except for a plural indicator. This is straightforward in Spanish, where an 's' is invariably used, and straightforward enough in French, where 's' (*homme*/*hommes*) or 'x' (*bureau*/*bureaux*) is very often a purely visual sign. Here the plural article is the true indicator of a plural: *l'homme* = /lɔm/; *les hommes* = /lezɔm/. Italian plurals tend to follow the Latin pattern, changing 'o' to 'i' and 'a' to 'e' (*ragazzo/ragazzi*; *donna/donne*). English, so progressive in other ways, uses a very mixed bag. 'S' – indicating /s/ or /z/ – we may regard as the regular pluraliser, but forms like 'ox/oxen', 'child/children', 'brother/brethren' represent an older and very Teutonic way of making plurals, as do 'man/men', 'woman/women' (/wʊmən/wɪmɪn/), 'mouse/mice', 'tooth/teeth', 'goose/geese', and so on. This latter kind of plural is to be found in Anglo-Saxon, and it seems to suggest some earlier -i ending which acted on the main vowel and (/i/ being a front vowel) dragged it towards the front of the mouth. If we imagine that something like /mus/ ('mouse') was pluralised as /musi/, then it seems reasonable for the /u/ to be brought forward to /y/ (the sound in *lune*), remaining there even after the pluralising -i had dropped off. This kind of assimilation (one sound influencing another) is common in the Teutonic languages, of which English is one. The plural of Anglo-Saxon *mūs* was, in fact, *mys*, and the /y:/ in the plural has become unrounded. The /miˑs/ – 'meece' – which a TV cartoon cat still favours – became /maɪs/ in the ordinary course of the vowel-shifts we have already discussed.

Children and comic songs ('Ours is a nice house, ours is: we've got no rats nor mouses') rationalise English plurals, and the few eccentric-seeming ones we have either fascinate foreigners (who delight in the 'child/children' pattern) or are easily avoided by them (I have an English-writing Russian correspondent who prefers to tell me about his 'kids'). German, however, is happier with this mutation of vowels on the 'man/men' principle than with any other of the pluralising devices available, and plurals like the following are regular and normal: *Bach/Bäch; Bogen/Bögen; Chor/Chöre; Drang/Dränge; Genuss/Genüsse*. The two dots are merely a 'fronting' signal.

Personal pronouns remain complicated in most Western languages, and they show a strange lack of willingness to 'generalise' which must be traced back to the unknown tongue which was the mother of the Indo-Germanic group. Thus 'I' bears no resemblance to 'me' in English, nor *Jeg* to *mig* in Icelandic, nor *Ya* to *mne* in Russian, nor *ego* to *me* in Latin. We see the same lack of sound-pattern in 'we'/'us', Russian *mi/nas*, German *wir/uns*, Icelandic *vjer/oss*. This is no law of linguistic nature, for Malay has *saya* and Chinese has *wo* as an invariable I-me form. English has tried to simplify its personal pronouns over the centuries, though earlier forms survive in dialect and colloquial speech. 'Bash 'em,' 'Give 'em hell' contain an abbreviated form of the old 'hem' (not 'them'), and the rural 'Tell un' ('Tell him') goes back to 'hine'. The Lancashire word for 'she' is 'oo' (/ɯː/), which is a survival of Anglo-Saxon 'heo', abandoned in favour of the demonstrative 'sio', whence 'she'.

English now recognises only two inflections for all pronouns – the subjective (or nominative) 'I', 'you', 'we', 'he', 'she', 'they', and the objective (or accusative) 'me', 'you', 'him', 'her', 'them', 'us'. The objective form is used after transitive verbs like 'love', 'hit', 'kick', and also after prepositions like 'after', 'between', 'for'. It is because 'you' has become an invariable form – both in case and in number – that the solecisms 'Between you and I' and 'Let you and I' are committed. It is through the operation of such analogies (if 'you' can be invariable, why not 'I' as well?) that languages can be simplified.

The greatest richness of inflection is to be found in the verbs of the Indo-Germanic languages, such richness seeming just and necessary if we remember that the verbs of the older tongues, like Latin, were not helped by personal pronouns. If we pervert an English verb, as we perverted an English noun, glueing the pronouns on to the end, we can see that the corresponding Latin verb is not so unreasonable after all:

English	*Latin*
loveI	amo
lovestthou	amas
loveshe, lovesshe, lovesit	amat
lovewe	amamus
loveyou	amatis
lovethey	amant

The tendency in the Germanic languages has been for the inflections of the verb to become simplified, leaving the work of person-indication to pronouns, so that the great majority of English verbs may some day follow the example of 'must', discarding even the '-s' of the third person ('he love'; 'she eat'; 'it bark').

Latin grammarians (meaning the classifying men of the Renaissance) never found it so easy to categorise verbs as to categorise nouns. This is why students of Latin have so many pages of principal parts of irregular verbs to learn by heart, some of them – like *fero, ferre, tuli, latum* – so fantastically irregular as never to be forgotten. The insistence on setting irregular verbs to be learnt is often misguided: it sets sheer form above meaning and forgets that one may go through life without having to use – or even to recognise in speech or literature – the more irregular of the irregulars. One may go quite a long way in French with the auxiliaries *être* and *avoir* and the verbs of the so-called first conjugation (those whose infinitives end in *-er*). The beginner in English can subsist equally well on the 'weak verbs' (eked out with 'to be', 'to have', 'to go') until he is sufficiently familiar with the 'feel' of the language not to be scared by irregularities.

'To understand all is to forgive all.' We have invoked this maxim in connection with the seeming illogicalities of English spelling. We can invoke it also with, say, 'go' and 'went', which do not seem to be part of the same verb at all and, indeed, are not. 'Go' is defective in that it lacks a past tense and has to borrow the past tense of 'wend' ('I wend my way'; 'I went my way'.) We see 'I sing'; 'I sang'; 'I have sung' (a 'strong verb') and wonder how it can inhabit the same linguistic world as 'I chant'; 'I chanted'; 'I have chanted' (a 'weak verb'). The fact is that all languages like to conserve, hate to discard, and the strong form belongs to an early stage of development while the weak one belongs to a later – and apparently more amenable – stage, and both subsist, cheek by jowl, in the same vocabulary. Only by creating artificial languages like Esperanto or Novial can we hope to achieve perfect logic and perfect regularity, and then we soon become sated with the mechanical deadness of perfection, longing for something more human and less regular – the 'madness' of Russian grammar, the waywardness of English orthography.

Grammar has its own fascination and, in a mystical way, its own peculiar truth. We may not know what the verb 'grobble' means, but we can be pretty sure that if I grobble, he grobbles and that, some time in the past, we both grobbled together. If 'grobble' is a noun, then 1 grobble + 1 grobble = 2 grobbles. There is a satisfactory *boniness* about grammar which the flesh of sheer vocabulary requires before it can become vertebrate and walk the earth. But to study it for its own sake, without relating it to function, is utter madness.

Chapter 10

The Science of Linguistics

The foregoing chapters may be taken as the regurgitation by a novelist of what he has read, thought, and experienced about language – the irreducible minimum of linguistic knowledge which a literary person ought to possess. It is now my duty to refer the reader to some of the great linguistic professionals.

Linguistics as a science hardly exists before the nineteenth century – despite some remarkable intuitions as far back as the medieval Roger Bacon – and the nineteenth-century linguists concentrated mainly on what is termed historico-comparative linguistics. Men like Rask and Jacob Grimm, for instance, were concerned with the processes which made the Germanic tongues emerge from the Indo-European mother-language (I shall have a little to say about Grimm in the second half of this book), and Schleicher attempted to reconstruct that remote and unrecorded language through comparison of the features possessed by all its children. One of the great enquirers into ancient phonology was Ferdinand de Saussure, but, though his dates – 1857–1913 – proclaim him as belonging to the age of historico-comparative studies, it is Saussure whom we take as the father of modern linguistics. This is the age of descriptive linguistics or structural linguistics, and the first man to present a full-blooded theory of the structural principle was Saussure.

Ferdinand de Saussure was a Swiss scholar whose lectures were collected and published after his death by two of his students – Charles Bally and Albert Sechehaye – under the title *Cours de linguistique générale*. The work appeared in English comparatively recently – in 1959, as *Course in General Linguistics*[1] – but the act of translation was probably supererogatory: the original has long sown its seeds. Saussure's importance lies mainly in the power of the definitions he made concerning the nature of language. Thus, he attempted to define the act of speech in terms of

[1] Ferdinand de Saussure, *Course in General Linguistics*, New York 1959; Fontana edition, with an introduction by Jonathan Culler, 1974.

a connection between thought and sound. A is talking to B, and the process of conversation is presented as a circuit which opens in A's brain, where mental facts or *concepts* are associated with sound-images used to express them. A given concept unlocks a sound-image – this is a psychological event. But then a physiological event supervenes: the brain sends out an impulse corresponding to the image, aimed at the organs used in producing sounds. The sounds travel from A's mouth to B's ear – a purely physical process. The circuit continues with B, but now there is a reversal of the process, with the sound-image going from B's ear to B's brain, where the psychological associations of the image lead to the corresponding concept. The concept itself is not a linguistic entity, but sound unrelated to concept is nothing but noise. Sounds are made meaningful by being related to concepts: in other words, language may be regarded as the link between a sound and a thought. To use Saussure's terms, the concept is the *signified* and the expression of the thought the *signifier*. What comes out of the association between the two may be called the *linguistic sign*. Our task is to understand the nature of this sign.

The sign, Saussure points out, is essentially an arbitrary thing: there is no inner relationship between signifier and signified. Signs are mostly immutable, language is peculiarly inert – we receive it from the remote past and pass it on to the remote future. No one can fight against accepting the forms which it takes. 'Because the sign is arbitrary,' he says, 'it follows no law other than that of tradition, and because it is based on tradition, it is arbitrary' (Wade Baskin's translation). Yet, as we know all too well, forms and meanings do change, and Saussure attributes these to a relaxation or displacement of the tie between signified and signifier. He takes as an example the German *Drittel*, which means 'one-third'. It used to be *Dritteil*, in which we see clearly the form *Teil*, meaning 'part'. The concept itself remains unchanged, but there has been a shift of relationship between the signifier and the signified: this has altered the *value* of the linguistic sign. This question of value is important, and it depends on the relationship a sign possesses to the total vocabulary. The English word 'sheep', the Spanish *carnero*, the French *mouton* have the same signification but not the same value: 'sheep' cannot mean the cooked meat of the animal – 'mutton' is used for that – but the French and Spanish words make no distinction between the beast in the field and the meat in the kitchen. Thus the *values* of the Romance terms differ from that of the English term, but the *signification* is the same.

Another distinction Saussure made which has become basic to linguistic thinking is that between *parole* and *langue*, aspects of the totality known as *langage* (translation of the terms is awkward, also unnecessary). *Parole* is language as the individual speaker uses it – the physical actuality that is never identical between any two speakers of the language. *Langue* is not spoken by anyone: it is the sum total of all the *paroles* spoken by individuals, but it remains abstract, generalised, a social phenomenon, an institution only minimally changeable by the individual speaker or writer. It is a social entity limited in time, as the structure of a society is limited in time: *langue* is contemporary to the society which expresses itself through it. Once 'time' is mentioned we find ourselves using two other Saussurian terms which have become fundamental to structuralist studies – *synchronic* and *diachronic*. Synchronic linguistics deals with linguistic events occurring in a given period of time – the 'vertical' approach – while diachronic linguistics is concerned with language moving through time and hence changing – the 'horizontal' approach. The two studies require totally different investigatory techniques, since what occurs in time – like a change in sound or structure – is unwilled and unconscious, while what happens in a static slab of time is conscious and willed. Thus, we can hear the difference between the vowels in *man* and *men*, but, during the period of the Great Vowel Shift, nobody was, presumably, conscious of the changing of the vowel of *shine* in the direction of the diphthong we use today.

An important movement in linguistics that found some of its starting-points in the writings of Saussure but then deviated from them was the so-called 'Prague School' (originally *le cercle linguistique de Prague*), whose leading figure was Nikolas S. Trubetzkoy (1890–1938), although Roman Jakobson (born in 1896), who became a professor at Harvard, was able to do more to publicise and extend the activities of the movement. It was the original Prague scholars who called their approach to language a 'phonological' one, proclaiming themselves as little concerned with what speech-sounds were like as acoustic entities, but very much interested in the *function* of those sounds, the manner in which they behaved within the total structure of a given language.

Trubetzkoy said that this approach was perhaps wholly Slavic in origin, and he expressed himself as indebted to J. Baudouin de Courtenay, a Polish professor at the University of Moscow, who saw as early as 1870 the need to distinguish between what a sound is in itself and how that sound is used in the structuring of a language. Languages, according to the Prague School, have their own special and idiosyncratic ways of ordering speech-sounds into patterns – *Sprachgebilde* – but essential to all such structures is the principle of opposition or meaningful contrast. In other words, we learn about /p/ through contrasting it with /b/ in such word-pairs as pole:bowl, pall:ball, rip:rib. Differences between sounds that do not signify semantic differences are not phonemic or (a term they originally preferred) phonematic. They are outside the field of phonological study. It was Trubetzkoy's mission to develop a set of 'contrast criteria' for identifying phonemic oppositions.

The point primarily to be made is that, while a middle C played on an oboe is a fixed and absolute and wholly mensurable sound, there is nothing so solid about a phoneme. A *significant* sound (that is, a sound concerned with determining meaning) is only *relatively* different from other significant sounds. Modes of opposition can vary from the very wide to the very narrow. For example, /a/ and /i/ are alike only in that they are vowels ('multilateral opposition'), while German /k/ and /x/ are totally alike except for the one distinguishing factor of the first being a stop and the second being a fricative: these exhibit the kind of opposition called 'bilateral'. 'Proportional opposition' occurs when one pair of contrasting phonemes has as its contrasting feature a property that is the distinguishing mark of other pairs – thus, /p/ and /b/ differ only in being respectively unvoiced and voiced (a contrast of 'sonority') but so do /t/-/d/ and /k/-/g/. 'Isolated opposition' is to be found subsisting between the /r/ of Spanish *pero* ('but') and the /r̄/ of *perro* ('dog'): the length of the sound is not a contrastive feature of any other pair of phonemes in that language. Phonemes can contrast in some positions but not in others (those two Spanish phonemes oppose each other only between vowels), and then 'neutralisation' occurs. This kind of pairing leads to an accurate and economical inventory of the phonemes of a language, and it also helps in the study of the history of a language, indicating why certain sound-changes took place (or presumably are likely to take place).

Saussure had said that the diachronic and synchronic approaches to language must be distinct and separate, but the special preoccupations of the Prague School led its most distinguished scholars – Trubetzkoy, Jakobson, and Karcevskij – to maintain (in 1928, at the first International Congress of Linguists at The Hague) that the phonological approach was as applicable to diachronic as to synchronic linguistics. A language, it would appear, wishes to observe certain principles of economy and symmetry – so the synchronic examination of the phonologists indicates – and the history of a phonemic system may show a movement in the direction of establishing a more harmonious and economic phonemic pattern. If, for example, a language has a /p/-/b/ opposition and a /t/-/d/ opposition but a /k/ that does not significantly oppose to /g/, then either the /k/-/g/ opposition will come into being to complete the pattern, or else all oppositions will disappear – leaving just /p/, /t/, and /k/ – or, a third possibility, /k/ will disappear, leaving /p/-/b/ and /t/-/d/. Italian can make no significant contrast of the *gli* in *famiglia* and the *li* in *Italia* (or the *gli* in *aglio* – 'garlic' – and the *li* in *olio* – 'oil'), so one of the two has to go. As one sees today from the political scrawls on Roman monuments, which often spell *Italia* as *Itaglia*, the *li* may be leaving the language. The opposition of 'high functional yield' – like the /p/-/b/ of English, which produces a great number of minimal pairs (peat:beat, pit:bit, pack:back, and so on) – is less subject to decay than one of 'low functional yield'. In the Spanish of Andalusia, the fact that no meaningful contrast exists between the *y* of *vaya* ('go!') and the *ll* of *calle* ('street') has meant the virtual disappearance of *ll* (and the willingness of uneducated workers in La Linea to spell *yo* as *llo* and *llegar* as *yegar*). All this signifies is that a phoneme can establish its identity only through the kind of opposition which determines difference of meaning.

One of the problems of linguistics resides in this very area of meaning. The study of meaning, semantics, tends to take the enquirer out of the area of language and drop him in the world of 'culture', where the establishment of meanings depends on the disciplines of such sciences as psychology, sociology, anthropology. The linguistic anthropologist may find it difficult to reconcile the two sciences he has yoked together and may end up – like Claude Lévi-Strauss – as a 'structuralist' looking in primitive societies only for the kind of pattern he has already found in language. Leonard Bloomfield (1887–1949), perhaps the greatest linguistic scholar America has produced, was logical in rejecting a system of language analysis which, as with the Prague School, depended on non-linguistic criteria for its results. He insisted that meaning had to be investigated through formal – that is to say, structural – differences in a language: it is structural differences that determine semantic differences.

This sounds mechanistic: it cuts out the Sassurian 'concept'; like Watsonian behaviourism, it is distrustful of the 'soul'. Bloomfield redefined the phoneme so as to cleanse it of its semantic significance; at the same time he saw that it could not, like the raw materials of the exact sciences, be measured accurately by instruments. If it is neither a determinant of meaning nor an acoustic entity, what can it be? He described it as a 'feature of language structure': the phonemes of a language, seen as a bundle of abstractions, are to be used to describe various properties of the utterances of that language. This does not mean that Bloomfield was indifferent to semantic enquiry. He saw merely that the 'statement of meanings is . . . the weak point in language-study'. We define by demonstration, by circumlocution, by translation, but none of these techniques is really satisfactory. 'We can define the names of minerals, for example, in terms of chemistry and mineralogy . . . but we have no precise way of defining words like *love* or *hate*.' He saw meaning as the situation in which utterance on the part of A and response on the part of B take place, and perhaps this is as far as the science of linguistics should go. The importance of Bloomfield lies precisely in his insistence that the study of language should be as rigorous a discipline as physics or chemistry.

The best-known name in modern American linguistics is that of Noam Chomsky, Professor of Linguistics at the Massachusetts Institute of Technology. His fame rests not only on his linguistic pronouncements but on his political radicalism, expressed in highly critical utterances on American foreign policy, and there are some admirers of Chomsky who see the linguistic and the political sides as cognate. For as Chomsky emphasises the fundamental structural similarity of all languages, despite surface differences to which too much attention is paid, so, by extension, he wishes to emphasise the fundamental oneness of mankind and the criminality of trying to impair this unity.

Chomsky has provided the theoretical basis of what is termed 'transformational-generative grammar' – or just 'transformational grammar' – which seems to derive from a view held as far back as the Middle Ages, to the effect that all languages have roughly the same sort of grammar. In the sense that a statement in ancient Sanskrit and one in modern Chinese both exhibit such features as substantive categories (parts of speech) and formal categories (subject and predicate), this is evidently true .Wilhelm von Humboldt, in the early nineteenth century, used the term 'inner form' to describe the basic make-up of all languages. Chomsky prefers 'deep structure', to which he opposes 'surface structure' – meaning the superficial divergences which mask the basic identity. Out of this notion glimmers the possibility of fulfilment of the old dream of a world language, based on the establishment of a corpus of 'linguistic universals'.

To put it simply, it seems rather astonishing that anybody is able to learn a language at all – let alone two, three or more. A language seems to contain an infinitude of structures, and it seems possible to go through life without repeating oneself unduly: there is the sense that there is always some new statement to create. The potentialities of a language seem so vast that we must wonder how it is possible for anybody to know so much. Language-learning has little to do with exceptional intelligence, and one has to conclude that what seems so complex is really quite simple – or else the rules of language are built into the human brain, are as much a human endowment as the instinct of self-preservation.

Chomsky says that linguistic competence is achieved when a speaker has mastered the set of rules by which language is generated. The rules are comparatively simple, and the human brain is somehow disposed to the mastering of them. To learn a language is not to memorise a vocabulary but to acquire a set of rules. To the transformational grammarian, a complete grammar of a given language is the full corpus of operational procedures needed for producing all the acceptable sentences of that language. This grammar would not be a 'creation' but a copy, or rather a model, of the 'grammar mechanism' already built into the human organism. Let us see how such a model is made.

A language, according to Chomsky's definition, is 'a set – finite or infinite – of sentences, each finite in length and constructed out of a finite set of elements'. He does not define a sentence, assuming, fairly enough, that such a structure can be recognized intuitively. Any 'well-formed' sentence in English (which we can call S) will contain a noun-phrase (NP) and a verb-phrase (VP) – in other words, a subject and predicate. A noun-phrase must at least have a noun – like 'man' or 'horse' – but it can also have determiners (D) like 'the', 'this', 'every'. A verb-phrase has to have a verb, but it can also have complements of various kinds (Compl), such as adjectives, adverbs, noun-phrases. In the following we have a set of 're-write rules' for generating basic sentence patterns in English. The arrow means 're-write as' and the items bracketed are optional.

Rule 1:   S
Rule 2: $S \to NP + VP$
Rule 3: $NP \to (D +) N$
Rule 4: $VP \to V (+ Compl)$
Rule 5: Compl $\to \begin{cases} (NP +) NP \\ Adj \\ Adv \end{cases}$

This 'grammar machine' can determine most of the basic sentences in the language. If we follow all the procedures indicated, these rules will give linear sequences of terminal symbols or markers – what Chomsky calls 'terminal strings' – in this manner:

1. $D + N + V + Adj$ ('The man is old'; 'This horse is strong')
2. $D + N + V + Adv$ ('All babies cry frequently'; 'The girl smiles sweetly')
3. $D + N + V$ ('The dog barks'; 'Every man dies')
4. $D + N + V (+ D + N) + D + N$ ('The boy writes (his brother) a letter')

With a complete list of terminal strings all the basic sentences possible to English can be worked out. By means of *transformations*, the phrase-structure grammar can be expanded to cover all combinations, rearrangements, additions, and deletions of the basic sentences. So far, however, we have in mind only sentences in the 'active voice'. To create a passive version of the example in 4. above – 'A letter is written by the boy' – we need a formula like this:

$$NP^1 + V + NP^2 \text{ Tpas} \to NP^2 + be + V\text{-}en (+ by + NP^1)$$

NP^1 stands for the first $D + N$ in 4., and NP^2 stands for the second. Tpas is the symbol for 'passive transformation'. V-*en* means the past participle of the main verb and *be* stands for the auxiliary verb which goes with it to make the passive construction.

Chomsky's contribution to modern linguistics is regarded by some scholars as of no great importance. The British linguist Robert Dixon has said that 'his linguistics is mostly concerned with formalising previous ideas of linguistics in terms of logical rules, and making explicit various intuitions about language patterns'. But this may in itself be a major advance – the provision of a new tool for grammarians. Chomsky himself stresses the implications of his theory for a deeper knowledge of the nature of language itself, not just any given language. One can hardly doubt the importance of 'the discovery that certain features of a given language can be reduced to universal properties of language, and explained in terms of these deeper aspects of linguistic form'.

I have mentioned briefly a few of the major names in modern linguistics. There are many more, and there are many books, all of them very forbidding to the amateur. The study of language is no longer an easily entered province for the mere 'lover of language'; it is as tough a science as nuclear biology or astrophysics.

PART TWO

Languages in Particular

Chapter 1

Learning Foreign Languages

1

The English, in their splendid isolation, used to regard foreigners as either a comic turn or a sexual menace. To learn a European language (other than the dead ones from which English had kindly borrowed) was, at best, to seek to acquire a sort of girl's-finishing-school ornament, at worst, to capitulate weakly to the enemy. Things are not very different now, but an uneasy awareness is dawning that linguistic isolation is no longer possible, that the tongues of these damned Europeans may have to be taken seriously if they persist in pretending not to understand English. Unfortunately, many educated Europeans *do* undertand English and are very ready to speak it to English travellers and write it to English business firms, thus soothing that uneasy awareness back into island complacency. But, in their soberest moments, most English people will admit that the attitude of 'Let them learn our language, blast them' will no longer do.

The ability to speak three or four foreign languages with moderate proficiency is looked on still with suspicion by English people of an insular bent. But by most it is grudgingly admitted to be clever, even a mark of genius. And yet many Welshmen carry their bilingualism very lightly; Swiss citizens know French, German, often Italian, as well as what they learn at school; a Chinese bar-boy in Malaya can cope with Malay, English, and often two or three dialects of Chinese; a Port Said dragoman will know at least ten languages (I met one who knew fifteen, as well as three English dialects). People like this are not towering intellectuals; they are people often of very moderate intelligence. What makes them good at languages is the fact that economic and social circumstances force them to be good. So far, the people of England have never really been forced out of their monoglot complacency, and the legend that there is something in the Englishman's genes that prevents his becoming proficient in languages continues to be fostered.

And yet English colonial administrators, as well as planters, have not merely mastered the languages of Africa and the East but given them dictionaries, grammars, even literatures. In any crowded public bar it will not be hard to find at least one man who can understand demotic Arabic, Urdu, or Malay. If a good enough motive can be adduced (soldier's hunger or loneliness, the colonial officer's proficiency bar), then a foreign language will be learned, and learned thoroughly. To find as urgent a motive in peace-time and at home is more difficult; the mood of exile is one thing, the cosy tiredness of after-work evening – the daily paper and the television beckoning – quite another.

I have in mind, of course, the learning of foreign languages as an adult undertaking, a matter of choice. Let us look first, however, at the reasons put forward for the learning of foreign languages in schools, where choice is hardly involved at all. In the grammar and public schools there seems to be no unification of motive behind the teaching of ancient and the teaching of modern languages. Latin and Greek are the tongues of two civilisations which have helped to make our own, therefore they must be accorded a peculiar reverence; learning them is an excellent mental discipline; they are logical and lucid and help us to write English well; they enshrine important literatures. These are the reasons put forward for their continuing high place in the curriculum, and – except for the last – they are not very convincing reasons. Ancient languages, with their batteries of irregularities, are far less logical than modern Chinese; only the study of English can help us to write English. On the other hand, there is a peculiar aesthetic thrill to be gained from reading Latin or Greek poets in the original, and this may well be the only justification for learning the languages: poetry, as Dr Johnson said, is untranslatable and hence, if it is good, it preserves the language it is written in. But to read Caesar's accounts of his conquests or Pliny on the habits of dolphins, one does not really need any Latin: a good modern translation will suffice. Herodotus, similarly, can be read with fair confidence in English, but the peculiar music of Sophocles cannot be rendered into any modern tongue – not even modern Greek.

The suggestion that secondary schools should teach only enough Latin and Greek (both languages; not just one) to enable a boy or girl to read Vergil and Homer with a crib will be regarded in many quarters as an heretical one. I make it seriously, however. The virtues of knowing how to write a good Latin or Greek composition are, surely, chimerical; unseen translation is of the same highbrow cross-word-puzzle order. We should only translate English into Latin for the benefit of a Roman, but all the Romans are long dead. If a 'key' will help us to work out the meaning of a Latin or Greek passage, why should we not use a key? There will always be classical scholars who will need more than the minimal training I suggest – editors of texts and makers of keys – but for the greater number it should be enough to be given a fairly painless entrée into the beauties of classical poetry and drama, the preservation of which is the only purpose behind preserving the languages they are written in.

We learn Latin not to juggle with subjunctives and gerunds but to get at the Roman spirit – that 'pagan night', for instance, which we find superbly expressed in Catullus and which had such a radical influence on our own seventeenth-century poets:

> *Soles occidere et redire possunt:*
> *Nobis cum semel occidit brevis lux,*
> *Nox est perpetua una dormienda.*
> *Da mihi basia mille, deinde centum,*
> *Dein mille altera, dein secunda centum,*
> *Deinde usque altera mille, deinde centum . . .*

A literal translation and a minimum of linguistic exposition should enable a teacher to give even a person with no Latin at all some notion of the meaning of this passage. Here, first, is a line-by-line translation:

> Suns can (may) set and return:
> For us, when once the short light has set,
> There is one perpetual night to-be-slept-through.
> Give me a thousand kisses, then a hundred,
> Then another thousand, then a second hundred,
> Then yet another thousand, then a hundred . . .

Following traditional learning methods, no student of Latin could except to approach a passage like this until the slow toil of learning paradigms and parts of irregular verbs had been completed. I see no reason why linguistic exposition of the passage should not follow a more empirical line – the breaking-up of words into their constituent morphemes. Thus, *sol-* means 'sun' (compare

English 'solar', 'solstice'); *-es* is a pluralising morpheme corresponding to English *-s*. *Occide-* means 'set' (of the sun), and it is to be found in the word 'occidental' ('western'); *-re* is an infinitive ending found also at the end of *redire*. *Poss-* has the root meaning found in the English derivative 'possible'. Of verb-endings found in this passage, *-t* always stands for third person singular (he, she, it), while *-nt* signifies third person plural (they). *Da* means 'give', the *-a* carrying an imperative force.

Apart from the characteristic morphemes of Latin which indicate the behaviour of the words, a good deal of the vocabulary of Catullus's poem is already possessed by the English student who knows no Latin at all. Even *basia* ('kisses') – though no English derivative exists – may be known from Spanish popular songs like *Besame* ('Kiss me') or *Eso beso* ('That kiss'). If *dein* and *deinde* (both meaning 'then') seem to denote an inconsistency, one must remember that this is a poem and that a certain poetic licence is admissible. But even in non-poetic English we use 'till' and 'until' indifferently.

The point about selecting a passage of verse or prose which shall give aesthetic pleasure, and then submitting it to linguistic analysis, is precisely that the end of learning a language can be presented along with the process of learning. In studying grammar, we swim miserably in a marmoreal sea of abstractions, wondering at the point of it all. In reading – however haltingly – even a very few lines of a Roman poet, we do not wonder; the point is there before us.

2

The purpose of teaching modern foreign languages is usually presented as primarily utilitarian: we want to converse with Frenchmen or Germans, to read their newspapers, understand their films, write and receive letters in their languages; it is also conceded that we may want to get to know their literatures. These aims are sound but rarely fulfilled. The tripper to Paris will find Paris only too happy to sell him everything in English, including the English newspapers; also he will find a minimum of pen-pals. Let us be honest and admit that few English people need foreign languages for the well-beaten holiday paths. In any case, one does not want to limit one's travelling to those countries which speak the languages one learned at school.

The final argument for learning the ancient languages is one of the most compelling for learning the modern languages as well – namely, that certain literary pleasures are unavailable in translation. The educated man, it is generally felt, should be able to read Racine, Goethe, Dante, Lorca – with, anyway, the aid of a crib. To know these only in translation is not to know them at all. And even prose literature (since the Renaissance, that is) does not yield all its magic in translation: Edmund Wilson rightly told us that we had better not deliver any literary judgement on *Doctor Zhivago* until we have come into contact with its wordplay and symbolism, which are, inevitably, confined to the original. One feels uneasy at reading Proust or Flaubert in translation, despite the excellent English versions that exist. The ultimate value of a translation lies in its power to ease our way into the original.

It would seem, then, that our formal educations should equip us with at least a reading knowledge of those major European languages that do not find their way into the curriculum for specialist treatment. 'Modern Languages' in most schools means French and German, mainly because there are so many French and German specialists available. But there are increasing signs that other Romance languages are finding their way in, as also Slavonic languages. One of the incontestable advantages of the British State Comprehensive School is the opportunity it grants for almost limitless choice in the linguistic field – in theory, anyway: we have still far too few teachers of Oriental languages and far too many teachers of French.

Any school should be able to offer, in addition to specialist courses in Modern Languages, a supplementary (or even alternative) course in Linguistic Elements, in which the bases of General Phonetics could be started in the first year (the eleven-plus year, that is), gentle comparative work on the Romance languages could follow in the second year, and reading German – and even Russian – could be added in successive years. One could envisage a pleasant elementary paper on General Language, in which questions like the following could be asked:

(1) Describe the organic processes involved in uttering the word 'thing'.

(2) Render your own pronunciation of the following into phonetic (IPA) script:

'Time and the hour run through the roughest day.'

(3) Break the following down into its constituent morphemes, describing the function of each:

'John's sister was unwilling to provide him with any financial assistance.'

(4) Transcribe the following phonetically:

fille (French); *figlia* (Italian); *filha* (Portuguese); *hija* (Spanish). Describe briefly the adventures that the Latin word *filia* has undergone in changing into these four words.

(5) German *Zahn* and English *tooth* are cognate with the Gothic *tunthus*. What processes of historical change do you think the German and English words have undergone since the time when they both resembled *tunthus*?

(6) Write down the following names in (*a*) Arabic (*b*) Cyrillic (*c*) Greek script:

Shakespeare; London; New York; Washington.

(7) Free translation of a passage from a French, Italian, Spanish, or German newspaper.

3

Our main purpose here is to ease the task of language-learning for the average adult. It is sadly true that we only begin to feel the urgent need to learn a foreign language when we have left school. The need may be commercial or social, or it may be an itch of sheer curiosity (it is often this last that produces the amateur student of Tibetan or Basque). Granted the need and the staying power, we can either enrol in part-time classes or – with the aid of books and records – teach ourselves at home. Firmness of motive is very important; any teacher of evening classes will know that those of his students who have no real reason for learning Spanish but 'thought it might be something useful to do in the winter evenings' will not last beyond the third or fourth lesson at most. The same thing can happen with the home learner: the books on French are not so immediately interesting as the latest Agatha Christie; the records of *Russian Self-Taught* are less soothing than a Frank Sinatra LP; one is tired; one has no gift for languages after all; everybody in Gambogia speaks English. The voices of these devils can only be stilled by a sense of the fundamental importance of what we are trying to do, and

also by a technique which makes the process of learning interesting in itself.

Unfortunately, most of the primers on modern languages
available to the home student are, where easy to follow, amateurish and, where professional, discouraging. Some primers still
inhabit a dream-world where the words for 'international cooperation' are available but the words for 'yes' and 'no' hard to
find. My own language library has a book on Finnish which
gives neither 'please' nor 'thank you', a Russian primer which tells
of a maggot on a cherry but not the lack of toilet-paper in the
toilet, a work on colloquial Arabic which is a miracle of scholarship but a daunting guide to the simple mechanics of touristic
need. When buying a foreign language primer, look first at the
guide to pronunciation, see if the author has any real phonetic
knowledge; then examine the range of vocabulary, see if the important things (drink, aspirins, bus-stops, traveller's cheques)
take precedence over the modern equivalent of lightning-struck
postillions; finally, see whether grammar is rejoiced in as an end
in itself or treated as a minimal skeleton to the flesh of speech.
You will, alas, find very few books which are really satisfactory.
You will end, as I normally end, by gutting the book you have
bought and using its materials to make a note-book primer of
your own.

Before enrolling in a language class, enquire discreetly as to the
qualifications of the teacher – particularly his qualifications in the
phonetics of the language he teaches, for without the basis of a
good pronunciation no real work can be done. Beware of the
teacher who sticks to the book. Question the wisdom of learning
paradigms for homework. Insist that language is for *use*, and
that the using of the one you are learning shall not be too long
delayed. If you find you are learning nothing, blame neither the
language nor your own incapacity. Re-consider your motive.
Do you really want to learn this language? If you genuinely do,
go home and start teaching yourself.

Ultimately, that is what all adults have to do. Adult language-
study is mostly self-study. In some of the ensuing chapters I
propose to give advice as to the learning of particular languages;
here I shall content myself with a few general pointers.

We will assume that you are going to visit the country where the
language is spoken. You will therefore require far more than a
reading knowledge. A writing knowledge will hardly matter at all.

But it is essential that you speak a little and understand a lot. Learning to speak and learning to understand are two separate techniques. Men excel at the first and women at the second, women having intuition on their side. Many learners become discouraged because, having attained a fair fluency in speech, they understand far less than they think they ought when they listen to the radio or a café altercation. They should not be discouraged. Anybody can speak if he has in his own hands the control of structures and vocabulary; he cannot control what the native speaker says. Some languages are easier to understand than to speak: Dutch and German are two good examples; German in particular does not slur its phonemes nor insist on great speed. On the other hand, French – because of its tendency to elision and nervous rapidity – is difficult to understand when spoken. That is why so many good English speakers of French like to keep talking all the time.

You are going to visit this foreign country in the summer. The time to start work seriously is after Christmas. First, if you have a new alphabet to learn (as with Russian), learn the alphabet before you learn anything else. Remember that it is only an alphabet. It is not the body and soul of the language, only its dress. If the Russians were to conquer Britain, the British might have to write English in the Cyrillic alphabet. And so imagine that this has happened; write English names and words in Cyrillic. Do not trouble about learning Russian handwriting; it will be enough if you can manage a decent print script. Start your new diary in Cyrillic script; use it as a code. A strange alphabet is never really so strange: it is amazing how quickly it will yield its mysteries.

Your next task gets closer to the heart of the language – the skin, the flesh under the clothes of the alphabet. I refer to pronunciation, and would emphasise again and again and again that nothing is more important than to acquire a set of foreign phonemes that shall be entirely acceptable to your hosts. It is so important that it is better to know twenty words with a perfect accent than 20,000 with the sorry apology that contents most English people. The English have produced the finest playwrights and the finest actors in the world, yet they still see it as somehow unnatural, even effeminate, to speak anything without the accent that their mothers or their public schools bestowed on them. Yet, if an Englishman is telling a funny story that is designed to disparage a foreign race, he will find little difficulty in contriving a comic, but quite passable, pastiche of the foreign accent involved. Speaking a foreign language is a kind of acting, a kind of imitation of a foreign person. It is not, however, funny when everybody else speaks in that way; it is we who become funny in persisting with our own native phonemes.

I might say here that a curious phenomenon in language classes run in Britain is the tendency of students to spoil their phonetic advantages by considering that a language class is a sort of social occasion. I refer, of course, to those dialect speakers who are equipped already with fine continental vowel-sounds (think of the Northern /a/, /o/, /e:/, /ɛ:/ – perfect for French). These people decide to put on a 'posh', 'hot-potato' accent when in the company of the strangers who are the other students of the class, and this, inevitably, is used when they are asked to speak the foreign language they are there to learn. It was a Lancashireman who noted, after a visit to France, that foreigners 'speak broad'. We must speak broad with them.

To master foreign pronunciation is not so difficult. First, we must listen – to broadcasts, to gramophone records, to the foreigners themselves, if there are any in exile among us. We will note that every language has its own phonetic trade-mark: English is full of the sound /ə/; French is heavily nasalised; German has a sobbing intonation; Russian is mad about palatalising everything; Malay will not explode its plosives. Let us learn these tricks and apply them to English. More, let us use foreign phonemes and none else when we are speaking English. Let us pretend we are Frenchmen or Russians or Germans or Malays speaking English. This will give us fluency and relieve us from the need of thinking about too many things at the same time. It is murderous to try to juggle with a foreign vocabulary, foreign structures, foreign phonemes, foreign intonations – all at the same time – but not difficult to speak English with a foreign accent. It is an act, it is comic, but it is a very valuable exercise.

Let us make sure first that we understand exactly what these foreign phonemes are. With the minimal phonetic information that is given in the first part of this book, any student should be able to find his way about the human mouth. If his foreign language primer tells him that 'the letter "i" in Middle Low Slobovian is like the sound in English "sea", "we", "three", but shorter and tenser', he will know that he is facing an /i/ that is pretty close to Cardinal Vowel Number 1. If his Russian primer tells him that 'the symbol ь softens the sound after which it appears', he should cry out for more information, write to the publisher, ring up the author, demand a scientific description. If his French book says that *thé* is pronounced very much like English 'Tay', he should ask for his money back. One has a right to an accurate description of the phonemic system of the language one is learning, and accuracy does not necessarily mean the use of scientific terms. To describe the 'll' of English 'belly' as a singing sound and the 'll' of Welsh 'Llanelly' as a blowing sound is good enough. To describe one of the Arabic back consonants as a 'dry gargle' is excellent.

When one is familiar with the sounds of the foreign language and, as far as possible, the intonations (much listening is needed here), a start can be made on the language itself. Let us not be told what words we need to learn first; we ought to know. Remember, though, that we are not machines trying to make a factual communication with other machines: we are concerned with establishing contact with human beings, convincing them that we too (who are now foreigners) are also human beings. Polite, smiling, friendly, deferential (where deference is called for), we are also courting sympathy and help. We need the following utterances before we need any other:

Excuse me, sir, madam, comrade, comrades, ladies, gentlemen.
I'm a (British, Irish, English, Scottish, Welsh) tourist.
I don't speak your language very well.

With these we can practise pronunciation. We need to get them right. We shall have to use them often.

In expressing our particular need, we must learn a sentence-frame –

I'm looking for . . .
Where is . . . (?)
Where, please, can I find . . . (?)

– and, to fit into that frame, various words and expressions:

a taxi; a doctor; a chemist; a tobacconist; a café; a porter; the Hotel Splendide; the Bureau de Change; the ladies' toilet

After this we must learn 'Thank you very much'.
Other frames follow:

I would like . . .
My wife would like . . .
We would like . . .

And these are completed with terms like

some tea; some coffee; some beer; some wine; some caviare;
an omelette; a bottle of brandy

Other words begin to suggest themselves now – demonstratives
like 'this', 'that'; the copula ('is', 'are') if it exists in the language
you are studying; adjectives like 'hot', 'cold', 'red', 'white'; the
numerals up to ten. Now, too, we are in a position to complete
our phatic battery with 'Good morning', 'good evening', 'how are
you?', and so on.

We have made a beginning. Our few simple frames can be completed with a host of nouns and phrases, and it is time now to say
something about the learning of vocabulary. First, let us not
subscribe to the notion that, although we cannot always think of
the right word in our own language, we must nevertheless never
fumble in a foreign one. We use 'er', 'what's-it', 'thingummy' to
fill in our gaps; one of our first tasks must be to find out the
equivalents for those in the language we are learning. Fumbling
for a word is everybody's linguistic birthright.

Next, we have to devise techniques for learning vocabulary. In
succeeding chapters I shall try to show how the English-speaking
peoples are helped in learning the vocabulary of both Romance
and Germanic languages by their own twin heritage – English
being a Germanic language with a large Latin vocabulary. But
what do we do when the language we are learning is utterly and
completely foreign, totally outside the linguistic family to which
English belongs? It is now that we have to use our most cunning
and ingenious techniques. Let me draw on my own experience
when, in early middle age, I had to learn Malay very quickly.

I have no very special linguistic aptitude; moreover, I have a
very bad memory. So I had to resort to the most fantastic of
mnemonics. The word for 'if' in Malay is *kalau*. This is easy
enough. Kipling wrote 'If'; 'Kipling' rhymes with 'stripling'; a
stripling is a callow person; 'callow' is close to *kalau*. The two
other, more literary, words for 'if' are *jikalau* and *jika*, easily
remembered when one has planted the strong mnemonic root of
the basic word. Some mnemonics are essentially personal.

Kawan is 'friend': I had a friend called Cowan. Others are ultra-ingenious. *Bermastautin* is borrowed from Arabic and means 'to settle in a country, be domiciled'. I formed an image of a stout-drinking Scotsman lying in somebody's else's bed, saying 'Ah'm settled here. Bear ma stout in'. To remember *mualif*, another Arabic loan-word meaning an editor of a newspaper, I had to make a tortuous rhyme:

'If you've been drinking, chew a leaf
    Of mint before visiting the *mualif*.'

This had to be pinned down in my head with an image of a hard-drinking newspaper reporter. I pride myself upon being able to devise mnemonics (some of them so childish as to be shameful) for any foreign word in existence.

Russian is a language that, though it belongs to the Indo-European family, contains many hard words, hard to learn and to remember. We can dispose of words like *brat*, meaning 'brother' ('my brat of a brother'), and *sad*, meaning *garden* ('a flowerless garden is a sad sight') with little enough trouble, but have to think hard with words like the following:

nozh – knife (try 'Eat your nosh with a knife')
vodá – water (try 'Mr K. is so fiery, he turns water to vodka')
karandásh – pencil (try 'Get into the car and dash off that note
    with a pencil')
sobaka – dog (try 'That dog is *so* much of a *barker*' or 'That
    dog is a sob-barker' or 'So bark a number of dogs')

Such a technique will not suit everybody, but I am persuaded that all language-learners need a mnemonic system of some kind.

The learning of autosemantic words – nouns, verbs, adjectives – is, of course, a great deal easier than learning such helper-words as 'with', 'like', 'when', 'in', especially as there is rarely any total correspondence between English and foreign usage (e.g. French *dans* cannot invariably translate English 'in'). Moreover, such words seem to lack body, to be too frail and elusive to be memorable. Russian helper-words, for instance, often consist of single phonemes – *i* ('and'); *v* ('in'); *s* ('with', 'from', 'since'). I suggest the composition of mnemonic rhymes. For any foreign student of English, the following should help to fix the spatial prepositions:

Out of the station puffs the train,
Under the bridge, then *up* the hill,

Down the hill, *across* the plain,
Through a village, *past* a mill,
Beside a river, till once again
It comes *to* a station and stands still.

Meanwhile, read. The Bantam dual language books and the Penguin anthologies of foreign verse are cheap and useful. They have literal translations next to the text. Whatever the view of poetry held by the average Englishman, most other peoples are fond of it. Read a French poem in a French café, and people will applaud. Read a Russian poem to Russians, and they will kiss you and buy you drinks. Learn short poems by heart. That is a sure way into the heart of the language and the hearts of the people.

Chapter 2

Language Families

You have met, in these pages, occasional references to the Aryan or Indo-Germanic or Indo-European 'family of languages'. The time has come to say briefly what this means and how it concerns us as language-learners.

We have to imagine, in that prehistoric past which is really a pre-alphabet past, a race – shadowy, dim, unknown, but undoubtedly real – which spread all over Europe and even further East, taking its language with it – a language which, because of the normal processes of linguistic change and the fact of geographical isolation, gradually split itself up into the main languages of Europe and India. Scholars of Hitler's Germany tried to persuade the world to call this race the 'Aryan' race (*Arya* is the Sanskrit for 'noble' or 'excellent') and even told the world what this race looked like – fair, tall, muscular – and what its qualities were – athletic, powerful, warlike. The image of the 'Aryans' was very much the official Nazi image of the Germans themselves. Because of the suspect nature of all Nazi scholarship, which was racialism in disguise, nobody has cared much to use the term 'Aryan' any more; even the term 'Indo-Germanic' implied that, because German scholars had done so much work in establishing the existence of a common ancestor for several European languages, the German nation had the right to plant its flag in the name to be given to this language. 'Indo-European' is accurate enough (though it leaves Persian out of the picture) and it is the term we shall use here.

Though the Indo-European language no longer exists (it split up before writing was invented), we cannot doubt the thesis that it was there, very solidly, in pre-history, the mother of the major languages of the modern West *in potentia*, disclosing itself shadowily today through the kinship that exists – sometimes under a mask – in those very languages. Just as English 'milk' is like German *Milch*, 'bread' like *Brot*, and 'water' like *Wasser*, so 'father' is like German *Vater*, Dutch *vader*, Gothic *fadar*,

Old Norse *faðir*, Greek and Latin *pater*, Sanskrit *pitar*; and 'brother' resembles Dutch *broeder*, German *Bruder*, Greek *phrater*, Latin *frater*, Sanskrit *bhratar*, Russian *brat*, Irish *brathair*. In other words, there is a family face, and from it one may even learn how to reconstruct probable forms in the ancient mother-language. Thus, the Indo-European for 'father' must have begun with a lip-sound; the middle consonant must have been dental or alveolar; there must have been a final r-sound. Again, the ancient form for 'brother' must have had an initial lip-sound, then an r-sound, a back vowel, a dental or alveolar consonant, a front vowel, and a final 'r'.

That, of course, would be the mere root of the word, for we cannot doubt that this ancient language was, like Latin and Greek, rich in inflexions, with special forms for 'to a brother', 'from a brother', 'with brothers', 'of brothers', and so on. In the late eighteenth century European scholars began to look at Sanskrit – that ancient language of India – and, in the nineteenth century, a dim notion of what Indo-European must have been like in its conjugations and declensions was formed from the rich grammar of the Indic tongue. Sanskrit has a far older literature than either Latin or Greek, and thus, in it, we can see what must be features of the mother-language more fully preserved than in either of the two classical European tongues. Here is the verb 'to be' (present tense) in Sanskrit and some of its sister languages:

Anglo-Saxon	Gothic	Latin	Greek	Sanskrit
eom (am)	im	sum	eimi	asmi
eart (art)	is	es	ei	asi
is (is)	ist	est	esti	asti
sindon (are)	sijum	sumus	esmen	smas
sindon (are)	sijuth	estis	este	stha
sindon (are)	sind	sunt	eisi	santi

We shrug our shoulders at the irregularities we find in our verbs to-day; it is interesting to note that, the further back we go, the more irregularities tend to disappear: the present tense of the verb 'to be' in Sanskrit is no different in its endings from other Sanskrit verbs. Here is the present tense of 'to give', with the Greek beside it for comparison:

Sanskrit		Greek
dadami	(I give)	didomi
dadasi	(thou givest)	didos

Sanskrit		*Greek*
dadati	(he gives)	didosi
dadmas	(we give)	didomen (*dialect* didomes)
dattha	(you give)	didote
dadati	(they give)	didoasi (*dialect* didonti)

When the study of the Indo-European family of languages got under way – early in the nineteenth century – a natural division was made between the 'older' languages – Latin, Greek, and Sanskrit – and the 'younger' Germanic ones. It was recognised – for, after all, this was a process that went on in recorded history – that Spanish, Italian, Portuguese, French were derived from Latin; it was similarly recognised that German, Dutch, English, Gothic, and the Scandinavian languages had a common origin in a primitive Germanic tongue which was lost (like the Indo-European language itself) because of lack of written records. But this primitive Germanic language could be guessed at as to its shape and content, and it seemed to be a 'young' language, one that had broken away from the older forms represented by Latin, Greek, and Sanskrit.

Jacob Grimm – one of the Brothers Grimm who produced the very grim fairy tales – formulated, in 1822, a law which accounted for the consonantal differences between Germanic and the older tongues. Really, he was trying to answer the question 'Why, if the Germanic and the classical tongues have a common origin, is "brother" (or *Bruder*) so different from *frater*, "father" (or *Vater*) so different from *pater* and so on? Why these big consonantal differences at the beginning and in the middle of words which are supposed to be fundamentally the same?' Grimm's Law could not explain, but it could formulate; it could show that the Germanic language, in separating itself from the 'classical' phase of Indo-European, had followed at least a regular pattern of consonantal change. The pattern can be summed up as follows:

The area of articulation of a consonant in the 'classical' phase of Indo-European does not change when Germanic comes into being: a labial sound in Latin, Greek, or Sanskrit corresponds to a labial sound in Germanic; a dental or alveolar consonant remains dental or alveolar; a velar consonant remains velar. If the following list represents the main consonants in these groups, then the changes will be horizontal, not vertical:

	Unvoiced	Voiced	Fricative
Labial	p	b	f (v)
Dental	t	d	th (z)
Velar	k (c)	g	ch (/x/) or h

Let us see how this works out in practice:

Classical	Germanic
Greek, Latin *pater*	father
Latin *pulex*	flea
Latin *frango*	break
Greek *odont-*, Latin *dent-*	tooth, *Zahn*
Latin *tenuis*	thin
Greek *kard-*, Latin *cord-*	heart, *Harz*
Latin *octo*	eight, *acht*
Latin *hortus*	garden, *Garten*
Greek *gonu*, Latin *genu*	knee
Greek *thugater*	daughter
Latin *fero*	bear

The rule seems to apply well enough: one kind of labial in the classical languages will correspond to a different kind of labial in the Germanic languages (here represented only by English and German), and the same will apply to the other areas of articulation.

Grimm's Law did not seem to give a totally satisfactory answer to many enquirers. For instance, why should the 't' in *pater* correspond to the 'th' in 'father', but the 't' in Latin *centum* correspond to the 'd' in 'hundred'? Surely, if the law is to apply consistently, the English word should be 'hunthred'? The Danish scholar Karl Verner proposed, in 1875, a law of his own to explain seeming irregularities like that. It was all a matter of accentuation, he said. Indo-European 'k', 't', 'p' became 'h', 'th', 'f' respectively in Germanic if the original accent was on the preceding syllable. But, if the accent was originally on a different syllable, the sounds became voiced – 'g', 'd', 'b'. Granted that *centum* is pronounced with the accent on the second syllable, the correspondence of 't' with English 'd' in 'hundred' is quite regular.

There is, of course, much more to these laws – Grimm's and Verner's – than can be presented here. Indeed, the modern student of language may be prepared to question the validity of linguistic laws that were formulated before phonetics existed as a science. But it is important to think in terms of regular laws of change when studying languages: the seeming caprice, the baffling irregularity, can always be explained. More, a knowledge of laws of sound-change helps us to ease our language-learning task, as we shall see later.

Let us now briefly see what languages make up the great Indo-European group. The long-dead mother left behind nine tongues which have, in their turn, split up into a number of languages spoken to-day. The nine principal groups corresponding to the nine old daughter-languages are: Indian, Iranian, Armenian, Hellenic, Albanian, Italic, Balto-Slavic, Germanic, and Celtic.

The great Indian language, Sanskrit, is, as we have already noted, the oldest surviving language of the Indo-European group. Its sacred writings go back as far as 1500 B.C., and it is still read, chiefly by devout Hindus and students of Hinduism. An important Western poem, T. S. Eliot's *The Waste Land*, bases its final section on three injunctions from the *Upanishads* – *Datta* ('give'), *Dayadhvam* ('sympathise'), *Damyata* ('control') – and ends with a triple Sanskrit blessing: *Shantih. Shantih. Shantih.* Sanskrit, like Latin, ceased to be a spoken language while it was still flourishing as a language of ritual and prayer. The local dialects that used to flourish alongside of Sanskrit have survived to become the living tongues of some hundreds of millions of Indians (one of them – Pali – has become also a literary and sacred language, the official tongue of the Buddhists). The main ones are Hindi, Bengali, Punjabi, and Mahrati. The Hindustani that, to most Englishmen, is the lingua franca of the country (especially the North), is a mixture of Hindi, Persian, and Arabic. Words like 'chit', 'pukka', 'chota peg', 'wallah', and so on are now established as part of the heritage of English, and they come from Hindustani. The tongue of the Gypsies – Romany – is a dialect of north-western India which, with the wanderers who speak it, has spread not only through Europe but into America as well. It is no mere 'thieves' slang': it is a genuine and ancient member of the Indian group of languages.

Iranian splits into two parts – the eastern language known as Avestan (or Zend, though this is not strictly accurate) which takes its name from the *Avesta* – the sacred book of the Zoroastrians; the western language known as Old Persian, which is preserved only in the records of the achievements of Darius and Xerxes, some 500 years before Christ. Out of Old Persian developed Pahlavi, which is the ancestor of the Persian spoken today. There is a good deal of Arabic in Persian, and the alphabet itself is Arabic, but there is no doubt of the Indo-European roots of what must be the simplest Eastern language of all for the Westerner to learn. The following words disguise very recognisable forms (read from right to left):

دختر   برادر

r t kh d   r d a r b

مادر

r d a m

– 'brother', 'daughter', and 'mother', in fact.

Armenian is spoken round the Black Sea and the Caucasus, and it probably got there about seven centuries before Christ. It seems to have crossed the Hellespont to get there, and there is evidence that the ancient languages Phrygian (the speakers of which were the Homeric Trojans) and Macedonian resemble it somewhat. Modern Armenian, which has a large but not world-shattering literature, has been much influenced by Persian and it has also come into contact with certain Semitic languages, as well as Greek and Turkish. But under the very mixed vocabulary the Indo-European origin shines clear. (Armenian, like English and Persian, has dropped grammatical gender.)

The Hellenic group is large and complex. The Hellenes – or Greeks – entered the Aegean area about 2000 B.C. and spread into the mainland of Greece, as well as on to the Aegean islands and the coast of Asia Minor. The older languages – Lydian, Lycian, Carian, Hittite – went under, and the four Hellenic dialect groups – Ionic (of which Attic was a member), Aeolic, Arcadian-Cyprian, and Doric – took control. Attic, being the dialect of the city-state of Athens, became the most important for obvious reasons – the commercial and political power of Athens, the great dramatists, philosophers, orators, and historians who wrote in Attic. The Attic dialect became the *koiné* or popular Greek which survives in the New Testament and in the Byzantine literature of Constantinople. It split up, over the course of the centuries, into the demotic Greek spoken by the ordinary people of Greece today, and the so-called 'pure' Greek of the schools, newspapers, and serious poets and novelists.

Albanian is spoken on the east coast of the Adriatic – the language of that Illyria which is the locale of Shakespeare's *Twelfth Night*. It has no great literature and its vocabulary is so bastard a mixture of Latin, Greek, Turkish, and Slavonic that it is rather difficult to dig out the original elements. Nevertheless, it is an original member of the Indo-European family.

The Italic group began, as the name indicates, in Italy. We must guard against identifying the Latin, or Romance, group with it, for Latin was once merely one of the old Italic dialects: it later became important because, as with Attic Greek, important or at least energetic people spoke it. Other Italic tongues were Umbrian and Oscan, and there was a language – now almost completely lost but certainly not Indo-European – called Etruscan used by a vigorous people that left something of its art behind. The district of Latium contained Rome, and its language became increasingly important as Rome's political influence grew. Latin became the tongue of an Empire, and it is still, in one form or another, with us at the present day. The daughters of Latin require, in fact, a whole chapter to themselves, and they will get it later.

The Baltic and Slavic languages are sufficiently like each other to justify our putting them into a common group. The Baltic languages are, however, of much more philological than literary, social, or political interest. German ousted what was once a lively Baltic language – Prussian – in the seventeenth century; Lettic is spoken by a couple of million people in Latvia. Lithuanian is of immense value to the language scholar because, of all living Indo-European tongues, it seems to conserve most of the elements of the ancient mother-tongue. It is said that a Sanskrit scholar can make himself understood in a Lithuanian village.

The Slavic group contains the giant Russian. This was first written down by St Cyril (who gave it the Cyrillic script) in the ninth century, in the form of Old Church Slavonic or Old Bulgarian – a South Slavic which is not too different from the old East Slavic which is the official mother of Great Russian. Great Russian (or just 'Russian') is obviously of immense and growing importance. Little Russian, or Ukrainian, is considered by the Ukrainians themselves to be an important branch of the Slavic original, and they emphasise its distinctness from the official tongue of the Kremlin, but with little justice. White Russian is found in Western Russia and adjacent parts of Poland, and it is the mother-tongue of some 5,000,000 people.

Polish is the most important language of the West Slavic sub-group, followed by Czecho-Slovakian. Sorbian or Wend is to be found in Germany, near Dresden, but it serves as the mother-tongue of less than 1,000,000. In South Slavic we have Bulgarian, Serbo-Croatian, and Slovenian – these last two spoken within the new holiday-maker's region of Jugoslavia. All these Slavic tongues are very much like each other – far more like each other than English is like German, for instance – and to learn one is to half-learn the others. The pan-Slav concept is very real as far as the languages of the Slavs are concerned.

The Teutonic or Germanic group of languages will require a chapter to itself. Its importance need not be emphasised here, as it contains both English and German, but we ought to note how the whole Teutonic family is divided. East Teutonic contained Gothic, the language of a powerful and aggressive people which survives in some fragments of Biblical translation carried out in the fourth century by Bishop Ulfilas (a Greek). In the same group were Burgundian and Vandalic, but these have not survived at all. There is a moral here somewhere. Despite the depredations of the Goths and the Vandals, the Latin language flourished. Conquerors seem to need a literature if they are to eternise their language. North Teutonic contains the tongues of Scandinavia – Swedish and Danish to the east, Norwegian and Icelandic to the west. We still think it important to learn Old Icelandic for the sake of the sagas. West Teutonic covers two branches – High and Low German, which came into being as separate sub-groups about 600 A.D., when a sound-shift rather like that ancient one described by Grimm started to operate. The old Low German tongues were Old Saxon, Old Low Franconian, Old Frisian, and Old English (or Anglo-Saxon). Out of Old Saxon came the modern *Plattdeutsch*, the homely day-to-day language of many Germans; Old Low Franconian turned into modern Dutch and Flemish; Frisian survives in Friesland and a few small islands. High German – which is divided into Old High German, Middle High German, and Modern High German – has become the official and literary language of Germany: it is what we mean when we talk of 'German'. It first gained its hold in the sixteenth century, when Luther translated his Bible into it.

The last of the Indo-European groups is the Celtic one, whose decline and fall makes a curious and sad story. Two thousand years ago the Celts were everywhere – France, Spain, Britain, Germany, Northern Italy; they had even, in the centuries before Christ, advanced into Greece and Asia Minor. But recorded history shows the Celtic languages giving way all over – Gallic in France replaced by Latin, Cymric (or Britannic Celtic) driven west by the Teuton invader, Welsh and Erse and Gaelic losing ground to English, Cornish dying out completely. Nationalistic movements in the 'Celtic fringe' of England have succeeded in reviving dying tongues, but it would be idle to pretend that such shots-in-the arm can do more than provide energy for waving a feeble banner.

These, then, are the languages of the Indo-European family. This, it will be noticed, by no means accounts for all the living tongues of Europe. Lappish, Finnish, Esthonian, Magyar (Hungarian) form a family of their own, called Finno-Ugrian. The language of Malta falls into that Semitic group which also contains Arabic, Ethiopian, Hebrew. The old 'sick man of Europe', Turkey, takes its language from that Turco-Tartar family which gives Tartar and Kirghiz. But, you will note, the motif of family, of relationship, prevails. Go East, and Chinese will be seen to be part of the Indo-Chinese family, along with Tibetan, Siamese, and Burmese. Malay in all its forms belongs with Fijian, Tahitian, and Maori – the Malayo-Polynesian group. To know what family a language belongs to is a huge help in learning it. To an Englishman, Frenchman, Greek, the task of learning Russian will be eased once the fact of its Indo-European nature is known. There will be genders, declensions, conjugations, and these conjugations will have a flavour of Latin or Sanskrit about them. Tackle Finnish and we are up against new territory, new principles – agglutination, word-building. The Semitic languages will behave mysteriously, staking out their three consonants to make a kind of word-ghost. Chinese will behave most mysteriously of all, clinging to single syllables and tones.

Let us look now at a few of the more important languages of the Indo-European family, starting with the ones that are closest to England.

Chapter 3

The Tongue of the British

The English call themselves British, but the true British are the Welsh. Those Ancient Britons whom the Romans fought and subdued – Boadicea is a Welsh heroine, not an English one – were driven to Wales ('land of the foreigner') by the invading Anglo-Saxons. English is a foreign language as far as Britain is concerned. Welsh, or Cymric, was the tongue for many centuries of what is now called England. King Arthur held back the barbarous invader for as long as he could, in the name of the Christian Roman Empire. He was a Romanised Welshman; the barbarous invaders spoke the ancestor of the language I am writing now. These facts ought to be pondered on occasionally. The Welsh language, dying, kept artificially alive in schools and eisteddfodau, deserves our respect and our homage.

The big difficulty that presents itself to the learner of Welsh is the tendency of nouns to change their initial sounds in the phenomenon known as *mutation*. This means that a dictionary is quite useless until we are well into the language: we cannot, as we can with almost any other Indo-European tongue, start reading right away. Look up *gadair* ('chair') or *bib* ('pipe') in a Welsh–English dictionary and you will find no entry. These, in fact, are mutations of the forms *cadair* and *pib* respectively.

Welsh has no indefinite article ('a' or 'an') but it has a definite article – *y*, *yr*, or *'r*. This causes mutations of the so-called 'soft' variety:

tref – a town	*y dref* – the town
basged – a basket	*y fasged* – the basket
desg – a desk	*y ddesg* – the desk
gardd – a garden	*yr ardd* – the garden

In the same way, soft mutation takes place with adjectives when these qualify a feminine noun:

llyfr bach – a little book	*fferm fach* – a little farm

hogyn drwg – a naughty boy   *geneth ddrwg* – a naughty girl
dwr poeth – hot water   *teisen boeth* – a hot cake

In addition, there are nasal mutation and spirant mutation, so that many words appear under four distinct forms (including the radical, or dictionary form). Look up 'horse' in the English–Welsh section of a dictionary and you will find *ceffyl*. But 'his horse' is *ei geffyl* (soft mutation), 'my horse' is *fy ngheffyl* (nasal mutation), and 'her horse' is *ei cheffyl* (spirant mutation). Similarly, the radical *tad* means 'father', but we talk of 'his *dad*', 'her *thad*', and 'my *nhad*'.

Not even the numerals are free from this initial consonantal change. *Un cant* is 'one hundred' (there is a shining indication of the Indo-European origins of Welsh), but note the following:

> 200 – *dau gant*
> 300 – *tri chant* (*ch*, as in German, = /x/)
> 400 – *pedwar cant*
> 500 – *pum cant*
> 600 – *chwe chant*

The *g*, *c* (/k/), and *ch* (/x/) are, of course, all velar forms, so that the mutation (look back at Grimm's Law) is 'horizontal'. But the change from *mil* (1,000) to *dwy fil* (2,000) can only be explained in terms of a bilabial fricative (/β/) bridging the gap between *m* and *f* (/v/).

This sensitivity of initial consonants in Welsh may be regarded as the trade-mark of its syntax, just as the unvoiced L (*ll* = /ɬ/) is the most idiosyncratic feature of its phonology. But to learners of Welsh there are attractive simplicities hardly to be found in other Indo-European languages. It is possible, for instance, to make any present tense form with the verb *bod* ('to be') and a present participle made out of an infinitive (*darllen* – 'to read'; *yn darllen* – 'reading'). The present tense of *bod* is as follows:

> *yr wyf i* – I am
> *yr wyf ti* – thou art
> *y mae ef* – he is   *yr ydym ni* – we are
> *y mae hi* – she is   *yr ydych chwi* – you are
>   *y maent hwy* – they are

The article *y* or *yr* has no meaning here, incidentally. Note that the pronoun comes after the verb. This is characteristic of Welsh, which prefers the following word-order: (1) Verb; (2) Subject;

(3) Object; (4) the rest of the sentence. 'I am reading' or 'I read' is rendered as *Yr wyf i'n (i yn) darllen.* 'We are learning to read' is *Yr ydym ni'n (ni yn) dysgu darllen.* A special form of the third person singular of *bod* – indifferently singular and plural – is used when a noun governs it as subject:

> *Y mae'r bachgen yn gweithio* – the boy is working
> *Y mae'r bechgyn yn chwarae* – the boys are playing

The vocabulary of Welsh is naturally rich, but it absorbed, under the Roman occupation, a fair number of Latin words:

llyfr – book (*liber*)	*pobl* – people (*populus*)
eglwys – church (*ecclesia*)	*pont* – bridge (*pont-*)
mur – wall (*murus*)	*gwin* – wine (*vinum*)
ffenestr – window (*fenestra*)	*coron* – crown (*corona*)

Inevitably, too, there are plenty of English loan-words:

bag	*desg* (desk)
banc (bank)	*ffatri* (factory)
basn (basin)	*ffilm* (film)
beisicl (bicycle)	*inc*
brecwast (breakfast)	*lamp*
busnes (business)	*map*
bws (bus)	*papur*
cwnstabl (constable)	*plismon* (policeman)

But the Welsh language has left its mark on a number of place-names in England, as, indeed, the various forms of old Celtic have survived in quite unexpected parts of Europe. 'Water' is /dur/ – *dwr* in Welsh – and it can be seen clearly enough in the following: Dour, Douro, Derwent, Dorchester, Dordogne. An alternative word for 'water' appears in the non-Cymric forms of Celtic as *uisge*; Welsh has *wysg.* The root is to be seen in the following: Esk, Usk, Isis, Exe, Ouse, Ischia, Aisne, Ausonne, Oise. The Welsh for 'river' is *afon* (/avon/), and cognate Celtic forms are found in these names: Aisne, Ain, Vienne. 'Avon', then, is not so much the name of particular rivers as the term for 'river' in general.

Here, now, are some Welsh words which, on the surface, do not seem to resemble any of the corresponding words in the Indo-European languages which are best known:

anadl – breath	*eira* – snow
annwyd – cold	*gair* – word
arian – money	*haul* – sun
brenin – king	*ia* – ice
blodeuyn – flower	*llaeth* – milk
bwyd – food	*llong* – ship
coeden – tree	*plentyn* – child
chwaer – sister	*telyn* – harp
diolch – thanks	*wythnos* – week

Out of *haul* and *llaeth* emerge the ghosts of *helios* (as in 'heliograph') and *lact-* (as in 'lactic'), but we are given no help from other languages in trying to master the other words. There is a hard lesson to be learned here. We have seen, in the section on Semantic Change, how the Italian *cattivo* ('bad') comes from Latin *captivus* ('captive'). The simple-minded might expect the Italian to develop the Latin *malus*; instead, though, they will find the adverb *male*. But, almost accidentally, a language will build its vocabulary out of what takes its fancy, choosing among a wide range of synonyms or even perverting, limiting, or extending the meaning of a word which lies quite outside the semantic area involved. It is not so much vocabulary that indicates origin as structure, and the structure of Welsh is thoroughly Indo-European.

Welsh is no longer a major language, but it has produced – and is still producing – a considerable literature. Unfortunately, the major literary talents of Wales turn to English, and we can be fairly sure that no modern Welsh-writing poet can match the achievement of, say, Dylan Thomas, who knew little Welsh but brought a Welsh 'bardic' quality to English verse. Still, there is an untranslatable charm in Welsh lyrical poetry, and the following folk song stanza will serve as a fair specimen:

> *Ffarwel i blwyf Llangower,*
> *A'r Bala dirion deg;*
> *Ffarwel fy annwyl gariad,*
> *Nid wyf yn enwi neb.*

It is worthwhile to learn this by heart. The pronunciation of the vowels follows the Continental or Latin pattern. *W* is a vowel symbol, standing for /u/; *y* after *w* is /i/, otherwise it approaches /ə/. *Ll*, of course, stands for the unvoiced L – /ɬ/ – while /v/ is shown as *f* and /f/ as *ff*. The Welsh lilt, so different from the English tendency to monotone, may be picked up from the radio or television. Now for the words and their meanings.

> *Ffarwel* (trilled 'r' and clear 'l') is a loan-word – 'farewell'.
> *i* is a preposition – 'to'.
> *blwyf* is a mutated form of *plwyf* – 'parish'; the soft mutation has been brought about by the preceding *i*.
> *Llangower* is a place-name.
> *a'r* is a combination of *a* ('and') and *yr* ('the').
> *Bala* is a place-name.
> *dirion* is a soft mutation of *tirion* ('gentle').
> *deg* is a soft mutation of *teg* ('lovely'). Both adjectives qualify *Bala*.
> *fy* is 'my'.
> *annwyl* is 'dear'.
> *gariad* is a soft mutation of *cariad* ('sweetheart'). The mutation is the responsibility of the preceding adjective.
> *nid* is 'not'.
> *wyf* is the middle portion of *yr wyf i* – 'I am'.
> *yn enwi* is a combination of the untranslatable present participle signaller *yn* and the infinitive *enwi* ('to name'). This gives 'naming', 'giving the name of'.
> *neb* is 'nobody'.

The whole quatrain therefore reads: 'Farewell to the parish of Llangower and to gentle, lovely Bala. Farewell to my dear sweetheart (I'm not naming anybody).'

The remaining stanza tells of going, with 'heart like lead', to live in the 'land of the Saxon'. Here, for English people, is the other side of the moon.

Chapter 4

Learning Teutonic Languages

From even the filmsy survey of the Welsh language we have just made, it will be clear that Welsh is close to English only in a geographical sense. In comparison with Welsh, which came to England in prehistoric times, English is very much an 'imported' language, and it has to leap back into Europe to find its near relatives. Though the Norman Conquest, and subsequent scholastic devotion to Latin, have given English the surface appearance of a Romance language, it is very much a Germanic dialect.

What is a dialect, and what is a language? My late wife was born in South Wales; I was born in Manchester. We went to live for a time in a small village near Preston, Lancashire. When we entered a pub one rainy day, my wife was greeted by the landlord with the words 'Art witshert?' (/a·t ˈwɪtʃ/ət/) I understood this, but my wife did not. It is a way of saying 'Are your feet wet?' ('Art thou wet-shod?') Later the landlord said of his own wife: 'Oo's getten showder-wartsh' (/uːz ˈgɛtn ˈʃaʊdə wǎ·tʃ/), meaning 'She's got a pain in her shoulder'. Again, I understood, but my wife did not. To her it was a foreign language; to me it was a kind of English I had often heard as a child but had never consciously got down to learning. We were hearing Lancashire dialect, or rather that particular kind of Lancashire dialect spoken in the Ribble valley. Native English, then; a tongue not spoken by foreigners. And yet, to my wife, as foreign a language as Finnish or Lithuanian.

We like to clear an English dialect of the charge of being a foreign language by pointing to elements in it that only seem foreign because they are archaic. Thus, the 'art' of 'art tha' in dialectal speech is a survival from what was good Queen's English in Shakespeare's time. In 'Oo's getten showder-wartsh' we can pick out the Anglo-Saxon 'heo' that was eventually replaced by 'she'. 'Getten' is a form of the past participle cognate with American and Elizabethan 'gotten' (it survives in modern Queen's

English in 'forgotten' and 'begotten'). 'Showder' shows a development of Middle English 'schulder' which, when one sees how 'hūs' became 'house' and the dark L of 'talk' and 'alms' disappeared, has as good a claim to be regarded as English as the standard form 'shoulder' (/ˈʃoʊldə/). 'Wartsh' goes back to Anglo-Saxon 'weorc' which, with a more generalised meaning than is found in this Lancashire form, is easily recognised as the ancestor of 'work'. All this, then, presents a paradox. Good honest native English can appear to another English-speaker as a foreign language.

The process of historical analysis is no way of separating 'foreign language' from 'dialect'. For, if I say: *Mein Vater ist ein guter Mann* or *Der Winter ist kalt*, the meaning is clear enough to the person with no German: there are elements in both German and English which are fundamentally the same. Indeed, the two German sentences may well be more intelligible to the Southern Englishman than the two Lancashire ones I have quoted. We must conclude, perhaps, that the terms 'dialect' and 'language' have very indistinct boundaries, and that 'foreign' has more social or ethnographical significance than linguistic.

The closeness of English and German is best seen in the earlier phases of the two languages. Here is some Anglo-Saxon poetry:

> Ða waes on healle   heardecg togen,
> sweord ofer setlum,   sidrand manig
> hafen handa faest: helm ne gemunde,
> byrnan side,   þa hine se broga angeat . . .
> . . . hraðe heo aeðelinga   anna haefde
> faeste befongen,   þa heo to fenne gang . . .

That is part of our national epic *Beowulf*; it means: 'Then was in the hall the hardedged (sword) seized, the sword over the benches, many a broad shield raised firmly in the hand: helmet did not remember the wide burnie, when him the monster seized . . . quickly she of the warriors one had securely seized, when she to the fen went . . .' The 'she' referred to is the mother of Grendel; both are foul murderous man-eating monsters. *Beowulf*, I have always maintained, would make a first-rate horror-film. Here for comparison, is a line or two from the German *Hildebrandslied* ('Song of Hildebrand'):

> Ik gihorta ðat seggen,
> ðat sih urhettun   .   aenon muotin,

Hiltibrant enti Haðubrant . untar heriun tuem,
sunu fatar ungo . . .

(A free translation: 'I have heard it said that two chosen men, Hildebrand and Hadubrand, met in single combat between two armies, the son and the father . . .') If one wishes to learn an old Germanic language, is there much to choose between these two?

When we look at older forms of the Germanic tongues, we tend to feel more at home than with their modern forms, chiefly because English has retained certain sounds once common to all the Germanic family but since – in all except English and Icelandic (an intensely conservative language) – shifted into sounds cognate but different. Take the two consonants /θ/ and /ð/, for instance, indifferently represented in English as 'th'. Icelandic clings to the old signs as well as the old sounds (this is from a newspaper: '*Um 90 pusand tunnur salta ðar alls á öllu landinu og i kvöld er búist við ad 200 pus . . .*') but look what has happened in German:

Dank – thanks	*Ding* – thing
dass – that	*Durst* – thirst
dann – then	*Distel* – thistle
dick – thick	*Dorn* – thorn
dünn – thin	*Dorf* – thorp = village

The initial consonant 'th', which, in the English words above, is sometimes a symbol for /θ/, sometimes for /ð/, has an invariable equivalent of *d* in German. But in Swedish there is a differentiation, so that *t* stands for English /θ/ and *d* for English /ð/:

tjock – thick	*det* – that
ting – thing	*dem* – them
tänka – think	*där* – there
tre – three	*fader* – father
tron – throne	*broder* – brother

Another shift that English has resisted is that from /w/ to /v/. German spelling does not show the true pronunciation of *Wasser*, *Wurm*, *Wort*, and so on ('water', 'worm', 'word'); we have to accept 'w' as a symbol for /v/. But in Swedish the spelling is honest:

vagn – waggon	*väder* – weather
vatten – water	*väl* – well

vild – wild *vid* – wide
verk – work *villig* – willing
varm – warm *ved* – wood

From this point on, we had better concentrate on German. It is, by virtue of its modern literature (from Goethe and Schiller on) as well as its philosophy and science, by far the most important language of the Germanic group (English, of course, excepted). The Scandinavian languages have their own interest, but only Ibsen and Hans Andersen are world literary figures, and they are available in translation: modern Scandinavian poetry is not, except of course, for the specialist, crying out to be read. As for Dutch, Holland shrugs its shoulders at the diminishing importance of this close relative of English; English is spoken by all educated Lowlanders. But German cannot be ignored by anyone.

The learning of German words is eased when we remember certain sound-shifts. First, English /t/ becomes an affricate /ts/, represented in German spelling as *z*:

tap – *Zapfen* tongue – *Zunge* to – *zu*

This is at the beginning of words; in the middle or at the end German goes the whole hog and has, for English /t/, a fricative – *ss*:

better – *besser* eat – *essen* foot – *Fuss*
kettle – *Kessel* let – *lassen* water – *Wasser*

(Note that German nouns begin with a capital – a time-waster to the typist.)

The English 'd' often comes out as German 't':

daughter – *Tochter* day – *Tag* drink – *trinken*

Two phenomena might, in addition, be noted in the above two first examples. The English 'gh', which used to stand for /x/, is now a mere sign of vowel-length, but, in trying to sort out the meaning of a German word, it is a good plan to substitute English 'gh' for German *ch* and see if any sense comes out of it – *Licht*, *lach(en)*, *Nacht*, for example. The *g* of *Tag* has softened to 'y' in English 'day'; sometimes it appears in English as 'w' (note that both 'y' and 'w' are semi-vowel symbols used to indicate /ɪ/ and /ʊ/ respectively as second elements of diphthongs). Thus, if the *v* of *Vogel* is pronounced /f/, what does the whole word mean? How about *pfennig*, *Bog(en)*, *Weg*?

The German *ch* stands for /x/ after a back vowel, /ç/ after a front one. It is sometimes equivalent to English 'k':

book – *Buch*	make – *machen*	week – *Woch* (/x/)
weak – *weich*	reek – *riechen*	rake – *Rechen* (/ç/)

English 'p' either becomes the affricate *pf* (/pf/) or else the full-blown fricative 'f' (/f/), according to position:

path – *Pfad*	pepper – *Pfeffer*	pipe – *Pfeife*
plant – *Pflanze*	sleep – *schlafen*	

This last example also reminds us that English 's' + consonant appears in German as /ʃ/ (spelt *sch*) + consonant:

sleep – *schlafen*	smut – *Schmutz*	snow – *Schnee*
swan – *Schwan*	sweat – *Schweiss*	

Finally, English non-initial 'v' often appears as German *b*:

give – *geben*	have – *haben*	love – *lieben*

In addition to these disguised identities, there are several words which are patently identical in English and German, though German prefers that older pronunciation still retained in, say, Lancashire English (e.g. *Butter*, *Mann*, *hier*, *Lamm*). And German sometimes gives a clearer indication of the English pronunciation of a word held in common than the English spelling itself – take *Haus*, *Maus*, for example.

It is not really possible to work out tables of vowel equivalents for the two languages. English 'o – e' will sometimes appear as German *ei* (/ai/); as in these examples:

one – *ein*	bone – *Bein* (leg)	home – *Heim-*

But there is no invariable rule to be made out of it. As with Semitic languages (there is a curious irony here, when one remembers the Nazi philosophy), German yields its secrets through the consonants.

One further point to be made about the German vocabulary is that it is 'pure': it hates to borrow from other languages. Where, for instance, English is only too ready to make its scientific words out of Greek elements ('oxygen', 'nitrogen', 'hydrogen'), German produces home-made terms like *Sauerstoff*, *Stickstoff*, and

Wasserstoff. Even with new sciences like semantics German resists the international term and chooses *Bedeutungslehre* ('meaning-lore'), and phonetics is taught as *Lautlehre* ('sound-lore'). Much of this native Germanic vocabulary has ceased to be used in English. The 'sore' of 'He was sore afraid' (equivalent to German *sehr*) has been replaced by the Romance form 'very'; a butcher is no longer a 'flesher' (*Fleischer*) and 'to dree' (*drehen*) is now 'to turn'.

It is a help when reading German to think in terms of the English of Shakespeare's day (or even earlier) rather than modern English. This will help with forms like *fast* ('almost') and *oft*. Tricks of inversion in German ('That have I oft seen') match earlier English usage. It is good training for German speech to play the harmless trick of inversion and verb-shunting with our own language: it is not, after all, so very un-native. We are sometimes surprised to find separation of verb and defining prefix (*anzeigen* – 'to advertise'; *Wir zeign nicht an* – 'We don't advertise'), but this is common enough in English: 'Put your hat on'; 'Kick the door to.' German is, when all is said and done, a dialectal kinsman of English.

The time has come to look at some German. Here is a passage from a modern poem by Friedrich Georg Jünger (born 1898). I have chosen it at random:

> *Mit dem Saft der Maulbeere haben die Kinder*
> *Ihre kleinen Gesichter beschmiert.*
> *Näscher sind sie, Koster der Süssigkeit.*
> *Sie tanzen in ihren geflickten Kleidern,*
> *Und mit ihnen tanzt der Westwind,*
> *Tanzt auf den Schnüren die Wäsche.*
> *Es ist, als ob ein Hauch des wunderbaren Lebens*
> *Die leeren Hüllen des Menschen fülle.*

After what has been said about the ultimate identity of German and English, it will be a disappointment to find words here that have no equivalent form in modern English. We have to remember again that it is all a matter of choice, of semantic change; one language prefers to render an idea with one word, another language with another: German still uses *Tier* for 'animal', while English took over a French word and made *Tier* ('deer') into a particular kind of animal. Take a deep breath and look carefully here; there are plenty of words which have maintained the same meaning, and almost the same form, in both languages. Here is a literal translation which retains the German word-order:

'With the juice of the mulberry have the children their little faces be-smeared. Fruit-stealers are they, tasters of sweetness. They dance in their patched clothing, and with them dances the west wind, dances on the lines the washing. It is as though a breath of wonderful life the empty hulls (husks) of man fills.'

And now a piece of prose, the beginning of the story *Ein Landarzt* by Franz Kafka. 'Land' has taken on the specific meaning of 'country' (as opposed to 'town') in German; a *Landarzt* is a country doctor:

Ich war in grosser Verlegenheit: eine dringende Reise stand mir bevor; ein Schwerkranker wartete auf mich in einem zehn Meilen entfernten Dorfe; starkes Schneegestöber füllte den weiten Raum zwischen mir und ihm; einen Wagen hatte ich, leicht, grossräderig, ganz wie er für unsere Landstrassen taugt; in den Pelz gepackt, die Instrumententasche in der Hand, stand ich reisefertig schon auf dem Hofe; aber das Pferd fehlte, das Pferd . . .

Let us keep very close to the German: 'I was in gross (great) embarrassment: an urgent ride (journey) stood me before (faced me); a sorely-ill-one waited on (for) me in a ten mile far thorp (village); stark (strong, heavy) snowstorm filled the wide room (large space) 'twixt (between) me and him; a waggon (carriage) had I, light, great-wheely, fully as it for our land-streets (country roads) was suitable; in the pelt (fur coat) i-packed (wrapped), the instrument-case in the hand, stood I ride-ready (ready for the journey) on (in) the yard; but the horse failed (was lacking), the horse . . .'

It will be evident from this how German and English have diverged from their common origin in respect of word-meanings or word-nuances. 'Stark' means less 'strong' in English than 'strongly plain'; 'waggon' cannot mean a vehicle in general, as it still can in *Volkswagen*. 'I stand' in German is *ich stehe* ('I stay'); 'I stood' is *ich stand. Strasse* is like 'street' but means a road as well as a town thoroughfare. *Dorf* ('village') is a word in its own right, as well as a suffix in place-names (Düsseldorf), but 'thorp' is only found in English in forms like Scunthorpe. *Pferd* has nothing to do with 'horse'. Still, the fact of kinship cannot be gainsaid, and there is fascination in looking for the family face under the whiskers.

Chapter 5

Daughters of Latin

Despite the closeness (and ultimate identity) of English and German, most British language-learners feel far more at home with the Romance sisters – French, Italian, Spanish, Portuguese. This may be a tribute to the beauty and hospitality of the Mediterranean countries, to the fact that they, unlike Germany, have done no real harm to Britain in the modern period, or, more likely, to the results of the Norman Conquest. William the Conqueror began the process of drawing English into the Latin family, and there is hardly a semanteme in the Romance languages which does not find a cognate word in English. In starting to learn French, Italian, or Spanish, we find ourselves already equipped with a vast number of words which, despite various phonetic disguises, bridge the distance between the lands of wine and the land of draught bitter.

It is interesting to see how English has entered into the Latin stream: it has dived into it both naked and wearing the clothes of Old French. For instance, the word 'count' comes from the French *compter*, or its earlier form, and *compter* comes from Latin *computare*. But English itself has the word, directly taken from Latin, *compute*, whose meaning is perhaps a little more rarefied and intellectual than that of 'count'. Here are other examples:

Straight from French	*Straight from Latin*	*Latin*
conceit	concept	*conceptu*
constraint	constriction	*constrictione*
dainty	dignity	*dignitate*
esteem	estimate	*aestimare*
feat	fact	*facto*
loyal	legal	*legali*
poor	pauper	*pauperi*
royal	regal	*regali*
sure	secure	*securo*

(Those interested in the inflexions of Latin words will note that the Latin ablative singular is given here: it was mainly from this form of the Latin noun that the Romance languages derived their own invariable noun-forms.)

English, then, absorbed many words direct from the French conqueror; ever since, it has been taking words consciously and deliberately from classical Latin. It is not too much to say that any Latin semanteme (or meaning-word) is potentially an English word, and we are always at liberty to coin new Latinisms whenever we feel like it. Thus, if I want to talk about the farmer's wife of the 'Three Blind Mice' round, I can – a little whimsically – refer to her as 'muricidal' or 'mouse-killing'. The word may not be in the dictionary, but it is a true English word for all that. Language is, of course, a potential thing rather than a completed and fixed body of forms and words.

When I talk of 'classical Latin', I am referring to a rather artificial, upper-class, literary kind of language, preserved in the work of Vergil, Horace, Cicero, and not generally used by the ordinary people of the Roman Empire. For instance, the patrician or literary word for 'beautiful' was *pulcher*, and we find this in the learned or facetious English word 'pulchritude'. But the common people used instead *bellus* (meaning, perhaps, 'pretty') and this survives in the French *bel, beau, belle*, and the Italian *bello, bella*. As a spoken form, there are no derivatives of *pulcher*. *Formosus*, however, meaning perhaps 'shapely' ('having form') has become the Spanish word *hermoso*. The upper-class or literary word for a horse was *equus*, and this appears in various English words – 'equine', 'equestrian', 'equerry' (though in this last word there was a bit of mistaken etymology, *scutaria* perhaps being the Latin word from which it ultimately derived). But the ordinary people called a horse *caballus*, from which has come the whole set of Romance words – French *cheval*, Spanish *caballo*, Italian *cavallo*. A gentleman – cavalier or *caballero* – is a man who rides a horse. Again, the upper-class Latin word 'to speak' was *loqui* (a whole host of English words has come out of this), but the word in common use was *fabulari*. This produced French *parler*, Italian *parlare*, and Spanish *hablar*, as well as the contemptuous form once used in British colonies – 'palaver'.

That, then, is our starting point: the Romance languages of to-day represent developments (involving a great deal of phonetic and semantic change) out of 'people's Latin'. Italian is, as it were, the domestic form that Latin took over the centuries; Spanish and Portuguese are the Latin taken to the Iberian peninsula; French is the kind of Latin that was spoken in Paris and eventually became the tongue of the whole country. The essentially national terms now in use – we give the language the name of the people who speak it – took some time to come about. There was a time when a differentiation between the various kinds of spoken popular Latin was made in terms of the words for 'yes': there was *langue d'oc* in the French southern provinces; *langue d'oïl* (*oïl* = *oui*) was spoken in the north; *langue de si* was Italian. This was as late as the end of the thirteenth century, very much a part of historical time. What we must do now is to show what happened to Latin in the various countries where it was spoken; this will give us a bunch of keys for opening the four main boxes – French, Italian, Spanish, Portuguese. This book, unfortunately, has no space for dealing with Rumanian or Catalan.

Let us look first at a number of English words derived directly from Latin: 'dictate' (Latin *dicto* – 'said'); 'fact (Latin *facto* – 'done'); 'lactic' (Latin *lacte* – 'milk'); 'nocturnal' (Latin *nocte* – 'night'); 'October' (Latin *octo* – 'eight': October was the eighth month of the Roman year). These all contain the consonants 'CT'. In Italian the Latin 'CT' changed to 'TT'; in Spanish it became 'CH'; in Portuguese and French it appeared as 'IT':

Latin	Italian	Spanish	Portuguese	French
dicto	detto	dicho	dito	dit
facto	fatto	hecho	feito	fait
lacte	latte	leche	leite	lait
nocte	notte	noche	noite	nuit
octo	otto	ocho	oito	huit

Note how the Latin ablative singular ending is retained in Italian, Spanish, and Portuguese. French likes to rid its words of endings, and even what is retained in the spelling at the end of the word disappears in speech: none of the 't's here are pronounced.

Let us now take three Latin words which begin with consonant + L: *pleno* – 'full' (English 'plenitude'); *clave* – 'key' (English 'clavicle', 'clavichord'); *flamma* – 'flame'. In Italian the L becomes I:

pieno   *chiave* (the *ch* is pronounced /k/)   *fiamma*

In Spanish the three forms – PL; CL; FL – all become LL (the palatalized 'l' somewhat like the 'lli' of 'million'):

lleno   *llave*   *llama*

Portuguese also uses the one sound for the three Latin consonant-combinations:

cheio   *chave*   *chama* (the *ch* is pronounced /ʃ/ – 'sh')

French, as if to make up for dropping the Latin endings, retains the initial Latin consonants:

plein   *clef*   *flamme*

To attempt to explain these changes, seemingly as capricious as the retentions, would require a great deal of speculation, bringing in questions of the influence of other tongues, for instance. But, a recurring motif in this book, the bilabial fricative /β/ has a lot to do with the following:

Latin	Italian	Spanish	Portuguese	French	English
capillo	*capello*	*cabello*	*cabelo*	*cheveu*	hair
lepore	*lepre*	*liebre*	*lebre*	*lièvre*	hare
sapere	*sapere*	*saber*	*saber*	*savoir*	to know
bibere	*bevere*	*beber*	*beber*	*buvoir*	to drink
habere	*avere*	*haber*	*haver*	*avoir*	to have

The *p*-between-vowels of Latin must have been very unsteady and wavering, and both the original and derived *b* must have had a fricative quality: only thus can we explain the present-day forms shown above, the French *v* a true 'v' as in 'very', the Spanish and Portuguese *b* with a soft 'buzzed' quality suggesting /v/.

Let us look now at what has happened to some of the original Latin vowels:

Latin	Italian	Spanish	Portuguese	French	English
pede	*piede*	*pie*	*pé*	*pied*	foot
petra	*pietra*	*piedra*	*pedra*	*pierre*	stone
decem	*dieci*	*diez*	*dez*	*dix*	ten
morit	*muore*	*muere*	*morre*	*meurt*	(he) dies
potet	*può*	*puede*	*pode*	*peut*	(he) can
foco	*fuoco*	*fuego*	*fogo*	*feu*	fire

You will notice that the front vowel *e* is diphthongised in Italian, Spanish, and French to *ie* (/ie/). The back vowel *o* has undergone three different kinds of diphthongisation, though in French the *eu* that was once *ue* has become a round front vowel – /ø/. The Italian *uo* merely seems to emphasise that we are dealing with a very round sound; the Spanish *ue* shows a pushing-forward of the original Latin *o* to the front of the mouth (/e/) and a preceding *u* to remind us that the changed vowel was once a round one. The Latin double vowel AU has become a simple vowel /o/ in the modern Romance tongues, though the spelling does not always show this. Thus, the *auro* ('gold') which we find in English 'auriferous' ('gold-bearing') or even just in the chemical symbol 'Au', has become *oro* in Italian and Spanish, *ouro* (same pronunciation /oro/) in Portuguese, and *or* in French. *Causa*, which we find in English as 'cause', has developed the meaning 'thing' in the Romance tongues, and appears as *cosa* in Italian and Spanish, *cousa* in Portuguese, and *chose* in French.

It will be evident from all our examples so far that, of all the daughters of Latin, French has strayed furthest away from home. English words like 'scripture', 'slave', 'space', 'spice', and 'scald' keep, in their initial sounds, very close to the original Latin, but see what they have become in French: *écriture; esclave; espace; épice; échauffer*. In general, the tendency of French is to get rid of an original Latin *s* where possible. Sometimes it is guilty about this and erects a circumflex as a kind of monument above the letter preceding the place where the *s* used to be. Compare the following:

Middle French	Modern French	English
bastard	bâtard	bastard
beste	bête	beast
feste	fête	feast
oistre	huître	oyster

English, you will see, is far truer to the traditions of old French than is modern French.

Another trick of French is to change the hard *c* of Latin (retained in Italian, Spanish, and Portuguese) to *ch*. This means that a /k/ has been pushed forward from the soft to the hard palate and turned into /ʃ/ (as in 'she', 'ship'). English has, incidentally, done the same thing with a few Latin words, so that *episcopus* appears as 'bishop' and *casius* became 'cheese'. But French is fairly consistent:

Latin	French	English
caballo	cheval	horse
capra	chèvre	goat
caro	cher	dear
cantare	chanter	to sing
capitulo	chapitre	chapter

The voiced velar consonant of Latin – /g/ – has been treated even more harshly than /k/ when it appears in the middle of a Latin word: *Augusto* ('August') has become *août* (pronounced /u/); *lege* ('law') appears as *loi*; *nigro* ('black') is Frenchified to *noir*. Elimination, shortening, has been really drastic in French: consider that *eau* (/o/) comes from *aqua* ('water'), and that *Noël* ('Christmas') derives ultimately from *Natalis* ('natal', 'relating to birth'). The paring-down is, of course, often really more drastic than it looks, so that *front* ('forehead'), though its spelling shows it to be derived from Latin *fronte*, no longer has an articulated *t*, and the *n* has been diminished to a mere snorting of the preceding vowel. *Front*, then, is pronounced /frɔ̃/.

Spanish and Portuguese show their own patterns of divergence – both singly and (as the two main 'Iberian languages') collectively. But both look more like Latin than does French. What gives Spanish its piquancy is its traces of the influence of non-Indo-European languages. The Basque tongue has no /f/, and this seems reflected in the following:

Latin	Spanish	English
fabulari	hablar	to speak
facere	hacer	to make
filio	hijo	son
folia	hoja	leaf

The *h* has no sound here, nor, indeed, in any of the Romance languages, though it seems to have had its full aspirate value in Latin. Note that the middle *l* of the last two Latin words on the above list has become *j* – pronounced /x/, the 'ch' of 'loch' – in Spanish. The inevitable Arabic influence on Spanish is mainly one of vocabulary, giving words like *mezquino* ('poor'), *alguacil* ('constable'), *aljibe* ('cistern'), *laúd* ('lute'), *ataúd* ('coffin').

Portuguese resembles French in having eliminated some of the nasals of original Latin and substituted nasalisation of the preceding vowel, or even (unlike French) diphthong. Spanish *lana* ('wool') appears in Portuguese as *lã*; Spanish *pan* ('bread') becomes Portuguese *pão*. And Portuguese, somewhat like Italian, is not always concerned about retaining an original Latin 'L'. Latin *caelum* ('sky') appears in French as *ciel* and in Spanish as *cielo*; but Portuguese has *céu*. Latin and Italian *volare* ('to fly') is *volar* in Spanish but *voar* in Portuguese. The 'L' has even disappeared in the definite articles, so that *lo* and *la* have become *o* and *a*. Occasionally Portuguese has *r* where other Romance tongues have *l*: what is *blanc* in French, *bianco* in Italian, and *blanco* in Spanish is *branco* in Portuguese. One is not 'much obliged' in Portugal; one is *muito obrigado*.

When we have considered all the sound-shifts, distortions, and disguises that make the modern Romance languages different from Latin and from the Latin part of English, we are still left with a corpus of transparent identities. If English 'experience' is *experiencia* in Spanish, *experiência* in Portuguese, and *esperienza* in Italian, we should have no difficulty in rendering 'impudence', 'indifference', and so on in those languages. Similarly, the ending '-ment' in 'argument', 'monument', 'element' will meet *-mento* in all three. The suffix '-ty' in 'identity' corresponds to French *-té*, Spanish *-dad*, Portuguese *-dade*, and Italian *-tà*. And words like 'education' appear as French *éducation*, Spanish *educación*, Portuguese *educação*, and Italian *educazione*. The recognition that our own language is, to some extent, as much a child of the Roman Empire as the true full-blooded Latin tongues of to-day should encourage us in our work on them. We may even eventually take breath and plunge into Rumanian, which has developed from the language spoken by Trajan's soldiers in the province of Dacia. There we shall find that the strange-looking *omul* is really *homo ille* ('the man'), and *lupul* is *lupus ille* ('the wolf'). Part of the pleasure of language-learning is the search for hidden identities.

Every schoolboy knows that the Latin verb is a nightmare. The nightmare has partly dispersed in the descendants of Latin, which still, nevertheless, make heavier going of verbs than English or German. But we ought to remember that the common people of the Roman Empire were already at work on a simplification and rationalisation which did not appeal to the patrician writers and their readers, and that this has left its mark on the modern Latin languages. Where Cicero or Vergil would write *amavi* for 'I have loved', the Roman plebs would prefer a form like our own:

habeo (I have) *amatum* (loved). In all the Romance languages you can make a past form, a future, and a conditional out of the verb 'to have', and this makes the learning of this verb an important – and not very difficult – task. Thus, the French *j'ai* – 'I have' – gives us the conversational past tense of *j'ai aimé* ('I (have) loved') and the future *j'aimerai* (infinitive *aimer + ai*). The past tense (imperfect) *j'avais* – 'I had' – will give not only the pluperfect 'I had loved' – *j'avais aimé* – but the conditional 'I would (might) love' – *j'aimerais* (infinitive *aimer + -ais*). The same process will be found in the sister languages of French.

Enough, perhaps, has been said in this chapter to indicate possible lines of study, the key-maxim being 'search for likenesses to English, identities in all languages of the group'. Ideally, one should know one Romance language really well, have a reading knowledge of the others, and be willing to acquire a conversational knowledge of any of those at, say, six weeks' notice.

Chapter 6

Piercing the Iron Curtain

Russian is as rich and satisfying as Christmas pudding, but what tends to dull the appetite for learning it is the apparent difficulty of the alphabet. I say 'apparent' advisedly, for it can be mastered in an hour or so. Once learnt, it will be seen as entirely suitable for the language it clothes, and Romanisation only makes Russian look clumsy. Compare the following:

Хрущёв

Kh r u shch e v

(The final consonant is unvoiced to /f/. Russian, like German, tends to unvoice its end-sounds.)

The following geographical names are useful for learning Cyrillic script:

Африка	Afrika	Africa
Брюссель	Briussel'	Brussels
Кембридж	Kyembridzh	Cambridge
Голландия	Gollandiya	Holland
Вальпарайзо	Val'paraizo	Valparaiso
Мельбурн	Myel'burn	Melbourne
Цейлон	Tsyeilon	Ceylon

Corresponding to the apostrophe in the second column above, you will notice the symbol ь, which puzzles most learners of Russian. It indicates that the preceding consonant is palatalised – that is, pulled from its normal mouth-position on to the hard palate. The difference between л (/l/) and ль (/λ/) is close to the difference between the 'l' of 'mill' and the 'lli' of 'million'. Any consonant which has this 'softening' symbol after it is, as it were, prevented from being exploded in the usual way: a 'y' (as in 'yes') comes along and chokes it.

The difference between a plain consonant and a palatalised one is not (as is the difference between dark and clear L in English) allophonic. The addition of ь makes a new phoneme, as is shown by the difference in meaning between the following:

угол – corner	уголь – coal
брат – brother	брать – to take

Palatalisation is dear to the heart of Russian, and there is a perfect opposition of plain and palatalised vowels:

А, а as in 'h*a*rd'	Я, я as in '*ya*rd'
Э, э as in 'd*e*n'	Е, е as in '*ye*s'
О, о as in '*o*n'	Ё, ё as in '*yo*nder'
У, у as in 'bl*ue*'	Ю, ю as in '*you*'

One Russian vowel which seems to have no equivalent in any other language is represented by ы. It is very much like the English /ɪ/ in 'sit', 'fit', but more centralised (properly 'ɨ') and sometimes pronounced with lip-rounding. For the rest, the Russian sound-system is straightforward enough, and Russian, like English, is willing to 'weaken' a vowel if it is not in a stressed position. Thus, *Doktor Zhivago* does not, as would be the case in a Romance language, preserve the rounded final *o*. The vowel is unstressed and becomes something like *a*.

The learning of stress in Russian is difficult: there are no stress-rules, and one is reminded again of English. But most Russian primers put a stress-diacritic (′) above the stressed vowel of a word, and this helps. Stress is vigorous, emphasising the very Indo-European nature of the language. The stressed vowel of the word, phrase or sentence takes up so much vocalic energy that none of the other vowels carry anything like their full quality. The tone of Russian is virile, suggesting that the sounds are pushed back into the throat rather than, as with French or Italian, placed in the front of the mouth. There is a grumbling bearish quality about a good deal of Russian speech.

Russian has plenty of grammar but, to anyone who has studied a classical Indo-European language like Latin, there will not seem to be anything unfamiliar. There are three genders, words ending in a consonant or the semi-vowel й (/j/) tending to masculinity, feminine words being, as with the Romance tongues, those with an *-a* or *-ya* ending, and neuter nouns terminating in *-o* or *-ye*. Adjectives (which come before the noun) have similar endings, and both adjectives and nouns have full batteries of inflexions. The endings of the various parts of the verb have a Latin flavour. 'I read' is *ya chitáyu*, 'he reads' is *on chitáyet*, 'we read' is *mi* (мы) *chitáyem*, and 'they read' is *oni chitáyut*. There is only one past tense, but its endings reflect the gender of the subject, so that 'I read' (/rɛd/) or 'I have read' will be *ya chitál, ya chitála*, or *ya chitálo* according to the gender of the speaker. The other persons of the singular ('thou', 'he, she, it') take the same endings as does *ya*, and the plural – whether 'we', 'you', or 'they' – has the invariable ending *-i* (*mi chitáli* – 'we read'; *oni chitáli* – 'they read', where 'read' = /rɛd/).

The Russian verb has only three tenses, while English has twelve. To make up for this deficiency, Russian introduces what are called 'aspects of the verb' – the *imperfective* and the *perfective*. If *chitál* means 'I have read', the addition of a prefix will produce *prochitál* – 'I have finished reading'; *budu chitat'* (the apostrophe indicates ь) means 'I shall read', but *prochitáyu* (a present tense form used with a future meaning) will mean 'I shall read (it) through'. The simple form of the verb, then, implies no completion of action and hence is imperfective; the prefix changes it to a perfective form or aspect, and completion of the action is the very essence of its meaning. Here are other examples:

Ya rabótayu – I work (continuously, habitually, or recurrently)
Ya porabótal – I did some work (i.e. completed some)
Ya porabótayu – I shall do some (a little) work (a present tense cannot indicate completion, so the present-tense form of perfective verbs has to convey a future meaning).

The bulk of the Russian vocabulary is pure Slavonic, but a vast number of loan-words (from Latin, German, French, even English) helps our learning task:

abort – abortion, miscarriage
abstraktniy – abstract
absurd – absurdity
ambitsiya – ambition
arka – arch
armiya – army
banknota – bank-note
bryesh' – breach, gap
bufyet – sideboard, buffet
vokal'niy – vocal
geroy – hero
gimn – hymn

dyek – deck
diplomaticheskiy – diplomatic
direktor – director, manager, chief
evangelist – evangelist
zal – hall (cf. French *salle*)
idyot – idiot
identichniy – identical
instruktsiya – instruction
kanal'ya – rogue, rascal (cf. French *canaille*, Italian *canaglia*)
karta – card, map, menu
katar – catarrh
konfyeta – sweetmeat
korpus – body, army corps
korrektniy – correct, proper
korryespondyentsya – correspondence
kortezh – procession, cortège
langust – lobster (cf. French *langouste*)
marsh – march
marshrut – itinerary, route-march
maskarad – fancy-dress ball
planyeta – planet
plug – plough
tabak – tobacco
talya – waist (cf. French *taille*)
tambur – drum (cf. French *tambour*)
tramvay – tram, tramway
tsyellyulyaniy – cellular
sharlatan – charlatan
shofyor – chauffeur

It is time to look at a little Russian in action, and we cannot do better than take a short poem by Pushkin, the Byron of Russian literature. Here it is, first, in Cyrillic script:

Я вас любил; любовь ещё, быть-мо́жет,
В душе́ мое́й уга́сла не совсе́м;
Но пусть она́ вас бо́льше не трево́жит;
Я не хочу́ печа́лить вас ниче́м.
Я вас любил безмо́лвно, безнаде́жно,
То ра́достью, то ре́вностью томи́м;
Я вас любил так и́скренно, так не́жно,
Как дай вам Бог люби́мой быть други́м.

And here is an attempt at transliteration into the Roman alphabet:

> *Ya vas lyubil; lyubov' yeshcho, bit'-mozhet,*
> *V dushe moyey ugasla nye sovsyem;*
> *No pust' ona vas bol'she nye tryevozhit;*
> *Ya nye khochu pyechalit' vas nichem.*
> *Ya vas lyubil byezmolvno, byeznadyozhno,*
> *To radost'yu, to revnost'yu tomim;*
> *Ya vas lyubil tak iskryenno, tak nyezhno,*
> *Kak day vam Bog lyubimoy bit' drugim.*

(Vowels have their 'Continental' values; 'y' always stands for the sound in 'yes'; 'g' is always hard, as in 'got'; the apostrophe stands for the softener or palataliser ь.)

The key-words are *Ya vas lyubil* (literally, 'I you loved'). Let us keep to the Russian word-order for our literal translation: 'I you loved: love still, perhaps/in spirit my has-been-extinguished (*ugasla*) not entirely;/but it you more let not trouble (let it trouble you no more); /I not wish to sadden you with nothing./I you loved without-(*byez*)-utterance (silently), without-hope (hopelessly),/now from joy, now from jealousy languishing;/I you loved so sincerely, so tenderly,/as grant you God be loved by another.'

Russian has a huge and important literature which cries out to be read (even with the aid of a crib) in the original.

Chapter 7

Malay

We have taken brief tastes of Indo-European languages and seen what they have in common – inflexions, conjugations, genders, and certain words. It will be salutary for us to move outside the great family and examine briefly one of the languages of the East. I choose Malay because of its interest and its importance. It is a lingua franca for South-East Asia and, as *Bahasa* (literally, 'The Language'), it is the national tongue of Indonesia. It is rich in dialects and cognate with the languages of the Dayaks and Ibans in Borneo, as well as (though more remotely) with Fijian and Maori, so it will be met in many forms. The Federation of Malaya accepts the dialect of Johore as its national language (the language of government announcements and official literature), and this is close enough to President Soekarno's *Bahasa*. The Muslim invaders of Malacca gave Malay a form of the Arabic alphabet (called the *Jawi* or 'Eastern' form), but Romanisation has proved easy. Dutch Romanisation differs from British, as it follows the spelling conventions of the Dutch language. Thus, the word for 'grandchild' is spelt *tjoetjoe* in *Bahasa*, but *chuchu* in Malayan Malay. We shall, naturally, keep to British Romanisation, not because it is British, but because its symbols hold close to the main European alphabetic stream.

Malay has no frightening phonetic curiosities. Final plosives like /t/, /d/, /p/, /b/ are initiated but not completed, and the letter 'k' stands for a glottal stop in words like *anak* ('child'), *sĕjuk* (cold), *itek* ('duck'). Words can begin with /ŋ/ (as in 'sing', 'song', 'thing'), something uncommon in Indo-European languages. The vowel symbols have roughly the same value as in Italian, but 'ĕ' stands for the neutral /ə/ of the second syllable in 'father', 'brother', 'mother'. There is a tendency for final *a* in a word like *ada* ('there is', 'there are') to be pronounced like the vowel of French *bleu*. Stress is either non-existent or too light to be important. Articulation is gentle and rapid. Malay is at the opposite pole to Russian and German: it is not a ponderous language.

What strikes the learner of Malay is the complete lack of those typically Indo-European properties – gender, inflection, conjugation. It is like diving into a bath of pure logic. Everything is pared to a minimum. Let us first look at the pronouns. *Saya* can be 'I', 'me', or, in postposition, 'my'. Thus 'I hit him' is *saya pukul dia*; 'he hits me' is *dia pukul saya*; 'my wife' is *istĕri saya*. *Dia*, as you will see, is as invariable as *saya*, and it can stand for 'he', 'she', or 'it'; in speech it can also mean 'they', the highbrow *mĕreka* being reserved for the written form of the language. 'His wife' can be *istĕri dia*, but *istĕri-nya* is perhaps preferred, that nasalisation of *di-* to *ny-* forming an interesting parallel to Welsh. The Malay word for *you* is slippery and variable, showing the influence of old taboos: it is as though there is something dangerous in using a second-person pronoun. And so a Malay will choose carefully in asking the question 'What do you want?' To a person of superior social status he will say *Apa tuan mahu?* ('What does the gentleman want?') or perhaps *Apa ĕnche mahu?* (slightly lower social status). There are other words which might be used: *lu* for a Chinese, *tuanku* ('my lord') to a ruler, *tĕngku* and *ĕngku* for rajas, *dato'* for chiefs, *'che guru* for a schoolmaster, and forms like *mika, awak, ĕngkau* among equals and near-equals. It is a difficult and touchy business, this choice of the right word for 'you', and offence can easily be taken. Malay has one advantage over the Indo-European tongues in its words for 'we': *kami* can exclude the person addressed, *kiya* includes him. In Borneo *kita* is used for 'you', so that one has a sort of governess flavour in statements like 'We mustn't do that again, must we?'

The noun is invariable, and does not even need to change in the plural. *Rokok* is 'cigarette', 'a cigarette', 'the cigarette', or 'cigarettes', the context making all clear. Pluralisation is often shown by duplication, but *rokok-rokok* (written as *rokok2*) implies a variety, different kinds of cigarettes, rather than a straight plural. When number is specified – 'two cigarettes' – or the nature of the pluralisation is significant, as in 'many cigarettes', a very Eastern device is used (it also found in Chinese). This is the 'numerical coefficient', and it varies according to the semantic nature of the noun involved. Human beings are preceded by the announcement 'human being', so that 'two clerks' is *dua orang kĕrani*, 'four soldiers' is *ĕmpat orang soldadu* (note the Portuguese loan-word *soldadu*, a relic of Portuguese Malacca), and 'many women' is *banyak orang pĕrĕmpuan*. The numerical coefficient for animals is *ekor* – 'tail' – and 'ten cats' is hence *sa-puloh ekor kuching*. Subtlety is required for inanimate objects. For instance, anything big, bulky, round has the coefficient *buah* (literally 'fruit'): 'a car' is *sa-buah kĕreta* and 'five hundred houses' is *lima ratus buah rumah*.

If one digs deeply enough into Malay, one comes to the conclusion that the Western concept of 'parts of speech' is alien to it. A word is a word is a word, and it can be used as any part of a syntactical pattern. Thus, *makan* expresses the notion of food, eating, and *makan saya* can, logically, mean either 'eat me' or 'my food'. *Tari* is either 'dance' (the noun), the idea of dancing, or the active verb 'to dance'. But, especially in written Malay, there is an interesting battery of suffixes and prefixes to call on which make more specific the function of the word in question. So *tarian* can only mean 'a dance' or 'the dance', while *mĕnari* (again the Welsh-type nasal mutation) has to be a verb. Much can be made out of little. The word *ada* means any of the following (I quote from Wilkinson's admirable Malay–English dictionary): 'to be present, to exist, to be at home (to a visitor), to exist in connection with, to appertain to, to have.' The root meaning is 'existence'. *Adakan* or *mĕngadakan* (the suffix *-kan* having a causative function) means 'to call into existence, to appoint'. *Bĕrada* is a polite way of saying 'to be present', but *orang yang bĕrada* means 'people of standing'. *Kĕadaan* (noun-suffix *-an*, abstract-noun-prefix *kĕ-*) means 'state, existence, condition of life, position'. One prefix, *tĕr-*, adds a remarkable nuance to a verb. If *kilat* has the primary meaning of 'a flash (of lightning)', and *bĕrkilat* means 'to flash', *tĕrkilat* means 'to flash suddenly, unawares', as of a darting fish.

Malay has certain words which cannot be assigned to any Western category. A good example is *pun*, literally untranslatable. It is an emphasising word, a word that 'lights up' the semanteme that goes before: *itu pun* means 'that also'; *sakali pun* is something like 'yet'; *dia pun pĕrgi* means 'he also went', the *pun* bestowing a past meaning on the invariable verb-form *pĕrgi*. There is no single meaning for *pun*, and it is hard to get at its roots and origin; its correct use is incredibly difficult to learn. The enclitic *-lah* is again untranslatable: it lends force to what goes before, so that *orang itu-lah yang pĕrgi* means 'It was *that* person who went'. Words like these are perhaps essential to a language that does not use vocal stress for emphasis.

The vocabulary of Malay is, in its fundamentals, entirely fitted to the needs of a people concerned with the concrete processes of everyday living – fishing, gathering fruit and coconuts, begetting children, lying in the sun. This makes it poetical, metaphorical, happier with proverbs than with abstract constatations. But the Arabs brought Islam and the religious and philosophical terms that go with it; loan-words from Portuguese and English are numerous; the need to cope – in education, newspapers, government directives – with the intellectual notions of the modern world has forced Malay scholars, teachers, and editors to fashion neologisms – usually out of Arabic or (and India has had its influence too) Sanskrit. There have to be trade unions, strikes, parent-teacher associations, co-operative societies. A new world of words, bewildering to the peasant, is being forged.

Whether Malay can be democratised is another matter. The feudal structure of Malay society has had a remarkable effect on the language. Words appropriate to the common man cannot be used in connection with a ruler – sultan or raja. I walk (*jalan kaki* – 'go with foot') but the Sultan must *běrangkat*. I eat (*makan*), but the Sultan *santap*. I sleep (*tidor*), while the Sultan *běradu*. This may seem a lot of unnecessary luggage (there are, of course, many other specifically 'royal' words), and, similarly, one is sometimes impatient at the unwillingness of Malay to *generalise* (there is no one word for 'you'; 'rice' is *padi* when growing, *běras* in the shops, *nasi* on the table; there is no single word for 'brother' or for 'sister'). But there is a fine economy and logic in the accidence and syntax of the language, just as there is in the numerical system. Malay starts its 'teens' at eleven (*sa-bělas* = 11; *duabělas* = 12; *tigabělas* = 13, and so on) and wonders why the West counts as though it had twelve fingers. The fact is that there is no occasion for the philologists of Europe to 'look down' on Malay as a primitive and outlandish language: it has solved linguistic problems that bother the speaker of English, German, or French; it has achieved a logic and simplicity which the Western tongues do not know. Every school curriculum in Europe should provide an opportunity for at least a dabbling examination of an Oriental language, in order to see how the other half of the world (very much more than a half) contrives not only to live but to think and express itself.

We shall end with two specimens of Malay writing, the first a poem. A popular Malay verse-form is the *pantun*, a quatrain which presents two contrasted ideas (two lines to each) which are made to show a kin-ship through similarity of sound. It is a subtle form, in which expression – as in all true art – matters more than content. Every Malay has a great store of *pantuns* in his memory; some Malays are adept at improvising them. Here is one of the loveliest of the traditional *pantuns*, known everywhere in South-East Asia:

> *Kalau tuan mudek ka-hulu,*
> *Charikan saya bunga kĕmoja.*
> *Kalau tuan mati dahulu,*
> *Nantikan saya di-pintu shurga.*

This means literally: 'If lord travel to-riverhead,/Look for me for flower frangipanni./If lord die first (before),/Wait for me at-gate heaven.' A freer translation would be: 'If you, my lover, go up-river, find me some frangipanni. Should you be the first of us two to die, wait for me at the gates of heaven.' Note the way in which the first and third lines, and the second and fourth lines, chime in assonance. Let us now look at the component words:

Kalau   if (met also as *jikalau* and *jika*).

tuan   literally 'master', 'lord', 'lady'. Used by a lover to his mistress, or vice versa.

mudek   an invariable verb-form whose meaning is 'travelling up-stream'. Malay is particular about the right word, hating to generalise with some such colourless form as *pĕrgi* – 'to go'.

ka-   to, towards, into.

hulu   the root meaning is 'head, upper portion'. An ordinary person has a *kĕpala* under his hat, but a royal personage has a *hulu*. *Hulu* can be the hilt of a weapon (*hulu kĕris*). With the addition of the noun-prefix *pĕ-* and a linking nasal we get *pĕnghulu* – 'headman of a village'. Here *hulu* means 'head of the river'.

Charikan   the root is *chari* – ' searching' – and the addition of -*kan* makes the verb 'to search for anything'.

saya   I, me, for me, etc.

bunga   flower.

kĕmoja   frangipanni (*kĕmboja* is another form). Like the cypress of the West, frangipanni is associated with graveyards.

mati   death, dying, to die.
dahulu   before, past, ahead of time.
Nantikan *nanti* means 'waiting' (it sometimes means 'shall',
           'will', and thus acts as a future auxiliary). Here the
           suffix *-kan* gives us the specific verb 'to wait for'.
di-   in, on, at.
pintu   door, gate.
shurga   (a Sanskrit loan-word) heaven.

Now let us examine a brief piece of modern Malay prose. It is taken from the introduction to *Pělita Bahasa Mělayu* – literally, 'Lamp of the Malay Language' – by Za'ba (an illustrious name in Malaya but hardly known here). Its theme is appropriate to this book on language in general:

Tiap-tiap (each, every) *bahasa* (language) *yang* (which) *hidup* (alive, living) *memang* (naturally, as a matter of course) *tabi'at* (character, nature) *dan* (and) *adat-nya* (behaviour-its) *tumboh* (sprout, spring up, erupt) *dan běrtambah* (increase, grow, develop) *sěrta* (with, together with) *běrubah* (being altered) *pěrlahan-lahan* (slowly) *dar* (from) *suata* (one) *masa* (time) *ka-* (to) *suata masa;* *jika* (if) *tiada* (there is not) *tumboh atau* (or) *běrtambah dan běrubah maka* (an untranslatable 'punctuation word' signifying the end of a subordinate clause) *ěrti-nya* (literally, the meaning of it = that is to say) *tiada běrgěrak,* (to move, to stir) *dan tiada běrgěrak itu* (that) *ěrti-nya 'mati'* (dead) *sa-bagaimana* (in the same way as) *bahasa Sanskrit dan Latin tělah* (have) *mati* (died).

Here is a free translation:

'The character and usage of any language which is living grow and develop – in a perfectly natural way – and change slowly with the passage of time; if there were no growth and development and change, then the language would be static, and when a language is static that language has died, just as the Sanskrit and Latin tongues have died.'

Look at the Malay once more:

Tiap-tiap bahasa yang hidup memang tabi'at dan adat-nya tumboh dan běrtambah sěrta běrubah pěrlahan-lahan dari suatu masa ka-suata masa; jika tiada tumboh atau běrtambah dan běrubah maka ěrti-nya tiada běrgěrak, dan tiada běrgěrak itu ěrtinya 'mati' sa-bagaimana bahasa Sanskrit dan Latin tělah mati.

It is evidently a fine, subtle, musical language, flavoursome with its duplications and repetitions. I have been haunted for many years by a phrase from an old Malay history, one which seems to sum up the suggestive possibilities of the language: *lima ratus orang orang pĕrang* – 'five hundred fighting men'. Could any language do better?

Chapter 8

The Breaking of Babel

The fact that the human race speaks many languages – most of them mutually unintelligible – has traditionally been regarded as a curse. The myth of Babel and the divine confusion of tongues converts an age-long process into a sudden and quite unexpected catastrophe. The 'unscrambling' of linguistic chaos is celebrated at Pentecost, one of the great feasts of the Church calendar. Quite outside the realms of myth and miracle, is it possible for man to redeem the curse, to create or choose a common language for the whole of the civilised world?

Certain men have thought so, and their thoughts have tended to run on the same lines: let every man be bilingual, with his first language his own regional mother-tongue, his second language a world auxiliary; let this world auxiliary be an artificial language, for only an artificial language can be truly supranational. One can see the point well enough: an existing language, like English or French or Spanish, is bound to have nationalistic associations unpleasing to all but its native speakers, and so it is not really suitable as a world auxiliary language. Hence – so the argument runs – the need for a sort of plastic language, something as neutral and aseptic as polythene.

Various artificial languages have, in fact, been painfully manufactured and some of them are – though not on a world scale – in periodic use. Volapük was the first (1880 – the creation of J. M. Schleyer, a German priest) and it swiftly died out because it was too complicated: a Malay would have fainted at the needless luggage of inflexions. From it we can learn how difficult it is for a language-maker to shed inborn prejudices: the messy grammar, the huge portmanteau-words of German, seemed natural to Schleyer, and he incorporated them accordingly in his brain-child. Volapük was logical (there were no irregular verbs, no exceptions to rules of noun-inflexion) but it was not simple. It took a long time for auxiliary-makers to learn how little grammar languages like Malay, Persian, and Chinese (and, for that matter, English) really require. Why should one have to slave over masses of grammar in one's world auxiliary when grammar hardly exists in one's mother-tongue? Schleyer could not see this.

1887 saw the birth of Esperanto, perhaps still the most popular of the artificial auxiliaries. Its creator, Dr Zamenhof, a Russian-Polish Jew, presented it as *Linguo Internacio de la Doktoro Esperanto*, this latter pseudonym meaning 'hopeful', and the name has stuck. Zamenhof saw that the great need was to have as little grammar as possible and he realized, from his studies of English, how unfunctional most grammar was. But he insists on an accusative case (*Ni lernas Esperanton* – 'we're learning Esperanto') and the agreement of adjective and noun. His vocabulary is eclectic – in other words, he draws from all the big European languages in fair proportion; what he does not do, however, is to remember how many international words already exist in those languages. If Latin has, for 'school', the word *schola*, and Swedish has *skola*, German *Schule*, Italian *scuola*, and even Malay *sĕkolah*, one is entitled to expect something like *skol* or *scolo* or *skula* in an international auxiliary. But Esperanto has *lernejo*.

Other man-made languages have followed Esperanto – Ido and Esperantido (simplifications of Esperanto), Interlingua (a kind of Latin without Latin grammar), Novial (a hybrid creation of the great philologist Otto Jespersen), Interglossa (a language very sensibly contrived out of Greek roots – Greek being our international scientific language – by Lancelot Hogben). But we tend to return, in our search for a bomb for Babel, to existing tongues. French has long been an international language of diplomacy and culture, ecumenical councils carry on in Church Latin. Now, more and more, it is evident that English will prove the great international tongue for all kinds of communication – not purely ambassadorial or ecclesiastical.

There are extrinsic reasons for the spread of English, and these are sufficiently well known. The English have long been a maritime people, concerned with exporting not only goods in their ships but also English-speaking communities. Of these America has become the most powerful, leader of the so-called Free World. Meanwhile, there remains a loosely-linked commonwealth in which English is either the first language or the chief auxiliary. Advances in technology have been associated with

English, and so has air communication between countries and continents: English is the language of international pilots. For a Dutch, Indian, or Chinese child, the first lessons in English already represent a key to the whole of the outside world, not merely the American or British part of it.

But there are certain intrinsic elements in English which render it suitable as an international auxiliary. It has far less unnecessary grammar than any other Indo-European tongue (with the exception of Persian); it has a considerable Graeco-Latin vocabulary, itself international; it can be polysyllabic, like Russian or German or Finnish, or monosyllabic, like Chinese. It has made its way, with no deliberate pushing, in the great world; it is felt that, with certain adaptations and deliberate simplifications, it can go still further.

This was the view of C. K. Ogden and I. A. Richards, the devisers of Basic English. In their *The Meaning of Meaning* they asked a fundamental question: what is the absolute minimum of English words required to define all the words in a dictionary? They came to the conclusion that it was something like 800. It seemed possible, then, to make out of English a very simple auxiliary, one that could be learned in two or three months. They proved, by a number of translations, that the most monumental work of English literature could be rendered accurately – though with an inevitable loss of 'magic' – into Basic, and that the average reader would be unaware of anything strange, forced, or insufficient.

The suitability of English for this reducing treatment is exemplified in its peculiar aptitude for verb-making. For instance, the colourless word 'get' can, in combination with various helper-words, do a remarkable number of jobs: 'I got to bed late but got up quite early, got my clothes on, got some breakfast, got on the bus, and got to the office on time. I got my ledgers out and got down to work, got a cup of coffee at eleven and got out to lunch at twelve-thirty. (I always get a good cheap lunch in the ABC.) I got back to the office at two and got away at five-thirty, got home safely, got my tea, then got out to the pub as quickly as possible: some friends and I were having a get-together . . .' Words like 'go' and 'put' show equal versatility. Meat can 'go off' in hot weather; when a woman nags she 'goes on and on and on' at her husband; if we like something, we say we 'go for it'. One 'puts up' with adversity, 'puts up' somebody for the night or for club membership; a vicious dog may be 'put down' by the vet; you 'put in' a good word for somebody. A language like French cannot say 'go up' or 'go down', only *monter* or *descendre*.

Teachers of English to foreigners are sometimes shy of the various 'get' combinations, chiefly because they have long – though foolishly – been considered vulgar or 'unliterary'. It is still regarded, in examination-setting circles, as more decent to 'propose' a new member than to 'put him up', to 'quell' a rebellion rather than 'put it down'. Thus, the huge advantages that the 'synthetising' powers of English have for the foreign student are snobbishly pushed into a dusty cupboard.

But, before English can be stripped to the bone and turned into a real world auxiliary, the academic pundits will have to learn a little more about practical semantics; they will have to submit to (or put up with) the most outrageous rationalisations. All verbs will have to become weak, forms like 'I swimmed' and 'I have swimmed' being semantically clear and hence thoroughly admissible. Verb-inflexions must go: if 'I must'/'he must' is accepted, then no noses may be wrinkled at 'I go'/'he go' (nor, of course, at 'I goed'). This process of simplification is, of course, regularly at work with uneducated foreign speakers of English; it is something, alas, that British children have to unlearn, along with 'mouse'/'mouses' and 'foot'/'foots'.

When Basic English first appeared, some people assumed that Ogden and Richards's proposal was to replace orthodox English with this new and simpler form. But such a thing, even if possible, could never be regarded by any sensible person as desirable. With our first language, we move in the direction of ever greater subtlety of distinction in meaning, sharpening the instruments for ever deeper probings into thought, emotion, and motivation; with an auxiliary, our aim is to achieve a contact – however minimal – with foreign minds. A foreigner learning some such simple type of English as Basic would not be precluded from using that as a way into 'total English'. It would be possible for the two – Basic and Total – to be used side by side as the various forms of the 'contact vernacular' known as Pidgin English ('pidgin' being a corruption of 'business') are used by Englishmen in contact with natives of New Guinea and the African ports. English has room, and has made room, for a large number of overseas English dialects, as the new and flourishing literatures of British Africa and the Caribbean clearly show.

What tends to happen to English, however, when spoken in foreign territories, is that it is absorbed too thoroughly, ceases to be an outward-looking auxiliary and becomes a mere dialect of the mother-tongue. This is certainly true of some of the communities of India, especially where the mother-tongue does not belong to the Indo-European family: Tamils, who speak a Dravidian language, are adept at turning English into a Tamil dialect – the phonemes, idioms, pace being so thoroughly Tamilised, that it is not possible for a non-Tamil English-speaker to understand very well. Writing and reading are, of course, a different matter. I could make no sense out of *bu lokkar* until it was written down for me as 'bullock cart'.

We have to reconcile ourselves to hard linguistic facts. Languages will always change, whatever we try to do about it, and out of local changes come local languages. English is already changing into new languages in various parts of the world, mutually unintelligible, unintelligible to the English-born. English – full of unstable diphthongs and vowels, carrying a stress-system not always properly understood – lends itself far more to change than does a language like Italian, whose simple vowels have hardly altered in 2000 years. But, if there is a confusion of English-speaking tongues, the written word remains constant enough, unifying as the ideograms of Chinese unify. And English is big enough to enclose any number of aberrations.

Chapter 9

The Future of English

We have already considered very briefly what part English is likely to play as a world auxiliary. It remains for us to illustrate one of our main themes, that of the changeability of language in general, by reference to what seems to be happening to English in those countries where it is a first language, and what will probably happen in the future.

Linguistic change is something so gradual that we barely notice it, though occasionally we will wake up to a sudden realisation that a new word or phrase, formerly unknown, is in general use, or that a form that was once 'wrong' has become 'right'. At school we were taught that 'owing to' and 'due to' are not interchangeable, that 'owing to' may begin a phrase but 'due to' only be used after the verb 'to be'. But British Rail have printed many thousands of posters announcing: 'Due to adverse weather conditions trains may be late.' What was once a solecism is now evidently acceptable: one hears 'due to' as a conjunctive phrase not only on the Independent Television News but also on the BBC – once a stronghold of linguistic conservatism. Again, the pronunciation /kənˈtrɒvəsi/ is now heard in official places, whereas the only accepted form was once /ˈkɒntrəvɜ·si/.

Changes in usage and in the placing of word-stress are more noticeable than the more intimate phonemic changes and changes in intonation-patterns. And yet millions of television-viewers must be dimly aware that the 'speech-tunes' of news-reel commentators in the nineteen-thirties (which they can hear regularly in programmes of a reminiscent nature) are very different from what we are used to to-day. Theatre-goers may notice that an acceptable 'a' in 'man', 'mad', 'hat', and so on is one much lower than the old statutory /æ/, and that young actors and actresses can now say something like /man/ or /mad/ or /hat/ (approaching the Lancashire /a/) without being rebuked. The vowel of 'mother', 'butter', 'shut' has always been unstable. With many actors it seems to be moving from /ʌ/ and drawing close to /ɑ/.

But what no British speaker of English can fail to have noticed is the tendency of transatlantic English to assume a greater and greater hegemony. Those specifically American forms that were once smiled at in Edwardian drawing-rooms have now to be taken very seriously indeed. American English was once regarded as an amiable aberration from the East Midland norm, a 'colonial' dialect of English. Now we have to recognise that there is an American language – capable of immense variety within itself, but possessing enough general characteristics to be described summarily.

American English differs from British English of the BBC or 'standard' variety in certain important phonetic respects. It has resisted changes that British English accepted more than a century ago and, for the language of a progressive country, is remarkably conservative. Thus, it will not accept the so-called 'long A' of 'bath' (/bɑ:θ/) and clings to the Elizabethan front open vowel /æ:/, giving us /bæ:θ/. It insists on retaining a pronounced 'r' in words like 'father', 'darling', 'park', even though the sound is purely vestigial. It rejects the 'clear L' and uses the 'dark' variety in all positions, so that it opposes /ɫaɪk/ to British /laɪk/ ('like') and /lɪɫɪ/ to British /lɪlɪ/ ('lily'). There are other differences, too, but these are the main ones, and, of all of them, the opposition between /ɑ:/ and /æ:/ is the most considerable. The Standard British pronunciation of 'path', 'dance', 'can't' actively causes distress and even hostility in the United States, and British actors making films for export to America have to learn a kind of 'mid-Atlantic' English whose main characteristic is that it meets the Americans on this question of the 'long A'.

American influence on pronunciation of English in the British territories is bound to be great, mainly because of the vast number of films, television programmes, and records of popular songs that fill our screens and record-players. For good or ill, the younger speakers of first-language English regard American pronunciation as a norm, and a teenager who wishes to disguise his regional or class accent finds it easier to do this by learning American rather than by attempting Standard English. At the same time, American educationists concerned with spreading English over the 'Free World' naturally teach American phonemes, and these are enshrined in primers and records of a quality, and at a rate of distribution, that the British cannot touch. Some of the finest work on analysis of English, as well as on second-language teaching method, has been done in the University of Michigan. We need feel no surprise at the wholesale planting of American phonemes in foreign territories.

American speech attracts a British generation that is touchy about 'class' and still hears in BBC English the voice of the squire with a whip or the sneering subaltern. There is about the best American English an informality, an ability to descend to solecisms like 'ain't' or 'the mostest' with no loss of dignity, that formal British English cannot match. On the other hand, American English – especially from the Pentagon – can be pompous with a pomposity that makes the hearer's heart sink like a plummet. Yet even the sesquipedalian 'affirmative' for plain 'yes' or such coinages as 'inhospitalisation' seem to derive from a love of the sheer sound of language – a joy in the rumble of English cognate with the creative zest of American slang.

American locutions have been absorbed into British English ever since American English existed, though the rate of absorption has notably increased in the last forty-five years – since, in fact, the coming of the talking films. Many American forms are, of course, native British English, usages which we abandoned long ago but which the conservative Americans have retained. 'Yeah' for 'yes' is as old as Anglo-Saxon 'gēa'; 'right now' and 'I guess' were common currency in the reign of Richard II. But other locutions point to immigrant Central European influence on American English, and many of them are too expressive to be regarded as the mere solecisms of the ignorant. 'This guy bugging you, honey?' is answered by 'He's offering me a film contract. You should bug me so good'. In this latter sentence we have a pure Yiddish construction, as also in the Rodgers-Hammerstein song: 'I'm a girl, and by me that's only great' (the singer is a San Francisco Japanese). Even the consonant-group 'shm' has come into American English from Yiddish; its appearance in duplicated forms has brought new nuances to the language: 'Œdipus-shmoedipus,' said the Jewish lady to the psychiatrist; 'what's it matter what he's got so long as he loves his mudder?' According to the American philological journal *Language*, the following was overheard in a university commonroom: 'Your theory won't hold; I've got data.' – 'Data-shmata; I *like* my theory.'

So much of the vigorous charm of American English derives from slang which, by its nature, must quickly die to make way for fresh slang. By the time 'That's the way the cookie crumbles' has gone into British currency, it is already old hat in America. Beatnik terms (-*nik* is Jewish-Slavonic) and beatnik syntax ('Like he's crazy, man') already have a lavender smell about them. The lure of the up-to-date is a sad one, but even flashy coinages keep language vigorous and remind us that it is a reflection of man's very mortal changeability.

There rests in American English, nevertheless, a sizeable body of usage which is there to stay and which points the American claim that its brand of language has a right to be regarded as distinct and different from British English. Such doublets as the following are well known (in each case the British word comes first:

braces/suspenders	unbeautiful/homely
suspenders/garters	flat/apartment
lift/elevator	tap/faucet
pavement/sidewalk	underdone/rare
platform/track	undertaker/mortician
muffin/biscuit	stupid/dumb
biscuit/cracker	petrol/gas

There was a time when both Americans and Englishmen would be confused by these, and the many more, divergences. Now, thanks to British familiarity with American films, no Englishman feels these transatlantic usages to be really foreign. On the other hand, Americans continue to have difficulty with specifically British terms. This is because the propaganda traffic is one-way: eastwards.

England gladly buys American; Americans have to be persuaded to reciprocate. It is interesting, and – for a patriot – disheartening, to see how many British-made television film series are designed with an American audience in view. British actors have to portray American characters, even when the locale is British; or else American actors are imported to fill traditionally British roles. There is one series in which Scotland Yard is virtually run by Americans, another in which a great hero of nineteenth-century Australia is an American carrier, yet another in which a Kenya police officer is Anglo-American (he derives his accent from his mother). In films like these, it is curious to hear odd Cockney supporting characters talking of seeing their attorneys, returning to their apartments, or waiting on the sidewalk.

It is all a matter of buying and selling, commerce paving the way for the ultimate victory of American phonemes and American usage.

Ought we to lament this or attempt to halt it? I think not. It is not really possible to resist such processes, however hard the forces of conservatism or inertia dump their dead weight on the threshold. English has a strange knack of doing well for itself, however much the old guard booms about threats to purity, the dangers of pollution. English did well out of the Danish and Norman invaders; it will continue to profit from the strange loan-forms and coinages of the mixed populations that – in both England and America – represent the new ethnological order. Whatever form of English ultimately prevails – the British or the American variety – it will still be a great and rich and perpetually growing language, the most catholic medium of communication that the word has ever seen.

But, if we cannot really resist change, we can resist inflation, that debasement of language which is the saddest and most dangerous phenomenon of a world dominated by propaganda-machines, whether religious, political, or commercial. Propaganda always lies, because it over-states a case, and the lies tend more and more to reside in the words used, not in the total propositions made out of those words. A 'colossal' film can only be bettered by a 'super-colossal' one; soon the hyperbolic forces ruin all meaning. If moderately tuneful pop-songs are described as 'fabulous', what terms can be used to evaluate Beethoven's Ninth Symphony? The impressionable young – on both sides of the Atlantic – are being corrupted by the salesmen; they are being equipped with a battery of inflated words, being forced to evaluate alley-cat copulation in terms appropriate to the raptures of *Tristan and Isolde*. For the real defilers of language – the cynical inflators – a deep and dark hell is reserved.

Yet language survives everything – corruption, misuse, ignorance, ineptitude. Linking man to man in the dark, it brought man out of the dark. It is the human glory which antecedes all others. It merits not only our homage but our constant and intelligent study.

Select Bibliography

BAUGH, A. C., *A History of the English Language*, London, 1954

BLOOMFIELD, L., *Language*, New York, 1953

CHOMSKY, NOAM, *Syntactic Structures*, The Hague, 1957

DINNEEN, FRANCIS P., *An Introduction to General Linguistics*, New York, 1967

FARB, PETER, *Word Play*, New York, 1973

FIRTH, JOHN R., *The Tongues of Men, Speech* (two works in one volume), London, 1964

FRIES, C. C., *The Structure of English*, New York, 1952

JESPERSEN, O., *Growth and Structure of the English Language*, Leipzig, 1930

JONES, D., *The Pronunciation of English*, Cambridge, 1956

OGDEN, C. K. and RICHARDS, I. A., *The Meaning of Meaning*, London, 1946 (8th edition)

POTTER, SIMEON, *Changing English*, London, 1969

QUIRK, R., *The Use of English*, London, 1962

ULLMANN, S., *Semantics – an Introduction to the Science of Meaning*, Oxford, 1962

WARD, I. C., *The Phonetics of English*, Cambridge, 1939 (3rd edition)

WATERMAN, J. T., *Perspectives in Linguistics*, Chicago, 1970 (2nd edition)

Appendix One

The International Phonetic Alphabet – 'Narrow' and 'Broad' Forms

The form of the International Phonetic Alphabet used in this book is 'narrow': it has a separate symbol for every phoneme, and sometimes separate symbols for allophones. The reader may encounter a less exact version of this alphabet, especially in books which do not dig too deeply into the facts of speech; this is the 'broad' form. It differs from the 'narrow' form only in the representation of vowel sounds, using lengtheners to show phonemic differences, thus:

/iː/ – as in 'see', 'sea', 'me', 'fee'
/i/ – as in 'sit', 'fish', 'win', 'dig'
/uː/ – as in 'blue', 'too', 'few', 'through'
/u/ – as in 'put', 'bull', 'cook', 'wool'
/ɔː/ – as in 'saw', 'for', 'war', 'daughter'
/ə/ – as in 'got', 'lock', 'fog', 'wad'
/əː/ – as in 'fur', 'her', 'shirt', 'word'

Sometimes, too, the reader may find that vowel sounds are doubled to indicate length, so that 'seat' is shown as /siit/, 'moon' as /muun/, and so on. Strictly speaking, we are at liberty to use whatever symbols we like, so long as we define them first.

Appendix Two

How English Has Changed

Various translations of The Gospel According to St Matthew, Chapter 8, Verses 1 and 2.

(a) Anglo-Saxon. 995

(1) Sothlice tha se Haelend of tham munte nyther astah, tha fyligdon hym mycle maenio.

(2) Tha genealaehte an hreofla to him and hine to him geathmedde, and thus cwaeth, Drihten, gyf thu wylt, thu miht me geclaensian.

(b) Wyclif, 1389

(1) Forsothe when Jhesus hadde comen doun fro the hil, many cumpanyes folewiden hym.

(2) And loo! a leprouse man cummynge worshipide hym, sayinge, Lord, yif thou wolt, thou maist make me clene.

(c) Tyndale, 1526

(1) When Jesus was come down from the mountayne, moch people folowed him.

(2) And lo! there cam a lepre and worsheped him, saynge, Master, if thou wylt, thou canst make me clene.

(d) King James Version, 1611

(1) When he was come down from the mountain, great multitudes followed him.

(2) And, behold, there came a leper and worshipped him, saying, Lord, if thou wilt, thou canst make me clean.

(e) The New English Bible, 1961

After he had come down from the hill he was followed by a great crowd. And now a leper approached him, bowed low, and said, 'Sir, if only you will, you can cleanse me.'

Index

He glanced at Kim. Her eyes were wide with fear.

Ahead was a sharp curve and a steep drop. At this speed they'd fly over the edge. Rick had no choice. He rammed into a scrub oak thicket. They fishtailed, then finally slid to a stop, dust enveloping them in a cloud.

"This was no accident," she said.

He crawled beneath the SUV and studied the damage. "You're right. Someone cut the brake line." When he came back out, his jaw was set. "I let my guard down, Kim. I'm sorry."

"I don't understand."

"I'm on the job. I should know better than to get so distracted by you."

"I wouldn't trade a second of what happened between us," she said, holding his gaze. "It drew us closer, and if you allow it, it'll make us even stronger."

It could also get them killed…

We've lost our brakes. Ho

Dear Reader,

Aimée always believed in the power of love, and the forty-three year romance we shared kept us together from the moment we met. I was with her when she died in February, just a few weeks after completing *Eagle's Last Stand*. We spent those days side by side—I had her back, and she had my heart. Those hours were precious because we were together, doing what we loved most. There were no regrets. Aimée was at peace, in our own home with her beloved pets, friends and family.

I'm proud to have been the husband, lover, best friend and writing partner of one of the most talented individuals I've ever known. We worked as a team, but it was Aimée who led the way, creating these stories of love, family, loyalty and honor that will live well beyond her life here on earth.

As you read *Eagle's Last Stand*, open your mind to the words, thoughts and feelings that flow from Aimée's heart into your own, and never forget that friendship, love and romance *can* last longer than a lifetime.

In Aimée's own words—"With love we can soar and accomplish anything."

David Thurlo

Published in Great Britain 2014
by Mills & Boon, an imprint of Harlequin (UK) Limited,
Eton House, 18-24 Paradise Road, Richmond, Surrey, TW9 1SR

© 2014 Aimée and David Thurlo

ISBN: 978-0-263-91379-8

46-1214

EAGLE'S
LAST STAND

BY
AIMÉE THURLO

MILLS & BOON

IN MEMORIAM

Aimée Thurlo was an internationally known bestselling author of mystery and romantic suspense novels. She was the winner of a Career Achievement Award from *RT Book Reviews*, a New Mexico Book Award in contemporary fiction and a Willa Cather Award in the same category.

Aimée was born in Havana, Cuba, and lived with her husband and writing partner, David, in Corrales, New Mexico, in a rural neighborhood filled with horses, alpacas, camels and other assorted livestock. David was raised on the Navajo Indian Nation. His background and cultural knowledge inspired many of the Aimée Thurlo stories for Harlequin Intrigue.

We at Harlequin are saddened by the loss of Aimée and collectively send our deepest condolences to David. Aimée was a genuine and lovely woman who we, along with her many fans, will miss greatly.

Chapter One

He'd wondered what this night would be like, and now he knew. Rick Cloud smiled as he looked around the private dining room his foster brothers and their wives had reserved for his homecoming. For years the Brickhouse Tavern had been one of their favorite watering holes, so it had been the perfect place for the celebration.

Gene Redhouse, the only rancher among the six Navajo men, came up and patted him on the back. "Welcome home," he said, then laughed as he saw their brothers Kyle Goodluck and Daniel Hawk clear away part of the heavy trestle table so they could arm wrestle. "They're at it again."

"Some things never change." Rick's eyes strayed to the pretty hostess as she moved around the room, making sure everyone's glasses were filled and watching over them like a beautiful guardian angel. She was tall and slender, with shoulder-length honey-colored blond hair and beautiful green eyes that didn't seem to miss even the tiniest of details. As he watched, she took away an empty dish of guacamole and replaced it with spicy salsa and blue corn tortilla chips.

"That's Kim Nelson. Do you remember her from high school?"

"I never met her. If I had, I would have remembered," Rick said without hesitation.

"She was a freshman when you were a senior," Gene said. "To hear her talk when we were discussing the plans for tonight, I think she used to have a thing for you. Kyle says it's because you were quarterback, but I fail to see the reasoning. You hand off or throw the ball, take some hits and run the option once in a while. Barely got your jersey dirty most games."

"Jealous, bro?" Rick said, and laughed.

"Nah. I'm the one who ended up with the prize," he said, looking across the room at the pretty brunette watching the match. "Lori's the perfect wife for a cowboy like me."

"You were born to be a rancher," Rick said. "I'm glad you're happy."

As Gene went back to join his wife, Rick found he couldn't take his eyes off Kim. Even the way she moved caught his attention. The woman possessed a presence; a dynamic combo of grace and confidence that kept him searching the dining room for her.

Finally he forced himself to look away. He didn't need this now. Though he'd never been the ladies' man his brothers thought him to be, he'd never had trouble finding company. Now that his face was marked by a scar that ran across his nose and cheek, a leftover from a deadly knife fight, things would undoubtedly be different.

As Kim worked the room, smiling but definitely staying in the background, he noted the way she'd sometimes glance in his direction. He was about to seek her out when she came over.

"You're the guest of honor tonight, Mr. Cloud. Is there anything special I can get for you?"

"No, I'm good, thanks," he said. She had spectacular green eyes that stayed on his, never shifting for a quick look at his scar. Kim couldn't have missed it, yet she still focused on *him*.

"I'm Kim, the events coordinator here at the Brickhouse."

He shook her hand. "Nice to meet you. And call me Rick."

"Your brothers wanted to make sure every detail of your homecoming was perfect, Rick. That's one of the reasons I stayed to handle things personally. The other, I've got to admit, is because I was curious to see you again. I knew who you were back in high school, but I don't think you ever noticed me," she said with a little smile.

"Definitely my loss."

She smiled. "When Preston Bowman came to book the restaurant for the private event, my uncle and I knew we had to make this evening super special."

His brother Preston, the lead detective on the Hartley, New Mexico, police department, had a way about him that intimidated most people. "Preston carries that much weight?"

"Actually he does, with me and my uncle, that is."

Something in her tone of voice caught his attention, but before she could say anything more, they heard a loud thump in the kitchen and the rattle of a pot or pan bouncing on the floor.

Kim jumped. "I better go see what happened," she said, excusing herself.

"Wait," he said, reaching for her hand. Something felt off. He took a shallow breath and caught the familiar scent of rotten eggs. It seemed to be growing stronger with each passing second.

"That's a gas leak," he told Kim, then called out to his brothers. "Everyone outside! Quickly."

"It's getting stronger," Daniel said. "Let's go, people!" He pulled his wife, Holly, toward the front door.

Rick's other brother, Paul Grayhorse, got there first but the door refused to budge. "It's locked!" He turned the knob and shoved, but the door didn't open. "No, it's stuck or jammed."

"Force it," Gene shouted. "Kick it open if you have to!"

"I'll check the back," Rick said, turning toward the kitchen.

"I've got to check on my uncle!" Kim rushed past him. She started coughing as she pushed through the double doors to the kitchen. "Uncle Frank? Where are you?"

As Rick caught up to her, they found Frank Nelson lying on the floor beside a long counter, blood oozing from the back of his head.

Kim knelt beside her uncle. "He's unconscious. We have to get him out of here," she cried out.

Out of the corner of his eye, Rick noticed movement. It was a flexible metal gas line against the wall behind the stove. Cut in two, it was fluttering slightly from the outflow of methane. Nearby lay a pair of heavy-duty, red-handled bolt cutters.

"We've got to get out of here before a spark sets off an explosion," Rick yelled. "Help me pull him out the back."

Her eyes narrowed as the foul stink of gas flooded the kitchen, but she didn't panic. Kim took her uncle's arm and Rick the other, and together they dragged Frank toward the rear exit.

Rick then pushed the left half of the double doors hard with his shoulder. It creaked, but only opened a few inches before it stopped with a rattle.

He looked down into the gap between the doors. "They're chained from the outside," he said, nearly gagging from the strong outflow of methane.

Putting his back into it, Rick pushed even harder. The doors squealed, but held tight.

"We're trapped! Maybe the front door?" Kim looked toward the dining area.

Following her gaze, Rick could see his brothers all leaning into the door. Slowly they forced it open enough to give Erin, Kyle's wife and the smallest of the women, room to slip through the gap.

"We can't wait. I've got to break the doors down." Rick pulled the unconscious man aside, lowered him to the floor and then took a step back. Bracing his arm against his body, he rushed the left door with a yell.

Rick's two hundred and twenty pounds of muscle crashed against the doors. The brass handles broke with a loud snap and the doors flew open. Rick stumbled halfway across the loading dock and crashed into the guard rail before he could stop himself.

Racing back into the kitchen, he reached Frank and Kim, who was down on her knees beside her uncle. Glancing through the kitchen toward his brothers, Rick saw Daniel, the last of the party, just ducking out.

"Time to leave," Rick yelled. He put Frank Nelson over his shoulder and strode quickly down the steps of the loading dock. "Hurry," he added, looking back at Kim.

Kim slipped under the guard rail, jumped off the edge of the platform and met Rick at the bottom of the steps. Just then, Kyle and Preston came around the corner of the Brickhouse, running toward them.

"Get back!" Rick yelled, jogging toward the street with the injured man over his shoulder. "The place can blow any second!"

With Kim beside him, Rick angled left, heading for the corner of the next building over, a former theater turned furniture store. He wanted a solid structure between them and the upcoming blast.

As he reached the sidewalk, he saw his family, en masse, racing across the street in a loose cluster. They had no time to find cover. "On the ground!" he yelled.

Rick dropped to his knees and lowered Frank to the sidewalk. Pulling Kim down and against the wall of the building, he covered her with his body.

Suddenly the earth shook, shaking him back and forth as a massive concussive wave and flash of light swept out into the street. A blinding ball of hot air and flames followed, shooting out of the alley to his left and reaching halfway across the avenue.

The windows on the real-estate office a hundred feet away shattered, raining glass onto the sidewalk. Turning his head slightly, he could see the people he loved, face-down on the far side of the street beside the curb, arms over their heads.

A cascade of falling debris became an ear-shattering hailstorm of bricks and building materials. This went on for several seconds, then began to subside, overwhelmed by the roar and crackle of the resulting fire.

Rick rose to his feet, his mind racing. "You okay?" he asked Kim.

"My uncle… Where is his pulse?" She searched the area around his neck with a trembling hand.

"He's breathing…he's alive. Put pressure on the head wound and I'll call an ambulance," Rick said, turning his back to the wave of heat from the burning building less than twenty-five feet away.

"I called 9-1-1," Preston said, coming up to him. He nodded at the older man on the sidewalk. "Let's get him farther away from the fire in case there's a secondary explosion."

Together he and Rick carried Frank into the recessed doorway of the furniture store. "Did you get a good look around the kitchen?" Preston asked. "What happened in there?"

"It was no accident. The gas line was cut," Rick answered. "I saw bolt cutters nearby. Somebody must have decked Frank, then cut the gas line and slipped out into the alley."

Preston's gaze swept over his brothers, their wives and the two waiters from the Brickhouse. They'd walked down the street several feet away from the fallen glass and stepped up onto the sidewalk as the first fire truck arrived. "Looks like we're all okay, and that's nothing short of a miracle," he said.

"I'm used to being targeted," Rick said, his voice reflecting the darkness inside him, "but the cartel I dealt with liked keeping things up close and personal. Cutting a gas line and hoping I'd be caught in an explosion just doesn't fit their M.O. My enemies are a lot more direct and efficient."

"Whoever it was didn't just come after you. They came after all of us brothers, and that was a big mistake," Daniel said, coming up beside them.

"Not necessarily," Rick said. Years of undercover work for the FBI, fighting human trafficking, had taught him that control and clear thinking spelled the difference between life and death. Emotions only got in the way. "Others were there, too."

"You mean they were after our wives?" Paul asked incredulously.

"More likely the restaurant staff," Rick said. "If the doors hadn't been blocked, another motive would have been to burn down the business so the owner could collect the insurance."

His gaze drifted back to Kim, who was crouched by her uncle. The bleeding had slowed from what he could see.

"Kim, who's the owner of the Brickhouse?" he asked, going over and placing a gentle hand on her shoulder.

"My uncle Frank is half owner," she said, never taking her eyes off her uncle. "His business partner is Arthur Johnson, but Art would never think of burning down the place or hurting anyone, especially Frank. Those two have been good friends for years, and the Brickhouse has always made money for both of them. You guys are off base on this."

"I'd have to agree with Kim. There's no way this place is losing money. It's always packed," Preston said.

"Gene's grabbed a big wrench from the toolbox in his pickup and he's going to shut off the gas at the meter. That'll help the firemen," Daniel said.

"Meanwhile," Preston suggested, "let's focus on what we know. Because of the timing, the firebug must have blocked the front first before entering the kitchen from the alley."

"If it was an inside job, it wasn't done by anyone who escaped with us," Rick concluded.

They heard the wail of an ambulance followed by the sirens of several police cruisers racing up Main Street. "Time for me to get to work," Preston said. "If any of you come up with a motive or a suspect, let me know. Right now, I've got to help secure the scene."

The big white rescue unit came up the street from the opposite direction, just ahead of a second fire truck. Preston stepped out into the street and motioned to the approaching vehicles.

Less than a minute later the firemen were working to suppress the fire. Two EMTs, having gathered their equipment, approached Frank, then crouched next to him.

Rick stood back with Daniel. "Frank's probably our best witness and may have some of the answers. There's a chance he saw the arsonist before he got clocked."

"Preston will follow up," Daniel said, "but there's something I need to talk to you about. Is it possible that the man responsible for the scar on your face came back to try to finish the job?"

"No, he's dead," Rick said, "but some of the ones he worked for in the Mexican cartel avoided arrest. They're still at large and fighting for control of what's left of their criminal operation. You never really defeat that kind of evil."

"Any chance you were followed home?"

Rick expelled his breath in a slow hiss. "To the U.S., then all the way to Hartley? My gut says no. They know I can't work undercover anymore. I've been marked in a way that makes it impossible for me to hide my identity. More importantly, I'm no longer a threat to them, so there's no profit in taking me out. I doubt they'd waste their resources."

"All right then." Daniel glanced at the debris strewed in every direction. "Taking on one of Hosteen Silver's boys is a bad idea, but taking *all* of us on is nothing short of a death wish. Whoever he is, he's going down."

"No doubt about it," Rick said. He looked over to where Kim stood watching the paramedics work. "I'm going to follow her to the hospital. I'd like to talk to her uncle as soon as he's conscious."

"Better wait for Preston. He's the only one of us who still carries a badge, and this is his turf, not ours," Daniel warned. "You know how he is about going by the book."

Rick gave his brother a mirthless smile. "Good for him. I started out that way, but undercover—"

"I know, but there are rules here," Daniel reminded him. "You're home now."

Daniel was right; he had to stand back. It wasn't his case.

Seeing Kim arguing with the paramedics, who wouldn't let her ride in the ambulance, he jogged over. "Come on, Kim, I'll take you to the hospital."

"Thanks, my car's at home."

As they strode to his rental SUV, Preston intercepted them. "Gene's going to take the women over to Level One Security, just in case it's a family threat. The kids will be brought over by the babysitters, too. Until we get a better handle on things, Daniel's office is like a fortress."

"What about Kim and the other two members of the tavern staff?" Rick asked.

"The servers have been told to stick around until I have the chance to ask them a few questions. Kim, you'll need to come back here after you check on your uncle's status," Preston said, looking directly at her. "Or you can meet me later tonight at the station. Your choice."

"I'll be sticking around at the hospital. If you need to speak to me before tomorrow, it'll have to be there."

"Fair enough. Under the circumstances, I don't blame you for wanting to stay close to your family, but it might be late before I make it to the hospital," Preston advised.

"As for you, Rick," Preston continued, "I'd like you to stick around. In your work I'm sure you've grown familiar with makeshift bombs, and I'd like you to go inside the building with me to help search for evidence."

Rick turned to Kim and held out his keys. "Take my SUV. It's the dark blue one toward the end of the block."

"Don't worry about it. I know Uncle Frank keeps a spare set of car keys. They're in a magnetic holder by the right front tire. It's okay if I take his car, isn't it?" she asked Preston.

"Yes. It'll have to be moved anyway once heavy equipment is brought in to clear the rubble off the street," Preston answered.

"Good," Kim said. "I'll be at the hospital, probably all night, if anyone else needs me."

"I'll catch up to you later," Rick said, watching her hurry down the sidewalk to a parked car. Kim was great-looking, and had guts. He'd only just met her but he sure liked what he'd seen.

As Rick strode toward what was left of the building, he saw it was now illuminated by floodlights placed strategically along the street and inside the dining room. Going into agent mode, he stilled his thoughts and allowed a familiar coldness to envelop him.

He stopped by the front door and studied it without touching anything. "What kept this from opening?" he asked Preston, who'd jogged over to meet him after speaking to the Hartley Fire Department station chief.

"A pipe was wedged into the wrought-iron security grillwork on both sides of the door, barring it from the outside. I bagged and tagged it before anyone else besides Erin touched it. It'll need to be processed for prints."

"The chains on the outside kitchen doors...those being processed, too?" Rick asked.

"Yes, including the lock and the metal door hardware. It's all been tagged for the lab."

"All right, then, let's go into the kitchen. I only got a quick glance before we got out, so I'm still not sure what actually set off the explosion—an open flame, some kind of timer, or something else."

Preston led the way through the front entrance where a metal door dangled by the upper hinge. Broken chairs, table lamps, dishes, utensils and other items were scattered all around them.

As they started to pick their way across the interior, a tall man carrying a camera and wearing an H.F.D. jacket stepped out of the shadows.

"Stop. The kitchen area is off-limits to everyone except fire department personnel right now." He identified himself to Rick as the fire marshal. "There's no surveillance footage here, so it'll probably take me until tomorrow to compile my report on what caused the explosion. For now, you guys have to get out of here." Without another word, he strode into the kitchen.

"That's Arnie Medina," Preston said. "He has jurisdiction here at the scene, so let's leave the kitchen to him and we'll concentrate on evidence that might help us determine who the suspect was, or how long he was inside the building. That would give us a time line when tracking people who were in the area."

Rick glanced around at the wreckage. Over the past four years, deep undercover, he'd worked alongside people who would have slit his throat just for practice. He'd looked forward to coming home and no longer having to sleep with his weapon at arm's reach.

Now his much needed R&R would have to wait. His family was in the line of fire. The first attempt had failed, but experience taught him that killers seldom gave up until they succeeded—or were put down.

As they entered an employee area adjacent to the kitchen, Rick noticed a canvas tote next to the wall and lifted it out from behind a fallen roof tile. He looked inside and saw several textbooks. There was also a small purse along with a set of keys. He held up the purse so his brother could see. "Still dry. Somebody got lucky."

Preston took the wallet and located the driver's license. "It's Kim's. I hope she doesn't get stopped. I'll make sure to take it with me when I go to the hospital later tonight."

Rick nodded absently, then taking a closer look at the books, realized that one of the volumes was a textbook on police procedures, another on criminal law and a third one on evidence collection. "What's this all about?" he asked, surprised.

"Kim's working on an associate's degree in criminology. Her dad was one of ours, and she wants to follow in his footsteps. Jimmy Nelson was a good man."

"'Was'?"

"He was killed in the line of duty," Preston said, noticing a crime scene investigator waving him over. "I'll be back in a minute."

Rick hung the bag from a wall bracket that was still intact, minus a shelf, and continued to search. It was becoming increasingly difficult to stay alert this time of night. He'd spent most of the day on the road and was physically beat. He was running on pure adrenaline.

Preston motioned him outside. "I think you should consider staying with everyone else at Daniel's tonight. I've got a late night ahead of me."

"Do what you have to," Rick said. "I was thinking of stopping by the hospital and talking to Kim."

"No. Not until I question her." Preston took a breath and let it out slowly. "I won't bother telling you not to get involved in this case, Rick, because you already are, but you need to remember you're not FBI anymore. Most important of all, you have no concealed carry permit."

"Actually, I do. The Bureau made sure of that before I left."

"Okay, one less problem. Where's Kim's purse?"

"Inside," Rick answered, telling him the location.

"Okay," Preston said with a nod. "Considering this might yet track back to your past, let me know if you'll feel safer carrying a badge just in case you have to mix it up with someone. I'm pretty sure the chief would deputize you, considering you're a highly trained former special agent with a distinguished record."

"Good. Do that as soon as you can. It'll be good backup."

"Consider it done. So, will you be going to Daniel's?" Preston asked.

He shook his head. "If someone's after me..." He let the sentence hang.

"There's no safer place on this earth than Daniel's compound," Preston told him, as if the issue was settled. He looked toward the brother in question, who was coming up the sidewalk.

For the first time since the blast, Rick smiled. Out of all his Navajo foster brothers, Daniel, the owner of a major security company, was the one he understood best. "I hear your place is as secure as Fort Knox."

"Did you expect anything less?" Daniel said as he stopped in front of them. "Speaking of safety, Rick, you're driving a rental SUV, but considering what happened tonight, you'd be better off with something from my company's motor pool. Tomorrow I'll match you up with a more suitable ride."

Preston excused himself and went to interview the two waiting employees, while Daniel walked with Rick back to the rental.

"Death follows me," Rick said as he climbed into the SUV. "Undercover, that's a given, but I never expected to find it here." His lips straightened into a thin hard line. "I guess they don't realize it yet."

"What?"

"Hosteen Silver's boys are damned hard to kill."

Chapter Two

After spending a restless night, Rick headed to the kitchen for coffee, desperate for a shot of caffeine.

Paul and Preston's adopted sons, Jason and Bobby, were playing a loud video game in the next room, and as he poured himself a mug of the dark steamy brew, Daniel intercepted him.

"Come on, time to work. This way."

Rick followed his brother into the main room, the office's planning and computer center. A huge horizontal computer screen the size of a table rested adjacent to four large monitors on the wall.

"I have access to intelligence chatter, courtesy of my Department of Homeland Security and National Security Agency contacts. There's been nothing at all to indicate you were specifically targeted last night. I contacted the Bureau, as well, and their sources agree with the other agencies. No flags were raised," Daniel said.

"So they might have been hoping to kill everyone, or maybe only one or two of us, while the rest of the family became collateral damage," Rick said. "That's pretty cold."

"There's no way to be certain, but my instincts are telling me that if they wanted one of us specifically, they would have taken their shot before now," Daniel said. "Their real target could have also been Frank, Kim, one of the two servers or the Brickhouse Tavern itself."

"The timing was linked to my homecoming, though," Rick said. "Besides that, was there anything special about last night?"

"Not that we know of," Daniel said, "but if your theory is right and this has nothing to do with your undercover work, then we should be looking for an enemy you made here, maybe during one of your infrequent visits."

"I can't think of anyone," Rick said, shaking his head, "but I'll give it some thought."

Preston came in just then. "Frank Nelson still can't be questioned. He's out of danger, according to the doctors, but they want to keep him sedated and are monitoring him closely for swelling of the brain. Kim gave us a preliminary statement late last night, but she was too shaken to remember anything we don't already know."

"It was close to home for her, but if she's going to be a cop, she'll have to toughen up fast," Rick said, his voice heavy.

Preston looked at his brother. "She will, but she's barely out of the starting gate. Her dad's gone and right now her uncle's her only living relative. The incident last night turned her world upside down."

For a moment Rick found himself indulging in an emotion he seldom experienced—sympathy. He knew what it was like to suddenly find yourself all alone.

"I'd still like to talk to her. Kim may know something useful. I'm not a cop, at least not anymore, so that might set her at ease and help her remember some details," Rick said.

Preston nodded. "Go for it."

"Before anyone leaves, we need to decide if our families need extra protection," Daniel said.

"I spoke to Gene this morning, and he agrees with me,"

Preston said. "The best solution is to get them out of town. Fortunately, Kendra has her U.S. Marshals training, so she'll keep them safe," Preston added, referring to Paul's wife. "We can also send two of your top security people along with them, Daniel, just to make sure."

"Where are you planning to send them?" Rick asked.

"To Gene's ranch," Preston replied. "You've never been there, Rick, but it's in Colorado, a few hours from here, out in open country where intruders are easily spotted."

"Since the trouble his wife, Lori, had a few years back, Gene's place now has surveillance cameras that feed to our computers here," Daniel explained. "With some handpicked men, and Gene and Kendra on the job, they'll be safe."

"Good plan," Rick said.

Paul came in just then. He still favored his shoulder when he moved, the result of the gunshot that had forced him to retire from the U.S. Marshals Service. "I'll be monitoring things from here."

"I'll handle the details," Daniel said, then looked at Rick. "You're going to need one of our special SUVs. Just leave the rental here and one of my men will take care of it. I've got a black one outside that'll be perfect for you. It's got extra Kevlar armor, a GPS tracker and run-flat tires."

"Good. I'd like to get going," Rick admitted.

"They wouldn't let Kim in to be with her uncle after I spoke with her last night, so she went home," Preston said. "If Kim isn't at the hospital this morning, you'll find her at Silver Heritage Jewelry and Gifts. The shop is owned by a member of our tribe, a Navajo woman, Angelina Curley."

"So Kim has two jobs, one at the Brickhouse and one at a jewelry store?" he asked.

"She's paying her way through college with gigs that let her keep flexible hours," Preston answered.

"I know she thinks highly of you. What's the story there?" Rick asked Preston.

"I put the man who shot her dad behind bars. Her uncle Frank really stepped up for her after that, but the P.D. kept an eye on her, as well. We wanted Kim to know that officers take care of our own, and if she needed anything, she had help. After she enlisted in the army out of high school, we kept in touch. She was deployed for a few years and then came home determined to follow in her dad's footsteps."

"So I should treat her with kid gloves, is that it?" Rick asked. It was a fair question, and there was no rancor in his voice.

"No, not at all. Just be aware that she's got a lot of officers watching out for her."

Daniel tossed Rick a set of keys. "Check in when you can. As soon as I get the family squared away, I'm going to dig into the backgrounds of each of the players, including Kim and her uncle. I have the contacts and clearance to get into databases the PD can't access without a truckload of paperwork."

Rick walked out and found the black SUV. It had a lot of extras and must have cost his brother's company a lot of money, but he was glad to have it. Something was telling him the case would be getting even messier soon.

As he drove down Hartley's Main Street, one thought continued to nag at him. He had to know if he'd somehow been responsible—if his arrival in Hartley had set off the attack. Maybe his instincts were still on overdrive, but he'd learned not to ignore them. They'd kept him alive.

KIM WAS CLEANING the glass-topped display case when she heard the bell over the door jingle. Glancing up, she saw Rick stride in and nod to Fred, the security guard, who was standing nearby.

She smiled. Rick had that elusive "it" quality that commanded attention without even trying. He'd been her secret crush back in high school. Rick had been the larger-than-life high school quarterback, and she'd been the nerdy freshman buried in homework. Back then, between her thick glasses and her braces, she'd barely got a glance from the popular guys. Of course, it also could have been because her father was a cop.

The boy she'd watched from a distance was gone now, and in his place stood a sexy, earthy, dangerous-looking man. The scar made him look tough, seasoned by a hard life and infinitely masculine.

As he walked around the counter in her direction, she couldn't take her eyes off him. He moved without wasted motion, sure of himself, aware of his surroundings.

When he saw her he smiled and for a moment his face gentled, but the emotion was gone in a flash.

"Good morning, Rick. What can I do for you?" she asked, going up to him.

"I know the police have already interviewed you, Kim, but I'd like to discuss last night again. When do you take your next break?" he asked in a voice so low only she could hear.

She glanced at the clock. Angelina wasn't in yet, so it wouldn't hurt to take her fifteen minutes a little early, particularly since they had no customers at the moment.

"Now would be fine."

She went to the coffeepot in the corner and offered him a cup. When he shook his head, she poured herself one. "I've been thinking of nothing else but the explosion. I barely slept last night, but I still haven't been able to remember anything that might help the police."

"Then shift your focus. Don't think about the explosion. Concentrate on what happened earlier that evening."

"Okay." As she looked into his eyes she saw something there that made her hold her breath. The angry scar across his face spoke of life-and-death struggles, but his steady gaze shone with strength, courage and determination.

"Your brother Preston asked the hospital staff for permission to speak to Uncle Frank last night, but the doctors refused. They had to sedate him. He was so scared, waking up in the emergency room."

"Did you get to talk to him at all?"

"For a bit. Uncle Frank told me he caught a glimpse of a big man wearing overalls, a blue ball cap and mirrored sunglasses right before he was hit on the back of the head. I should have asked him more, but all I could think of was how lucky we were. We'd all nearly died." She stopped and looked up at him. "Does that make me sound like a coward?"

"It makes you sound human. When it counted, you stepped up. Your first thought was to find your uncle, then you did everything you could to get him out of danger. You worked to save a life, and did a lot more than was expected of you. In my book, that's the definition of a hero."

She shook her head and gave him a quick half smile. "Thanks, but no. There were no heroes there. We were all just people doing what we had to do."

"It was a crazy time," he said quietly.

"The person who did this took a huge risk. If my uncle hadn't had the Cowboys game going full blast, he probably would have heard the guy sneak up behind him."

Hearing the jingle at the front door, they both glanced in that direction and saw the security guard hold the door open for Angelina. "That's my boss," she said quietly. "She's got a bad temper, so I better get back to work. We can meet later for lunch at the Desert Rose Café and talk some more if you want."

Rick looked at Angelina and suddenly remembered meeting her before. Smiling, he went up to her. "Angelina Tso! I'm not sure if you remember me," he said. "You got stuck in Copper Canyon after a hard rain several years ago after working with my father, and I towed you out to the highway."

"I'm Angelina Curley now," she said curtly.

"Weren't you studying with Hosteen Silver to become a medicine woman?" Rick asked, using the Navajo equivalent of Mister that most of their tribe preferred. "Did you find another mentor after my foster father's death?"

Her expression darkened, and Kim, who'd been watching the exchange, recognized the signs instantly.

"Kim, I'm paying you to work, so find something to do!" Angelina snapped. "And you," she added, looking at Rick. "I'm warning you right now to stay out of my store. Neither you nor your family is welcome here. Hosteen Silver cheated me. He took my money and then wouldn't let me come back for more instruction. He robbed me of my chance to become a Navajo healer, then tried to ruin my reputation."

"There's got to be more to the story. *Integrity* was more than a word to Hosteen Silver," he said, biting back his anger. "Why don't we talk about this in private?"

"I'm not saying another word to you. Fred, show Mr. Cloud out," Angelina said, looking at the security guard.

"I know my foster father, and what you're telling me isn't something he'd do. Let's talk and figure things out," Rick insisted, taking a step closer to her and gesturing to the empty office behind them. "We can talk in private in there."

"Keep your hands off me," Angelina shouted at him.

"He didn't—" Kim started, but in an instant everything went crazy.

As Fred rushed forward, squaring off in front of Rick,

fists clenched, Kim squeezed in between them, facing the security guard.

"Fred, he didn't touch her. Just calm down," Kim urged, anxious to avoid a stupid confrontation.

"Do something, you fool," Angelina yelled at Fred.

"Out of my way, Kim," the security guard ordered.

"No. Just chill out, Fred, okay?"

"Throw him out, damn you!" Angelina screamed.

The guard grabbed Kim by the shoulders and pushed her aside. Kim stumbled and slammed her ribs against the edge of the counter. Groaning, she reached out with both hands and, getting a grip on the display case, managed not to fall.

Rick instantly grabbed the man by the belt and collar and hurled him facedown across the tiled floor.

Fred careened into a freestanding metal display filled with souvenirs and cheap Mexican pottery. The display rocked, sending a cascade of key chains, postcards and clay pots tumbling to the floor.

Angelina reached for the low shelf behind the front counter, brought out a revolver and pointed it directly at Rick. She was breathing hard, shaking and clearly out of control.

"No!" Kim lunged toward her boss, but Rick beat her to it.

In a blur he yanked the weapon from Angelina's hand and looked over at the guard, who'd grabbed the display and managed to keep it from tipping over.

"Everyone, *calm down!*" he ordered, opening the cylinder and dumping the bullets onto the floor before placing the revolver on the counter.

Kim froze in place. Even without a weapon, he still commanded the room. "I'm leaving now," he said, holding out his hand, palm up, as a signal for Fred to stay put. "See you at lunch, Miss Nelson?" he asked softly. Assessing the situation with a steely gaze, he never turned his back until he was out of the shop.

As the door swung shut, Angelina, still shaking, turned to Fred, who was down on one knee picking up the scattered merchandise. "You're my brother's son so I gave you a chance, but you stink as a security guard. Turn in your gear and get out. You're fired." Then she turned to Kim. "And you—"

"Angelina, I didn't do anything wrong this morning, and you know it." She wasn't going to take any abuse from the woman, but she couldn't afford to lose her job. If she could only manage to calm her down....

"He came to see *you*."

"All he wanted to do was follow up on last night," Kim said, struggling to keep her voice low and controlled. "That explosion at the Brickhouse could have killed fifteen people. Most of us got lucky, but my uncle is in the hospital with a fractured skull. You must have seen the burned-out building and street barricades. We were lucky to get out alive."

"You were hosting a dinner for the sons of Hosteen Silver. What did you expect? That bunch brings nothing but bad luck. Look what just happened here," Angelina said, then shook her head. "Forget it. Get out. You're fired."

"I doubt Mr. Cloud will ever be coming back, so why let me go?" she insisted. If she ended up jobless, how would she be able to stay in school?

"I'm not interested in an employee who's friends with my enemies. I know you're having lunch with him," she snapped. "I'll mail your last paycheck. Now get out."

Kim picked up her purse, jacket and lunch bag and walked out while Angelina searched for the bullets still scattered on the floor.

"I'M GLAD YOU called to tell me what happened, Rick," Preston said, looking around the interior of the Desert Rose Café, studying the smattering of diners there.

"I had to. That woman lost it completely. When she screamed at me to take my hands off her, her guard moved in, but I never touched Angelina Curley. Kim can verify what happened," Rick said, reaching for his spicy breakfast burrito.

"Angelina's well known around town and has friends in high places despite her erratic behavior. Stay away from her. It's unlikely that she's involved in what happened at the Brickhouse, so tread carefully. You don't want to turn her into an enemy."

"We already are enemies." His gaze snapped to the shop across the street as an old saying played in his mind. "Hell hath no fury like a woman scorned." One way or another, he was going to find out what had happened between Angelina and Hosteen Silver.

Chapter Three

Though it was only ten-thirty and way too early for lunch, with nowhere else to go at the moment, Kim decided to stop by the Desert Rose Café for a cup of tea. As she walked in, she was surprised to see Preston and Rick sitting at a table near the window.

Kim approached them slowly, wondering if she was making a mistake. Maybe Rick was bad luck. Look at everything that had happened so far, and he'd only been in town since yesterday afternoon.

She discarded the thought immediately. There was no such thing as luck. She remembered the quote by Louis Pasteur her father had hung in his office at home. "Chance favors the prepared mind." People made their own luck.

Rick and Preston stood as she came over, and Rick gestured to the chair beside him. "What brings you by so early, Kim? If you're hungry, I can recommend the breakfast burrito. It's terrific. The coffee...not so much."

She smiled. "I know. I usually order tea."

The waitress came over and smiled. "Hey, Kim. What'll you have?"

"How about a job, Sally? Only kidding. I just got fired," she said, "so a cup of honey tea will do."

"I'm so sorry to hear that," the young waitress answered.

"So am I," Rick added. "Order what you want and consider it part of my apology. I owe you that, at least."

Kim shook her head. "Tea will be enough." As the waitress left, she touched Rick's arm briefly. "I appreciate the offer, but all you really did was speed up the inevitable. I've never liked the way Angelina treated her employees and, frankly, I only stuck around because the work fit my schedule."

Preston spoke up. "If you need some financial help—"

She shook her head and held up a hand, interrupting him. "I've got skills and experience working retail, so I'll find a new job soon. However, if you hear of a part-time position with flexible hours, let me know."

"I've got to get back to work," Preston said, removing a few dollars from his wallet and placing them on the table. "Kim, keep thinking hard about last night. Sometimes the answers don't come all at once."

"I will."

As the waitress brought over her cup of tea, Kim eyed the piece of Rick's burrito that remained but said nothing. Pride always stopped her from asking for favors or help.

"We changed our minds. How about a breakfast burrito for the lady, too," he said.

"Be back in a jiff," the waitress said.

Kim smiled at Rick. "You didn't have to do that, but thanks. The aromas in here always make me hungry."

"No problem. Now I feel a little less guilty."

A lengthy silence ensued until Sally returned with her food and, wanting to know more about Rick, Kim decided to start the conversation. "So tell me, Rick. Are you really home for good?" she asked, taking a bite of burrito.

"Yes."

"Are you glad to be back among family or do you miss your old job?"

"Both."

He obviously wasn't much for small talk. She took several more bites, enjoying the flavorful explosion of green chili. Remembering how procedural books said that people often opened up just to fill the lapse in conversation, she let the silence stretch.

It didn't work. Rick had probably read the same book years ago.

"I appreciate that you bought me something to eat and are letting me enjoy the burrito in peace, but I get the feeling there's something on your mind," she said, taking the last bite. "So how can I help you?"

"I know Angelina Curley had dealings with my foster father, then one day she stopped coming around," he said. "I don't believe her accusations at all. Any idea what really happened between them?"

"I've heard pieces of the story here and there, but because they originated from Angelina I'm not sure how accurate they are," she warned.

"Go on."

"Hosteen Silver accepted cash and jewelry in payment for her instruction and apprenticeship, but then, according to Angelina, he made sexual advances. When she rejected him, he got angry and refused to continue her training."

"My foster father would never have done anything like that. The woman's lying."

"Uncle Frank knew your foster father. I met him once at the Brickhouse, too. He didn't strike me as that type of person, either," she admitted. "But in my experience, Angelina isn't above lying if it suits her. I've seen how she twists things around when she's dealing with customers and vendors. She keeps things legal, but she's completely unethical," Kim said. "Maybe she was the one who made a pass and got shot down. She doesn't take rejection well, I can tell you that. Or maybe she just didn't have what it takes to be a medicine woman and needed someone to blame. Considering Angelina doesn't remember details, I'm surprised she's as successful in business as she is. She'll often ask us the same question two or three times."

"That might explain her failure as my father's apprentice. The Sings have to be memorized perfectly and some last for days," Rick answered. "One mistake and the gods won't answer, or they might make things worse for a person out of anger. Getting it right shows respect."

"It took days for her to remember the combination of the new safe." She paused for a moment. "Angelina's not stupid, far from it, but she's easily distracted."

"My foster father could be very exacting. If Angelina wasn't measuring up, he would have told her that in no uncertain terms."

"Angelina would have blamed him, not herself," she answered.

"I was surprised to see her pull a gun this morning. Was that all a bluff, or is she capable of violence?" he asked.

"I don't think she would have fired at you. She's a bully and wanted you afraid. If you'd started pleading with her to set it down, that would have made her feel in control, and you would have made her day."

"I get it."

"For what it's worth, that's my amateur attempt at profiling. Although I've worked at Silver Heritage for the past ten months, she and I aren't friends, or even friendly. I don't even recall having a conversation with her that wasn't business-related."

"Fair enough," Rick said.

Kim watched him for a moment. He knew a lot about her, but she'd yet to learn much about him. Mystery clung to Rick like dust from a hot summer's whirlwind.

"I think my brother said something about Angelina owning another business as well as Silver Heritage," he said.

"That's true. She has a high-end Southwest design jewelry business across from the regional hospital. If you want, we can go over there after I finish class. The manager's a friend of mine. Although Angelina goes over there every day just after lunch, she usually comes back to the downtown shop after an hour or so. If you let me come along, I can watch out for her."

She checked her watch. "Right now I've got to walk over to campus. I've got class at noon."

"Mind if I tag along? It's a nice day to be outside."

"Glad for the company."

After they left the café, he fell into step beside her. It was a beautiful October day and the air was brisk but not cold. "So tell me, what makes you so determined to become a cop?"

"I want a career doing work that matters."

He nodded. "And you think you can make a difference as a cop."

It hadn't been a question, but she answered him anyway. "Good people are needed to keep the bad ones in check."

He smiled. "That's what Hosteen Silver used to say. It's part of the Navajo belief that says balance is necessary for happiness."

Rick's entire face softened when he smiled. The edginess that was so much a part of him disappeared and gave place to calmness. It even made his scar look less daunting. "You should smile more often, Rick."

He grew serious again. "I don't usually have many reasons to do that."

"Then find them," she answered with a smile of her own.

Seeing a homeless man she recognized sitting on the sidewalk against the wall of a laundry, soaking up the sunshine, she quickened her pace. "That's Mike. I brought him leftover food every night at the end of my shift at the Brickhouse. He's going to have to find other help now."

As they neared, the man looked over then jumped to his feet. "Mike, don't go. I need to talk to you," she called out.

The homeless man stood around six feet tall, with a red beard and brown hair. He was wearing a camouflage jacket, jeans, lace-up boots and was carrying a backpack.

Mike glanced at her, then Rick. A second later he stepped off the sidewalk into the alley and disappeared.

As they reached the alley, they saw his back just for an instant before he slipped around the far corner of the building.

"Rats!" she grumbled. "The weather's going to be turning cold pretty soon. Mike's going to need food and shelter. We have a food pantry over on 4th Street that feeds the homeless, but they already have to turn people away. One of the churches plans to take up the slack, though, and I wanted to make sure he knew."

"Mike is behind the Brickhouse every night?" Rick asked quickly.

"Yeah. He always sits on the steps of the furniture store's loading dock, waiting for me to come out into the alley."

"If he was there last night, he may have seen something important," Rick said. "Maybe even the guy who clobbered Frank and sabotaged the gas line. We have to find him again."

"That's going to be tough. You saw how he can disappear in a flash," she said. "I know I mentioned talking to him, but except for a few rare times, it was mostly a one-way conversation. My guess is that even if he saw something, he won't talk about it."

"He may be emotionally disturbed. Whatever the situation, I want to talk to him," Rick said. "Even if all he does is nod or shake his head, it might be enough to give us a lead."

"Good luck."

SEVERAL MINUTES LATER they arrived at the small community college campus and walked up the wide sidewalk toward a large, white, concrete-and-stone building. "This is my stop." Kim met his gaze. "If you find Mike, be kind but careful around him. Some things can't be forced. He's been living on the street for years now, and he's wary of everyone."

"It never hurts to try. Did you ever learn his last name?"

"I don't even know what his real first name is. I've always admired the football player Michael Oher, particularly after seeing *The Blind Side,* so I asked him if I could call him Mike. He nodded."

"All right. Let's see what I can do."

She checked her watch. "I've got to go. Class lasts an hour. Should we meet afterward and go to Turquoise Dreams, Angelina's other shop?"

"Okay, sounds good."

"See you later, then," she said.

AFTER LEAVING CAMPUS, Rick headed back to the center of town, deliberately choosing the side streets and alleys along Main, watching carefully as he approached restaurants and fast-food establishments. Mike undoubtedly already knew about the explosion at the Brickhouse Tavern and would be searching for a new place to score a meal.

At first Rick had no luck, but eventually he spotted Mike standing on a wooden pallet as he searched through the big green trash bin behind Hamburger Haven.

Instead of approaching him, Rick circled the block and came up the alley, looking down at the pavement and never making eye contact. About twenty feet away, he sat on a flattened cardboard box, his back to the wall. He was wearing a turtlenecked sweater and jeans, not his usual jacket, which often served to hide a handgun at his waist. Instead he had it in his boot for emergencies, but he knew what he was dealing with here and doubted there'd be a problem. Unless cornered, with no escape possible, Mike was unlikely to turn violent. He'd run. Though Rick pretended to be looking toward the street, he could see Mike in his peripheral vision. He knew that Mike, aware of him from the moment he'd entered the alley, had been watching him.

As Mike stepped down off the pallet, Rick saw the tattoo on the man's left forearm. It was the outline of a horse head with a diagonal line beneath it—the insignia of the Army's First Cavalry division.

"Ooorah, soldier," Rick said in a barely audible voice.

Mike looked at him, his gaze focusing on Rick's scar.

"Some scars are easier to see than others," Rick said, still avoiding direct eye contact. "You like cheeseburgers? I'm hungry. I'm going to get myself one. I'll pick one up for you, too, if you want."

Rick glanced at Mike and noted the vacant expression on his face. For a moment he wondered if the man was beyond the ability to answer questions.

Then it happened. A spark of intelligence lit up Mike's face for an instant. Rick realized that what he'd seen before was the thousand-yard stare: the blank look of someone who'd seen too much suffering and death.

"Cheeseburger. And fries," Mike said.

"Coming right up."

Rick went inside the small fast-food place, eager to return but afraid to look as though he was in a hurry. He'd just found his first asset and, with luck, he'd also be able to help the man.

One thing he knew about was adversity. It either broke or remade you, but sometimes finding your strength again required retreating to a place so deep inside yourself, the world couldn't reach you. He understood that. He'd done it himself.

When Rick returned to the alley, Mike was gone, but Rick could sense he was being watched. Mike was nearby, probably trying to make up his mind about him. Rick placed the sandwich bag filled with food on a cardboard box next to the wall where he'd been sitting. Mike would find it there.

"I'm after the man who nearly killed Kim, her uncle and my family," Rick called out as clearly as possible without shouting. "You see things most of us miss, Mike. Whatever you tell me will stay between us, but I could really use your help. Whoever it is may not be through yet."

Rick left the alley and crossed the street. As an undercover operative he'd lived engulfed by a darkness most sane people would do anything to avoid. Yet it was there, in that world of senseless violence, that the true measure of a man was often found...and sometimes lost.

Chapter Four

Rick picked up a soft drink inside the fast food place, then walked back to where he'd left Daniel's loaner SUV. He'd drive rather than walk back to campus. With time to spare, he took the long way, reacquainting himself with Hartley. Eventually he pulled into campus.

When he'd taken classes here right out of high school, the community college had been nothing more than a multi-classroom structure and administration building. Now the campus comprised about three acres, with a grassy commons area and central fountain.

Rick took the road leading to the visitors' parking area and pulled into the first slot he found. After a short walk, he found Kim standing just down the hall talking to a man who looked vaguely familiar. It hit him a moment later when the guy turned and Rick saw his face clearly for the first time.

"Karl Edmonds. It's been a lifetime," Rick said.

"You know my professor?" Kim asked.

"*Professor?* That's one career I never would have expected you to choose," Rick said, looking at Karl.

"I'm technically an instructor, Cloud. I teach part-time, and work full-time for the Hartley P.D. I run the bomb squad," he said.

"Now *that* fits the kid I knew," Rick said.

Karl looked at the scar that ran across Rick's face, then

glanced away quickly. "Looks like you came in second in a knife fight, dude. Hope you've brushed up on your hand-to-hand since then."

Rick remembered why Karl had always annoyed him. They'd always been competitors, never really friends. Karl's biggest problem, which had obviously followed him into manhood, was that he never knew when to shut up.

"We'd better get going. Kim and I need to meet with Preston," Rick said.

"It was good seeing you, buddy," Karl said.

"I'm sure we'll run into each other again." Rick held Karl's gaze for a moment longer than necessary. Instinct was telling him to be careful around the man. Was it that old competition between them or something more? He couldn't tell, but until he figured it out, he wouldn't lower his guard.

KIM FOLLOWED HIM to his SUV. "You and Karl... You weren't ever really friends, were you?"

"No, but we attended school together and played on the same football team. We were friendly—at times."

"I can't believe how rude he was to you," Kim said. "Do you really need to meet your brother or was that an excuse to walk away?"

"Both. It's a bad idea to make enemies with someone Preston may have to depend on someday," he said. "Right now, I'd also like to get clearance to take a look around the Brickhouse again in daylight," he said. "Afterward we'll head to Turquoise Dreams. Angelina certainly got my attention today."

"Are you sure your brother's going to be okay with you investigating on your own?"

"Under ordinary circumstances, no, but the Hartley P.D. is badly understaffed. I can be an asset to them because I've got the best law-enforcement training in the world."

"Will I need clearance, too?"

"Yes. I need you there because you're familiar with the place and can help me reconstruct the scene. If something's off or doesn't belong there, it might stick out to you but slip right past me."

AS THEY RODE to the station, she remained quiet. Although she never looked directly at him, Kim was aware of the way his strong hands gripped the wheel and how he seemed to completely focus on whatever he was doing at the time. She wondered what he would be like in bed—all that intensity, all that drive.... Everything about him spoke of endurance and masculinity.

She shifted in her seat. This was not the time for thoughts such as these. Still watching him out of the corner of her eye, she saw him rub the bottom tip of the scar near his cheek.

"Does it ever ache?"

"What?" he asked, focusing on her.

"The scar."

"Not generally. The skin around it feels tight sometimes, but that's about it." He glanced at her, then back at the road. "When we first met, you never looked directly at it. Most people stare when they see me for the first time, then try to pretend they weren't."

"Your eyes drew me more," she said.

"My...what?"

"You have a way of looking through people, not at them."

"I observe. It's how I stay alive."

"Is the scar one of the reasons you left the Bureau?"

"Yeah, it ruined me for undercover work. I became too easily identifiable."

"You could have still been involved in routine investigative work," she said. "Why leave?"

"I preferred undercover assignments." He shook his head. "No, it was more than that. I knew it was time for me to come home and try to reconnect."

"With your brothers?"

"With myself."

THEY ARRIVED AT the police station a short while later and Rick led her down the hall to his brother's office. Preston waved them inside.

"Anything new?" Rick asked.

"No, but it's too soon. The lab's backlogged."

"I'd like clearance to search the crime scene," Rick said. "I know the arson investigator and your crime scene team has already been through there, but maybe Kim and I will see something that'll trigger a memory. It can't hurt."

"You're right. In fact, I've already asked my captain about getting you officially involved. He's agreed."

Preston reached into the drawer and brought out a shield. "I'm deputizing you. Raise your right hand." Preston swore him in with a short phrase.

"At the end of this case, if you want to join the force officially, your application will go to the top of the pile."

"Thanks."

Preston looked over at Kim. "Stay with Rick and follow his orders to the letter. You are *not* a police officer, you're just an observer."

"Understood," she said.

"All right." Preston looked at his brother. "Remember to wear gloves," he added, handing him and Kim a pair each.

After they left the station, Rick asked, "What were the names of the servers last night?"

"Bobby Crawford and Kate Masters."

"How do we find them?"

"Kate's probably in class right now. She carries a heavier

load than I do and is just a few credit hours away from her business degree. She probably won't be much help. Kate's a hard worker, but her mind's always on some test or paper. She rarely even goes into the kitchen."

"What about Crawford?"

"Bobby comes in on time and does his job, but never has much to say. We don't talk about anything other than job-related things."

As they neared what remained of the Brickhouse, Rick slowed down to study the heavily damaged structure before parking across the street.

"Look down the alley. The back wall was pretty much blown out last night, but it looks even worse this morning. More bricks and roof beams must have come down since then. The loading dock and half the alley are blocked."

"At least all that flying debris didn't penetrate the side wall of the furniture store. These old downtown buildings were built to last," Kim noted.

"Well, whoever cut the gas line and blocked the door counted on the initial blast and resulting fire to do their work," he said. "If we hadn't escaped and lived to tell the real story, it might have been written off as an accident caused by faulty connections."

Kim peered ahead at a young man ducking beneath the tape and walking into the alley. "I think that's Bobby Crawford. See him over there? He's wearing jeans, a gray sweatshirt and ball cap," she said, pointing.

Rick caught a glimpse of the man just as he climbed over a pile of rubble and headed toward the loading dock. "Come on. Let's go talk to him."

By the time they'd crossed the street and reached the crime scene barrier, Bobby was nowhere in sight. Rick slipped beneath the crime scene tape and climbed up the rubble-filled stairs of the loading dock to look inside.

"Stay here," Rick said, then slipped though the gaping hole where the blown-out kitchen doors had once stood.

Rick moved slowly and carefully, picking his way through the mess. Only a few wall studs and pieces of wallboard remained between the kitchen and the dining room. The left wall of the kitchen facing the street had also lost most of its roof structure. From where he stood, Rick could see blue sky and part of the parapet. As he turned to look back out into the alley, Rick noticed that the remaining outside brick wall on both sides of the gap was bowed, ready to crumble.

At the far end of the dining area was a set of brick-littered stairs leading down into the basement. Except for a few inches of water, it was probably the least damaged room in the tavern.

He stood still for a moment, listening. Someone was going through the rubble in the north end of the dining area, the side farthest from the street and hidden by the remaining walls. He turned toward the sound. Despite his size, Rick could move silently when he hunted man or beast. He had a tattoo over his heart with the word *chaha'oh*. It meant shadow.

"Federal agent. Don't move." As he stepped through what remained of the doorway, he realized he'd spoken out of habit. He was now working with the Hartley Police. "Turn around slowly."

"Just don't shoot, okay? I work here," he said. "Remember me from last night? I'm Bobby. Bobby Crawford."

Hearing footsteps behind him, Rick turned his head for a second and saw Kim. She'd come in the same way he had, through the door cavity, and was wearing a white hard hat and holding another.

"Dude, just chill, okay?" Bobby said, his hands up. "In the rush to get out last night, I lost something important.

I was hoping to find it before they brought in the bulldozers. It was a gift from my mom."

Rick sized Bobby up in a glance. He was around eighteen or nineteen, stood five foot six and had dark hair and brown eyes.

"Did you mention this to the police when they took your statement?"

"No, I didn't realize it was gone until this morning. It's a gold crucifix I wear around my neck on a chain."

"You shouldn't be here. That's why the yellow tape's there," Rick snapped. "It's not safe for the public to be rummaging around, moving things around."

"Dude, are you *listening?* It's not evidence. It's a family heirloom."

"Forensic experts and the fire marshal will continue to sort through the debris and recover items. If your crucifix is found, you'll get it back," Rick told him. "Let me see your driver's license."

When Bobby handed it over, Rick took a quick look, then returned it. "All right. Get going. If anything belonging to you turns up, I know how to find you."

Bobby backed out through the kitchen and quickly disappeared down the steps.

"I ran into the fire marshal out on the sidewalk," Kim said, and handed Rick the hard hat. "Preston had called to tell him we'd be here, so Medina came over to make sure we followed safety protocols. He said no one's allowed inside the Brickhouse without hard hats and he intends to stand by until we're ready to leave."

Rick gave her a tight-lipped smile. "Medina give you hard time?"

"No, not really," she replied softly, gesturing to the street to indicate the man was close by. "He told me not to lean on anything or to move any structural elements. Then he gave me these and insisted we wear them."

"All right," he said, putting the hard hat on. "Let's take a look around, then we'll go into the kitchen, where all this started."

She stood in one spot and turned around in a circle, slowly surveying the wreckage. "I can't believe what this place has become. You could always hear laughter here."

"Everyone's okay and we have another chance at life. That's a reason for laughter. You ready to go into the kitchen?"

She nodded. They picked their way back, stepping over and around the remnants of the shattered interior.

They were barely in the kitchen when Arnie Medina poked his head in through the front door and yelled. "This place is coming down! Get out. *Now!*"

Rick grabbed Kim's hand and moved toward the gap in the wall facing the alley. Before they could reach the opening, a cloud of dust descended and bricks began to tumble from overhead, raining down on their escape route.

Rick turned back toward the dining area when a roof beam sagged, then cracked as the ceiling gave way.

Chapter Five

Rick spun Kim around and pushed her toward the basement stairs. "Down! Jump!"

Because the wooden steps were littered with chunks of bricks and debris, Rick and Kim ended up sliding into the basement, flat on their backs. As dust and ash billowed down the steps with them, Rick rolled on top of Kim, his body protecting her from the building materials that bounced down the steps. One brick struck his hard hat like a stone fist.

Within seconds the earthshaking cascade was replaced by a loud rattle, then a dozen or more solid thumps from somewhere above. When it was quiet again, Rick rose and looked down at Kim, who still had her eyes tightly shut. It was a good thing, considering her face was covered with dust.

"Keep your eyes shut and I'll blow away some of the dust."

He tried, but they both started coughing. He helped her sit up.

For a moment she kept her head down. Finally she opened her eyes and looked up at him. "We're alive, I take it?"

Rick smiled. "Pretty much. You okay?"

"I feel like I just went down a rock slide, but all I've got are bumps and bruises, I guess," she said, looking down at herself.

Shaken, she turned to look at the stairs. They were piled high with bricks and rubble, but light was coming in as the dust began to disperse.

"At least we're not totally trapped," Rick commented. "But we're going to need help digging out of here."

"Can you hear me?" came a man's voice from up above.

"I hear you, Medina, and we're both fine. There's a lot of debris in the way, but once we clear a path we'll have enough room to crawl out," Rick called back.

"No! Don't start moving things around. Something else could come down. Wait until my people have a chance to check the situation here. Stay away from the stairs, hang tight and we'll get you out."

TWENTY-FIVE MINUTES later Rick and Kim were standing in the alley at the rear of the Brickhouse. The firemen had braced the remaining walls as well as the sagging roof beams, then cleared a path for them.

"Did I ever tell you how much I *hate* closed-in spaces? I felt like I was smothering down there," she said, coughing.

"That was poor air quality, not claustrophobia," he said, clearing his throat. "At least you did all the right things, including the most important of all—keeping your head."

Arnie Medina came to meet them. "Speaking of keeping your heads, good thing I handed you the hard hats, huh?"

"Yeah, but I still don't get it. I made sure we stayed in sections that looked stable," Rick said.

"You had someone working against you. A guy with mirrored sunglasses, dressed in sweatpants and a gray sweatshirt, gave it a push with a two-by-six. He stopped the second I saw him and yelled, but I have no idea how long he was out there."

"Wait. Sweatpants or jeans?" Rick asked, instantly thinking of Bobby.

"No way," Kim said, reading Rick's thoughts.

"You know who it was?" Medina asked.

"Maybe," Rick answered. "What color hair? Height? Give me anything you've got."

The fire marshal shook his head. "He was wearing a hoodie, and his face was turned away from me when I saw him leaning into the wall. I went to confront him, but he dropped the board and took off like a jackrabbit. Practically knocked a homeless man to the ground, too."

"The homeless man—six feet tall, red beard and brown hair?" Rick asked.

"Yeah, that fits. He was over by the furniture store's loading dock for a moment and then he disappeared down the far end of the alley," Medina said.

"Thanks for everything," Rick answered.

"You're through here, I assume?" Medina asked.

"For now," Rick said, then added, "Would you and your men keep an eye out for a gold crucifix on a chain? The male server who worked here last night—Crawford—was hanging around when we first arrived. He claimed he lost it last night and came back to look around."

"We can do that."

Rick hurried with Kim back to his SUV. "I'm going to drive around to see if I can spot Mike."

"I'll help you look."

After twenty minutes of Rick circling downtown and driving down alleys, he glanced over at her, shaking his head. "It's like he vanished off the face of the earth."

"Mike's like that," she said. "I've tried to help him, get him connected with people who'll give him food and shelter, but he didn't want any part of it. He sets his own rules and comes and goes as he pleases."

"There's something to be said for that, I suppose."

"There's one thing I'm sure about. If he knew someone was out to hurt me, Mike would find a way to let me know. He's not a bad guy. He's hiding—from the world, from himself, I just don't know—but there's a lot of good inside him."

"And you know this how?" Maybe Kim was still an innocent, a woman determined to see the best in everyone.

"I'm not just another idealistic do-gooder, if that's what you're thinking," she said. "One time after I handed him a sack of food, I reached into my purse and my wallet fell out. It was late, I was in a rush and I didn't discover it missing until I was finally home."

"Did you have cash in it?" he asked.

"Oh, yeah. My salary, my tips and my one credit card. I canceled the card, but my driver's license was also gone. Replacing it and buying groceries for the week was going to be difficult without any cash."

"Couldn't you have asked your uncle for help?" he asked. "Or at least for an advance on your salary?"

She shook her head. "I wouldn't have done that until I'd exhausted every other option."

He bit back a grin. He was the same way.

"The next afternoon when I went back to the Brickhouse to start my shift, Mike met me by the back door and handed me my wallet. He'd kept it safe for me. I tried to give him some money as a reward, but he wouldn't take it. He just asked that I bring him a *sopaipilla* with green chili for dinner—but only if I wouldn't get into trouble. That's the only time he ever spoke to me in full sentences."

Rick smiled, glad to see she'd made a logical decision, not one based on pity, an emotion that often conspired against a man, destroying him from the inside out.

To this day, he still remembered the pity he'd seen in almost everyone's eyes after his mother had abandoned him at six years old at the trading post. Those looks had completely sapped his confidence, continually reminding him that no matter how sorry they felt, few would ever open their doors to him. They had their own lives, and he wasn't included.

Last year, after surviving the knife fight, he'd wondered if the scar on his face would arouse a similar reaction. He'd made it a point to carry himself ramrod-straight, determined not to give anyone an occasion to feel sorry for him.

As it turned out, the agents he'd been working with had looked at the scar as a badge of honor and respected it. Outside the Bureau he'd held his head high, went about his business without hesitation, and in the end his efforts paid off. He'd seen fear in some and shock in others, but pity had been absent.

"I know we were supposed to go to Turquoise Dreams, but do you mind if we stop by my place first? I live in a duplex that's on the way and I'd like to drop off my books and notes. I also want to make sure that the mail carrier picked up a job application I left in the PO box."

"What kind of job are you applying for?" he asked as he followed directions to her home.

"One that's connected to law enforcement," she said, crossing her fingers. "There's a security company in town that hires and trains, and it would give me the kind of experience that could come in handy when I apply for the police academy."

He glanced at her quickly. "Exactly what position are you applying for?"

"The only part-time they've got at Complete Security right now—monitoring cameras at night. There's more to it, but they're very tight-lipped and don't give out job details until after they do a background check."

"How's the pay?" he asked, knowing they were talking

about his brother Daniel's firm. Level One Security was the parent company of Complete Security, a new venture for his brother. CS was an electronic service Daniel had started up for small businesses in the area.

"The pay's just average, but they could really teach me a lot—if I get the job." She pointed. "Here we are, up ahead on the right, 1916 Pine Street."

Seeing the For Rent sign, he tensed. "The other side of the duplex is empty?" he asked, not liking the tactical complications that presented.

"Not for long. The rent's reasonable and the owner advertises on campus."

He quickly parked. As he got out of the SUV, the hairs at the back of his neck prickled. Something was wrong, he could feel it.

Rick looked around, but everything appeared peaceful.

As they stepped onto her small porch, he noticed that her door was slightly ajar. "Do you have a housekeeper or a nosey landlord?"

"A housekeeper? Me?" Kim laughed and then, following his gaze, saw what he was looking at. "I always lock it before I leave, but my landlord, Mr. Hopson, has a set of keys. That might be him, replacing the furnace filter," she said. "Come in. I'll introduce you."

"No." He pulled her back. "Wait outside."

She froze. "What did you see?"

Rick reached for the pistol inside his boot, then moved forward quietly, holding the weapon down by his side, the safety now off.

Chapter Six

Rick pushed the door back hard, to make sure no one was hiding behind it, then went in. At a glance it was obvious there'd been a break-in. An older model TV had been dumped off its stand and kicked in, and ceramic figures and books had been swept off the shelves. It was difficult to say if Kim had been robbed or if this had been the work of vandals.

He searched each room, moving carefully, but the intruder was nowhere around so he put away his weapon. An open bedroom window and a footprint on the dresser beneath it showed how the intruder had gained entry. Pulling out his cell phone, he called Preston and reported the break-in. He then walked back to Kim, who was standing in the doorway, looking inside as she shook her head in obvious disgust.

Rick waved her inside. "Brace yourself, it's like this everywhere," he advised. "And put on those gloves Preston gave you before you touch anything."

She stepped inside, pulling on one of the gloves, and cursed aloud. Basically everything that had been on the shelves was now on the floor.

Looking through the doorway she could see the kitchen was a mess, too. All the chairs had been overturned and every drawer upended.

When she walked into the bedroom, she discovered that the futon had been sliced down the middle with something sharp, like a box cutter. "Why would anyone do this to me?"

"It looks like they might have been looking for something."

"Hidden inside a cheap mattress that was completely intact?" She shook her head. "No, this was done to hurt me."

"Hey," he said, gently pulling her into his arms.

He liked the way Kim fit against him. She was soft and warm. He pressed his lips to her forehead and then, as she looked up, he kissed her.

She melted against him with a sigh and parted her lips.

That was one invitation he couldn't refuse. For those precious seconds, nothing existed except her and him. He caught the scent of wildflowers—her shampoo, or maybe her perfume.

She was sweet, yet passionate, and he loved the way she clung to him. He'd only wanted to comfort her, but other infinitely darker needs soon rose inside him. Knowing he might lose control if he didn't release her, he forced himself to step back. "It'll be okay, Kim. Don't let them get to you."

Kim stepped back as well, and took a long look around the room. "The bed…" she said at last, avoiding his eyes. "I need to try to save the mattress. I can't afford to replace it. Could you hold the two torn sides together while I sew them up?"

Pulling on his latex gloves, Rick went over to help her, but as he brought the two sides of the slashed canvas together, he felt something hard underneath the surface in the bedding material. "There's something in here." Putting his gloved hand inside, he pulled out a bone about six inches long.

"What the heck is that?" she asked.

Rick cursed under his breath. "Do you have a paper

or plastic bag?" he asked. "We need to turn this over to Preston."

She ran to the kitchen, then hurried back. "You think that could be a human bone?"

"Maybe. The lab'll tell us more."

"This sure has the earmarks of Angelina's skinwalker stuff."

He looked at her quickly. "Say again?"

"Angelina never became a medicine woman. She said she found something more useful. She claimed she could put a curse on just about anybody who deserved one."

"She *admitted* she's a skinwalker?" Rick asked, surprised. Even if she had become one somewhere along the way, it seemed unlikely she'd let anyone know. Witches were despised among The People, and the evil ones, as they were often described, kept their practices a secret.

"She didn't say it in so many words. She just mentioned that she found the opposite of a medicine woman—a skinwalker—much more interesting. She said their ways were more practical," Kim explained. "I don't believe in stuff like that, so I never paid much attention."

"So maybe the break-in was someone's way of warning you to stay away from me," Rick said.

"Angelina's already fired me. She has no more say in my life. Whoever did this is just plain mean."

"Even if you don't believe in Navajo witchcraft, the people who choose to practice it are usually unbalanced," Rick said. "The further into the practice they get, the more likely they are to get out of control."

"From what I've seen, Angelina's all talk. She wants people to fear her, but it'll take more than a bone and a dead spider to scare me," she said.

"She pulled a gun on me today," Rick reminded her.

Kim nodded slowly. "That's in another class entirely."

"Since you're interested in police work and need a job, I have a suggestion. I've been away from Hartley for years, so you know the community better than I do. I could use your help," Rick said.

"Does that mean you want to hire me?" she asked, surprised.

"In a way. With your permission, I'd like to talk to Daniel. In case you didn't know, Level One Security is Complete Security's parent company—and my brother owns and controls both. Maybe you can become a paid intern and work with me. I can teach you investigative techniques. In return for the training and job, you could agree to stay with the company for at least a year at the same salary. If I can pull this off, how does that sound?"

"I won't be earning my degree for at least another eighteen months, so it sounds perfect. I'd gladly work for your brother for a year. Having been employed by a company like his will look great on my résumé."

"Okay, then." He went to the window and glanced outside. "It looks like Preston and some of his officers are here. While you fill him in and show him around, I'll give Daniel a call."

While Preston spoke to Kim, Rick moved away to call his brother, telling Daniel what he had in mind.

"So what do you think?"

"I've done that before for people with potential, so it's fine, but there's something I need to know. Is she getting under your skin? Is that why you're doing this?"

"No, it's not that. I was the reason she lost her job. It was unintentional, but it's a fact."

"As logical as it sounds, my gut tells me there's more to it," Daniel replied.

Rick ended the call just as Kim and Preston came over to talk to him. From their expressions, he could tell something else was wrong.

"What's up, guys?" Rick asked.

"In a normal break-in we'd have dozens of usable prints, but this place was wiped clean. The only prints we found were on the lock and the door itself, which makes me think they belong to you and Kim."

"That settles it. This was no ordinary burglary or act of vandalism," Rick said somberly.

"I'd advise you not to stay here," Preston told Kim. "It's no longer safe."

"I have no other place to go. I can't stay with a friend or relative and put them in danger, too, nor do I have money for a motel."

"There might be a way of getting around that problem," Rick said, pulling out his phone. "But I'll need to check something out first. Excuse me for a minute," he added, then stepped outside.

Rick returned a short time later. "My brother Kyle and his wife, Erin, are willing to give you a room at the family home in Copper Canyon. It's northwest of Shiprock, on the Rez. Except for last night, when I didn't want to add a long drive to my evening, I'm staying there, as well. I can drive us back and forth."

"I don't know.... I hate to intrude," Kim said.

"We're going to be working together, so that'll make it simpler all the way around," Rick said.

Rick noted the pleased look on Kim's face and the surprise on Preston's.

"It's a logical solution," Rick added.

"How soon do you want to leave?" Kim asked.

"As soon as you're ready. So go pack what you'll need."

"Not so fast. Let's take one last look around," Preston said.

Rick's eyes narrowed. "You think you missed something?"

Preston nodded slowly. "Yeah, call it cop's instinct."

"Is it still okay if I pack a few personal things while we look around?" she asked Preston, who nodded.

In her bedroom, the two men waited as Kim placed her laptop in her suitcase and then opened the dresser drawer. As she began to remove essential clothing, something fell to the floor.

"Drop a button?" Rick said, bending to look. "I guess not," he added, picking up the curious-looking object with a gloved hand and holding it up for Preston to see.

"What on earth is that?" Kim asked. "A...tooth?"

"A *long, hollow* tooth," Rick observed. "Like a rattler's fang."

"Does that have any special significance?" Kim asked. "Other than the obvious?"

"According to our creation stories, witchcraft started before mankind emerged from the earth. First Woman passed it out to the others, but Snake didn't have pockets, so he took it in his mouth. That's why snake bites can kill," Preston explained.

She shuddered. "Sorry, but I don't think that was meant for me. If you hadn't explained, I wouldn't have known, and the point would have been lost. This was left for you guys," she said, looking at Rick, then Preston.

They exchanged glances before Rick nodded to his brother, who bagged and tagged the evidence.

SEVERAL MINUTES LATER, after signing the required incident report statements, Rick and Kim drove southwest through downtown Hartley.

"The incidents we've seen so far don't make a lot of sense if you put them together," Kim commented. "No one motive seems to fit. What we saw at my place was a result of creepy maliciousness. What happened at the Brickhouse was attempted mass murder. One was intended to scare, the other to kill. If the same person was responsible, you'd think the sequence of events would have been reversed. We may be dealing with multiple suspects."

He nodded slowly. "Solid deduction."

Kim glanced around. "Heading out of town in this direction will take us past the hospital. Can we stop there for a few moments so I can visit my uncle?"

"Yeah. In fact, that's a good idea," Rick said. "Are you two close?"

"He was there for me when my dad died, but Uncle Frank's not someone who invited a girl's confidences. Nor is he the huggy-kissy type at all," she said with a wry smile. "Dad's brother is a man's man. I'm sure he'll come through this—and just as sure that he'll never talk about it again."

"Is he financially secure enough to weather what happened at the tavern?"

"Yeah, the place was well insured. As long as he can reopen the restaurant, he'll be fine, but I bet he's glad he didn't actually buy his partner out as he'd planned."

"Arthur Johnson, right?" Rick asked and saw her nod. "What can you tell me about him?"

"He and my uncle go way back. Art's wife got sick a few years ago, and although they had health insurance, there were a lot of deductibles and collateral expenses that nearly bankrupted him. After she died, he sold almost everything he owned except his share of the Brickhouse," she explained. "I think Art kept it mostly because of my uncle."

"How involved is Johnson in running the Brickhouse?" Rick asked.

"Art's a silent partner all the way—always signing off on Uncle Frank's operating decisions without question."

"He hasn't showed up on the scene yet, so I'm guessing Arthur doesn't live in Hartley?"

"No, he doesn't. Art's got a rustic cabin he just loves for some odd reason. It's in the Sangre de Cristo Mountains above Santa Fe."

Rick pulled into the hospital parking lot and glanced across the street to the west. There were several businesses there, including a few small warehouses and a low block building with a big sign.

"Turquoise Dreams. Isn't that Angelina's other shop?"

"Yes, and we can go over afterward, providing Angelina's pickup isn't still there," she said, pointing to the vehicle on the east side with a custom license plate that read *'lina*.

They entered the hospital, officially a regional medical center, and stopped at the front desk. After a short wait they were directed to Frank Nelson's room. He was alone in the semiprivate room, watching TV.

Frank looked over at them as they entered and smiled. "Good to see you two! I've been hoping for some news. Is the restaurant a total loss?"

"Pretty much," Kim said with a nod. "We'll have to file a claim with the insurance company as soon as the fire marshal has completed his preliminary investigation. There'll probably be some delays because it was clearly arson."

"That place was all I had," Frank muttered. "Who would have done something like that?"

"You co-own the Brickhouse Tavern with Arthur Johnson, I understand," Rick mentioned off hand, hoping to start a conversation.

"Yeah, and I have to let him know what's happened. Unfortunately he's probably still out of reach. He left on one of his late-season fishing trips a few days ago, out of state, I think. Art likes to hike deep into the mountains, going to places where he can't be reached except on foot or horseback. I know he's still grieving for his wife," he said, his voice heavy. "He'll call me when he's available again."

"Any idea when that'll be?" Rick asked.

"A few more days, maybe a week, depending on the fishing. Art doesn't have to answer to anyone these days."

"I understand that the restaurant was doing well," Rick said.

"Oh, yeah. We have a lot of loyal customers and always manage to stay in the black. The insurance won't be enough to cover all the losses, though, just in case you're thinking along those lines."

"Will you reopen?" Rick asked.

"I guess it'll depend on my partner. Art might want to just take his share of the insurance settlement and walk. I'll do my best to talk him out of it, of course, because I love that place."

"Has there ever been any bad blood between you and Angelina Curley?" Rick asked, and to his surprise, Frank barked out a laugh.

"That lunatic? The woman's nuts, but at least she doesn't mess with me. Your foster father and I were friends, and he gave me a leather pouch with flint arrowheads, corn pollen and some other items he referred to as medicine. They were supposed to work together to keep evil at bay. I showed it to her once when she was complaining about some parking meters I was pushing the town council to approve. I don't know if that was what did it, but ever since then, she's kept her distance."

Kim stepped closer to the bed. "Uncle Frank, I came by to tell you that I won't be at my place for a while," she said, explaining about the break-in.

"She'll be safe where I'm taking her," Rick added.

"Aren't there any surveillance cameras around your duplex? I don't recall seeing any, but what about the street side?" Frank asked.

She shook her head. "It's a low crime neighborhood except for the usual college parties that can get a bit loud. Anyone who lives on my block is too busy getting by, Uncle Frank. Not much to steal."

"My brother will canvas the neighborhood and check out traffic cameras," Rick said as they readied to leave.

"I'll be out of the hospital in a day or so and be able to take a look at what's left of my restaurant," Frank said. "If you need me, Kim, call my cell phone number."

Outside in the parking lot a few minutes later, Rick noted that Angelina's pickup was still parked in front of the jewelry store. "Looks like we'll have to come back later," he said, nodding across the street.

"You're right. There's no sense in another confrontation right now," Kim replied, climbing into the passenger side of the SUV.

Once they were on their way again, Kim glanced at Rick. "From the questions you asked my uncle, I gather you're thinking that this could be a case of insurance fraud. Since my uncle was struck on the head and left to die, he can't be a suspect. So that leaves whom? Art?"

"He's one possibility. Preston's people will check the evidence and then we'll see where we stand. Patience is the key."

"Sorry, I'm fresh out."

AN HOUR LATER they'd left the wide river valley far behind them, and were well on their way into the Navajo Nation. The dry mesas were scattered in the distance, those to the north and west topped by junipers and piñons. Beyond those formations were the foothills, leading to mountain ranges and forests filled with pines and fir.

"I love this open country. It's not houses backed up against houses. The skies are blue and you can breathe out here."

"I gather you're a country girl at heart?"

"No, I belong in a town or small city, hopefully wearing a badge someday. To me, coming out here is a chance to decompress. Everyone needs that." She saw the flicker of approval that played on his features. "Is that why you're staying at Copper Canyon?"

"Yeah. The place is small but it's a three-bedroom. Kyle and Erin invited me to stay with them until I could figure out what was next for me."

As they drew closer to their destination, a high mesa that curved into a blind canyon with a single outlet at the base, he smiled.

"This is Copper Canyon—home. My brothers and I know this place like the backs of our hands."

She glanced around, a worried frown on her face. "It's really isolated here, Rick."

"This is the safest spot around. There's only one way in for vehicles—a narrow road easily monitored. We're on it now. Also the place transmits sound like a giant megaphone. From the moment we crossed the wooden bridge, Kyle and Erin could hear the rattle of the timbers even though the ranch house is still some distance away."

"I don't see a house anywhere," she said, looking around.

"It's farther ahead. Maybe a quarter of a mile."

"From what I can see, there's a series of trails. That means there has to be more than one route to the ranch house once you're inside the canyon," she said, observing her surroundings. "This particular pathway is super rough," she said, holding on to the armrest as the SUV rocked from side to side. "How about taking the one to our left?"

"That's a common mistake, and a bad idea. The other

trails may look smoother, and people who haven't been here before often choose those, which explain their presence. Before long, those people either get bogged down or high center their vehicle," he said. "There's also an arroyo ahead that intersects the other routes. That'll stop anyone not on horseback or foot."

She looked around her. "I see what looks like a big, plowed field, but other than that the trees and undergrowth are pretty thick. I've already seen rabbits and quail. Is there any other wildlife around?"

"Big cats occasionally hunt here, and so do coyotes. Then there's the occasional bear that comes down out of the mountains. But the bigger predators avoid people. The trick is never to corner them."

Kim soon spotted the rectangular, sand-colored, stucco-and-wood-framed house, not far from one of the steepest cliffs. The metal roof shimmered in the sunlight. Beyond that she noted the log corral with two beautiful piebald horses.

"Horses!"

"Women and horses," he said, smiling. "Those belong to Kyle and his wife. She fell in love with them from the moment she saw them at Gene's ranch," he said. Then pointing ahead, he added, "Looks like Erin's just finished feeding them."

Kim saw a petite brunette brushing hay from her clothes as she walked toward the house.

As Rick pulled up and parked by the side of the house, a short distance from a small storage shed, his brother came out the back door to greet them.

"Welcome, guys," Kyle said.

"So you heard us coming?" Rick asked with a grin.

"Yes, but only a few minutes ago. I'm not as good as Gene and Preston at picking up visitors at long range."

"Yeah, you and me both," he answered and looked at

Kim. "Some of my brothers are incredibly attuned to nature here. For example, the absence of birds or their sudden flight lets them know when anyone's around. Gene,
in particular, can listen to a coyote's howl and tell you if
everything is okay."

Erin joined them and gave Kim a hug, having first met
her at the Brickhouse. "You'll be safe and comfortable here,
Kim. Come inside and help me fix dinner."

As they reached the small porch, Kim heard an ominous
rumble. Looking off into the distance, she noted the billow-
ing clouds beyond the canyon walls to the west.

Rick followed her gaze and glanced at his brother.
"White Thunder. Remember what Hosteen Silver used to
say about him?"

Kyle nodded. "None of the medicine men ever called on
White Thunder during ceremonies because it was said he
only brought trouble."

"So that's a bad sign?" Kim asked.

Rick shook his head. "Not necessarily. Thunders have
the power to find things, too."

They'd just reached the front door when a silver-gray
hawk cried overhead and landed in a tall piñon about a
hundred feet from the house. It remained there, gazing
down at them.

"Isn't it beautiful? It hangs around here a lot," Erin whispered.

"Hosteen Silver's spiritual brother was Winter Hawk,"
Rick told Kim.

Kyle nodded slowly. "White Thunder and now Winter
Hawk…. It's a welcome and a warning."

"Well, if there's danger ahead, Copper Canyon's the
place to be. Let's go inside," Rick said, his voice tense.

Chapter Seven

Kim felt Rick's tension as clearly as her own. She didn't believe in omens, but she didn't dismiss them outright, either. She'd learned at an early age that New Mexico was the land of the unexplained. Here, the mysterious existed along with the ordinary, each finding its own place.

As she stepped inside the main room, she smiled, feeling instantly comfortable. It looked like the interior of a rustic cabin, very similar to those in country magazines. Though sparsely decorated, it had an undeniable elegance.

To her right the room opened up and against the far wall was the kitchen. Closer, and in the center of that space, was a large dining table pieced from several pine logs.

Centered in the room was a sofa covered in rich brown leather. Beautiful wool Navajo rugs were hung on the wall opposite a huge stone fireplace with vents that probably circulated the warm air generated from the fire.

On the wall opposite the dining side was a walk-in closet that had been converted to fit either computer equipment or TV screens.

"What a special place!" she told Erin. "I can see why you wanted to live here."

"The brothers all agreed that we could make it our home, so I sold my place in Hartley and Kyle and I moved in," Erin explained. "It's the perfect place for us. I can irrigate and have more land to grow my crops. The fields have already been leveled, and this coming spring we'll be putting in rabbit-proof fencing. I'm a chili farmer and Kyle's in the family security business. He runs Complete Security for Daniel and often works from home."

Kim smiled. "I work for Complete Security now, too, as a paid intern."

"I've heard," Erin replied, leading the way to the kitchen. Rick and Kyle were already there, coffee mugs in hand.

"It's hot and it'll warm you up," Rick said. "Want a cup?"

"It's *hot*? That's the nicest thing you can say about my coffee?" Erin said, laughing as she handed Kim a mug.

Sipping her coffee, Kim watched them kid around with each other as they all pitched in to fix dinner. Although the fare was simple, she had to admit the green chili hamburger, thick and on homemade buns, was the best she'd ever tasted.

After dinner, they retreated to the sofa and chairs. The blazing fireplace would keep them warm and comfortable. "Your letter, the one Hosteen Silver left for you, is on the third shelf of the bookcase," Kyle said to Rick.

"Although I'm tempted not to read it, that would be showing disrespect, and I owe Hosteen Silver everything," Rick said, walking over to pick it up. They'd all been left letters to read upon their foster father's death, but Rick's undercover work had kept him away. This was the first time he'd ever even seen the envelope.

"We've all read ours, so yours is the last," Kyle said.

Rick sat on the hearth and stared at the envelope in his hand.

"The longer you put it off, the harder it'll get," Kim warned softly.

Rick tore open the sealed envelope, his expression hard.

In a gesture of solidarity, Kyle came over to stand beside his brother as Rick pulled out the small piece of paper.

No one spoke as Rick read it silently. "As cryptic as ever," he said at last, then read it out loud. "'It's not Eagle's nature to accept what seems to be. As what is hidden comes to light, your fight will begin. You will walk in beauty only after blue overcomes red and your eyes are opened to a truth that eluded me.'" Rick placed the paper on the coffee table so they could all see.

"There's something different about your letter, bro," Kyle said. "First, it doesn't really look like Hosteen Silver's handwriting. It's shaky. Then look at the date on top. That's the same day we think Hosteen Silver disappeared."

Rick took a closer look at the letter. "It's his writing. Look at the *f* with that extra loop in its center. The *g* is also not connected to the letter following it." After a moment Rick added, "I'm guessing his hand was trembling."

"The man was without fear. Maybe he was sick at the time he wrote it," Kyle said.

"That's what I think, too," Rick answered.

"What's that stuff about blue overcoming red?" Kyle asked. "It sounds vaguely familiar, but I can't nail it down."

"It's part of the story Hosteen Silver used to tell us about the Hero Twins and their special prayer stick."

"Who were the Hero Twins?" Kim asked.

"Navajo creation stories tell us about the sons of Changing Woman and Sun. The twins were great warriors, so their father, Sun, sent them on a great quest to destroy mankind's enemies. Before they left, they were given a special prayer stick that was covered with blue paint and sparkling earth, symbols of peace and happiness. They were told that anytime the prayer stick turned red, a deadly battle lay ahead."

Kyle nodded. "Now I remember."

"I think he was telling me that there's a mission I have to complete here, a wrong I have to right before I can find peace," Rick said.

"But if he didn't tell you, how will you know what that wrong is?" Kim asked.

"That's the essence of all of Hosteen Silver's predictions," Rick answered. "You don't have to go looking for answers. Eventually what you're after, or what you need, will come to you."

After the revelation, everyone's mood turned somber. Although they remained by the fireplace for several more hours, they were quiet for the most part, all lost in their own thoughts.

Finally, Erin stood and stretched. "I'm going to bed. I can show you your room if you like, Kim."

"Tonight I want to keep a lookout, so I'll be sleeping on the sofa," Rick said.

"How about we trade off keeping watch? You could crash in the remaining bedroom when I'm on duty," Kyle said. "We've got cameras rigged up at a few key points, too, so we'll get an alert the minute anything larger than a coyote comes down the road or approaches the house. The system immediately starts to record, too, so just open the cabinet and check the monitors if we get a hit."

"Works for me," Rick said. "I'll take the first watch and wake you up in four hours."

"I could help," Kim said. "I'm a good observer. Right now I can tell no one's around. There's a coyote howling in the distance, and I don't think it would announce its presence if humans were around."

Kyle smiled. "No one ever hears Rick move—not unless he wants you to, that is. We used to call him Shadowman."

Rick smiled. "It's a gift."

"You said you'd train me, and here I am. Let me help," she insisted.

"All right," Rick said at last. "Neither of us got much sleep last night, but together we can keep each other alert." Rick looked at his brother. "I'll come get you when it's time."

When Kyle and Erin left, Rick turned off all the lights. Only the glow from burning piñon logs in the fireplace—and the monitors—illuminated the room. "I'm glad you volunteered to stay up. I'm tired and it'll be easier to stay focused with a partner."

She smiled, glad to be considered a partner. "Tell me more about that note," she said, taking a seat on the hearth. "If I read you right, there was something else about it that troubled you."

He nodded slowly. "My gut's telling me that Hosteen Silver wrote that after he knew he was dying. Since I'm the youngest, he probably put me last on the list when it came to his final message. I think that's why his handwriting was so shaky," he said. "I know Hosteen Silver was trying to tell me something, but he always overestimated my ability to understand him."

"I have a feeling he knew exactly what he was doing when he deliberately chose you to do what needed to be done," Kim said. Rick could be gentle, but his strength never wavered. Remembering the way he'd kissed her, she felt her skin prickle. "How are you different from your brothers?" she added, forcing herself to focus on the conversation.

"They prefer team efforts, but I like working solo. That's why I volunteered for undercover work." He stood by the side of the window, pulling back the heavy curtain to look out into the canyon. The desert was bathed in moonlight and every rock and patch of open ground wore a faint, glowing blanket.

"You're fine working with your brothers, though," she said.

"That's because I trust them, but I still like taking point."

"Wow, talk about double-speak. Or is it ego?"

He chuckled. "Maybe both." He walked to the note Hosteen Silver had left for him, picked it up off the table, folded it and placed it in his back pocket.

"What I don't understand is the reference to Eagle. Who or what is he?" Kim asked.

"That's also linked to our Traditionalist beliefs. Hosteen Silver gave each of us a special fetish, and mine's Eagle. The spirit of the animal is said to become one with its owner, and by sharing its special qualities, it enhances my own."

"You mean you can see things that are far away?" Kim asked, trying to understand.

"No, it's not like that. Eagle stands for vision and power through balance. It's not distance vision, however, it's the ability to see the overall picture, something any investigator has to learn to do." As he checked the monitors, he added, "Eagle's about honoring knowledge by knowing when it's okay to share it and when it's better to withhold it."

"Sometimes I get so sidetracked by details, I lose the overall perspective. I wish I had Eagle's ability to see the whole picture." Kim took a deep breath. "When I lost my job at Angelina's I was terrified. Having my apartment wrecked after that made things even worse.

"Now that I have a new perspective," she added, "I realize that getting fired from Silver Heritage was one of the best things that ever happened to me."

"Angelina made it that tough?"

She nodded. "I liked to take time to talk to the customers, to get a feel for what they were really looking for, but Angelina was all about making the sale—" She stopped abruptly and her eyes widened. "I just recalled something that may be important."

Rick nodded. "Go on."

"About three weeks ago there was a curious incident at the store. An Anglo man in his late forties came in. He was a professor at a college in Durango. He asked if we could connect him to a local Navajo medicine man who was said to occasionally use Hopi fetishes in blessings for protection."

"Did he mention Hosteen Silver by name?"

"No, but I was sure that's who he meant, so I suggested he speak to Angelina. At the time, I didn't know about the bad blood between her and Hosteen Silver. The instant I mentioned her by name, the professor politely declined and left the store. That's the last time I saw him."

"You don't have a name?"

"Sorry. I never asked, but I'd recognize him if I saw him again. If he's still teaching up in Durango, there's got to be a photo of him somewhere."

"Good thinking. We'll look that up in the morning."

They kept each other alert until 2:00 a.m. when Kyle came into the room, unannounced.

Rick grinned. "So I see your internal clock is still working."

"Go to sleep, you two," Kyle said, ushering them out. "You'll have a long day tomorrow."

Rick walked Kim to her bedroom. "Sleep well."

"You going to be in the next bedroom, Rick?" she asked.

"Nah, I'll crawl into a sleeping bag in front of the fireplace. I prefer to be on hand in case Kyle needs me."

She went inside the room and, exhausted, stripped down to her underwear and crawled in between the heavy blankets. Almost as soon as her head hit the pillow, she was fast asleep.

Kim never woke until the sun peered through the curtains, yet it wasn't the daylight that had nudged her awake. Unsure of what it was, she went to the window and peered out.

It was dawn, but the canyon floor was still in shade because of the cliffs. Rick was already outside. She saw him check the immediate area, including the shed beside the house, then head up the canyon.

Curious, she dressed quickly then went into the living room. It was empty. Kyle had gone back to bed. Making an impromptu decision, Kim slipped out the front door. Being Rick's backup was part of her job now.

Bundling her coat around her tightly, and trying to protect herself from the cold breeze, she followed the trail Rick's boots left in the sand.

Chapter Eight

Rick looked up at the pine trees dotting the top of the mesa. They glowed in the sunlight that had yet to penetrate to the desert floor. The cliffs were layered top to bottom in a kaleidoscope of color, from yellow-orange to a pale cranberry-red that turned purple above the shadow line. It was more beautiful here than he remembered.

This was his turf, but he still didn't feel at home. Maybe he just needed to reconnect. He jammed his hands inside his leather jacket and continued walking.

Every day at this time Hosteen Silver would leave the ranch house to go offer his prayers to Dawn at a spot high atop the sandstone bedrock. His voice, filled with power and conviction, would echo in the walls of the narrow canyon.

Without charting a course, Rick moved farther up slope, deep into Copper Canyon.

It was here that he'd heard his foster father cry to the morning sky, *"Hozhone nas clee, hozhone nas clee,"* which translated meant "Now all is well, now all is well." Then he'd scatter pollen from his medicine bag as an offering to Dawn, so he could continue to walk in beauty.

Memories crowded Rick's mind as he stared into the brightening cliff wall to his left. That's when he remembered the other reason he'd come this way as a boy. Hearing the spring-fed creek that ran the length of the canyon year round, he smiled.

As his brothers before him, he'd staked out his own special place, one too private to share. Although his brothers' spots were soon known to the rest of the family, no one had ever discovered his.

He smiled, wondering if his sole treasure still lay nestled in that hole carved into the rock face, hidden by the thick spread of junipers that scented the air year-round. There was a gap in the cliffs here, one cleverly hidden from the curious by nature herself.

Rick stepped around the tall rock that seemingly blocked further passage. Pressing his way sideways between the plants that formed a natural barrier, he walked up a rabbit trail that was almost obscured by permanent shadows.

He never would have found this place as a boy, as a matter of fact, if he hadn't seen a cottontail disappear into the cliff side. About twenty steps into the narrow opening, which closed off completely just around the curve, he stopped and searched for the familiar crevice created by the splitting of a sandstone layer centuries ago.

He'd just reached in when he heard footsteps—not animal. He spun in a crouch instantly, gun in hand.

"Whoa! It's me," Kim said, hands up in the air.

"You followed me?" he asked, surprised. No one had ever been able to do that before. But then, he'd been on a walk, not trying to evade the enemy.

"Yes, I'm supposed to be your backup. That's part of my training, too. What if you ran into danger?"

"If I had, what could you have done? You're not armed."

"I can fight. I was deployed in Afghanistan as a cargo specialist," she said. "And I'm armed, not with a gun, but with this," she said, holding up a can of Mace.

He smiled. "What they sell as Mace these days is usually just pepper spray. Anyone who's drugged up or has any training won't be deterred by that."

"I wasn't thinking that you'd run into humans. I was thinking more of wild animals."

"I'm armed," he said, putting his pistol away.

"What if you'd fallen off a cliff or stepped on a rattler?"

He decided not to argue the point. Her motives had been right on target, but he was curious how she'd pulled it off. "I know you didn't follow me from the house, not visually. I'd have seen you."

"Tracks," she said, pointing to the sandy earth. "I learned it at Boy Scouts. Actually, I had a friend who was a Boy Scout and he'd teach me what he was learning. It was far more interesting that what my Girl Scout troop was doing."

He laughed. "Yeah, that fits you."

"So why are you out here?" she said, changing the subject.

He grew serious. "I was trying to reconnect with the place I called home for so many years. This was my special spot. When I first arrived at Copper Canyon, after Hosteen Silver convinced family services that I wasn't beyond hope and took me in—as he had before with my foster brothers—I went hiking a lot. One day I found an arrowhead. It wasn't particularly valuable, but I chose to see it as something this place had meant for me to find. It fit the image I had of myself back then—a survivor and a fighter."

"You still are," she said softly.

"Yes, I'm that—and more," he said. Parting some branches, he reached into the shallow crevice in the sandstone wall. "Let's see if my arrowhead is still…" He paused for a moment. "There's something else back here."

He pulled out a pocket-size, metal breath-mint box containing the arrowhead and, along with it, a small, spiral notebook enclosed in a plastic freezer bag.

Curious, Rick put the box that held the arrowhead back for a moment, then opened the plastic bag and took out the notebook. Inside, on each page, were ink drawings. "The Plant People."

"Who are they?" she said, trying to get a closer look at the drawings.

"A Traditionalist Navajo believes our native plants are people who go where they will, and can harm or bless, depending on how you appeal to them," he said. "These particular ones are the plants Hosteen Silver used for his ceremonies...but look at the top of the page. That's some kind of code."

"Do you recognize it?"

"No, but he obviously left this here for me, so he thought I'd be able to decipher and read it." He studied it for a moment longer.

"This was your special hiding place, but you shared the location with Hosteen Silver?"

"No, but it doesn't surprise me that he knew," Rick said. He held the notebook and leafed through its pages again. "I think there's a good chance that he left this here for me the same day he went for his final walk into the desert. The numbers that make up the code are shaky, like the handwriting in his note to me."

"I don't understand," Kim admitted. "Why would your father just walk off like that to die? Why not pass away in his house or call 9-1-1 and get help?"

"That's not the way of a Traditionalist Navajo," he said, his voice heavy. "Had he passed away at home, many would have believed that the ranch house would have drawn his *chindi* and become cursed."

"You mean by his ghost?"

"No, the *chindi* is not a man's spirit. It's only the evil

side of him that has to remain earthbound because it can't unite with universal harmony."

"Do you and your brothers believe in the *chindi?*"

"No, not really, we're all Modernists. But like most Navajos, we still respect the old ways," he said. "The things I've seen on the Rez, and what I've learned from our Traditionalists, have taught me that there's a lot more to life that what we see and can easily explain."

"Listen. I hear a voice," Kim said.

It was Kyle, yelling for Rick.

Rick yelled back. "We're okay." He glanced at Kim. "It's time to head back, but there's something I need to do first."

He took the arrowhead out of the mint box and placed it in his pocket. Then, using his cell phone, he photographed each page of the notebook, enclosed it in the plastic bag and placed it back in the crevice.

"Why are you leaving it here?" she asked.

"My foster father hadn't been suffering from any obvious terminal disease. It's impossible that my brothers, and the people who lived in the area and saw him often, would have missed something that important. Whatever caused him to walk off and die like that came on very suddenly.

"Over the past several months we've all begun to think it's possible that he was murdered—maybe by some toxic substance, or more likely, a plant-derived poison that wasn't detected until too late. That would explain why he left this documentation of the Plant People. The notebook may be the single most important clue we have. If I take it with me, and people come after us, I risk losing or damaging it," Rick said. "The notebook has remained safe here all this time. For now, this is where it should stay."

"Will you tell your brothers?" Kim asked.

"Yeah, and as soon as I can I'll send Daniel and Paul the pages. Both of them are good at breaking codes."

"We're heading back to Hartley this morning, then?"

"Yes, but on the way back to the ranch house we need to rub out our tracks. I trust my brothers, of course, and you, but I want to make sure no one else who comes into the canyon can track us here," he said.

Rick broke off a juniper branch and showed her how to erase obvious marks in the sand left by their shoes. "Carefully scoop up handfuls of sand, smooth over those scoop marks, then scatter the sand lightly over the trail the branch leaves as I run it over the ground. Just don't pour the sand onto any leaves if you can help it."

It took them several minutes to finish the job around the cliff exterior, but the rest was easy. They were back at the ranch house a half hour later.

Kyle met them at the door and Rick told him what they'd found.

"The fact that he didn't leave the notebook here makes me think his enemy was familiar with our home and where things were kept," Kyle noted.

"That doesn't narrow the list very much," Rick responded.

"Yeah, I hear you. Let's see if Paul and Daniel can break the code, but I have to tell you, Hosteen Silver meant for *you* to find it, so it stands to reason you hold the key," Kyle said. "You two had a special connection."

"That's because I could read people, just like Hosteen Silver did."

"I understand you kept in touch with him even when you were undercover, south of the border."

"It was only a sporadic note that would appear on a website set up by Daniel. Hosteen Silver would let me know when I had a new niece or nephew, or tell me he'd done a special Sing for my protection. Stuff like that."

"I suppose the notes were in code?"

"Yeah. He would give it to Daniel to encrypt and I had the software needed on my end to decrypt."

"Do you think he used a variant of the same system in the notebook?"

"Not likely. He didn't like computers, but it is possible it's based on a number-letter substitution with a specific book as the key. If I'm right, finding that particular book is going to require patience and a lot of luck."

AN HOUR LATER, after a quick breakfast with Kyle and Erin, Kim and Rick were in the SUV heading back to Hartley. "I remember when your foster father came to visit Uncle Frank," Kim said. "All eyes in the tavern would automatically turn to him. His white headband and of course his long silver hair made him stand out even in a crowd."

"That's why he was known as Hosteen Silver. *Hosteen* means Mister, I'm sure you know that already, having worked with Angelina. And Silver...well, that was obvious. His hair seemed to glow with a silver sheen that's impossible to describe."

"I agree. One time I was stressed out, hurrying to finish cleaning the tables so I could get to class. He came over and told me that I already had my place in the pattern of life. I didn't have to rush to make it so."

"That sounds like him."

"I wasn't sure what he was talking about, but I didn't have time to ask," she said. "The next day when I went to work, Uncle Frank said that he'd left a note for me. I read it but it made no sense."

"What did the note say?"

"It had a tiny hand-drawn figure of a horse, and a note saying that the horse had a lot to teach me." She held up her hands, palms up and shrugged. "No explanation, nothing. Just that."

He smiled. "He was telling you that Horse is your spiritual sister."

"Why a horse? I love them, but I've never even ridden one."

"As far as he was concerned, what Eagle is to me, Horse is to you."

"Does the horse symbolize strength?" she asked, taking a guess.

"Yes, and cooperation, too. Horse is all about knowing when to exert control and when to yield. It's a reminder that you get better results when you don't try to do everything by yourself."

"I wish he would have just said that."

Rick laughed. "That wasn't his way. He liked letting things unfold in your own thinking."

After a while, her thoughts still on the case, she glanced over at him. "Do you still want to stop by Angelina's second store? Jeri, the manager, worked at Silver Heritage before her promotion and she might remember the professor's name."

"What makes you think she'd remember?"

"She thought he was hot."

"You didn't?"

She took a deep breath. "What attracts me to a man isn't looks. It's attitude. Like confidence. Integrity is essential, and courage works, too."

"Are you telling me that you're never swayed by packaging?" he said, giving her an incredulous grin.

"Hey, I like eye candy as much as the next person, but keeping my interest takes a lot more than that," she said, laughing. "I'm picky. When I met you for the first time since high school, what got my attention was the way you looked at whoever was speaking to you. That person had your undivided attention. You also took time to savor your food; you didn't just wolf it down. I knew that you were a man who took his time to do things right." Realizing the double entendre, she glanced away and felt her cheeks burning.

"I don't like to rush," he said, his voice low and deep. "Like wine, women and investigations, some things just need that extra attention."

The masculine timbre of his voice felt like a warm caress on a cold winter's night. Realizing the turn her thoughts had taken, Kim forced herself to look directly ahead.

As she peered off into the distance, something on the road caught her attention. "Slow down. There's some kind of animal in our way." She squinted, then quickly added, "It's a snake."

"Pretty common sight this late in the year. They sometimes sun themselves in the morning just to get warm. Let me see if I can prod it off the road." He braked and came to a stop.

"Why don't you just drive around it? If it's a rattler you'll be safer keeping your distance."

"The road isn't wide enough. And if I try to straddle it, it might just move and get struck. Wait here," he said, climbing out. "I don't want to kill it unless I have to."

She watched him approach the snake, then stop and glance all around. Maybe it was already dead.

She watched him use the tip of his boot to prod it, but to her surprise, part of the snake suddenly disappeared. That's when she realized it wasn't real. She got out of the SUV and walked over. "What is it?"

"It's a fake, constructed out of colored sawdust, ash and charcoal. The pattern and materials remind me of the dry paintings Navajo witches use."

"Skinwalkers?"

He glared at her. "Don't say that word. Not here." Looking around, he added, "Get back in the SUV. Hurry."

She heard the urgency in his voice and moved quickly. Before they were halfway there, the sharp blast of gunfire echoed against the canyon walls behind them and two holes appeared in the windshield.

"Ambush!" Rick said, grabbing Kim's arm and pulling her to the driver's side. "Get down!"

Chapter Nine

"Crawl underneath the SUV," Rick yelled as more bullets kicked up dust inches from his head.

As soon as she was beneath cover, he rolled in and lay next to her.

"We're trapped!" she said, her voice shaky.

"For now we're out of his line of sight with a lot of heavy engine metal between him and us," Rick said, reassuring her by putting his hand on her shoulder. "But we can't afford to stay pinned down under here. If we're unable to move, that'll give him time to change positions and maybe get a clear shot."

"We need to call for help."

"That's the plan." Rick rolled onto his side, brought out his phone and handed it to her. "Tell Kyle we're about a hundred yards from the highway and that the shooter is on high ground to the northwest, a couple hundred yards away from us at the moment."

"What are you going to do?"

"I'll put myself in a position to return fire and keep him from flanking us. Best case scenario, I'll pin him down or force him to move. Then we might be able to climb back inside the truck and get away."

"Okay, but be careful, please!"

"I'll be fine," Rick said, crawling prone to the passenger's side then inching out. Scrambling to his knees, he moved to the rear of the SUV and took a quick look around.

Hearing a boom and a thud as a bullet struck the rear bumper about a foot away, he ducked back.

"You okay?" Kim called out, fear alive in her voice.

"Yeah. Make the call."

"I'm waiting... Okay, he's answering," Kim told him.

Rick brought out his pistol, slipped off the safety and considered his next move. The glare off the vehicle should interfere with the shooter's sight. He moved toward the front passenger door and rose up for a look.

He watched carefully for movement and finally saw the shooter's exact location. If only he had a rifle with a scope. A direct hit with a pistol at this range would be unlikely, but he might be able to either discourage movement or, better yet, force it.

Another shot rang out. This time the bullet struck somewhere up front.

Rick looked to his left, then his right. There was no cover to speak of. If they decided to make a break for the canyon they'd get shot in the back.

"Kyle called the tribal police, but it'll take at least a half hour or more for them to arrive," Kim called out to him. "Kyle's circling around, coming from the northeast. He says he'll be within range in fifteen minutes or less."

"Okay. Just stay where you are."

"How's Kyle coming around from the east? I thought there was only one way in or out of Copper Canyon, the trail that's right behind us."

"There's another way, providing you travel on foot. Only my family knows it, though."

"So what do we do now, wait?"

Rick kept his eyes on the shooter's location and saw movement. Someone was standing. "Hang on a second."

He moved to the hood, stood and fired two shots at the sniper. Though he missed, the bullets got the shooter's attention and he dropped to the ground instantly.

A few seconds later the shooter fired again, one bullet high, the second striking the SUV in the side, passing through and whining down the road.

"That was close," Kim called out. "You okay?"

"Yeah, but he'll have to think twice about trying to work his way around us now," Rick said, looking back at the exit hole in the passenger door.

That ruled out any attempt to get behind the wheel. "Come on out, Kim, I want you behind the engine block."

He bent and looked into her dusty face. Her expression was grim but calm.

"How do we fight back?" she asked.

"We survive. Backup's on the way. Till then we have to stay alive and protect ourselves from being outflanked." He reached down and lifted her up to a crouching position. "Keep your head down."

After the longest five minutes in history, Rick's phone rang.

"He's gone." Kyle's voice was clear. "There's a truck in the distance, about a quarter mile down the highway and picking up speed. I'll call the tribal cops to see if they can set up a roadblock."

"You sure that's him?"

"Pretty sure. There's nobody on that hill anymore. All I can see through my rifle scope is a depression in the sand where the guy was lying."

Rick motioned for Kim to stay down, then looked out through the windows toward the north. There was Kyle, about a hundred and fifty yards away. Rick glanced to the south, then swept the area all around them, including back toward the canyon. Nobody was in sight.

"It's okay, Kim," he said, reaching over and taking her hand. She stood and he brought his arm around her, pulling her close. "We made it."

AFTER THE TRIBAL officers arrived, they went over to the three-dimensional charcoal-and-ash snake left for them on the road. "This was meant to get your attention, a setup to make you stop and present an easy target," Officer Begay said, taking a photo of it. "It's not really Navajo witchcraft. All the elements don't fit. Scattering ashes about in the daytime is insulting to Sun, but that's not scattered."

"So we may be talking about someone with limited knowledge of Navajo ways," Rick added.

"An Anglo maybe?" the other tribal cop, named Henderson, suggested. "Certainly something to consider." Both officers looked at Kim.

"Might be someone who works with members of the tribe who aren't Traditionalists," she replied.

"I agree," Rick said. "How about we check out the sniper's position?"

They climbed the low hill to join Kyle, who'd remained near that spot.

Officer Henderson crouched down and studied the ground. "He ignored the impression his body left in the sand, but rubbed out his footprints before he left," he said. "He wasn't trying to erase his shooting position, but he was determined to prevent us from finding a boot or shoe print to identify. No shell casings, either, or cigarette butts or hard evidence of any kind. At least we'll be able to identify the tread patterns from the pickup tires. We photographed them beside the highway."

"There are reports that you've had other problems recently," Begay said, looking at Rick. "If we go from the assumption that the two incidents are related, then you must have been the target today."

"Or perhaps your companion," Henderson said, looking at Kim. "You were at the restaurant, too, correct?"

Kim nodded. "Anyone out to hurt me could have done that weeks ago. This began after Rick returned home."

"My gut says she's right," Rick said, then told them about the falling wall. "The perp failed to take us all out at once, so now maybe he's decided to come for us one a time." He looked at Kyle and added, "Stay on your guard, just in case that's it."

RICK AND KIM signed statements that were included in the tribal police report while Kyle caught a ride back to the ranch with Erin, who'd driven up once her husband declared it to be safe. After checking to make sure the SUV was still functional, Rick and Kim were on their way to Hartley.

"I'm thinking all this has something to do with Hosteen Silver and you," Kim said, "but I'm not sure what the connection is."

He pushed the cell phone over to her. "Call Daniel and send him copies of the notebook pages I photographed."

A moment later Daniel called back. Rick put him on the speaker, which was clearer than the cell phone.

"I'll put this through a decryption program, but I don't think we'll get far," Daniel said. "It's not the same code you and our father used earlier. You probably noticed that already."

Paul was also on the line. "I think we need to talk to Gene. He was the last one to speak to our foster father before he went missing. Hosteen Silver had asked him to go pick up the horse and board it for a while. Maybe he'll remember something useful."

"Gene's up at his ranch?" Rick asked.

"No, he's staying here at the compound," Daniel said. "And here he is now."

Gene's voice came through next. "After Preston told me what was going on, I decided to put some distance between me and my family. If someone wants to off me, I'm not running, but I want my family out of the line of fire. Some of Daniel's men are taking care of things at the ranch in case I'm on somebody's target list. In the meantime I made sure I was seen in Hartley."

"Good plan," Rick said, giving him the highlights of their conversation before he joined in. "So what can you tell me about the last time you spoke with Hosteen Silver?"

"There was no grand revelation. He said he seldom went riding anymore and asked if I could use another ranch horse. Later that day, I went to pick up the gelding, but Hosteen Silver wasn't around. I went inside to check on things and that's when I realized something was off."

"Considering he left his private journal, the letters and the keys to his truck right there on the table, I'd say he planned things carefully. He knew he was going for his final walk," Daniel said. "Did he say anything about a code when you spoke to him?"

"No, not a thing. Just about his horse," Gene replied. "Preston came over soon after that and we searched the entire canyon, but there was no sign of him."

"He didn't want to be found," Rick said.

"By the way, Preston heard from the fire marshal. He claims that the explosion at the Brickhouse was triggered when a small piece of wood placed on the heating element of an electric hot plate produced a flame," Daniel reported.

"A very simple setup that would have probably escaped detection if the fire hadn't been put out so quickly. That establishes arson for sure," Rick replied.

"Time for a war council," Daniel said. "Are you on your way to town, Rick?"

"Yeah. I have one stop to make, then I'll head over to your compound," he answered.

"Good. We need to come up with a viable tactical plan."

After he ended the call, Kim looked at him. "Turquoise Dreams—is that where we're going?"

"Yes, I want to see if your friend remembers the professor's name and if she can give us some useful insights."

As they approached the business, they made sure Angelina's pickup wasn't there before parking.

The store was smaller than Silver Heritage, but catered to a more affluent clientele. A guard sat on a bar stool near the door and nodded to them as they came in through the small glass foyer.

Jeri ran around the counter to give Kim a hug. "I heard what Angelina did to you, and I'm so sorry! I wish I could talk her out of it, but you know how she is."

"It's okay, Jeri. I've landed an even better job." She gestured to Rick. "Have you met my new supervisor?"

Jeri smiled widely and held out her hand, offering to shake. "I'm Jeri Murphy."

"Rick Cloud," he answered, shaking her hand. He was no Traditionalist and had no problem shaking hands with a stranger.

"So what brings you here?"

"We're trying to find someone—the young professor who came looking for Hosteen Silver," Kim said. "Do you remember him?"

"Oh, yeah. Those blue eyes…" She sighed. "What's to forget?"

"Do you recall his name, or what he teaches? All I remember is that he said he was from Durango," Kim said.

"He teaches at Fort Lewis College, and introduced himself as Tim McCullough," she said. "Why are you interested in him?"

"We wanted to know why he was interested in Rick's foster dad," she said. "If you hear anything, or if he shows up here again, let me know?"

"Sure," Jeri said. "If you find him first, tell him we carry high-quality, hand-carved fetishes here at this shop. Maybe he'll stop by. It sure would be nice to see him again. He's easy on the eyes."

Kim smiled. "I'll remember."

They started to leave the store when Rick stopped by the security guard, took a closer look at the man's face and smiled. "Big Joe! I haven't seen you since high school. I always thought you'd be playing football with the pros someday."

"Me, too, Rick, till I got injured and sat out my senior year."

"Now you're here in the security business," Rick said.

"Who'd have thought it, huh?" Joe said, laughing. Then he turned serious. "I've got friends in the P.D. who've kept me current on the situation with you and your family. Anything I can do, just say the word. When I came back from Afghanistan, Hosteen Silver helped me get my head together by doing a pollen blessing over me. I got my life straightened out again 'cause of him, so if his sons need me, I'm there."

"I never saw you as a Traditionalist, or a new Traditionalist, either," Rick said, surprised.

"The older you get, the more the Navajo Way makes sense," he said, referring to the path traditional members of the tribe followed. "It's in our blood, brother."

"I hear you. I still carry the medicine pouch my foster father gave me," Rick told him.

"Your old man definitely had what we call *'áli·l.*"

Rick nodded and then, glancing at Kim, explained. "It means supernatural power, something that goes beyond what we can explain rationally."

"That's why he made enemies," Joe added. "People continually came to him wanting to become his apprentice. They all wanted to do the things he could, but he turned almost everyone away. Remember Nestor Sandoval? The little guy in our chemistry class who never said much to anyone?"

"What about him?"

"Nestor began to walk the path of a Traditionalist and wanted your foster dad to take him on as an apprentice. After about a week, they had some kind of falling-out."

"Any idea what happened?" Rick asked.

"Hosteen Silver took his work very seriously, and in my opinion, he figured out that Nestor wanted to manipulate people, not help them."

"Interesting. What's Sandoval doing these days?" Rick asked.

"He's mixed up with a gang of Rez thugs, and let me tell you, he hates your family, especially your foster dad. To hear Nestor talk, Hosteen Silver prevented him from following The Way."

"Good to know, thanks. Any idea where I can find him?" Rick asked.

"His crew sometimes hangs out at the Taco Emporium on East Broadway. It's next door to Augustino's Pawn Shop, where they do business."

"Sandoval sounds like a good suspect," Kim said as soon as they left the store.

"I'll have my brothers run him through the system. If he has a record, we'll get a better idea of who we're dealing with."

After he made the call, Kim shifted in her seat, facing

him. "I never imagined that a medicine man would make deadly enemies."

"It's not unusual. Sings gone wrong.... Jealousy.... Hosteen Silver had a strong personality and high standards."

They were soon traveling down Hartley's main street. "I was really surprised to see Joe. I always liked him, and from what I can tell he hasn't changed much, despite all he's probably been through. I don't think he ever noticed the scar on my face. To him, I'm still just Rick."

"That's because of *you,* Rick. When you walk into a room, you own it. That's why I can't picture you working undercover anywhere. You stand out, and it's not the scar on your face."

"Is that a compliment?" he asked, enjoying the stirring he saw in her eyes and the flash of heat that coursed through him.

"It's a fact...and a compliment," she added with a tiny smile. "So how did you ever make it undercover? You just don't blend in."

He laughed. "Going undercover is tricky. You have to play a role, much like an actor, and create a whole new personality. Sometimes you do it so well, you start to forget who you really are. That's when it's time to get out," he said, his voice somber. "The fight that left me with the scar you see on my face gave me the final push I needed to come home."

"What happened?" she asked.

"That's for another time."

He'd kept his eye on the rearview mirror as he drove through Hartley. "We're being followed," he said at last.

Chapter Ten

Rick's hands tensed as he gripped the steering wheel, trying not to make any sudden moves. Patience was required until he came up with a strategy.

A few blocks farther down the street, Rick checked the mirror again. "He's staying well back, but he's still there."

Kim was about to turn around in her seat when he reached over and touched her on the shoulder. "Don't look. Glance in the side mirror, but don't do anything that'll attract his attention and signal that we've spotted him," he said. "I want to see if I can draw him out."

Rick took a slower route and paced himself to catch every stoplight. The beat-up '60s Ford pickup followed his lead and remained at least three to four car lengths behind.

"I could call my brothers and see if we can trap him between us, but he's being too careful. He'll take off the moment he smells a trap."

"When did you first notice him?"

"A few minutes after we left Turquoise Dreams." Rick slowed and turned the corner. "He's not there anymore. I think something spooked him."

Rick continued moving slowly for several more minutes, giving the tail a chance to catch up, but the truck had disappeared. They rode in silence for a while longer, then he heard a faint electronic click coming from somewhere up front.

He looked around, trying to find out what might be making the sound. Nothing was on at the moment except for the engine—not the radio, heater or anything else. "Did you just hear something?"

"That click? I thought maybe you'd switched on the cruise control or something like that," she replied.

He glanced below the instrument panel in the area of the steering column. The low tone was coming from beneath the floorboards; a hum he'd never heard before.

"I have a bad feeling about this." He pulled into the lot of an empty store with a For Rent or Lease sign in the window. "Something's wrong. Get out and get away from the vehicle."

"What is it?" she replied, throwing the door open and jumping out quickly. "Aren't you coming? What's wrong?"

"I don't know, but I want to check this out. Stay clear until I'm done." Taking a flashlight from the glove compartment, he studied the steering column, then directed the beam slowly down toward the floorboard. "Nothing."

"You think it's a bomb?" she asked, her voice unsteady. "If you do, get away from there right now and call the police."

"It's not a bomb. I've never heard one that sends out a warning. That would defeat its purpose." He climbed out his side, dropped to the asphalt and aimed the flashlight underneath the vehicle. Attached to the frame just inside the left wheel well was a black vinyl box that looked like an eyeglass case.

"I found something," he said. Where it was attached to the wheel well he saw a chunk of gray metal that had been glued to the bottom of the case. "It's attached by a magnet, like one of those hidden car key things."

He put on his gloves, detached the box and then set it on the ground about ten feet from the SUV.

"Let me take a look," she said, inching closer.

"No, stay around behind the engine block until I'm sure what this is. Could be a jerry-rigged tracking device of some sort."

"You think maybe one of your brothers put it there?" she suggested.

"My brothers wouldn't have attached something that had a tone anyone in the front seat could hear. Listen."

"It's humming."

"Stand back," he said, reaching for it with a gloved hand.

Holding it away from him, he turned his head and opened the top.

It popped loudly and threw confetti into the air. Rick automatically flinched and dropped it to the ground. A moment later, realizing that there was no danger, he bent to pick it up. "Someone's messing with us," he growled.

Kim came closer and looked at the container. "Was it some kind of firecracker?"

"No, it's a party popper. Whoever did this fixed it so that when I opened the top, it pulled a hidden string, setting it off."

"I've heard of those, but never seen one."

"Back in high school I hooked one inside Kyle's locker. He opened it up one morning and *bam!* He dropped his books, jumped about three feet and ended up looking like an idiot. He caught me and there was all hell to pay later," he said with a quick half grin.

"What's the little plastic box in there?"

"Some kind of battery-powered noisemaker, like the ones you find in some stuffed animals and toys," he answered. "Reach into the glove compartment. Dan keeps evidence bags there. I want Preston to see if he can lift prints from the case or the box."

"This may be the work of the person who left the snake fang in my apartment and that fake snake on the road. If the arsonist had done this, there would have been more than confetti and a pop by now." She'd meant to sound brave, to shrug in the face of danger, but her voice broke.

"We're okay," he said in a quiet, steady voice. "Don't let him get inside your head."

Within minutes they were on their way again. Rick drove around the block slowly, checking out the immediate vicinity.

"You're hoping to spot the old truck again?" Kim asked.

"Yeah, sure, though the odds are against it," he answered.

"Considering what Big Joe told you about Nestor Sandoval, wouldn't you say that this kind of stunt fits something he'd do?"

"Back in high school, maybe, but now that he's gang connected, a brick through our windshield might be more his speed."

As they drove past the lot where they'd been parked, Kim noticed someone enter the alley behind the empty building. "Circle the block," she said quickly. "I think I just saw Mike."

He turned the corner and drove to the other end of the alley.

"Mike, are you in here?" she called after rolling down the window.

The big man came out from the recess of a doorway. He was wearing a backpack and thick camouflage jacket.

"Hungry?" Rick called out. "I think we can rustle up a cheeseburger and some fries."

Mike didn't answer, but he pointed down the street.

"Total Burger? No problem," Rick said. "Hop in. We'll give you a ride."

Mike shook his head.

"How about if we all walk there?" Kim suggested.

Mike smiled, so Rick inched forward and parked beside the curb in a legitimate parking spot.

They strolled down the sidewalk side by side in silence. Then to their surprise, Mike spoke.

"Saw a guy watching from the alley when you removed the confetti popper from beneath the SUV. He was Navajo, five ten, maybe...jeans and a red sweatshirt that said Chieftains. When you were done, he got in a pickup and drove off."

Kim's look of surprise quickly turned into a smile.

Rick recognized the name of the Shiprock high school team. "What was he driving?"

"Old truck," Mike said. "But at least there were no bullet holes in it," he said, a trace of a smile on his face for a moment.

As they reached the fast-food place, Rick walked to the entrance and held the door open for all of them, but Mike shook his head.

"It's okay, Mike, we'll eat out here," Kim said. Looking at Rick, she reached into her purse for her wallet. "Wanna get us all something?"

"I've got it."

Rick came back moments later and placed a sack filled with food and a milk shake in front of Mike. He had another bag with burgers and fries for himself and Kim.

They all dug in quickly and after a few minutes Rick spoke. "We're both glad to help you, soldier, but we could use your help today."

Mike took another big bite out of a burger, chewed

silently for a while, then swallowed, all the time avoiding Rick's gaze. "No one will believe anything I say."

As Mike continued to eat, Rick allowed the silence to stretch out.

"You're hoping I saw someone the night of the explosion. But I didn't see anything until the day after," Mike said. "When you two were inside looking around, I saw a guy pushing against one of the damaged walls."

"Did you recognize who it was?" Rick asked instantly.

"I didn't see him clearly, just his gray hoodie and sweatpants," he said.

"Could it have been Bobby Crawford?" Kim asked, knowing Mike would have known the staff at the Brickhouse.

"Too tall for the boy."

"Was he the same height as the man you saw watching us today?" Rick asked.

"Maybe." Mike wadded up the hamburger wrapper and tossed everything in the trash. "People don't want to look at me. That makes it easier for me to keep watch. If I hear or see anything else, I'll find you."

"Mike, there are veteran organizations—" Rick began.

Mike held up a hand, interrupting him. "No thanks. I can take care of myself." With that, he walked off down the alley.

Wanting to give Mike a card with his cell phone number, Rick raced to catch up with him, but by the time he got to the end of the block, Mike was gone.

"I should have known," he said, shaking his head as he returned.

"He's like a puff of smoke, here one second, gone the next. How does a big man like him do that?" Kim asked.

"He's learned to become invisible on the streets. It's

how you keep breathing." Rick stopped at the trash can and picked up the clear plastic top to the empty milk shake container. "Let's see if I can find out who he really is."

"Mike won't like that."

"I don't have to tell him I know. I just want to know who I'm dealing with."

Hearing the haunted tone in Rick's voice, she wished she could have asked him about his life, but a man like him didn't share personal information easily. First, she would have to earn his trust and respect. Yet having him see her as an equal promised to be a tough proposition, particularly since she was now his intern.

THEY WERE IN Daniel's tactical room some time later with three of Rick's brothers. Preston had accessed Sandoval's record, which was extensive, and had sent it to one of the wall monitors.

"Nestor lives on the Rez. He's out of my jurisdiction unless he commits a crime in the city and I'm in pursuit," Preston said. "I've got his file thanks to my contact in the Shiprock P.D. I'll be meeting him later today to see what else I can find out."

"You may not be able to question Sandoval, but I can," Rick said.

"Not officially, you can't. Give me time to persuade tribal detective Bidtah to go with you. That's his turf."

"I've got practically nothing on Bobby Crawford," Paul said, looking up from the big tabletop computer. "A couple of parking tickets is all."

"My uncle would have had a background check done," Kim said. "He was always careful who we hired."

"Anything on the transient, Mike?" Rick asked Preston.

"Yes. Once I had his prints, the rest was easy. His real

name is Raymond Weaver. Ray made sergeant in the army, serving with the First Cavalry. A week before he was scheduled to rotate home his recon unit was ambushed. He managed to recover and evacuate the wounded in his troop, carrying them to safety one at a time. Most of the men died while being treated, but Ray saved four lives. One of those survivors, who lost a leg, later committed suicide. Sergeant Ray Weaver, the man you know as Mike, was awarded several medals. After being diagnosed with post-traumatic stress disorder, he left the service at the end of his enlistment and dropped out of sight. No credit cards, no bank accounts, and his driver's license has expired."

"He's lost until he heals from the inside out," Rick noted in a taut voice. "PTSD isn't something you can overcome without a struggle."

"You want me to have one of our officers pick him up?" Preston asked. "Maybe we can convince him—"

"No." Rick cut him short. "That's the worst thing you can do. He can't be pushed. He has to do this his own way."

Rick remembered his days in the hospital after being pulled out of his undercover assignment. The scar on his face had been only one of many wounds. Long months of recuperating and rehab had challenged him at every turn, and during the dark days that followed, he'd battled his own demons.

"Something about you drew him out, Rick. Was it something you said?" Kim asked.

"Not so much. I think he senses that in a lot of ways we are two of a kind." He shook his head, signaling her not to ask him any more questions.

From across the room Gene spoke up. "Kim, I think your uncle Frank might still be able to add something to the arson side of the investigation. You should talk to him."

"He was released from the hospital yesterday," Preston added. "He's home."

"I'm ready to pay him a visit as soon as you are, Rick," Kim said.

"First, you two better get another ride. The one you're in looks a little too conspicuous," Preston joked.

"Good idea." Rick grabbed a set of keys to one of Daniel's other SUVs from a hook on the wall.

"Let's go, but stay focused on Sandoval, Preston. He's involved in this and I want to know how," Rick added.

"On it," Preston answered. "I'm also going to take a real close look at Angelina Curley. For all we know, the person who clocked Frank Nelson was a woman."

"Did any of you look into Frank's silent partner, Arthur Johnson?" Rick asked.

Preston nodded. "He's a former lieutenant colonel in the marines, honorable discharge, has no record other than an old speeding ticket and drives a 2001 green Mercedes with a vanity plate that says *Ellie*. That was his wife's name. She died about eighteen months ago."

As Rick drove out of the compound in the new SUV, Kim leaned back in her seat. "I don't know much about Art, but Uncle Frank doesn't make friends easily, and he trusts him completely. That should count for something. Do you want me to ask Uncle Frank about him?"

"Sure, but don't dive right in. Ease into it."

"Do you think my uncle's hiding something?" she asked, curious about his suggestion.

"Not necessarily, but I've learned that people speak more freely and tend to remember important details when they don't feel pressured."

They were driving past what remained of the Brickhouse when Kim noticed three muscular teenage boys circling

Mike, feigning punches and grabbing at his backpack. One was waving around a small baseball bat like a club.

"Those punks are taunting Mike. Ray, I mean," she said, pointing. "He needs our help."

Chapter Eleven

Rick slammed on the brakes and pulled over to the curb, but before he'd even come to a stop, Ray Weaver had taken away the bat from the first teen, flipped the second over onto a pile of plastic trash bags and was facing off with the third. The tall kid with peach fuzz sideburns tried to land a knockout punch, but Ray blocked the move easily. The kid, realizing he was out of his league, spun around and raced on the tail of his fleeing companions.

"Guess you don't need anyone covering your six," Rick said, using the military expression for watching your back.

Ray shrugged. "Not with those sorry punks. They just need to learn a little respect for their elders, but thanks for stepping up."

"No prob. They won't be bothering you again, that's for sure." Rick reached for his wallet and gave Ray a card with his telephone number. "When you're ready, Sergeant, call me. I can help you land a job and find a warm place to crash."

"You know who I am." His eyes met Rick's and something clicked. "My fingerprints were on that plastic lid you pulled from the trash."

Rick didn't answer directly. "As I said, Ray, when you're ready."

On their way again, Kim gave Rick directions to Frank's

home, then opened up to him. "I experienced combat when our supply convoys came under attack. Whenever we hit the road, my nerves were always on edge, waiting to see if our vehicle was going to take an RPG strike or run over an IED. That uncertainty and fear really gets under your skin. Even after I came home, I was always looking around, gauging the threat environment. It took me a long time to become a civilian again," she said. "Is that what you think happened to Ray?"

"To a degree, yes. Right now he's trying to make his peace between who he was as a soldier and who he's supposed to be stateside," he said. "He needs to withdraw from the world to find himself again."

"You went through something like that when you left undercover work, didn't you?" she asked softly.

He nodded. "After my last assignment, I spent a lot of time in a hospital recovering from three bullet wounds and the cut you see on my face. The pain was a daily reminder of how close to death I'd come. Once the doctors had done all they could and we reached the cosmetic surgery stage, I'd had enough. I said no more and walked away. I rented a cabin up in the San Juan Mountains and stayed there for ten months. I didn't shave. I bathed in a creek. And didn't speak to anyone," he said, his voice distant. "Time—and that daily silence—mapped my way back."

"My healing came little by little on campus. A group of us would get together after class and relax by talking about inconsequential things like a new purse, or shoes, or the latest coffee flavor at Fresh Cup. Slowly I became me again."

"Finding your way back can take you down many roads, but in the end all that matters is that you made it."

As they arrived at Frank's home, Kim sat up and looked directly ahead. "The Silverado is Uncle Frank's pickup. I don't know who owns the white Toyota."

Rick got some immediate feedback from Preston, who ran the plates as they parked. "It belongs to Arthur Johnson," Rick said, viewing his phone as they walked up the sidewalk. "Looks like we got lucky."

They entered the house and Frank ushered them into the living room. Although he got around slowly, he seemed on the mend.

"I'm so glad to see you up and about, Uncle Frank," Kim said.

"Me, too. Hospitals scare me spitless," he admitted with a wry grin. "Your dad would tease me unmercifully about that," he said and laughed. "It's a good thing I was unconscious when they brought me in."

Frank looked at Rick. "Have you found any answers yet?"

"Not definitive ones, no, but we'd like to ask you a few more questions," Rick said. He could hear someone in the kitchen—no doubt Arthur—but avoided glancing in that direction, not wanting to distract Kim's uncle.

Frank gave his niece a hard look. "You convinced Mr. Cloud to let you help investigate the blast, didn't you? I know you're taking law-enforcement classes, Kim, and that you learned a lot from your dad, but you're still not a police officer."

"This is all part of my new job, Uncle Frank. I've accepted a paid internship with Level One Security, and Rick's giving me on-the-job training. It's an opportunity I couldn't pass up."

Frank's gaze hardened and he looked directly at Rick. "This is also his chance to keep you close and figure out if you know anything about who might have done this."

"I can protect her," Rick said.

"Looks to me like you haven't had much luck protecting yourself in the past," he said, his meaning clear.

"The fact that I'm standing here now proves I can handle myself."

"Good point. So how can I help you?"

"Have you given any more thought to the events leading up to the explosion?" Rick asked.

"I've thought of nothing else," Frank admitted, touching the large bandage above his right ear.

"Now that you've had a chance to look back, were there any red flags you somehow missed?"

Frank nodded. "When I went to take out some trash I heard someone in the alley behind the Brickhouse. I saw the back of someone in a hoodie walking down the alley, but I just assumed it was the homeless vet Kim feeds every night."

"How'd you know he's a vet?" Rick asked.

"He has a tattoo I recognized—some cavalry unit—and he carries himself like a soldier. I served and I recognize that walk."

"The hoodie person—you know it was a man, not a woman?" Kim asked.

"Strode like a man. Didn't have hips, either. I guess I should have taken a closer look, but I was watching the Dallas game while cleaning up."

"Do you keep the kitchen doors locked?" Rick asked.

"Not when we're open. Someone's constantly going outside to throw out trash or to take a break. We've never had any trouble before."

A moment later a man came into the room holding a mug of steaming coffee. He stood around six foot one and had silver, close-cropped hair, the perfect image of a no-nonsense former military officer.

Frank stood to introduce them. "This is my partner and friend, Arthur Johnson."

"Call me Art," he said, extending his hand and shaking Rick's. Art sized up Rick at a gaze. "I imagine your family has run a background check on me by now. What can I add to what you already know?"

Something told Rick that Art was a man who'd prefer the direct approach. "Where were you two nights ago at approximately 9:00 p.m.?" he asked, not wasting any time.

"Right to the point. I like that," Art said with an approving nod. "I was on the first leg of a flight back here from Oregon. I had a layover in Phoenix, and I didn't arrive in Hartley until around noon yesterday. If you're looking to me, or Frank, for a motive, you're wasting your time." He took a long sip of coffee from the mug.

"I understand the insurance settlement will be substantial," Rick said, though in truth he didn't have any details yet. Preston needed a court order, and going through the red tape always took time.

"I always make sure I can recoup my losses should something happen to one of my investments," Art said. "That's just good business. As it stands, though, even if the structure and contents of the Brickhouse are replaced quickly, Frank and I will still face a substantial loss of revenue during the rebuilding process."

"Is it true you aren't involved in day-to-day business at the tavern?" Rick asked.

"Never have been. I was a silent partner, and Frank made all the operating decisions. After my wife passed away, I liquidated most of my investments, but held on to the Brickhouse mostly because it always ran in the black."

"So you plan to rebuild?" Rick asked.

Art set the coffee mug down. "Frank and I haven't had time to discuss that yet. First, I want to see for myself just how big a hit the building took. Would you like to come with me? I'm going over there now."

Rick shook his head. "I've already seen what I need there."

"Then I'll say goodbye," Art concluded. "I hope you catch the weasel who jumped my partner and burned down our place."

Frank gazed out the window as Art drove away. "He's a good friend. I know he sounds cold, but Art always steps up whenever he's needed."

Rick glanced at Kim. "I need to call my brother, so I'm going to step out onto the patio and give you two a chance to catch up in private."

Rick walked out the French doors onto the flagstone patio to call Paul. He needed someone willing to cut a few corners.

"Run a careful check on Arthur Johnson's finances," Rick told him. "Look beneath the surface."

"Am I searching for anything in particular?"

"For starters, tell me if he's in debt. He mentioned selling most of his assets, and that backs up what Kim has already told us. But we don't know his current financial situation. I'd like to know if there's any reason other than personal considerations."

"Will do. Hang on and I'll do a credit check." Paul put him on hold but quickly came back on the line. "He's got a lot of outstanding medical bills, mostly alternative treatments his health insurance refused to cover. The payments are high, but he's never late."

"That doesn't necessarily mean he's not about to go broke. Check into his bank accounts and get back to me," Rick answered.

Ending the call, Rick entered the living room just in time to catch the tail end of an argument.

"You're getting sidetracked by taking on what could be a low-paying, full-time job, Kim. Nothing's more important than your education. That's your ticket up," Frank said.

"I'll benefit from this work almost as much as I do my classes, and I won't have to work two jobs just to make ends meet. I'm staying on course, and at the end of the road, I'll be wearing a badge," she said in a quiet but firm voice.

They lapsed into silence the moment they saw Rick standing there. "You ready to go?" Kim asked Rick, her face slightly flushed.

"Sure," he said.

As they walked back to the SUV parked across the street, he asked the question foremost on his mind. "Are you having second thoughts about taking an active part in the investigation?"

"None," she said flatly. "Karl Edmonds, who teaches my Police Procedure class, called me while you were outside and Uncle Frank heard me talking to him. Edmonds doesn't think Daniel's company is a good environment for a future law-enforcement officer. He wants to talk to me at school."

"I know Edmonds doesn't like me, but there might be some bad blood between Karl and Daniel, too. Any idea why?" Rick asked.

"I don't know for sure, but there's always been friction between the police department and private investigative firms in our area—everything from salaries and rivalries to conflicting interests."

"Let's go over to the campus and we'll both talk to Edmonds."

"Sounds good to me," she said, liking the way he'd offered to stand with her on this. Rick was a rock in times of trouble. His mixture of testosterone and gallantry was one she couldn't resist.

Once they arrived on campus, they headed directly for

Karl's office, actually a cubicle among a dozen others in a large metal portable building. Except for Edmonds, the building was empty at the moment.

Edmonds smiled at Kim when she knocked on the doorless partition, but once he noticed Rick standing beside her, he scowled. "I'd like to talk to Miss Nelson privately, if you don't mind, Mr. Cloud." His wording was polite, his tone not even close.

"It's okay with me if Mr. Cloud remains, Mr. Edmonds," Kim answered without emotion.

Edmonds kept his eyes on Kim as he ushered them to seats. "I wanted to speak with you about your work at Complete Security. I don't know if you're aware that private investigation agencies in our area are known for cutting corners. They walk a thin line between legal and illegal practices, and that's going to hurt your chances of getting into the police academy."

Rick replied before Kim could speak. "Level One Security is led by a highly trained former military intelligence officer with a higher clearance level than anyone currently serving with your department.

"The company also works under contract for state and federal agencies. Local public law enforcement often enlists their services for special investigations."

Karl shrugged, ignoring Rick's remarks. "You're free to make your own decisions, Kim, but the way security firms conduct their business is a lot different from the way the police department works. You're headed in the wrong direction, no matter what Rick's telling you."

Rick leaned closer. "Exactly what am I telling her, Karl?"

Edmond's gaze locked with Rick's. "You're placing this woman in danger she's not trained to face. Your entire family has enemies here, Cloud, and Kim isn't ready for the truckload of trouble you and your brothers can bring her way."

"I'm already involved, Mr. Edmonds," Kim said. "Someone tried to kill me two days ago, and I'm not going to sit back and let them have another go at me."

"That's another reason you shouldn't be involved. You're too close to it. Cops aren't allowed to investigate cases they're personally involved in." Edmonds stopped, then gave Rick a stony glare. "Or are you using her as bait?"

Rick moved forward but Kim grabbed his arm. "Come on. We're leaving."

Once they were on the sidewalk, Kim shook her head angrily. "What's gotten into him? He was sure doing his best to provoke you into taking a swing. No way that was all about me."

"Let me call Daniel to find out the history between them."

As they walked to the parking lot, Rick made a quick call. A few minutes later he had his answer.

"Before Karl got the job with the bomb squad, he'd applied for a job at Daniel's company. Something about him rubbed Daniel wrong, so he ended up hiring someone else."

"What exactly was the problem?" Kim asked.

"Daniel wouldn't say," Rick answered, "but he wants Preston to know what went down today."

"Do you think Karl Edmonds might have had something to do with the explosion? He was angry at Daniel and you, so maybe after three or four years of stewing on it, he decided to take action."

"As far as theories go, that's not so far-fetched. This was the first time Daniel and I have been together in years, at least in a place that was vulnerable to attack."

"And Edmonds does know how to blow things up," Kim said.

"Still, I'm not ready to put him on my short list—not without a stronger motive," Rick said. "Right now I've got another idea I want to check out."

Chapter Twelve

"We need to think outside the box on this," Rick said as they drove away from the campus. "My gut's telling me that you and the rest of the staff at the Brickhouse were just in the wrong place at the wrong time. My family seems to be the focus of the attack, and somehow I think it ties back to Hosteen Silver."

Kim watched him. He looked so relaxed behind the wheel, but his gaze was restless, taking in everything around them. That intensity was part of what drew her to him. He was a man who lived on the edge, one who'd dealt with brutality and conquered it, but had yet to open his heart to gentleness. She wanted to be there for him, to soothe all those rough edges, yet it was difficult penetrating the steel walls he'd built around himself.

Annoyed with herself because she'd allowed her thoughts to wander, she focused back on business. "Even if we accept that there's someone out to kill all your family, why did he wait till now? What's changed?"

"Good question. My gut tells me that once we get an answer to that, the case will crack wide-open," he said, giving her a quick smile.

His entire expression softened when he gave her one of his rare smiles. Despite what he thought, the scar didn't diminish his looks. It added to that earthy quality he possessed, and made him even more appealing.

"What are you thinking about?" he asked, his eyes dancing as if he'd already guessed.

Flustered, she thought fast. She couldn't admit to fantasizing about his looks. "I'm sure some of the answers we're searching for will come to us after you crack the code your foster dad left you."

"Good point. Let's go pay Daniel a visit to see if they've made any progress on that front."

When they arrived at the compound they joined Daniel and Paul in the main room. Rick immediately asked them about the code.

"We've run every decryption program we have and we've still got nothing," Daniel said.

"If you ask me, you're both going too high-tech on this," Paul said, looking at Rick. "The old man thought you could figure things out without a mainframe computer, so the key has got to be something you two did together or spoke about."

"A lot of time has gone by since he and I spoke at any length, but we never really talked about private stuff beyond day-to-day decisions. Even as a kid I avoided the touchy-feely stuff, and he never pushed it."

"Yet he left the book with the code in a place where only you'd be likely to find it," Daniel insisted.

After a long thoughtful pause, Daniel continued. "I have an idea. Kyle and Erin will be gone from Copper Canyon for a day or two. They're meeting potential clients in Albuquerque, so you'll have complete run of the place. Relax, look around, and maybe something will come to you. The key is, don't force it."

"I agree with Daniel," Paul said. "We'll concentrate on finding and interviewing Professor McCullough, and you work on trying to find any possible link between what happened to Hosteen Silver and the explosion at the Brick-house."

"Okay, but there's someone I want to meet face-to-face first. What do you have for me on Nestor Sandoval?" Rick asked Paul.

"He was picked up for drug trafficking six months ago, but the case fell apart when witnesses recanted and he walked. Sandoval's stayed under the radar since then, but the police suspect he's dealing weapons now," Paul said. "He's bad to the bone, Rick, so if you're going to go searching for him, take Detective Bidtah, like Preston suggested."

Rick considered it, then nodded. "I'll head back to the Rez. See if Preston can arrange for Bidtah to meet us at Sandoval's residence."

AFTER GETTING SANDOVAL'S ADDRESS, Rick and Kim left Daniel's compound and headed west. Rick finally asked the question that had been on his mind. "Are you okay staying at the ranch alone with me? As you pointed out once before, backup's a ways off."

"Of course."

He smiled. He'd been like her at the beginning of his career—eager to work, wanting to do the right thing and refusing to back away from danger.

"We both know there's more going on between us than business," he said in a quiet voice. "That's bound to complicate things."

She sat a little straighter. "No, it won't. I barely know you, Rick. You're not exactly an open book."

"No, I'm not," he admitted.

"From what you told your brothers about your relationship with Hosteen Silver, that's just your way."

"Maybe so," he answered, not bothering to argue the

point. "Life teaches all of us different lessons—or maybe it's the same lesson and we all react differently to it."

She saw the muscles on his face tighten.

"My brothers and I were all headed in the wrong direction when Hosteen Silver found us. He helped put us back together again, though unfortunately, old wounds don't always disappear. They turn into scars, reminders that none of us is as tough as we'd like to be."

"It's hard to trust a perpetual stranger, Rick. I want to know the man who'll have my back."

"Fair enough," he said after a beat. "Ask me whatever you want."

"How did you end up in foster care?" When he didn't answer right away, she added, "Do you want me to ask you something else?"

"No, it's okay," he said, then continued. "I was born to a single mother and abandoned at a trading post when I turned six. I never saw my mother again after that. By the time Hosteen Silver found me, I'd gone through a series of foster homes. I was trouble and most families couldn't wait to get rid of me. That was fine. I'd already learned never to count on anything or anyone outside myself. He found me in family services, offered me a chance to turn my life around, and it worked out, though it wasn't easy for either of us."

He'd told her his story quickly, factually and without emotion. He didn't want her to realize how painful his past still was.

"Before you start feeling sorry for me, you should know that I like my life," he added quickly. "My brothers and I are close and I've achieved what I set out to do when I left the Rez."

"And now?"

"I've left the Bureau, so I'm in transition again. Life will show me what's next."

"You need a new passion, something that calls to you like the work you did for the Bureau. You need to find a new dream."

"I'm not a dreamer. I'm a doer."

"The two go hand-in-hand. What would you like to see in your future—a family and kids, like your brothers?" she pressed.

"I suppose I'll marry someday, but if I do, it won't need to be out of love. That emotion can change in the blink of an eye."

"So you'll marry…out of expediency?"

"No, more out of friendship and respect. Those tend to last longer."

"I've heard of worse reasons for getting married," she said, "but I won't settle for anything less than love."

"You're a beautiful woman—independent, smart," he said. "I can't imagine you not having guys lined up at your door, wanting to take you out."

"Thanks, but the truth is I'm hard to deal with. Back in high school my friends would go for the predictable guys, the pretty boys, the bad boys or the ultramacho jocks. I wasn't into any of them."

"What type of guy do you want?"

She shrugged. "I'll know him when I see him. He'll speak to my heart and be someone who needs me as much as I'll need him."

They were on Highway 64 just east of the town of Shiprock when he saw the emergency lights of a white tribal police SUV coming up from behind. "I have a feeling that's Detective Bidtah. He knew which road I'd be on."

Rick pulled over and a moment later a plainclothes officer approached, his badge clipped to his belt.

"Rick?" he asked. "I'm Detective Allan Bidtah. One of our undercover people found out that Sandoval was evicted from his old residence. He's moved to a new place north of Shiprock on the Cortez highway. There's a rumor that he's involved with a particularly violent gang that's been causing problems in Rez communities south of Shiprock. If that report's correct, you're going to need armed backup."

"All right. Lead the way. We'll follow you."

Ten minutes later they were heading north in the direction of Colorado. They left the highway just past Monument Rocks and entered a run-down rural area, what appeared to be the beginnings of a housing development that had fizzled out. All that remained was graveled roads and a grid of scattered single-wide mobile homes. Some stood on concrete pads laid as foundations for permanent homes, and most were surrounded by chain-link fences.

Bidtah parked on a dusty road between two single-wides, then stepped out of his vehicle. He pointed to the front end of a black Nissan sedan behind the closest trailer.

Rick nodded. "You're not armed, Kim, so you should probably stay in the vehicle," he said.

"No chance. I'm supposed to be learning from you, and I can't do that if I duck and cover."

He bit back a smile. He hadn't expected anything less. "Follow my lead, stay behind me and keep your eyes open for anything that doesn't look right."

With Bidtah, they walked over, keeping space between them, not wanting to present too easy a target.

"Sandoval, open up. Detective Bidtah, tribal police," the detective said, knocking hard on the metal door. Rick watched the corner of the trailer, making sure nobody came out the back.

Several seconds went by before there was the sound of

footsteps inside. The door opened slowly and four young men in their late teens, wearing baggy pants and hooded sweatshirts, came out onto the stacked warehouse pallets that served as the step. If they were armed, no weapons were visible.

"Sandoval's not here, officer. Hasn't been around for several days, maybe a week," announced a big, barrel-chested guy with a shaved head crowned with a red bandanna.

"Where can we find him?" Bidtah demanded.

"Don't know. If you get to him first, tell him Billy's looking for him."

"That makes you Billy. How about a last name?"

"Why get all cops-and-robbers on me? I ain't done nothing," Billy said.

"Talk to me here, Billy, or at the station," Bidtah said, looking back and forth at the other three, who'd stepped off the pallets and were slowly starting to form a circle.

Rick recognized the flanking maneuver. He got set, used to being the first target because of his size. He knew what was coming.

Billy nodded slightly to the others, then rushed Rick, jabbing for his throat.

Rick sidestepped the punch, dropped his shoulder and sent the big guy flying into the air. Billy hit with a thud and Rick immediately moved in, placing his foot at the guy's throat. "Don't move."

Bidtah had his weapon out now, covering two of the others, who had their hands out, palms up, to show they were unarmed.

Out of the corner of his eye, Rick saw the fourth young man lunge for Kim. The teen threw his forearm up around her neck in a choke hold, but Kim sagged suddenly, elbowed him in the gut and stomped on his instep with her heel. As he gasped, letting go momentarily, she turned and punched him in the groin with her fist.

In agony, he sank to his knees.

Kim stepped away, turning to face the others. "Come on, guys, now that you've stood up to the cops, let's talk. Obviously you like Sandoval even less. And guess what, we don't like him, either. If you give us a lead so we can track him down, we'll all come out ahead. Make sense?" she asked, remaining perfectly calm.

"Or we can go to the station and talk breaking and entering, assault on a police officer and civilian and whatever else I can come up with between now and then," Bidtah added. "One look at the broken latch on the trailer door tells me you didn't gain entry with a key. Whose screwdriver is that anyway?" He pointed at the tool on the ground.

"So we help you find Sandoval and we're off the hook?" Billy asked.

"There's a saying, 'my enemy's enemy is my friend,'" Kim said. "At the moment, that means we're all on the same side."

"Yeah, okay," Billy said, nodding to the others. "Sandoval burned my crew. We don't owe him anything except the big hurt. What's your game?"

Kim held his gaze and kept her cool, not looking over at Rick or Bidtah for support. She knew that the gang members would probably see that as a sign of weakness. "Sandoval's in the wind. Any idea why?"

"He's worried about some heavy hitter Navajo guys, the sons of a *hataalii* he ripped off."

"Ripped off how? Money?" Kim pressed.

"Not even. The old man had taken on a student, Angelina something, so he could teach her medicine man stuff. Anyway, when the *hataalii* found out she'd been recording his Sings and sneaking photos with her cell phone, he grabbed it from her and ran her off. Sandoval heard Angelina had been planning to sell the Sings to a local college professor writing some book, so Sandoval offered to get the phone back for maybe two hundred bucks."

"But how do the sons of the *hataalii* figure into it?" Kim asked.

"When Sandoval went looking for the cell phone, the *hataalii* caught him red-handed. Sandoval roughed him up a little and got away, but not long afterward, the *hataalii* disappeared. Now Sandoval's afraid his sons will think he offed the old man."

"You got that from him?" Rick asked.

"Yeah. I can't say for sure, but I think Sandoval's also the one who placed a bounty on one of the *hataalii*'s sons. Word reached us a few days ago that anyone who takes out the marked man is in for some serious cash." He looked at Rick and studied his face. "I'm guessing that's you."

"But you're not sure of the source?" Rick persisted.

"No, and I didn't bother to find out. We're not stepping into a gig like that. We do our own thing," Billy said.

Rick suddenly heard the sound of a car engine moving toward them at high speed. As he turned his head, he saw a plume of dust trailing behind the beat-up silver sedan racing up the dirt road. There were three people inside. Two of them on the passenger's side, front and back, were wearing baseball caps. The car made a hard right, then headed directly for them.

As the car swung around broadside to the trailer, the two passengers reached out their windows, pistols in hand.

"The Diablos," Billy yelled, diving to the dirt just as bullets started to fly.

As Detective Bidtah dropped to one knee and returned

fire, Rick grabbed Kim's shoulder and pulled her to the ground.

The attack only lasted a few seconds before the sedan accelerated and disappeared into the freshly generated smoke screen of sand, dust and gravel.

Chapter Thirteen

They got up slowly, looking around to see if anyone had been hit. Rick concentrated on Kim, and as soon as he verified she was okay, turned to Bidtah. The tribal cop was on his cell phone, calling in the incident as he brushed the sand from his pants with his free hand. He seemed no worse for wear.

Rick looked over at Billy and saw pure hatred in his eyes. "Cool down, man," Rick warned.

"How do I know you didn't bring them here?"

"We were *not* followed," Rick assured him. "The detective and I know how to spot a tail. At least nobody got hit," he added, looking at the other gang members now on their feet and dusting themselves off.

"The Diablos know where we hang, bro," one of the three boys said. "After last week—"

"Drop it!" Billy ordered, turning toward the boy. "Don't be putting our business out on the street like that."

He looked back at Rick. "From me to you, dude, you stick out—the big Navajo with the scar on his face—so watch your back. And don't worry, lady, if we see Sandoval I'll pass the word along." He turned to the detective. "You're Bidtah, right?"

Bidtah nodded and gave Billy his card. "Cell number is on the back."

After the four gang members drove away, Bidtah went to his unit. Rick noticed Kim reach up to touch her shoulder and wince.

"I thought you were okay," he said.

"I am. I just landed wrong."

"Putting something cold on it will help," Rick said, walking with her toward the SUV. "We'll get you an ice pack."

Bidtah came over and joined them. "Patrol cars are out looking for the silver sedan. I don't know if Preston mentioned it to you, but the Rez gangs have changed a lot since you and your brothers lived here. They're trying to control some parts of the Rez turf. If there's a price on your head, you're going to need to be on full alert. What they lack in training, they more than make up in brutality."

"I hear you," Rick said.

Bidtah handed him his card. "If you have a problem or need some backup don't hesitate to call me."

"Thanks for all your help," Rick said as they parted ways.

Once they reached the main highway again, he and Kim drove west toward Copper Canyon, his gaze continually darting to the rearview mirror.

"Once we get home and take care of your shoulder, I'm going for a long, slow walk around the house and the shed. Maybe what I need to break Hosteen Silver's code is one particular memory, something I haven't thought about in years."

"Become the teenager you were back then. See things through his eyes."

Rick called Preston on the car phone to update him.

"That professor keeps coming into the picture, and it's got to be the same guy."

"Probably, but I have a hard time seeing a professor as a

hit man," Preston said, his sour voice mirroring his mood, from what Rick could tell.

"McCullough's cultivated sources in the Four Corners that seem to be at the heart of this case," Rick noted. "Don't write him off yet."

After hearing that they were on the way to Copper Canyon, Preston said, "I'm not sure if that's a safe place for you anymore, particularly if you're being targeted by the gangs."

"Let them take one of their low-slung rides into the canyon. They'll either high center on sandstone or be so worn out from getting unstuck they'll turn around and head back down the highway," Rick said.

Preston laughed. "Probably so," he said, adding, "I'm going to send you the photo I found of Professor McCullough. It was on a college social website. I don't know how old the photo is, but see if Kim can make a positive ID. I'm also sending you a copy of a paper he wrote for an anthropology journal.

"One last thing," Preston added. "I ran a background on Angelina Curley. Although her husband's death was ruled a suicide, there were some unanswered questions."

"Like what?" Rick asked.

"The man died in his garage from carbon monoxide poisoning, and there was a suicide note next to him that matched up with his desktop printer. The department spoke to friends and neighbors, but the only person who claimed he'd been acting strangely was Angelina. There was no real evidence of foul play, however, so Angelina inherited his money and the business."

"Good to know, but at the moment, Nestor Sandoval's at the top of my list," Rick said and ended the call.

Kim turned in her seat to face him. "I don't think Sandoval should be our prime suspect. Maybe he played a role, but we're dealing with a multilayered case. Until we have a lot more answers, nothing is going to fit together."

"What makes you so sure?"

"Intuition," she said.

"Intuition's good, but you have to make sure it's not just wishful thinking or your own bias. You want it be Angelina, don't you?"

"Maybe I do," she admitted grudgingly, "but unfortunately she has an alibi. She was scheduled to speak to an association of minority businesswomen during your welcome-home event. She'd been practicing that speech for weeks."

"Yeah, and the brief glances we've gotten of the suspect suggest it's a man."

"She could have hired out," Kim said.

"She may also have canceled her plans at the last minute," Rick said, then called Preston back. "Did you ever speak to Angelina Curley about her alibi for the night of the explosion?"

"I checked it out. She was speaking to the MWA—Minority Women in Action. People saw her there and there's a DVD of the event that shows her staying late to talk to the participants."

"Okay, thanks," Rick said, disconnecting before he told Kim what he'd learned. "She's still a viable suspect, but stop trying to make the facts fit. It's an occupational hazard, I know, but what we need is hard evidence."

THEY ARRIVED AT the house thirty minutes later. The weather had turned cold, with the jet stream bringing down much cooler air from the north. Rick built a fire while Kim checked out the materials Preston had sent them.

"How's your arm?" he asked. "We keep reusable ice packets in the fridge. I'll get you one."

"Ice packs on a cold day. Brrrr," she said, pressing it to her shoulder when he returned.

He smiled. "Don't use it for more than twenty minutes," he said. "I remember that from my high school football injuries."

His concern washed over her like a gentle warm breeze. He was the toughest, strongest man she'd ever met, yet he could still show gentleness.

"Preston said he copied the file from your phone onto the computer over here," she said, walking to the reconverted closet where the electronics were kept.

He pulled up a chair and sat beside her in front of the computer as she opened the file folder. She could feel the warmth of his body envelope her, and that made it hard for her to think clearly.

Locating the photo that Preston had sent, she took a moment to study it and nodded. "McCullough was much younger when this photo was taken, but it's him."

They used the link in Preston's email to read Professor McCullough's paper.

"The prof refers to his primary source only by initials, but A.T. could be Angelina Tso," she said. "He also admits that there were other *hataaliis* he'd wanted to interview, since most specialize in two or three types of Sings only, but they wouldn't cooperate."

"That doesn't surprise me," Rick said. "The spoken word has power, so Sings would lose their effectiveness if everyone discussed them freely. Anglo professors interested in padding their résumés with tribal ceremonial secrets are generally avoided like the plague."

Kim sat back, thinking. "This paper is interesting, but it's far from a motive for killing anyone."

"I agree."

Rick stood and turned, looking across the main room.

"We've made some progress. Now let's see if there's something else I can do. It's time for me to visualize what this place looked like when I was growing up. My brothers updated it, but the past is still here. Like those bookcases," he said, pointing across the room. "I helped Hosteen Silver build those."

"He read a lot?"

"Yes, we all did, usually together. We had a TV, but it only got local channels and we were limited to two hours a night. Our dad loved reading history books, particularly those covering the Southwest or anything dealing with the Navajo code talkers."

"They were radio operators for mostly Marine units in the Pacific theater, right?" she asked and saw him nod. "We read about them in school."

"They transmitted messages the Japanese were never able to figure out by developing a sub code using Navajo words for military terms. For example, the word for *navy* was comprised of the Navajo words for *needle, ant, victor* and *yucca.* And the code word for *tank* was the Navajo word for *turtle.*"

"Do you think that's the code Hosteen Silver used?"

"No," he said. "That required those at both ends of the message to know the code, which never varied," he said. "But his interest in codes was always there. That may have led him to use one that required something simpler, like a reverse-sequence key based on identical books. Anyone reading the message would just see numbers, but those numbers might indicate the page number, line number, word number or character number within that word. For instance, a number sequence 39, 14, 25, 5 could mean you look at the fifth letter of the twenty-fifth word on the fourteenth line on page thirty-nine of the book. That letter could be an *a*."

"Okay, so each set of numbers gives you letters to spell words, and once you know the words and the sequence, you know the message," she said.

He nodded. "The reason it would be hard to break is that the letter *a* could have a different number sequence every time it appeared. No pattern. Unless you had an identical copy of the book, you couldn't decode the message."

"If you're right, figuring out which book he used is going to be tough," she said.

"There are several dozen books still on the shelves, but over time the majority of what was there has been given away, taken home by one of my brothers or lost. We may not even have the particular book Hosteen Silver used anymore." He was about to say more when his cell phone rang. Looking at the screen, he saw it was Preston.

"I did some more digging on McCullough," Preston told him. "He took a sabbatical to conduct field research and he's currently at an Anasazi dig on the Rez."

"Where?" Rick asked.

"About twenty miles southeast of the ranch house. It's on a low bluff about a quarter mile above the old riverbed. A recently formed arroyo apparently exposed some artifacts."

"I think it's time we went to talk to him," Rick said.

"Something else... I spoke to Detective Bidtah. The professor's already been warned twice about straying off the site. Once more and he loses his permit."

"Okay, good to know. If I don't find him at the dig, we'll look around."

"I'll text you the GPS coordinates for the site," Preston added.

After Rick disconnected, he glanced at Kim and filled her in. "Let's go pay him a visit."

"Excellent idea."

En route he decided to take a shortcut, using the GPS on

his phone to zero in on the location. Turning off the graveled road, Rick headed across an area of sandstone bedrock and shallow depressions where pools formed during the rainy season—when there was one.

The next half mile was filled with jarring, gut-crunching drops as they bounded along the desert landscape.

"This washer-board road is more like a death wish than a shortcut," Kim said.

"We should be able to cut a few minutes of travel time this way and, coming in from another direction, we'll arrive without giving anyone much warning."

As they topped a rise he said, "There they are, just below us."

Below was a narrow arroyo leading to the river through a break in a sandy plateau that extended for miles. An angular section of hillside had been carved out of the side of the arroyo. It was about three feet deep and wide, with neat, squared corners. A man in tan-colored pants and jacket was crouched within the dug-out section, examining the strata with the help of a small, bright lantern.

Around him wooden stakes and posts were laid out in a pattern that defined the site, which extended in a string-outlined rectangle about the size of a large house. Wooden screens with wire mesh bottoms were being loaded into the back of a white Land Rover carry-all by two college-aged men wearing green boonie hats. Beside the first vehicle was a light green Jeep.

"When you said a 'dig,' I envisioned more than three people," Kim said. "I had in mind a camp with tents or RVs, floodlights and a dozen or so student volunteers."

"This is clearly a low-budget operation," he said. "It's getting late, too, and this isn't the kind of place you want to be once the sun sets. You could easily drive off a trail and end up stuck all night."

"Good point," she said, watching as the younger men finished loading their gear and climbed into the carry-all. The vehicle started up and then headed out along two ruts that comprised a route to the site. "Now that the students are gone, looks like we'll have the professor all to ourselves, assuming he's the guy still at the excavation."

As Rick parked beside the Jeep, the man in the arroyo looked up.

Just as soon as Kim got out of the SUV, the man smiled, recognizing her. Then he took another look at Rick, turned off the lantern and walked over to meet them.

"I'm surprised to see you out here, Kim," he said. "That's your name, right?"

"Yes, Professor McCullough. I'm glad you remembered. I'm helping investigate what happened at the Brickhouse Tavern," she said.

"I heard it was a case of arson," the professor said.

"From who?" Rick asked.

"Just here and there," he answered, then focused on Rick. "Are you the son of the medicine man known as Hosteen Silver?"

"I am," Rick answered.

"Well, talk about serendipity! I've been trying to find out what happened to the *hataalii*. All anyone would tell me is that he's gone."

"We believe he walked off into the desert to die. It's the way of our Traditionalists when their time draws near."

"I know, and I'm sorry to hear that," he said. "I was hoping to work with him. I've been trying to preserve and document Navajo healing traditions. Word of mouth is uncertain because it's subject to opinions and memory, but a written record would be there for generations to come. Would you or your brothers be willing to help me?"

"Our medicine men don't allow Sings to be recorded or

written down in their entirety. Sharing that kind of knowledge indiscriminately is believed to be dangerous."

McCullough's eyebrows knitted together. "You don't strike me as a Traditionalist."

"I'm not and neither are my brothers, but we respect our foster father's wishes on something like this."

"All right, I understand. How about this instead? His paraphernalia—the artifacts used for the Sings... No one will use them now because of the *chindi*. If I could buy them from you, or maybe you could donate—"

Rick held up his hand, interrupting McCullough. "We have no idea what he did with them. He clearly took care of those things before he left for his final walk." Rick paused, then added, "Tell me something, professor. Do you normally offer to pay people for information?"

"I did at the beginning. I thought it might speed things along, but it didn't," he admitted. "Angelina Tso, a former medicine woman, seemed more cooperative after I offered to pay for her time. She delivered a few of the Sings, but when she found out that I'd have to verify their accuracy with another healer, she refused to have anything further to do with me."

"You didn't trust her?" Kim asked.

"My reputation is on the line with every monograph or article I write, and having two or three independent sources is standard practice," he said. "I was sorry to lose her, but it was the weird stuff that happened afterward that bothered me most."

"Like what?" Kim queried.

"A few weeks later someone vandalized my car and office. I was sure it was her because I found ashes scattered everywhere—a bad omen for most Navajos—but I couldn't prove she was responsible."

"You'd had problems with Angelina but you still came to her shop looking for help? How come?" Kim was curious.

"I made sure she wasn't there before I went in. I knew she had contacts, so I wanted to talk to the clerks. I'd hoped to get the names of some high-end carvers. One of the papers I'm currently researching deals with the power of fetishes and their role in the Hopi and other Southwestern tribal cultures," he said, then checked his watch.

"All right then," Rick said, sensing this was all they'd get for now. "Thanks for your time."

"If you find anything among your foster father's possessions that might shed light on what it was like to be a *hataalii* of his stature, I'd appreciate the chance to catalog it—keeping the name of the source confidential, of course. A copy of my paper will go to the Navajo community college at Tsaile, so you'd be adding to the tribe's storehouse of knowledge."

"I don't think we can help you with that, not yet anyway," Rick said.

"You want closure first," he said, nodding.

Rick didn't reply. As was customary, he didn't say goodbye, either, he simply walked back to the SUV with Kim.

"He's right about one thing," Kim observed gently. "You and your family need closure. Once you know what really happened to your foster father, the rest will fall into place."

"Let's go back to the ranch house. I need a chance to think."

Once they were on the highway again, Rick's attention focused on something on the road ahead.

"What's going on?" she asked.

"Maybe nothing. There's a pickup coming in our direction, and he's really making time. Could be kids, a drunk or just someone in a hurry. Seat belt on?"

"Always. Better give him as much road as you can," she advised. "He's not slowing down."

As she spoke, the pickup eased toward the center line of the two-lane highway.

Rick touched the brakes again and eased to the right, hugging the shoulder. Though they'd avoided a head-on, the pickup driver tossed something out his window.

Glass shattered onto the SUV's reinforced windshield and quickly coated Rick's side with a black, flowing goo that completely blocked his view.

"Hang on!" he yelled.

Chapter Fourteen

Rick held the SUV's steering wheel steady, took his foot off the gas and looked out the side window to gauge his position on the road. He already knew the big vehicle tracked well, so if he could keep it on the highway...

"Can you see anything ahead?" he asked Kim, whose side of the windshield wasn't completely covered.

"You're doing great, drifting just a little to the right. Just hold us steady," she advised.

As they slowed to a crawl, he looked over. "How close to the shoulder am I?" he asked.

"About three feet. You can come over just a little more. Gently... That's good."

He braked and came to a full stop, flipping on the emergency blinkers to warn oncoming traffic, despite not seeing any vehicles.

"You okay?" he asked, glancing over.

"I'm fine, just a little rattled. I knew something was wrong after the way he raced up to us like that, playing chicken like in the movies. For a second I thought we were dead."

"Did you catch the plates?"

"No, he went by in a flash and I was too worried about where *we* were going," she said, her voice thick with fear and adrenaline.

"I'll call Bidtah. That's paint on the windshield. You can tell by the smell."

"Maybe he can get prints from one of the pieces of glass," she suggested. "Good thing it was a glass bottle, not a big rock...or bullets."

"We're both okay and the SUV is still in working order, so let's take it as a win," Rick said.

"Some win," she muttered.

BIDTAH AND TWO crime scene techs arrived twenty minutes later. At their insistence, Rick and Kim stayed inside the SUV as they collected evidence.

"This SUV is built like a tank," Bidtah said, coming over to them. "The impact of the paint-filled jar didn't even crack the windshield."

"Were any of the pieces of glass big enough to lift a print?" Rick asked.

"No. All we know is that the container was a twenty-ounce pickle jar—still had the label attached. But we did get a partial from the lid, which escaped being coated with paint except on the inside surface."

"If possible, can you share your findings with my brother Preston?"

"I sent him what I have and will keep him updated," Bidtah said. "One more thing. I took a close look at a sample of the paint, and there's something else mixed in there. I could see the particles. They could have been small clods, I suppose, except some were porous."

"What do you think it was?" Rick asked.

"My guess is either bits of pumice or corpse powder."

"Pumice, I know about," Kim noted. "We use it to clean the grill at the Brickhouse. But corpse *what?*"

"It's said our skinwalkers dig up the bones of the dead,

grind them into powder, then use that as a weapon," Bidtah told her.

"Ugh," she said with a grimace.

"There's something else you need to be aware of," Bidtah added, looking at Rick and then at Kim. "If people around here see you as cursed, or subject to being cursed, they'll avoid you. People will stop talking and you'll be ostracized," Bidtah pointed to his belt. "That's why my men and I carry a medicine pouch."

"I have one, too," Rick said, pulling it out of his pocket, "but I think it's time I fastened it to my belt and made it easier to see."

"Excellent idea," Bidtah said, then added before leaving, "You should consider carrying one, too, Kim."

She nodded. "Thanks."

Fortunately, the paint was water-based, so after wiping away the paint with paper towels and bottled water from their emergency kits, they'd managed to restore enough visibility to make it to a trading post and hose down the SUV.

"I've decided to push my brothers into helping me find our foster father's body," Rick said as they made their way back to Copper Canyon. "It's too late to follow a trail, but we know he left on foot, so together we can make some intelligent guesses concerning where he might have gone. Then we'll know, once and for all, if he died of natural causes or if he was murdered."

"Most of you have law-enforcement training. How come you never checked into this before?"

"We talked about it, but the truth is none of us was ready to accept his death. As long as there was no body, we could all hang on to the hope he'd turn up again someday. There was also the matter of accepting his wishes and respecting Traditionalist ways. We all believed, at first, that he had gone off to die."

"Do you think they'll help you look for his body now?"

"Yes, but it won't be easy for any of us." He glanced over at her. "Bidtah was right, though. If you're going to continue to take part in the investigation, you'll need a medicine pouch. First, we'll get you the fetish of a horse. You can carry it in the pouch with pollen, a symbol of well-being, and a crystal, which stands for the spoken prayer. Together they have the power to make your prayers come true."

"What a beautiful tradition."

"That it is."

SURPRISINGLY, ALL HIS brothers were in agreement with the plan to search for Hosteen Silver's body. Kyle had also abandoned his trip in favor of joining in. Those who could attend met at the ranch house at nine the next morning, accompanied by Detective Bidtah, who, as a tribal cop, had official law-enforcement jurisdiction.

The two newcomers joined Rick, Kyle and Kim at the kitchen table while Erin was out feeding the horses.

"Rick, searching for our foster father's remains is going to be very difficult," Preston said, taking a sip of freshly brewed coffee. "First of all, no one on the Navajo Nation is going to feel comfortable speaking of the dead. That means establishing his whereabouts on that last day is going to be nearly impossible."

"I agree with Detective Bowman. You're not going to get any cooperation. There isn't a crime to speak of, so most will see what you're doing as disrespecting the old ways and the *hataalii*'s wishes," Bidtah said. "If I were in your boots, I'd concentrate on the battles you have a chance of winning."

"We can still question possible witnesses, and we will," Preston said. "We just have to remain respectful and not be so direct."

"Kim and I will try to retrace the likely steps Hosteen Silver may have taken when he left here for the last time," Rick said. "I recall that he liked to go to the Totah Café in the mornings. It's an hour's walk from here, a short distance by Navajo standards. There's always a chance that he might have gone there the day of his final walk, just to say goodbye to the café and his life here on Mother Earth. It would have also been easier for him to catch a ride there, too, if he'd decided to go farther from Copper Canyon."

"Our dad walked off almost three years ago. The employees at that café aren't going to remember much now," Preston warned Rick.

"It's still worth a try," Rick said. "The fossil fuel industry in our state has grown these past few years, and a lot of oil and gas field workers take this highway to and from work. I've only passed the Totah a few times since returning, but there always seems to be several industry-associated vehicles parked there."

In a somber mood but with a solid plan now in mind, they set out to find answers.

Rick and Kim were the last to leave. Reaching the highway, he watched beyond the fences that paralleled the road. "There are a lot of sheep herders around here. Perhaps we can find some to talk to."

As the sun got higher in the sky, they saw an elderly Navajo woman sitting on a low hill, watching her goats and sheep.

"Let's go talk to her, if she's willing to speak with strangers. From the way she's dressed, and what she's doing, she's a Traditionalist. Do not mention skinwalkers," Rick warned.

"Got it."

They left the SUV parked on the side of the road and crossed the fence some distance from where the animals were grazing.

The woman turned to study them as they approached, her eyes narrowed, but seeing Rick, she relaxed.

"Do you know her?" Kim whispered.

"No, but she's probably heard of me," he answered. "If you hadn't noticed, there's a scar on my face."

He greeted the woman in the traditional way. "Aunt, do you have a moment?" Rick asked. "I'm the medicine man's foster son. His clan was the Salt People, and he was born for the Near the Water People," Rick added, referring to his foster father's mother's clan, then his father's.

Normally he would have mentioned his own clan and that of his father's, but those were unknown to him. Considering no one had ever claimed him, he'd never been motivated enough to find out.

"I know who you are, nephew," she said with a nod. "It was a sad thing about the *hataalii*. His medicine was strong."

"Did you ever see him walking in this direction along the highway after leaving the canyon?"

"Many times. Then one day he stopped coming."

"Does anyone else pass by on a regular basis? Maybe another Navajo on his way to work or an oil worker?"

"Not that I've noticed," she said. "I visited with your father often because he was my friend. I also warned him not to accept rides with company men on their way to or from work. The days when we could trust people so easily were gone. He never worried, though."

They spoke for a little longer, but soon it became clear she had no more information to give him.

"Thank you, aunt," Rick said. As they headed back to the SUV, he added, "Let's go check out the Totah Café."

"What's 'Totah' mean?" she asked.

"Where three rivers meet. It's a place of rest."

They made their way back slowly, careful not to spook the sheep and goats.

With Rick leading the way, they went in and out a small arroyo recently formed by runoff. Rick stopped to pick something out of the small ditch. "What a rare find! I haven't seen one of these in years."

"What is it?"

"A flint arrowhead, probably made for hunting smaller animals, like rabbits." He showed it to her. It was small, gray, with one pointed end. "Flint is sacred to the Navajo. Our creation stories say it came from the hide of monsters that preyed on our land. It has power because of its hardness and its ability to reflect light."

He admired it for another minute, then handed it to her. "Carry it with you. Flint brings protection against evil."

She studied the arrowhead, noting two small notches toward the base, probably where leather sinew was wound, attaching it to the shaft of the arrow itself. The find had meant a great deal to him, yet he was giving it to her. "What a wonderful gift. Thank you."

"We'll get you a proper *jish* soon. That's a medicine pouch," he added.

They crossed the low wire fence, then were soon on their way to the café.

She thought of the qualities she'd always envisioned her ideal mate would have. She'd promised herself to find a romantic man who'd sweep her off her feet, one who'd bring her flowers for no reason at all…someone filled with surprises.

She looked over at Rick. This morning he'd surprised her by giving her something he valued, a gift far more precious than flowers he could have picked up anywhere. Today he'd given her a memory wrapped in flint.

THE CROWD INSIDE the Totah Café was sparse at the moment. Most of the customers were Navajo or Anglo oil workers who'd taken a coffee break between shifts. "Let's ask around quietly," Rick said. "I recognize the guy over there in the far booth, so we'll start with him."

As they moved across the room, Rick saw people glance at his face then quickly look away, as they often did.

From day one, Kim had been different. She'd never pitied him, nor made him feel different in any way. Kim saw him as a man—nothing more, nothing less.

"Donnie Atcitty," Rick said, looking at the man who was wearing a tan uniform, handgun and badge on his shirt that identified him as private security. "Haven't seen you since high school. Now you're carrying a weapon and working for Sunrise Energy."

"Yeah, I'm directing company security for over sixty company wells," Donnie replied, offering them a chair. After exchanging a few pleasantries, he focused on Rick. "I heard you were back and I've been meaning to pay you a visit. You back for good?"

"Yeah, that's the plan. For now, I'm staying at the ranch house with my brother and his wife."

"I was sorry to hear about your father, Rick. He was a good man."

Rick nodded. "We're still not sure what really happened to him, so now that I'm back, we're trying to piece things together. From what I've been told, he didn't appear to be sick."

"That's Anglo thinking," Donnie said, shaking his head. "Our people know when it's time to die, and they leave so that the house will be safe for the family. The *chindi* can make problems for the living, you know that."

"Are you a Traditionalist?" Kim asked him.

"Not me, but I'm married to a Traditionalist woman. The way I see it, it's about respecting old beliefs. You can accept the way things are here on the Rez, or not, but you can't change what is."

Kim nodded slowly.

"All true, but before I can let this go, I've got to make sure he walked off on his own free will, Donnie. You get me?"

"So that's what you're thinking," Donnie said in a quiet voice. "You may have a point. The old man made enemies, *hataaliis* often do, just like doctors or preachers."

Rick nodded. "I found out it was pretty cold the day he disappeared, so he may have hitched a ride. It's not unusual for an oil worker or truck driver to stop and lend a hand to someone on foot."

"I'll pass word among the crews and my staff via the radio net. But you're talking years ago, and we've got a lot of new people."

"I'd appreciate you giving it a try, Donnie. Here's my telephone number. You can reach me anytime. If you hear from anyone who remembers giving him a ride, give them my number. Hosteen Silver wasn't the kind anyone forgets. With that long silver hair of his, he was nothing if not memorable."

Donnie smiled. "No argument there." He stood. "Gotta go back to work. I hope you find the answers you need."

After a quick lunch, they climbed into the SUV and Rick dialed Kyle and Preston. Pressing the conference call button, he told them about his conversation with Atcitty.

"By the way," he said before ending the call, "do either of you know what happened to the rest of the books that were on the bookcase when I moved out?"

"You think the code's in one of those?" Preston asked almost immediately.

"It's a possibility. That's why I've got to track them down."

"Call Gene," Preston said. "He took quite a few of Hosteen Silver's books. He also made a list of the books we donated to the high school library."

"Okay, I'll talk to him."

Rick called Gene immediately.

"I did take them, and read quite a few, but I didn't keep them here. I stored them in a metal chest at the old cabin," Gene told him, referring to the place where he and Daniel had first lived when Hosteen Silver fostered them.

"I'll go up there and take a look. Spare key still under that flat rock?" he asked.

"Didn't think you still remembered after all these years," Gene answered.

"Hey, I love that place. I spent two weeks up there alone one winter break, remember?"

"I remember you burned up all the firewood," Gene recalled, chuckling.

After ending the call, Rick glanced at Kim. "I'd like to go right now. Any objections? The cabin's an hour west of here and north into the mountains. All in all, a very rough ride."

"Let's do it."

He started to switch directions when his phone rang.

"Mr. Cloud? My name's Larry Blake. I got your number from Donnie Atcitty. I'm calling about your father."

Chapter Fifteen

Rick arranged to meet Larry Blake and a friend of his, Victor Pete, who'd also seen Hosteen Silver that last day. The site of the meeting was to be the parking lot of a well-known trading post just off Highway 64, a few miles inside the Navajo Nation. Just to play it safe, Rick had asked Bidtah to run a background check on the men. Both had come up clean.

The drive took them about twenty minutes. As they pulled off the highway into the parking lot, they saw two men standing beside a pickup parked to one side of the lot. One man, an Anglo, was leaning against the truck bed, holding a can of soda in his gloved hand. The second man, a Navajo around five foot nine with a barrel chest, sat on the lowered tailgate, smoking a cigarette.

Rick pulled up and parked. "Stay alert," he told Kim.

"You're thinking it was too easy?"

"That, and I just don't like the looks of these guys."

"Oil and gas field workers are known for being tough. It comes with the job. I've met a few hard cases myself at the Brickhouse," Kim told him.

"All the more reason to be careful," Rick responded, stepping out of the SUV.

"Rick?" The Anglo came toward him and extended his

hand. "Larry Blake. Victor and I gave your old man a ride that day. I remember because it was as cold as hell and he was just walking down the side of the road, real casual-like, his hair blowing in the wind."

A long silence stretched out, but Rick didn't interrupt. Anglos often felt uncomfortable during long pauses in the conversation and would begin talking just to fill the silence. He'd gotten his best leads that way over the years.

"From what I recall, he looked like he knew exactly what he was doing," Larry said. "When I asked him where he was headed on such a crappy day, he said he had some unfinished business. He asked us to take him as close to Big Gap as we could. That being several miles from the highway, in the middle of nowhere, I advised him to let us give him a ride home instead. It was getting stormy, and whatever business he had would wait until tomorrow, but he just shook his head."

"Where did you drop him off?"

"It was near one of the old oil wells about a mile from the highway in the Navajo Field."

"Show me."

"It's about forty-five minutes away, south of Shiprock, but Victor and I worked the graveyard shift, so we're done for the day."

"Good. I'll follow you," Rick said.

They rode east through the town of Shiprock, then south and west to an area filled with low hills and pines.

Rick followed Larry's pickup down a long, narrow, grav-eled road.

"What's bothering you?" Kim asked, no doubt picking up on his mood.

"I don't remember any oil wells this far off the high-way. That's not to say there weren't any, because drilling has picked up in the past few years. Still, we should be watchful."

The road quickly deteriorated to nothing more than a few ruts across the desert. Ahead of them, the men in the pickup were bouncing around but refused to slow down. "It doesn't look like the oil companies ever did any drilling around here, or we would have seen some capped wells," Rick said. "I'm getting a bad feeling about this."

Just as he finished speaking, the truck ahead came to a stop. There was a wide arroyo ahead, blocking their way.

"Maybe they took a wrong turn," Kim suggested. "It's been a few years."

"Let's see what they have to say," Rick answered, climbing out of the SUV. Kim followed.

"Guys, sorry, I think I'm lost," Larry said, stepping out of the pickup. "This arroyo shouldn't be here."

"It happens," Rick said, shrugging. "Want to give it another try?"

Just then Victor came around the truck. He'd put on mirrored sunglasses and now had a pistol in his hand. "Bring out your weapon slowly, with your left hand, and drop it on the ground."

Rick, knowing he'd never be able to draw his pistol in time, did as he was asked. Silently, he noted that Larry didn't appear to have a handgun, though there was a long hunting knife in a sheath clipped on his belt.

"Now step back ten feet," Victor ordered, waving the barrel of his pistol back and forth.

Larry came forward, picked up Rick's weapon and stuck it into his waistband.

"Those sunglasses. *You* were the one who pushed the kitchen wall of the Brickhouse down on us," Kim said to Victor.

"Finally put that together, did you? You two are really

hard to kill. I cut the gas line, blocked the exits, and you and the others still managed to get out without even a blister before the place went up in flames. Then I buried you under a ton of bricks and you tunneled your way out like prairie dogs," he said. "This is your third strike. Nothing personal, though. Larry and I are just the hired help. We never even met your old man."

"You plan on killing us, I get that. So why don't you tell us who's behind this?" Kim asked.

"Don't know, don't care," Victor answered. "Word got around at a cockfight up near Bloomfield that some local had enemies he wanted put down. I needed the money, so I stepped up and called the number. The voice was altered, but I said I'd do the job. An envelope was left for me at a drop site and inside was half the payment, photos and instructions. The party popper under the SUV was something special we added to the mix just to mess with you. Bet you jumped when it went off."

Rick ignored the comment. "So my foster father never came this way. It was all a con?" he asked, slowly moving away from Kim and edging closer to Victor. If he could take Victor's gun away from him, Kim could fend off Larry before he pulled his weapon. He'd seen her hand-to-hand skills.

"Once I heard the company security guy asking for help over the radio net, we made up stuff to draw you in."

"If anything happens to us, he'll know it was you," Kim pointed out.

Larry laughed. "Hey, all we have to say is you never showed up. And when nobody finds your bodies…"

Victor motioned with his pistol. "Enough talk. Walk over to the truck, slowly, hands away from your body. Don't try anything that'll get you killed before your time."

Larry reached the truck first and, bringing out two

shovels from the bed, tossed them on the ground. "Pick
them up and start digging." He pointed to the arroyo. "Find
a soft spot if you want. The hole's got to be at least four feet
deep and let's say six long."

"You want us to dig our own graves?" Kim demanded,
sounding more outraged than scared. "Forget it! Dig them
yourselves." She tossed the shovel down into the arroyo,
then stepped back.

"Go get it—now!" Victor swung his handgun around,
waving it at Kim.

Wielding the shovel like a bat, Rick connected with the
pistol. Victor screamed in pain and the weapon went flying.

Larry looked down to grab Rick's pistol, which he'd
tucked in his waistband, but Kim was already on the move.
She dived at the man, who looked up in surprise, tried to
dodge, then dropped the gun. Kim grabbed for it in mid-
air, but missed and ended up knocking it into the arroyo.

Rick swung at Victor with the shovel again, but the guy
blocked it with his arm, howling with pain. The handle
broke and the shovel slipped from Rick's grip.

Victor reached down to his boot, no doubt for a backup
pistol, but Rick, seeing the opening, attacked. With his left
hand, Rick pinned Victor's neck, swinging him around toward Larry and using the man as a shield.

Rick reached down for Victor's small handgun, slipping
off the safety with his thumb as he yanked it from the ankle
holster and raised it toward the man.

Larry had managed to grab Kim, and now had the tip
of his hunting knife next to her neck. "So what'll it be, Indian? Can you kill me before I cut her throat?" To make
his point, he pressed the point of the blade into her neck
until a drop of blood appeared.

Kim tried to lean away from the knife. "Take the shot!"

He should have done it. He was an excellent marksman. Yet the risk to Kim made it impossible for him to shoot. "I'm not letting your pal loose, or allowing you to walk away, either, Larry. Think hard, because you have one chance to live. If anything happens to her, you're next."

Kim suddenly went limp, collapsing out of Larry's grasp. As Larry tried to grab her, Rick squeezed the trigger. Larry fell to his knees, then onto his back, a bullet hole in the center of his forehead.

Victor elbowed Rick in the gut, twisting around and reaching desperately for the pistol. As the weapon fell to the ground, Rick knocked Victor back with a stiff arm to the chest.

Rick turned for a brief second, trying to catch sight of the pistol, and then realized Victor had picked up Larry's knife.

This was one fight Rick had hoped to avoid. He wanted to take this guy in alive.

Victor slashed at him with the big blade, but Rick feinted left and dodged right, keeping his arms up to block any jab or sweeping motion.

Out of the corner of his eye, Rick saw Kim pick up the pistol. Before she could fire, Victor rushed Rick, jabbing the blade toward his gut.

Rick sidestepped, slipping outside the motion, and grabbed Victor's extended knife hand at the wrist and twisted. The man screamed in pain as bones cracked.

Rick kicked the man in the gut, then pushed him to the ground, overpowering him with a choke hold that quickly rendered Victor unconscious.

Rick rolled Victor so he was facedown and put his knee on the man's back. He looked over at Kim, who was now aiming the pistol at Victor.

"Find something to tie this guy up," he said, never easing his hold.

She looked into the back of the pickup and brought him a jumper cable. "No rope, but this should do."

After Victor was secured, Rick stood and quickly looked her over. "Are you okay?" Seeing the spot of blood on her neck, his gut tightened.

"I'm fine. It's just a scratch," she said, dabbing at the puncture wound with her hand. "It's already stopped bleeding."

Rick called Bidtah next and quickly filled him in, giving him directions and GPS coordinates. As soon as he ended the call, he looked back at her. "We're going to wait here for the tribal cops. Do you need to sit?"

She pulled down the pickup's tailgate and took a seat. "For a moment or two I thought that was it for both of us. Why didn't you take the shot?"

"I didn't have a clear line of fire," he said.

"Yet you were able to hit the exact spot you were aiming at while he was moving. When he had the knife at my throat, he was basically still, a much easier shot," she said.

"I couldn't risk hurting you," he said, grasping her shoulders and looking squarely at her. "Do you understand what I'm saying?"

She shook her head. "Talk to me. Help me understand you," she said, her voice unsteady for the first time.

"I care for you, Kim, more than I should. I'll do whatever I can to protect you, but you should run away from me. Go as far and as fast as you can. The man you see before you—that's only half the picture."

Before she could respond, they heard sirens coming up the road from the highway. He moved away from her. "That'll be Detective Bidtah and the Crime Scene Unit. They'll have a lot of questions, so get ready."

BIDTAH AND RICK stood aside, watching the Navajo M.E. and the other crime scene specialists work with the body.

"This is one of the cleanest shootings I've ever seen. One head shot, small caliber, instantly fatal. That's some marksmanship," Bidtah said.

"A necessary skill in my last occupation," Rick answered.

"We've got the deceased's address and we'll check out his place. I'll let you know what we find. We'll also be questioning Victor Pete at length. Preston will be present when we do," Bidtah added.

"Good."

Bidtah looked over at Kim, who joined them after having her small puncture wound photographed for the record. It had already stopped bleeding.

"If you're through with us here, I can take her to Copper Canyon and clean off her wound," Rick said.

"Go. I know where to find you," Bidtah answered.

As they walked back to the SUV, Rick caught a flicker of light coming from just beyond the highway. He hurried with her to the vehicle.

"What's going on?" she asked as they got under way.

"Someone's watching from that stand of cottonwoods we passed on the way in," Rick said. "It might just be a curious passerby who saw the tribal police and decided to take photos to post on the internet."

"Or not. You going to tell Bidtah?"

"Yeah, but I also intend to check things out for myself." He slowed, brought out his cell phone and called Bidtah.

Several seconds later Rick ended the call and looked over at Kim. "He's sending one of his officers." He brought out his pistol and placed it on the seat between them. "You up to this again, so soon?"

"You bet. Let's go."

He smiled. He loved her spirit.

Chapter Sixteen

They drove past the grove of trees and parked out of sight around a curve in the road. On foot, they advanced quietly, circling around from the opposite side of the stand of cottonwoods. Rick finally stopped about fifty yards from where he'd seen the flicker of light. Using the binoculars he'd pulled from the glove compartment, he searched the low, marshy area carefully. "No one's there now, but I'd like to take a look around anyway."

They walked up a small wash that drained the marshy spot—Rick was alert every step of the way—but there was very little ground cover. Soon he caught a flicker of motion to his left.

"Officer Sells," the man said, immediately identifying himself and stepping out from where he'd been crouching beside a juniper. "I swept the area coming in from the west at the other end of this wash. Subject's gone. Wanna take a look?"

Rick followed Sells to the location and saw a small medicine bag lying on the ground. It was made of the skins of horned toads. "That's a witch bag," he explained to Kim. "It's the opposite of a medicine bag." He paused, gathering his thoughts. "The flicker of light, whether it came from a mirror, rifle scope or binoculars, was no accident. Someone wanted us to find this. It's a way of saying they're not through yet."

Officer Sells radioed Bidtah, explaining that they'd found no shoe or boot prints, just faint moccasin impressions.

"Someone sure hates you," Sells told Rick after ending the transmission.

"Yeah, but they don't know me very well. If anything, this just makes me more determined to find them."

Sells nodded, then began the walk back to the crime scene.

ONCE INSIDE THE SUV, Rick gazed at her for a long moment. "If you're in this for the duration, so be it, Kim, but you'll need to carry the right weapons."

"I qualified with several infantry weapons in the army, including handguns," she said.

"Not those kinds of weapons."

"You're referring to traditional Navajo protection, like fetishes and medicine bags, aren't you?" she asked.

"Yes. It'll show respect for our culture and traditions, which means people on the Rez will be more likely to trust you. It'll be late by the time we get there, but Pablo Ortiz lives at the rear of his store. He'll welcome us even if it's after hours for him."

"Mr. Ortiz of Southwest Treasures?"

He smiled as they drove east toward Hartley. "You know him?"

"Only by name."

They pulled into the rear parking lot of Southwest Treasures instead of parking at the curb.

As Rick got down from the SUV, Pablo Ortiz, a short, rotund Zuni tribesman with gray hair and a wide smile, came out to greet them.

"Welcome, Rick! You picked a great time to visit. After hours is always best. No interruptions."

After Rick introduced Kim to Pablo, they went inside and Pablo led them up the stairs into a tiny kitchen.

"My friend needs a *jish* and a special fetish. She's helping me on a case," Rick said.

"Then come with me into my work area." He took them into the small living room. At the center of the room beneath a bright overhead light was a sofa, a leather recliner and a metal tray with various grinding and polishing tools.

Following her line of sight, Ortiz smiled. "My special pieces are finished there, but the initial work requires a more secure surface." He pointed to a bigger wood table on the north side of the room. Above it was a shelf containing handsaws, mallets, chisels and stone rasps and files of all sizes.

"I have three finished fetishes. I don't know who they'll go to yet, but the spirit inside the stone will know its owner."

Kim walked over to the larger table. "Is it okay for me to take a closer look?"

"Go ahead," Ortiz said.

"We were looking for a—" Rick started but grew silent when Ortiz held up his hand.

The first fetish was a small bear made of jet. The second was a beautiful blue-turquoise lizard. The third was a horse made of alabaster, with a turquoise heart line etched from its mouth to its heart. Feathers adored its back.

"This one is gorgeous," she said.

Ortiz smiled at Rick, then glanced back at her. "Horse chooses you, as you've chosen it," he said.

"What do the feathers stand for?" she asked.

"They are an offering to the spirit of the fetish and increase its power. Feathers, blue ones in particular, are powerful medicine."

Ortiz looked at her for a moment. "What led you to choose Horse?"

She told him about Hosteen Silver's note, adding, "This one reminded me of fearlessness and freedom." She looked at the small figure in her palm.

Ortiz smiled. "Good. The match is complete."

"Thank you, uncle," Rick said. "We'll also need a *jish,* one with protective qualities."

His uncle walked across the room and picked up a small leather bag from a collection of five. "This has pollen, a crystal and a sprig from a powerful good luck plant. It's perfect for Horse and you," he said, handing it to Kim.

She carefully placed the small fetish in her pouch and, following Ortiz's directions, sprinkled it with pollen. Then after asking permission, she added the flint arrowhead to its contents.

Rick paid the customary amount and Pablo Ortiz thanked him. "Be careful, both of you. Something tells me you've yet to face your worst enemy."

"Thank you for the warning, uncle. We'll remember," he said.

As they left, heading back to the Rez, Kim felt different somehow. "Thank you for this," she said, her hand on the small pouch now attached to her belt. "It was pretty amazing how your foster father mentioned Horse, and the right one was here waiting for me."

"Pablo's got an instinct for things of this nature. I was the hardest to read of all my brothers. Even Hosteen Silver was unsure which fetish would be right for me, so he brought me here. We stayed for several hours, shared a meal and just talked. Pablo wanted to know what my plans for the future were."

"How old were you?"

"Sixteen, but even back then I knew what I wanted. I told

him I needed to lead a life with a clear purpose. One where I'd be challenged and each day was different from the last. My goal, even back then, was to join a federal agency and do undercover work."

"So you became someone else for a while and brought some bad people to justice. Yet the act of surviving isn't the same as living life, either."

He looked at her for a moment and then focused his eyes on the highway. The SUV's headlight beams were quickly swallowed up by the yawning black void ahead. The only other lights were stars in the dry desert sky.

"Rick, no warrior wears his armament all the time."

She wanted to reach him, to connect. She understood why he'd closed himself off, yet she knew he'd never find happiness until he learned how to lower his guard and let people in.

Silence ensued but she didn't press him. Looking around into the darkness surrounding the SUV made her feel claustrophobic. "I've lost track of where we are and where we're going," she said at last.

"My foster father's old cabin. I have a feeling that the code I need is inside one of the books Gene is storing up there."

"Tell me more about the cabin," she said. "What can I expect?"

"Daniel and Gene lived there with Hosteen Silver the first year they came to stay with him. It's small, just two rooms, and when they arrived there was no running water. They had to carry containers uphill from a well that was near a spring on the property."

"Even a few gallons of water are heavy. That would have been a tough workout."

"Yeah it was, but Hosteen Silver saw it as a way of making the guys too tired to stir up trouble. They were both pretty wild back then, so he'd decided to challenge them and teach them to work together."

"Did you have heat?" she asked. "A woodstove or anything?"

"There's a woodstove for cooking and a well-designed fireplace. The temperature tonight will go down into the low forties, so I'll make a fire as soon as we get there and warm us up. Since Daniel uses the cabin when he goes hunting, we've added a generator and electricity."

"And running water?"

"Just cold, and trust me when I say *cold*."

She smiled. "We can heat some up on the stove if necessary."

Almost two hours later, Rick pulled up to a wood cabin in the middle of a small clearing a few miles inside the pine forest.

It took a few minutes to find the key, but they were soon inside the solid-looking log structure with its corrugated metal roof.

Kim looked around. It was small, yet despite the frigid temperature in the room, had the comfy feel of an oasis, a touch of civilization in the middle of the wilderness. It was furnished simply, just a couch and one easy chair, but the beautiful, cream-colored sheepskin rug by the fire caught her eye. It looked incredibly soft and fit the cabin's rustic atmosphere.

"I'm going to build a fire," Rick announced. "My brother stacks the wood next to the generator shed, so I'll turn the electricity on while I'm out there."

As he left, she kept her gloves and coat on to ward off the chill, and looked around. There were no photos on the walls, but on the desk near the corner there was a framed photo of Holly, Daniel's wife, holding a baby.

After Rick came back in, she watched him start the

fire, using wadded-up newspapers to get the kindling lit in a hurry. Rick moved with purpose and confidence, the quintessential man.

Once the fire was going, he glanced up at her. "You're freezing, aren't you?" he asked, standing to full height again.

She'd wrapped her arms around herself tightly; her gloves were still on. "Guilty," she said with a tiny smile. "My heavy coat is still at my apartment."

He came over and, opening his own jacket, pulled her against him.

The gesture had been completely unexpected and took her by surprise. Nestled against him and his warmth, she felt protected, secure. She loved feeling his heartbeat against her. He was strong and steadfast, and she melted against his rock-solid chest.

He tilted her chin up and kissed her tenderly. "You're safe with me—always."

His heat was intoxicating. "I just wish…"

"What? You can tell me anything, you know that, don't you?

"You've told me before that I don't see the real you, Rick, but how can I, when you won't let me in? You want me to trust you, to lose myself in your arms. I want that, too, but you've put up a wall between us," she whispered. "Let go. Trust me, just as I trust you."

He didn't ease his hold. He kept her pressed against him. "I learned to protect myself by keeping everyone at bay. It was the only way I knew to keep life from kicking me in the gut. As time went by I guess those instincts became part of who I am."

"It's a good enough way to live if you plan on spending your life alone, but most of us want more than that."

"I wanted no part of love. At best it's an illusion, a fantasy that quickly fades. At its worst, it's a tool used to manipulate people you care about."

"But you're close to your brothers. You love them."

"What binds us are loyalty, integrity and honor. Those attitudes—commitments—are more reliable than romantic love."

"For those to remain strong, they have to be rooted in love," she murmured, her face nestled against his neck.

"I have feelings for you, Kim, the kind you can always count on. I'll be there for you no matter what," he said, easing his hold and brushing his palm against the side of her face.

"But you're still fighting this. Why?"

"Because of what I see in your eyes when you look at me."

"I don't understand."

"You see who you want me to be, not who I really am."

"What I see is the man who protected me, who shielded me with his own body. You saved my life."

"And took others," he said. "I'm not a choir boy."

"What you are is a man who'll risk everything to do what's right, one who isn't afraid of anything—except letting people get close," she said. "But for us to have more than just a snapshot in time, you have to open your heart."

He released her and stepped back. "Kim, there are things about me you don't want to hear. Once they're said, we'll never be able to go back to the way things are now."

"You care for me, but you'll never trust my feelings for you until you stop keeping me at arm's length."

Rick nodded slowly. "All right." He brushed a kiss on her forehead and moved farther away. Restless, he began to pace, his hands jammed deep into the pockets of his leather jacket. "I thought I was perfect for undercover work—cold, focused and able to think on the fly, but there was more to the job. White hats versus black hats are a myth. There are many shades of gray. The longer you're in, the more you understand bad guys are seldom totally evil."

He ran a hand through his close-cropped hair, struggling to find the right words. "When you begin to see parts of yourself in the people you're there to bring down, you start to question what you're doing. That's when things begin to unravel."

"So why didn't you ask to be pulled out?"

"It had taken me more than a year to infiltrate that human trafficking cartel, and my work was finally providing valuable intel—names, places and events. I was real close to shutting down the entire operation," he said, staring into the fire.

Minutes passed, but she didn't interrupt. Some things couldn't be forced.

"Then the head of the cartel ordered me to kill a man—his competitor, another trafficker. I would have been doing the world a favor, but I wasn't there to do the cartel's dirty work."

He shook his head and rubbed the back of his neck. "I made the decision to let fate handle the outcome. I arranged a meet, knowing he'd try to kill me and that only one of us would walk away. Self-defense was something I could live with."

Another silence ensued before he continued. "We met in a church parking lot, which turned out to be an ambush. I was set up. A wedding was going on inside, so he'd planned to use a knife instead of a gun. It was a brutal fight. The man was strong and fast—a former soldier. My training was better, though. Soon I had him pinned against the side of a car. I was about to finish him off when he looked directly at me—helpless."

Rick turned away from her to lean against the brick fireplace and stare out the window.

She came over to him and placed her arm around his waist.

He turned and held on to her. "It wasn't until I saw myself reflected in that man's eyes that I realized what I'd become. I'd wanted to kill him and had been looking for justification. I pulled back, intending to let him go, but he grabbed his fallen knife and took the swipe that gave me this scar. Then he moved in for the kill. In the end, I survived, he didn't."

"You did what you had to do," she said. "You gave him a chance. Your humanity came through."

"And it nearly cost me my life. As I walked to my car, half-blinded by the blood, his bodyguard stepped out of hiding and shot me three times. A few seconds later, a local cop took him down.

"Later, in the hospital between surgeries, I had plenty of time to think about what I wanted to do next. I decided to come home and reconnect with myself. Figuring once I was back on my turf, I'd be able to find a new purpose for myself, a reason to get up in the morning."

"And the mystery behind your father's disappearance has given you that?"

"No, *you* did," he said. Tilting her chin up, he kissed her slowly and tenderly.

When Rick released her, a small tremor ran up her spine. "You've gone through hell, Rick, but you're a man of honor and compassion. You're everything I thought you were—and more."

He kissed her hard then, forcing her lips to part for him as he drank her in.

FIRE COURSED THROUGH HER. She'd met men over the years who'd attracted her, but she'd never felt this overwhelming need to give her love without demands or conditions. Maybe real love didn't need a reason, just the freedom to exist.

Though Rick hadn't said he loved her, it didn't seem to matter now. She pushed his jacket back and opened his shirt, wanting to feel his muscled chest. As she looked up at him, she saw the dark fire in his eyes. He was holding back, keeping a tight rein on himself. His jaw was clenched, and as she left a moist trail down his chest, he sucked in his breath.

There were two scars on his chest, both up high, by his collarbone. Below, over his heart, was a Navajo word: *Chaha'oh.* She ran her fingertips over it. "What's it mean?"

"Shadow. That's what many claimed I was like when I hunted man or beast."

She kissed his scars one by one and felt him shudder. When she moved to unbuckle his belt, he placed his hand over hers. "It's not too late to change your mind, but it will be in another second or two."

"Rick, I'm not afraid of you. Open your heart to me. Let me show you that love doesn't have to hurt."

She undid his belt and caressed him.

"Slow down," he whispered, pulling her hands up and placing them on his chest. He slipped off her jacket, then tugged at her sweater and pants until she stood naked by the fire. Lifting her into his arms, he lowered her onto the sheepskin rug.

In the flickering firelight, a world of light and shadows, they came together. Heat became a living force. The roughness of his touch drove her wild. This was love—and their destiny.

She knew Rick struggled to maintain control for as long as he could. Yet the fire coursing through him seemed to increase with each second. With a groan, he surrendered and completed what was meant to be.

Even after their breathing evened, Kim held on to him, refusing to let him move away. "For now, you're mine and I'm yours. Don't go."

"I'm here."

Chapter Seventeen

Time passed and the air in the room began to grow cold.

"The fire's almost out," Rick said, moving away from Kim's arms and getting dressed. "Too bad it's not summer. I would have loved seeing you walk around naked."

"You're not so bad yourself," she said, her gaze taking him in slowly.

He laughed. "Scarred and worn, but not too bad?"

"I've got no complaints," she said, reaching for her clothes.

He gave her a hand up. "We'll warm up sooner if we get to work. Let's find the books and take them out to the SUV. I'm not leaving them here. This place doesn't have the electronic protection the ranch does," he said. "More importantly, we don't know who else knows of this place besides family."

"Did your brother tell you where he put the books?"

"No, just that they're in a metal trunk. I don't see them here, and they weren't in with the generator, so I'm sure they're in the bedroom," he said, gesturing with his head toward the door.

"I can't remember ever being this cold," she said, wrapping the sides of her jacket tightly around herself.

"I do, but it was a long time ago," he admitted. "Once I get the fire going again, it'll heat up fast. Don't worry, I can build a fire in the stove, as well. Daniel's a wuss about cold, so he sold the old potbellied stove and added this beauty." He pointed toward the steel stove with its two big doors, the right one with a glass window. "No gas, no electricity, just firewood in the left side."

"Daniel doesn't seem like a wuss to me," she said, laughing.

"Well, he is. Just don't tell him I said so. He's the one who paid for the upgrades."

A short while later they'd pulled two large boxes from a big trunk in the bedroom. They were clearly labeled Books and marked with the date they'd been packed. "That's Gene. He's organized about everything," Rick said.

They carried the boxes into the main room and placed them on the heavy pine table. "I want to sort through these before we load them into the SUV. I'm not taking back any passengers, like mice, to my brother's house."

"Yeah, I saw the chewed corner," Kim said. "He must have kept the boxes outside the trunk at one time."

Rick opened the flaps of the first box and reached for a fat, clearly water-damaged paperback that had long lost its cover. "I remember this one. It's signed by one of the Navajo Code Talkers, a man Hosteen Silver greatly admired. Kyle was reading it one summer and accidentally dropped it into the horse tank. I helped Hosteen Silver dry it out, but it looked ruined to me. Since he'd read it a million times, I assumed he'd chucked it," he said, leafing through the loose, brittle pages until he found something of interest. "There's a torn page from another book stuck in here at the halfway point. It's from a book about Richard Sorge, from what I can tell."

"Who's Richard Sorge?" Kim said.

"Don't know. Once we have internet access, we can do

a search. If the code I found in the notebook is based on a book about, or by, Sorge, maybe we're on to something."

She helped him return the books to the box before they opened the other one. "You want to go directly to Daniel's place instead of to the ranch house? Paul and Daniel seem to know more about codes than Kyle."

"Yeah, let's go to Daniel's. I have a feeling we're close to answering some important questions."

He doused the fire and they locked up the cabin, loading the boxes into the SUV.

Rick took it slow as they went down the narrow road, which was basically a bumpy trail cut into the hillside by vehicle use, not road equipment. After a quarter of a mile, needing to slow before crossing a dip in the road, he touched the brake.

"The brakes feel spongy," he said in a taut voice, his hands clenching the wheel. "Not good."

The SUV bounced hard as they crossed the shallow trench. Kim grabbed the armrest and adjusted her seat belt.

"We've lost our brakes," Rick said. He pulled the handbrake and it grabbed, slowing them a little. "Hold on," he said, turning the wheel slightly to the right and trying to skid to a stop as he reapplied the handbrake.

The SUV rocked to the left and the right rear tire rose off the ground. When he swerved left, the wheel touched down again. Even though they bounced heavily, the road was steep and they picked up speed once more.

He glanced over at her. Kim had pressed her back against the seat, her eyes wide with fear as she hung on to the armrest.

Ahead was the steepest part of the trail, a sharp curve and a fifty foot drop to the left. At the speed they were going, Rick knew he wouldn't be able to hold the turn. They'd fly right over the edge.

For a second he thought a forced roll would be safer—they were buckled in and the air bags would help. Then he remembered the brush ahead. There was still a chance...

"Hang on, this is going to get rough," he yelled, veering off the road to the right and ramming into a scrub oak thicket about three feet high. The soft impact knocked him into the steering wheel, enough to cost him a breath, but not enough to trigger the air bag.

Rick hung on to the wheel, whipping it back and forth, fishtailing as they rammed their way through the thicket, racing up slope. There was a loud, jarring thump somewhere underneath them and Kim bounced into the air, bumping her head on the roof.

Their speed dropped and the rear wheels grabbed on to something. As the SUV slid to a stop, dust enveloped them in a cloud.

Rick reached down and turned off the ignition. The engine rattled for a few seconds. The front end vibrated. Then suddenly it was dead quiet.

After a second Rick's ears stopped ringing and he looked over at Kim.

She smiled weakly. "Are we there yet?"

"Take it as a win. This may be as far as we can go, but at least we're in one piece." He looked around carefully before glancing back at her. "Stay in the vehicle for now. I'm going to take a look underneath to see if I can figure out what happened."

"No, I'm going with you. I can hold the flashlight while you check the brakes. I can also keep an eye out for anyone who might be lurking about. This may not have been an accident," she said, climbing out her side.

Rick crawled beneath the SUV and studied the damage. "From the smell of brake fluid and the crimp in the line, which is now dangling loose, you're right. This was done on purpose." When he came back out and stood, his jaw was set. "I let my guard down, Kim, and brought this on. I'm sorry."

"I don't understand. How is this—" She stopped abruptly. "You mean because we made love?"

"I was on the job. I should know better than to get so distracted."

"First, you don't know exactly when the person sabotaged that brake line except that it was after we arrived. We may have been searching for the books at the time, or maybe it was done right after we arrived and you were busy building a fire," she protested.

"More importantly," she added softly, "I wouldn't trade a second of what happened between us." She held his gaze. "It drew us closer, and if you allow it, it'll make us even stronger."

He smiled. "You look like an angel, but you've got a core of steel, Kim."

"Most women do," she answered.

He studied the area around him, taking everything in slowly and thoroughly. "Escape and evasion. I'm trained for this. Let's get moving, in case whoever did this stuck around to watch. There's a tool bag in the back. Let's empty it out and put the books inside. I'll carry it while you take the binoculars in the glove compartment. They're infrared."

"Okay."

"It's a half-hour hike to the main road. Once we're there I'll be able to get a cell phone signal. I'll call Daniel and let my brothers know what happened. Preston will be able to get the tribal police moving on this. There's no second set of tracks on the road, so the guy must have approached on foot. His vehicle is probably parked in the vicinity."

Rather than stick to the trail, they moved directly downhill, sticking to cover whenever possible to avoid being spotted. Rick scarcely made a sound even through the rough terrain, but Kim knew she was probably alerting wild animals for miles.

"Do you think the person's still out there? They haven't done anything directly, like shoot at us," she noted. "Not yet anyway," she added, looking over her shoulder.

"My gut tells me our enemy is around here somewhere. There's no way for him to have predicted how effective tampering with the brakes would be. Once he sees we've walked away unhurt, he'll probably try something else."

DANIEL PICKED THEM UP at the highway and before long they were inside Daniel's office in the computer room, all holding freshly brewed hot coffee. Preston had just arrived and Paul was already behind the computer.

"Let me look up Richard Sorge for you. Then we can go from there," Paul said, typing in the name.

He then looked up at them. "He ran a Soviet spy ring in Japan before and during World War II. They used OTPs—one time pads—that required both sender and recipient to have the identical page to decipher the message. Although it was more secure than what the code talkers used, it was also a lot more time-consuming to decode," he said. "Do you still have the photos of the code you found in the notebook Hosteen Silver left for you?"

"Yes, I do." Rick handed Paul his cell phone and Paul transferred the images to the central screen.

"They're sequences of numbers separated by commas," Daniel said. "But it isn't a simple grade-school code, where the number one equals *a,* two equals *b* and so forth. We've already checked some of those patterns."

"A common substitute for those OTPs is one that requires both sender and receiver to have identical editions of the same book—a popular novel, reference book, even a dictionary. If we can find the book our father used to create the code, we can figure out the message," Paul concluded.

Rick studied the well-worn paperback in his hands. Although they'd looked for a book about Sorge, it hadn't been in either box. "I think he mentioned Sorge to tell us he was using a variation of the old-style OTP code," Rick said. "Let's check the books, starting with his favorite, and see what we get."

"Go from the premise that the first number corresponds to the page, the second is the line number, the third is the word and the fourth is the letter in the word," Paul said.

Rick checked the old paperback and followed the sequence. "First letter is an *s*." A few minutes later Rick looked up and smiled. "First word is *she*. Second is *fed*. Third word is *it*."

"That can't be a coincidence," Kim said, looking from brother to brother. "*She fed it* is not random. And the only woman who's a suspect in all this is Angelina Curley."

Rick nodded and continued matching numbers with letters, writing them down. "The next word is *to*. Last word…" He paused. "There's water damage on this page, but I think the last word is *me*."

"*She fed it to me.*" Kim looked around the room. "What did Angelina feed your father?"

"This was in a notebook with information about the Plant People, so I think Hosteen Silver was trying to tell us he was poisoned," Rick said.

"He hid that notebook in a place only you would find," Kim said. "I think it's safe to assume he was concerned his enemy, probably Angelina, would sweep the ranch house to make sure no evidence of what she'd done was left behind."

"What I don't get is why he didn't call you, Preston, or the tribal police, and identify Angelina," Daniel interjected. "Or just name his killer outright."

"Maybe he wasn't one hundred percent sure, and didn't want to make what was essentially a death-bed statement, naming the wrong killer," Kim suggested.

"He may also have known help wouldn't arrive in time, or that nothing could be done, so he used his remaining energy to do what he felt was honorable—die as far away from his home as possible," Paul said.

"Or maybe he thought he might be able to reach Angelina in time and she'd have the plants necessary for an antidote," Daniel said. "But, as Kim suggested, that doesn't necessarily make her guilty. She might have simply shared his love for the Plant People."

"But Angelina doesn't live anywhere near Copper Canyon," Kim pointed out.

"This all happened before she married," Paul responded. "Let's see where she lived before then. Hang on." Paul typed something into his computer and a minute later looked up. "According to MVD records, Angelina lived just three miles from Copper Canyon. It's possible that since his truck wouldn't start, our foster father set out on foot to her house but never made it."

"Great theory, but without a body, we still have zero," Preston conceded. "We can't prove how he died or even that he *is* dead."

"There's something that still doesn't make sense to me," Kim said. "Why would Angelina try to kill Rick after all this time? Even if she did kill Hosteen Silver, she'd already gotten away with murder. No body, no witnesses, no real evidence except the coded message—and that doesn't identify her, not really."

There was a long silence as everyone considered the possibilities.

"She may have been afraid that once Rick was back, he'd somehow be able to tie the poisoning to her," Preston said. "Rick was the only one of us who could think like Hosteen Silver. That's scarcely a secret."

"Makes sense, but finding the body is totally up to us now," Daniel said. "We need to hike away from the ranch house to the location of Angelina's former home. We should take the most likely direct routes, and search along those trails. If he didn't make it to her place, his body has to be around there somewhere."

Paul used his computer to locate an aerial view of the area, and showed the others what was on the monitor.

"The shortest route passes through a section with no homes or signs of habitation. Just nature and wild animals," Preston observed, not needing to explain the gruesome possibilities. "His body may be long gone by now."

"We still have to do this, and we can't depend on help from anyone else," Paul said. "No Navajo would go searching for a body under these circumstances, at least no Traditionalist."

"Let's get a few hours of sleep, then start first thing in the morning," Rick said, stifling a yawn. "Kim, we'd all understand if you want to sit this one out."

"Give me a good strong cup of coffee and I'll be ready when you guys are," she answered.

Rick's phone rang. "It's two in the morning. This can't be good."

Chapter Eighteen

Rick identified himself to the caller and immediately recognized the rough voice at the other end.

"It's Ray," he said, no longer using "Mike," the name Kim had given him. "Detective Bowman let word out that he was looking for Nestor Sandoval and I've found him. He's in Hartley, lying low, but I know where he is."

"Give me the address," Rick said quickly.

"The numbers aren't there anymore, but it's the abandoned building behind the gas station on Pine. The station is closed for the night but there's a light in the alley. I saw Sandoval go in through the back. He hasn't left, so he must still be inside. He's also alone, from what I can tell."

"How do you know Sandoval?" Rick asked.

"He's the guy I bought a combat knife from—a KA-BAR. I needed a weapon to defend myself if it came to that," Ray answered.

"Can you keep an eye on the place until we get there?" Rick asked.

"I'll stay here by the pay phone and follow him if he leaves."

"Observe, but don't engage. Is that clear?" Rick said crisply.

"Copy," Ray answered, all business now, as if the soldier in him had awoken. "Avoid approaching using the street north of the station. He's placed boards with nails and broken glass all over the ground to discourage visitors."

"You know a better way in?"

"Affirmative," Ray replied. "Approach from the east and circle south around the gas station. That'll screen your approach and place you on the east side of the house. There's a vacant lot full of weeds there, and no road access, so he won't expect anyone to come from that direction. You'll have darkness on your side, as well."

"Good job, soldier," Rick said, then ending the call, filled everyone in.

"I can call for police backup," Preston said, "but going through channels will come at a cost. You all know I prefer to go by the book, but this may be our last chance to get Sandoval. I don't think we can afford to wait for SWAT and risk losing the element of surprise."

"Then let's move," Rick said.

"He won't come easily," Daniel said. "He's facing three strikes now."

"At least there's less risk to the public. That area is commercial and industrial and at this hour nobody should be around. We'll do what we have to," Preston said.

"I've seen combat, I can help," Kim said.

"No. This is an entirely different situation, and there are different rules to follow," Preston said.

"Why don't you come and watch our backs in case someone tries to sneak up behind us?" Rick asked.

"Consider it done," she answered.

PAUL WAS ASSIGNED to cover the northern approach, a likely escape route for Sandoval considering he knew where he'd placed the obstructions. Rick and Preston would approach from the east, as advised, while Daniel moved in from the southwest corner to prevent any exit south. There were no west-facing windows or doors.

They all carried radios with earplugs, remaining in constant contact as they advanced. There was a full moon, so they wouldn't be groping around in the dark, at least.

Rick reached the east wall of the single-story building first, staying low to avoid being seen from any of the building's windows. Preston was to his right, farther north along the same wall. Each was approaching a window. The plan was for one of them to enter through whichever opening offered the easiest access, while the other provided cover.

Rick noticed a heating unit on the ground close to the southernmost window and silently pointed it out to Preston. He then contacted Kim, who was back at the corner of the garage, watching both north and south with infrared binoculars provided by Daniel.

"You're all still clear," she said.

"I'm going in," he whispered into the radio before climbing onto the unit and through the window.

A minute later he was crouched low beside the open doorway of the room he'd entered, listening and watching the hall as Preston climbed in. The room was unlit, but the moon was bright, the windows large and the walls light-colored. There was no way he'd miss seeing a man-size figure. As his brother lowered himself onto the floor, his shoe landed on a chunk of glass, making it crunch loudly.

Rick turned and waved him toward the corner just as footsteps raced down the hall. Aiming a pistol into the room from out in the hall, Sandoval fired blindly, not presenting a target. Two bullets hit the wall beside the window.

Rick shifted his aim, but the shooter's pistol, which had been barely three feet from him, disappeared before he could acquire a target.

"Go," Preston ordered over the radio, signaling for Paul

and Daniel to close in. There was the sound of footsteps as Sandoval ran down the hall.

"Police! Put down your weapon and give up before you get hurt!" Preston called out. "The building's surrounded."

"I'm not going back to prison," Sandoval yelled from somewhere inside.

Rick took a quick look out to his left, seeing only a blind corner, and stepped into the hall, hugging the far wall. Weapon aimed, he looked over at Preston.

"Got your back," Preston whispered.

Rick inched down the wall to the corner, ducked low and took a quick look. Sandoval was crouched behind a stack of wood pallets, his pistol aimed right at him. Rick ducked back just in time. Two bullets came his way, one taking a chunk out of the corner.

Rick leaped across the hall and through an open doorway, firing toward the pallets as he moved. Once inside the room, he glanced around. It was empty and smelled of mold and damp wood, probably the results of a leaky roof.

From his position near the door, Rick looked back at Preston and nodded, ready to provide cover.

Preston crept to the corner where Rick had been just seconds earlier and looked up at the shot-out chunk of masonry.

"Move in carefully, guys. I'm going to draw his fire," Preston whispered over the radio. "I got a look at his weapon. It's a revolver. Two more rounds and he has to reload."

Preston stuck out his pistol and then pulled it back.

Sandoval fired once, hitting the wall.

Rick put his pistol back in its holster and looked across the way at Sandoval. He'd turned to look out a north window just as Preston fired two more shots, striking one of the pallets.

Sandoval fired back, then Rick heard a click. Sandoval was out of ammo.

Rick rushed into the room, leaped across the pallets and tackled Sandoval.

Sandoval went down, Rick on top. In a matter of seconds Preston was there, along with Daniel and Paul, both carrying bright flashlights to illuminate the scene. By then Sandoval was on his back and Rick had pinned him to the floor.

Preston cuffed him and read him his rights. "Come on. I'm taking you in."

"You know who we are?" Daniel asked Sandoval.

"Yeah, and you think I had something to do with the explosion at the restaurant," he said, looking at Rick.

"Let me guess. You're completely innocent," Rick said.

Sandoval stood as Preston held on to his arm. "No one over the age of five is completely innocent."

"Did you know what was going down or not?" Rick prompted.

"Hell, no. I had nothing to do with your old man's disappearance. I do have information to trade, if you're willing to cut me a deal."

"Let's go to the station," Preston snapped, leading him out the north side toward Main Street. "We'll talk there."

RICK WATCHED PRESTON get into his cruiser, parked at the curb one block down from the gas station, and drive off. Paul and Daniel left next.

Rick met Kim at the SUV, which had been next to Paul and Daniel's vehicle. "Have you seen Ray?" he asked.

"Not since we arrived."

"I'd like to try to find him."

"He probably didn't go far. We'll have better luck on foot," she said.

They set out together, walking down the alley on the

north side of Main Street. They'd gone halfway down the block when Ray stepped out of the shadows. "Looking for me?"

The change in him was subtle, but nonetheless there. He stood straight, his gaze steady.

"Sure am, Ray. We wanted to tell you personally how much we appreciate your help tonight."

"No prob, and thanks to you guys, too. You reminded me what it was like to have something important to do again," he said. "I got in touch with an organization that helps local vets. Now I have a place to sleep and a job. As it turned out, one of the volunteers over at Warriors in Transition is an old friend. He runs a dog-training operation at the edge of town. He and I were both handlers and loved working with the dogs," Ray said. "He's invited me to teach basic obedience classes for problem dogs."

"Congratulations," Rick said, shaking his hand.

"Me, too, Ray," Kim said softly.

As Ray walked off, Rick smiled. "The man's taking control of his life again. He'll be okay now."

"I think so, too," she said. "You made a real difference when you treated him like an equal and asked for his help."

"Everyone needs a hand at one point or another. I'm glad I was there. The road back is tough, but the first step is the hardest."

Rick walked with her to the SUV. "Let's go find out what Sandoval's holding back."

"Do you think Preston's going to offer him a deal?"

"Eventually, but first he'll want to make sure the information is worth it."

KIM WAS LOOKING through the two-way glass, listening to what was going on in the interrogation room. Preston and

Rick had gone inside and Daniel had gone home, but Paul was keeping her company.

"My brother has strong feelings for you, Kim," he said. "I've never seen him relax around anyone except us—until now. He needs you."

"I need him, too," she said quietly. "If you're worried I'll hurt him, please don't be. What we have isn't exactly Romeo and Juliet, but it is right for us."

He nodded. "Good to hear."

Looking at Sandoval, who was handcuffed to a table, they focused on what was being said inside.

"I want full immunity," Sandoval said. "Give me that and I'll steer you in the right direction."

"Do you know who cut the gas line at the Brickhouse?" Preston demanded.

Kim looked over at Paul. They already knew that answer.

"Patience," Paul whispered. "Preston is good at this."

"No, but I've got a pretty good idea who was behind it and why," Sandoval responded.

"Keep talking. We need to know that what you have is worth something," Preston said.

He shook his head. "No way. You first."

"Okay, I'll drop the charges for attempted assault on a police officer," Preston said. "Your turn."

"No weapons charge, either," Sandoval said.

Preston shrugged. "*If* what you've got leads to a conviction on an attempted murder case, I'll take this to the D.A. Otherwise, no deal."

"Maybe you should rethink that. I'm also probably the last person to have seen your foster father alive, and it wasn't under the best of circumstances. I was there to take something back, and he caught me."

As she watched, Kim saw Rick's face turn to stone. His jaw was clenched and so were his fists.

"I went to retrieve something for Angelina Tso—now Curley."

"We already know she recorded some of his Sings," Preston said.

"There was more to it than that. Angelina also went through your foster father's stuff and took photos of other things, like the list of Plant People who could harm. He caught her and demanded she erase everything, but she refused. He grabbed the cell phone but couldn't erase the images without knowing her password. He refused to give it back until the photos were erased."

"Why didn't he just take the memory card?" Preston asked.

"Maybe there wasn't one, or he didn't know how to delete the files. Anyway, Angelina hired me to steal the phone back, so I did. The old man caught me, though, and we had a...confrontation. He lost and I took the phone."

"You—" Rick dived toward him, but Preston got in the way and pushed him back. "Not now!"

Rick pulled himself together in an instant. Only the deadly set of his jaw revealed the rage inside him.

"Do you believe Angelina retaliated against Hosteen Silver after that?" Preston asked.

"Yeah. He threw her out, so she couldn't become a medicine woman. Angelina was really pissed off. She didn't think she'd done anything wrong, since she'd paid to learn from him. When you came back home," he said, looking at Rick, "she offered me a new pickup if I got rid of 'the marked man.' She said you were the only one who could connect her with his disappearance. I told her to go fix her own problems."

"You turned her down? Why should I believe that?" Preston asked.

"Taking on one of you amounts to taking on the whole damned family. I'm not afraid of jail, but I'm not stupid," Sandoval said.

"You seem to know a lot, Sandoval," Rick said. "How was my father poisoned?"

"Angelina's niece—Bonnie—likes to talk, so I can make a good guess. Before she became his apprentice, Angelina and Hosteen Silver were friends," he said. "He loved breakfast burritos, and Bonnie sold homemade ones with *naniscaadas*—handmade tortillas. Angelina would deliver some to him every morning when she came for her instruction. One time, after a rain, she got stuck driving through Copper Canyon. I understand you dug her out," he added, looking directly at Rick.

"Was she still bringing Hosteen Silver food at around the time he disappeared? *After* they'd had the falling-out?" Preston queried.

"She wasn't welcome there anymore, so no, but Angelina often helped get the orders ready and it's possible her niece continued with the deliveries to Hosteen Silver."

Rick turned to Preston. "We done here?"

"For now," Preston responded, standing.

"What about me?" Sandoval asked.

"Once we confirm your story, we'll discuss the deal," Preston responded.

They were leaving the room when Rick's cell phone vibrated, indicating a text message.

Rick looked down at the display as Preston closed the door behind them. He showed his brother the message from Detective Bidtah.

"'The substance in the black paint splashed on your windshield is bad news,'" Preston read aloud.

"There's more," Rick said as a new message appeared.

Chapter Nineteen

As soon as they were out in the hall, Rick and Preston met with Paul and Kim. "The paint thrown onto the windshield contained corpse powder, just as I suspected," Rick reported.

"There are some nasty things going on, then," Preston said. "If we want to get to the bottom of it, we're going to have to find Hosteen Silver's body and have it tested for traces of poison. Without it, proving he was murdered will be impossible."

"Let's crash at Daniel's, get some sleep and set out from the ranch house at first light. Each of us will choose a different path to Angelina's old home. We can stay in contact via satellite phone," Rick said, adding, "We'll want Gene on this, too, so we need to get him down here ASAP. That means calling him tonight."

"What about Detective Bidtah?" Paul asked.

"This kind of search isn't tribal police business, not unless we find a body," Preston said. "If we can prove there was a murder, then he has reason to open an investigation."

"It would also be best not to tell anyone outside the family what we're doing," Preston advised. "It'll upset members of our tribe. They'll see what we're doing as dangerous."

"Maybe it is," Rick admitted, "but it's the only shot we've got left."

Kim woke up suddenly to the blast of a coach's whistle. Paul, on the floor a few feet away, sat bolt upright.

"What the—?" Paul growled.

Daniel grinned, holding up the silver sports whistle. "We needed to wake up ready to go, and I thought this would help."

"The aroma of coffee would have been nicer," Kim muttered. She'd insisted on sleeping in one of the sleeping bags just like the others. The only way to be treated as an equal was never to ask for preferential treatment.

She reluctantly scrambled out of the warm bag, then quickly rolled it up and stowed it out of the way, memories of her days in the military flooding back to her.

"We'll have a light breakfast and get under way. Take some of the protein bars and water bottles in the kitchen and put them in your backpacks, too."

Rick stood. "One last thing. We all have to wear our medicine bags where they can be easily seen. If we need help or if another Navajo sees or guesses what we're doing, we don't want to be mistaken for skinwalkers."

"Good thought," Paul said.

After breakfast, they set out in separate vehicles. Preston rode in his private SUV in case he had to return to Hartley unexpectedly on police business. Daniel and Paul were together in one of their company SUVs.

Once they reached the entrance to Copper Canyon, Daniel would be taking a foot trail toward the site of Angelina's mobile home, joining up with Kyle, who'd meet him on the way. Paul would circle the outside walls of the canyon, looking for undiscovered trails that might have been a possible route if their father had actually continued out of the canyon. Later, he'd join Daniel and Kyle on the other side near the highway.

Gene had decided to take his pickup and drive outside

the canyon along the highway, searching for foot trails crossing the main road. Later, he'd join Erin at the ranch house, where they'd act as a control center, coordinating the search and passing along information to the others.

Rick and Kim were to hike to the spot in the canyon where he'd found the notebook, then pass through the secret passage behind the house that led through the cliff walls to the highway. From there, they'd take the quickest route to Angelina's old residence, based on the trails Gene or one of the others discovered.

It was ninety minutes into the plan when Rick and Kim stood beside the highway just west of the hidden passage. Rick consulted a topographic map that Daniel had provided to each of them. "Our trail will take us through that dry canyon I always avoided as a kid," he said as they crossed the highway. They soon entered a wide, shallow arroyo that extended for miles in a sinuous path. "It's that one, on your left," he added, pointing. "This wash narrows up there, and passes right through the gap."

"What bothered you about that place?" she asked, working to keep up with him in the soft ground. The trek, which would require them to walk uphill for at least three miles, was going to be harder than she'd expected.

"This becomes a narrow passage up there between two sandstone cliffs, and the shadowed side is full of caves dug into some of the softer layers of rock. I used to imagine mountain lions or coyotes hiding up there, waiting to pounce."

"A boy's imagination at work," she said with a smile.

"One day I decided to face my fears, so I went up there with a flashlight and a pointed stick—my spear. It was near dusk, and I discovered that some of the shallow caves were habitats for bats. They all came flying out when I stepped inside with my flashlight. I've never been back since."

"They don't come out during this time of day, right?" she asked, not eager to face a dark cloud of bats.

"No, but because this is the quickest route to Angelina's old home, it's probably the path Hosteen Silver took. If I'm right about that, and he found he couldn't make it all the way, he may have sought shelter, hoping to gather his strength. There are some bigger caves up there."

"Makes sense."

They approached a narrow pass flanked by steep hillsides, climbed out of the arroyo, which had narrowed and deepened, then walked along the steep slopes above the dry channel.

"Are those the caves you were talking about?" she asked, pointing up their side of the canyon. "They don't seem so high off the ground."

"You're right. I guess my perspective has changed over the years." He gazed at the caves, lost in thought. "If he was getting weak and the weather was turning bad, my gut tells me he'd have chosen the closest one large enough for a man to crawl into." Rick reached down and touched his medicine pouch. "I'm going in."

"Rick, let me check. This will be easier on me if we find a body. I'm also a lot smaller than you. Hand me the flashlight and I'll take a look."

"No, I have to be there. We can do it together, though," he said, offering his hand. "Let's climb."

The cliff face was by no means vertical, sloping only about forty five degrees, and they didn't need any special gear because of the many handholds and footholds available.

They reached the opening of the shallow cave several minutes later. On their knees at the entrance, he held out his arm, holding her back. "Let's make sure there are no animals inside first."

He brought out his flashlight. "No bats, but there's a stationary figure deep in the shadows."

"I see something back there, too," she whispered.

Angling the flashlight as he leaned forward, resting on his elbows, he finally managed to illuminate the prone shape. He moved the beam around for a few seconds before turning it off.

"Is that him?" Kim asked softly.

"Yes, the heat and the desert appear to have mummified his remains, but that long silver hair and the custom belt buckle tell me all I need to know." His voice was taut.

"He's on his back, like he went to sleep. Would you like me to go over and check for a wallet or something else?" she asked, placing a gentle hand on his arm.

"No. I'll radio my brothers once we're back outside. Once they arrive we'll photograph everything, check the cave for evidence, then put the body in a bag. If the tribe approves, we'll take it to the office of the regional medical investigator in Hartley. Forensic people can check it out. If he was poisoned, then it'll fall to Bidtah to investigate," Rick said, his tone flat and emotionless.

Despite his determination to keep his emotions well under control, she knew he was hurting. Without thinking about it, she threw her arms around him. "I'm so sorry, Rick."

"Searching for his body seems like a betrayal, but if he really was poisoned, letting his murderer go free would have been worse," he said, holding on to her tightly.

"You followed your highest sense of right. He would have expected nothing less from you," she said.

He eased his hold. "I have to let my brothers know," he said, clearing his throat.

Once they were outside the cave, he contacted them. "Make sure we have two sets of gloves for everyone," he added before ending the call. "Not for us but out of respect for him. Hosteen Silver would have wanted it that way."

IT TOOK THEM two hours to get the body into the back of Preston's vehicle.

"Gene, if you can help Preston deliver the remains, I'd like to continue on to where Angelina's mobile home stood at one time and have a look around," Rick said, then glanced at Kim. "You can come with me, or go back to the ranch house and we'll meet there later."

"I'm sticking with you," she said.

"I'll conduct a grid search from the cave where we found the body to see if there's any other physical evidence that'll explain his reasons for coming here," Daniel said. "I'll be in the area, so when you're done, give me a call and I'll either come and get you or meet you someplace."

As Rick and Kim set out, she noticed how quiet he'd become. "Are you okay?"

"I guess."

She took his hand. "You don't always have to be so tough, Rick. We're all human and that means we're all vulnerable," she said gently.

He gave her hand a squeeze. "Right now, you and I have to focus on one thing—life. We're still in danger, so stay alert."

Their route led them away from the canyon and onto a long, downhill slope with low, scattered piñon and juniper trees and waist-high sagebrush. They moved steadily but carefully, on the alert for danger now that the vegetation provided cover for anyone wanting to ambush them.

Soon, they spotted the worn tar-paper roof of a red outbuilding and a flat area cleared of everything but low grass and tumbleweeds. "That's her barn, and to the left is the concrete slab where Angelina's mobile home stood. Let's go take a look around there." He turned and looked back toward the canyon.

"My foster father got within a mile of her trailer before he died," Rick observed. "There's also the possibility that he actually got here, then crawled up into the cave on his way back. Let's see if we can find a lead."

"Like something that belonged to Hosteen Silver, or evidence she overlooked?"

"Exactly."

As they approached, a flock of blackbirds flew up into the sky. He held up his hand and stayed perfectly still, listening.

Kim froze and searched the area, her heart beating as fast as it had when on convoy duty in Afghanistan. Even little clues mattered in life-and-death situations.

Staying behind the cover of a thick juniper, they waited. Then she saw movement and, getting Rick's attention, pointed.

Chapter Twenty

A moment later a coyote come out of the brush with a rabbit in its mouth. The successful hunter then trotted off, quickly disappearing.

"He's found food, so he's not interested in us," Rick said, remaining on alert.

Sensing his uneasiness, she whispered, "What's wrong?"

"I don't know. Maybe it's seeing Coyote, the Trickster. That's how he's known in our legends," he said. "Stay watchful and expect the unexpected."

"All right."

He looked around carefully, then called Daniel. "We're going to move in on the property, but I've got a hunch someone is out there watching. Have you seen anyone, any vehicles?"

"Just a dust trail a while ago along a dirt road east of you. Probably a local. I'll drive over to see if they parked or kept going. It'll take a while for me to get there, so give me a call if you need anything. Be on the lookout for any surprises, like a bear or coyote trap. Whoever is doing this has tried just about everything so far."

"Stay safe," Rick added, ending the call. "All right, then," he said to Kim, "let's move in. Search for footprints or any indication that someone's been by here. Daniel advised us to look for traps, just in case."

He moved forward cautiously, but the birds had come back and all seemed normal as they approached the concrete pad. They circled the area, searching for anything interesting, but only found a few cinder blocks that had probably been used to help level the mobile home.

There were no signs that anyone had been there in quite a while. Cockle burrs, goat-heads and Russian thistle had already appeared in what had been a cleared area. The chain of succession had begun.

"Barns aren't that common out here. Most people have sheep pens," he said, looking over at the dark red building that was about the size of a one-car garage.

"It's old, the paint is fading and the siding is starting to warp. I have a feeling there's not much to see, but let's go take a look inside anyway," Kim suggested.

"Hang on a minute." Rick's gaze took in the area. "I'm getting some bad vibes here." He called Daniel again. "I'm going to check inside the barn," he told his brother after filling him in, "but I want you to call me if it turns out that vehicle ended up heading in this direction. Something still feels off to me."

"Okay. Preston and Gene are on their way to the lab with the remains, but I'll ask Paul to head in this direction. Kyle's monitoring the ranch."

Kim waited till he'd ended the call. "If someone's out there, wouldn't they have done something by now, like shoot at us?" Kim challenged. "They did before."

"If it were me, I'd lay low and wait until the target got real close. Patience can be a reliable weapon."

They went up to the barn doors, but before going inside Rick looked around one more time. Nothing seemed out of place, and there were no footprints, yet the feeling that they were being watched persisted. "We'll take a quick look inside, then walk down the old road leading from here to meet up with my brothers."

They went in just as a gust of cold wind slammed against the side of the barn. The entire building seemed to groan. His uneasiness increased.

"It seems sturdy enough," Kim said, looking around. There were two stalls against one wall, an area with pallets for storing hay, and a crude rack with wooden pegs that held a rake with missing tines and a rusty shovel with a third of the handle gone.

As another hard gust hit the building, the door slammed shut.

"Those gusts are making my skin crawl," she said.

"Wind's said to have power to carry news. Whether it's good or bad, that's for someone else to say."

He studied the wooden walls, full of gaps where the planks had warped and twisted. "At least we don't need the flashlight to find our way around."

The wind had generated a combination of dust and plant debris in the air, and Kim sneezed. "There's nothing in here anymore. Let's leave before my allergies start to kick up," she said.

Rick pushed against the entrance doors, but they refused to yield.

"Is it stuck?" she asked, coming over to give him a hand.

Stepping back, Rick looked through the crack between the barn doors and quickly identified the problem. "The bar that keeps the door shut must have dropped down into place somehow. I'll need something sturdy and slim to slip through the gap and lift it up and out of the way."

"That gap is too narrow for the rake or shovel handle. If we could find a piece of wire, maybe we can wrap it around the bar and lift up."

He sniffed the air. Something else was wrong. "Do you smell it?"

"Dust and moldy hay that's making me sneeze. Is that what you mean?"

He glanced around in the dimly lit interior and by the time he brought the flashlight from his backpack, smoke was visible against the north wall.

"Someone set the outside of the barn on fire." He tossed her the phone. "Get Dan. We need him here in a hurry. I'll grab the shovel and try to lift the bar using the blade."

Through the gaps between the boards, he could see the stack of dead tumbleweeds piled up against the side of the barn. Each ignited one after the other into white smoke and flame.

Kim made the call, then ran over to Rick. "Daniel's on his way, but it'll take him several minutes to get here."

Rick picked up the shovel, but the blade was curved like a scoop. He tried to make it work, but there was no way he could angle it through the opening to raise the bar.

As he turned his head to check the progress of the fire, smoke was flowing up the wall, entering through the gaps between the boards. Flames were visible in places and the tumbleweeds burning outside crackled loudly as they were consumed.

"Daniel won't get here in time, will he?" she asked, her voice shaky.

He didn't answer. "Look for a weak spot in the wall. I'm going to make our own door."

Kim coughed as the white smoke became thicker and the sharp scent of burning wood began to penetrate her lungs.

"Put something over your nose and mouth, or pull up your shirt and breathe through the fabric," Rick directed, leaning against the wall, looking for a place to smash through.

"This is a weak point," Rick said. "Some of the planks

are split." Using the blade of the shovel as a spear, he began to work. After the third jab, the plank broke in two, leaving an eight-inch, waist-high gap.

The next plank was tougher, but in four jabs he'd knocked it loose from the uprights and it fell to the ground outside.

"One more plank and we can crawl out," she yelled, her voice raspy now as she gasped for air.

The wind and smoke picked up quickly, intensifying the fire, which was crackling louder than ever.

Coughing, he pulled Kim to her knees close to the hole he'd made in the side of the barn.

There was a loud whoosh across the barn. The opposite wall was a sheet of flames leading from floor to roof. "We've got to get out of here *now!*"

He dropped the shovel, lowered his shoulder and charged the gap he'd made in the side.

The building shook as he hit the wall, and several planks snapped from the impact as he broke out into the open, nearly falling to the ground.

Turning his head, he saw Kim stumble out through the gap. Catching her with both arms, he brought her up against him.

"We're okay now," he reassured her, kissing her forehead tenderly.

Hearing running footsteps, Rick pushed her behind him and aimed his gun at the far corner of the barn. Had the firebug come back to finish them off?

As Paul and Daniel came into view, Rick lowered his weapon.

"Easy, bro," Daniel said. "We're the good guys."

DETECTIVE BIDTAH ARRIVED a half hour later, finding them quickly thanks to the black smoke rising from the smoldering wreckage of the barn. He was not happy to see them, judging from the first words he spoke after climbing out of his SUV. "You're investigating on *my* turf but you didn't call me till now?"

"We weren't sure this was a police matter, so we gave you plausible deniability," Rick said. He quickly explained that the purpose of the removal of Hosteen Silver's body was to try to determine the cause of death.

"If the death proves suspicious, it's my case," Bidtah reminded him. "Now tell me more about you and Ms. Nelson being locked inside this barn."

"Here's how it went down," Rick said, then explained.

"There are lots of footprints around," Bidtah said after Rick had finished. "At a guess, I'd say most belong to you two or your brothers," he added, looking at their boots. "There's a strong scent of charcoal lighter here, too. That must be what the arsonist used to ignite the tumbleweeds."

Rick nodded. "I can smell it now."

"Any of you find anything else I can use?" Bidtah asked, looking from Kim to the brothers.

They shook their heads. "The cave where we found the body is about fifty feet up the south wall of the canyon," Rick told him. "You'll be able to spot it from our tracks."

"Not looking forward to it," Bidtah said. "Your dad was a good man. You let me know as soon as you hear from the lab," Bidtah ordered. "And email me all the photos you took of the scene."

"Absolutely," Rick replied.

"The murder of a highly regarded medicine man is going to send ripples through our community," Bidtah said, rubbing his chin pensively.

"Probably, but it'll be up to you to determine how much you want to divulge to the public," Rick noted.

"It's hard to keep secrets on the Rez," the detective commented.

Rick nodded slowly. "I know."

Bidtah glanced over to where the mobile home had once stood. "I'll have to speak to Angelina Curley as soon as possible. Like your place, this land belongs to the tribe, and if she's not occupying it, the land should go to another Navajo family," Bidtah said. "I also intend to ask why she chose to move away. If she was running from something, I want to know."

THEY WERE BACK at Daniel's a short while later, but a somber mood had settled over them.

"How soon will we hear from the medical investigator?" Kyle asked.

"That depends," Preston answered. "All they've got to work with is hair, bones, bone marrow and a few viable tissue samples. Jack's given it top priority, however."

"While we wait for results, we need to find out more about Angelina's niece and her homemade burritos," Rick said. "That's the only possible vector for the poison we know about right now."

Paul, who was at the computer, spoke up. "The woman's name is Bonnie Herder. She's a single mom with three kids. She owns her own small business, has a catering truck and usually parks by the public high school in Shiprock."

"School lets out in less than an hour. I'm going to go talk to her," Rick declared.

"I can't question her because she's out of my jurisdiction," Preston said. "If I try, I'm going to stir up a real hornet's nest. The way things stand, Bidtah would take it as an affront."

"You shouldn't go, either, Rick, because she's bound to know exactly who you are," Kyle said.

"Let me talk to her," Kim offered. "I'll just pretend I'm a substitute teacher on a break. I'll get further if it doesn't look like an interrogation."

"Kim just might get away with that," Preston agreed with a nod. "But you'll need to stay out of sight, Rick, or you'll blow it for her."

"I'm not happy with this plan," Rick said.

"Why?" Kim countered. "I can handle this. By keeping it friendly, we may get the information we need without her realizing it could be a problem for her aunt."

"I agree with Kim," Daniel said.

Rick shook his head. "We're after a killer. Kim will be unarmed as well, so she runs double the risk."

"Not if you're close by, backing her up," Preston said. "She's not likely to get violent that close to so many potential witnesses anyway."

TWENTY MINUTES LATER, wearing a change of clothes so she wouldn't smell like smoke, Rick and Kim set out in one of Level One's SUVs.

"Have you ever met Bonnie?" she asked him.

"Not that I recall. But a single mother with three kids and a business has a lot to lose. If she knows anything or if she's involved, she'll be on her guard. Be careful how you ask your questions and don't target Angelina specifically. Find out if Bonnie's family helps her prepare the food or if she has regular helpers, and so on."

"I've got this, trust me," she said.

"I do, but I still hate having you take point."

"You won't be far. Why are you worried?"

He kept his gaze focused on the road ahead. "You're more important to me than anything else, including this case. Do you understand me?"

"No. Are you saying that you think I can't handle this or that you're afraid you can't?" she added with a tiny smile.

"Maybe both. I love you, Kim," he said. Pulling over onto the side of the road, he hauled her into his arms.

Before she had the chance to react, he kissed her hard, moving his mouth over hers until her lips parted.

He was rough, desperate for more, but with a groan, released her. "No matter what happens, I'll have your back," he said, putting the SUV back in gear.

Dazed, happy, her heart pounding overtime in her ears, she nodded, not trusting her voice. He loved her! He'd shown her in countless ways and now he'd actually said the words.

She smiled. No matter what happened from this point on, she'd always have this.

Chapter Twenty-One

"I shouldn't have told you that, Kim, not right now," he said, cutting into her thoughts less than a mile later. "We have to focus on one thing—survival."

"But I feel the same way about you, Rick. I—"

"No. Don't say anything else, not until the danger's past. Do this for me. For us."

She wasn't sure if he thought he'd change his mind after the dust cleared or whether he thought she might. Either way, she wouldn't press him. Trying to hide her disappointment, she nodded. "Okay."

Twenty minutes later they reached the high school south of the main highway. "School hasn't let out yet, so she probably won't be surrounded by students," he said, passing by without slowing. "There's the catering truck parked just down the road."

"Good. That'll make my work easier," Kim said, not looking directly as they passed the truck, which now had the sliding panel up and counter out, ready for customers.

"Listen to me carefully, Kim. If you sense trouble, cut it short and head back to the SUV."

"Sure, but remember I'm not going to confront her. I'm going to talk to her—one working woman to another."

"All right. I'll park here, out of sight." He turned into a big empty lot a few hundred yards farther down.

KIM TOOK A deep breath, smiled and went up to the catering truck's window. "I'm starving. What do you have that I can eat fast?"

The young woman smiled. "Lucky you're going to just beat the after-school rush."

"Which means I've got to hurry. What can you recommend?" Kim asked.

"My bestseller is the green chili burger on homemade tortillas."

"Sounds good. I'll have one," she said. "Mild."

As the woman assembled the burger, Kim introduced herself.

"I'm Bonnie," the woman answered. "You're new around here, aren't you?"

"At this high school here, yes. I'm substituting today. But I grew up in Hartley."

"Half an hour drive. That's not too bad," Bonnie said.

Kim rubbed the back of her neck with one hand and made sure the woman saw the gesture. "I've been sitting at the desk way too long. Time for stretching exercises. I just wish I could find something to ease the sore muscles. The over-the-counter pills give me stomach problems and the ointments smell like a locker room."

"Have you considered herbs? Our medicine men are very knowledgeable about things like that."

"That's what I've heard. Can you recommend someone?"

"No, not really. The one I knew isn't around anymore," she said, placing the snack-size burger in a small microwave oven as she spoke.

"My friend got a cream from a local medicine man, Mr....something. Ruby swore by it, but I can't remember the man's name."

"Hosteen Silver?" Bonnie asked. Seeing Kim nod, she smiled sadly and continued. "He was really nice, and a great healer. My aunt would take him some of my freshly made breakfast burritos every morning. She was his apprentice for a time." Bonnie took the warmed burger out of the microwave and placed it on the counter.

"Your aunt is a medicine woman?" Kim asked, paying for the food.

"No, she didn't want to spend half her life in training. She got married instead."

"This burger's excellent," Kim said after taking a bite. "When the kids are out, like for lunch, I'm sure business is nonstop. Do you have any helpers?"

"My aunt used to help me get the *naniscaadas* ready each morning, but now she has her own business."

Hearing a bell, Kim turned toward the high school's main building. "I better get back to my room before I get run down by the fleeing kids," Kim said.

She left quickly and within a minute was surrounded by teens hurrying toward the food truck. Kim reversed course and walked back to the SUV, this time passing behind the food truck and staying out of view.

She ate the last bite as she slipped inside the SUV. "Now we have confirmation that Sandoval was telling the truth. Angelina used to help Bonnie make the *naniscaada,* then would take freshly made breakfast burritos over to your foster father every morning."

"Let me call Preston. This doesn't constitute proof, but it's something to work from."

Preston answered on the first ring and Rick put his phone on speaker. "I'm at the medical investigator's lab now," Preston announced. "The preliminary tests run on tissue samples drew a blank. One of the lab techs found a dried leaf in his shirt pocket, however. At first it looked like parsley, but the botanist recognized it as *Aethusa cy-*

napium, known commonly as fool's parsley or, get this, garden hemlock."

"Hemlock is deadly, remember Socrates?" Kim commented.

"Exactly," Preston responded. "According to what I was told, death can take anywhere from hours to days. If that's what killed him, Hosteen Silver might have known what was coming. The problem is that it's hard to prove it is the cause of death, because the only postmortem sign of hemlock is asphyxia. That can't be established, not now."

"That leaf didn't end up in his pocket by accident. In his last hours he must have suspected the source and kept that leaf for someone—maybe us—to find," Rick said.

"Problem is, we can't prove who put that poison in his food, or even if that's what killed him," Preston pointed out.

"If you come up with any ideas, let me know. I'll do the same." Rick ended the call.

Pulling to the side of the road, Rick stopped the SUV and turned to look at Kim. "Looks like we have to force the issue. Angelina's easily angered, so I think it's time to push her and see what happens."

"I agree. Today's Friday, her day to go see two silversmiths who live up by Teec Nos Pos, just inside the Arizona state line. The drive usually stresses her out, but she's always insisted on going herself. The woman doesn't trust anyone else to bargain hard enough. If we catch her on the road, I'm willing to bet it won't take much to rattle her."

He considered it. "I'm going to bluff her out to see if I can make her blink first," he said. "Any idea where these silversmiths live?"

"Yes. Angelina kept a map in the store so we could track her down if she got stuck in bad weather or had car trouble. She takes the northwest road out of Shiprock to Teec Nos Pos, turns south at mile marker twenty-nine just past the local Chapter House, then continues on a dirt road into the foothills for about five miles. The silversmiths are father and son, but she has to deal with them separately."

Rick called his brothers and asked them to meet him at mile marker twenty-nine.

RICK AND KIM were already halfway there, so they arrived first and pulled off the main highway, positioning the vehicle so they could see anyone coming their way up the dirt road. Daniel, Paul and Preston would be delayed by a half hour.

"She normally arrives back at the store before six, and it's about fifty-five miles from here. If her business is done, she should be passing through here before long."

After ten minutes she pointed. "That looks like her pickup coming in our direction."

"All right then." Rick pulled out and blocked the road.

A minute later the truck was close enough for them to confirm who was driving. Angelina honked the horn, slowed and finally stopped about fifteen feet up the road.

She climbed out, a thirty-thirty Winchester rifle in her hand. "What's going on here?"

Rick got out and walked over to the front of the vehicle. "Remember me?"

"Like a disease. When you're around, nothing good ever happens. Get out of my way."

Rick took a breath, determined to keep his cool. "I need to talk to you. It's important."

"Forget it. I'm not interested."

"You better be, because the Navajo police are on their way here as we speak," he answered, lying through his teeth.

Angelina watched Kim as she came out the driver's side and walked over to stand beside Rick. "You traitor."

Kim said nothing and Angelina kept her rifle in front of her, not aiming at the moment.

"You'll be interested to know we found my foster father's body," he said. "It was up in one of those caves, easy walking distance from where you used to live in that mobile home. Did he die on the way there or on the way back? Tell me."

Angelina's eyes widened slightly, then settled down. "After nearly three years, you finally went looking for that old fool?" She shuddered. "How do you know it was even him?"

"There was no mistaking his clothing, his belt and, of course, his hair. That remains long after death when preserved in a dry cave," he said. "But here's where it gets interesting, Angelina. His final act was to scratch out your name on the wall of the cave."

Her eyes narrowed for a second. She cleared her throat. "He had a thing for me. I must have been the last person he thought of before he died."

"No, he was poisoned and the police think he did that to name his killer. He also kept a leaf in his pocket. A leaf of fool's parsley—garden hemlock. Where'd you get that anyway? Grow it on a windowsill, maybe?"

Angelina stood rock-still, but her right index finger inched toward the rifle's trigger.

"And we know how you delivered the fatal dose, too," Kim added. "You brought food from Bonnie's truck out to Hosteen Silver every morning. You helped her fix them, as a matter of fact. A little extra chili on it…and something that looked like parsley. He never even noticed until it was too late."

"He taught you all about plants, and you used that against him," Rick snarled. "Before the police get here, at least tell me why you killed him. That's the only part I still don't get."

Angelina levered a shell into the rifle chamber. "If only you'd just run off that cliff…"

"Don't get stupid, Angelina. If you shoot us, any chance you have will go right out the window. We're standing in Arizona now, and they have the death penalty."

He pointed down the road toward the west. A white sedan was heading their way. "There's the Arizona highway patrol right now." He was bluffing.

As Angelina swung the rifle barrel around, Rick dove behind the engine compartment, pushing Kim down ahead of him. "Stay low," he yelled, rolling up into a crouch.

Angelina fired, the bullet ricocheting off the reinforced hood.

Rick poked his head out around the front bumper and ducked back as she fired again, shattering the front headlight inches from his head.

Rick reached down for his pistol, but his holster was empty. Glancing around, he spotted the pistol lying in the sand a few feet away. It must have slipped out when he'd dived to the ground. He lunged for it just as Angelina jumped into her pickup.

As he brought the pistol up, shaking sand from the barrel, Angelina sped by Rick's vehicle on the passenger side, sideswiping the SUV with a teeth-shattering screech.

Rick, on one knee, spun around, aimed carefully and fired two rounds into the rear of her truck as it reached the highway.

"She's getting away," Kim yelled, racing around to the passenger side as Angelina sped east toward Teec Nos Pos.

Rick jumped in and handed her his pistol. Whipping the vehicle around, he pulled onto the road right behind a frightened-looking elderly couple in a white sedan. They were clearly not Arizona Highway Patrol officers.

As they accelerated after the fleeing silver pickup, Rick looked over at Kim. "You okay?"

She looked down at her right hand, which was on her lap on top of his pistol. "Scrapes and stickers, but mostly I'm angry."

"Me, too."

His phone rang, and with a flick of his finger, he put it on speaker, keeping both hands on the wheel. Doing eighty, Rick whipped around the white sedan as if it was standing still.

"Hey, Rick, where are you?" It was Preston's voice. "A silver pickup almost ran us off the road. Was that—?"

"Angelina," Rick confirmed. "We're coming up fast. Once we pass you, turn around and give chase."

"Copy. I see you now."

Kim signaled the men as they raced past Rick's brothers at ninety miles per hour.

"You're flying, bro, slow down." Preston's voice came over the phone instantly.

"Can't. Unless I keep her in sight, she could pull off anywhere."

"She won't get far. I see a trail of fluid on the road. I'm guessing she's losing gas," Preston told him.

Kim looked down at the road ahead. "I see the shine on the asphalt."

Rick slowed to eighty-five. "Okay. I'm slowing down. I have the truck within sight now."

"Her new home isn't far from here, a few miles past Beclabito, on the right," Kim advised, referring to the small community ahead, just inside the New Mexico state line.

Rick nodded. "Hear what Kim said, guys?"

"Copy," Preston acknowledged. "Once you confirm her route, let us know. We're about a mile behind you now."

About three minutes later, the Beclabito trading post fading in the rearview mirror, Kim pointed toward a cloud of dust ahead, to the right of the highway. "That's the turn-off. Did she wreck?"

Rick took a long look and spotted a vehicle emerging from the right side of the cloud. "No, she may have spun out, though. She's headed home, guys," he said loud enough for Preston to hear over the speaker.

A minute later Rick turned, pointing to skid marks on the asphalt and road shoulder. "Look at those ruts. She nearly lost it making the turn."

"Her home is a few miles ahead, just on other side of those cliffs, up against a hill," Kim reported. "With that rifle, she might be planning to ambush us when we go through the road cut."

Rick slowed, noting the trail of damp earth in the center of the dirt road. "Still losing gas. Once she runs out, we've got her."

They topped a small rise and saw the pickup in the middle of the road about two hundred yards ahead. Steep cliffs rose on both sides of the road cut. "How many rounds did she fire from that Winchester?" Kim asked.

"Three, maybe four. Her rifle holds six to seven rounds normally, so she's still armed and dangerous. With that weapon she also has a range advantage and hitting power over our pistols."

"We need to play it smart," Kim said. "Make her waste her ammo."

Rick slowed to a crawl, then turned, blocking the road. "My feelings exactly. Follow me out on my side. Once the guys arrive we can move in. They'll cover us."

"Assault tactics."

"Exactly, except they won't open up unless Angelina actually starts shooting," he said. "We'll advance along both drainage ditches. Stay low and be ready to go prone if she opens fire."

Preston, already briefed on the tactical plan, pulled up behind them. With backup now in place, Rick and Kim moved ahead to the silver vehicle. The smell of gasoline was thick in the air.

Rick looked around. "Her footprints don't lead down the road toward the house. They lead off to the right. I can still track her."

"Maybe she's just circling around, hoping to lose us by climbing up some trail to the top of the mesa. Once she's up there, she could shoot down on us," Kim said.

"If she wanted to make a last stand, yes, but I don't think she wants a fight, Kim. I think she's looking to hide. She'll head someplace she feels safe."

He stood back from the cliff, looking along the upper third of the formation. Feeling the vibration on his cell phone, he brought his brothers up to speed. "There are shallow caves up there. My guess is she made it to one of those. Someone needs to keep watch for a rifle barrel poking out. Once we start our climb, she'll have to poke her head out to shoot at us."

"We'll provide suppressive fire if she shows herself," Preston replied.

Rick put the phone in his pocket and glanced over at Kim. "From this point on we'll have to be as silent as possible."

"All right. Let's go."

Pushing some dried tumbleweeds out of the way, they worked their way up. This slope was a lot easier to climb than the cliff where they'd found Hosteen Silver's remains.

The first few caves were nothing more than low overhangs and were easy to see inside. He moved past them, signaling for Kim to remain in place. He then headed alone toward what looked like a deep cave.

He immediately found a small path and shoe prints. Angelina had come this way.

He glanced back and, spotting his brothers below, pointed ahead. He then signaled Kim to follow him.

As Rick got closer to the cave, he saw what looked like the barrel of a rifle lying on the floor of the cave. He motioned for Kim to hold her ground, then carefully advanced to a position beside the opening.

From where he stood, he could see that the lever of the rifle was half-open, a bent cartridge in the breech. A jam, probably caused in panic by an inexperienced shooter. Reaching over, he grabbed the barrel, pulled out the rifle and slid it down the slope. It hung up on some brush about fifteen feet from the opening.

Rick pulled a wide-beamed flashlight out of his pocket and examined the cave from outside. It was much bigger than the one he'd been in earlier that day, about five feet high toward the rear, maybe ten feet wide, and at least double that distance deep. At the back were what appeared to be two shrines.

Rick entered on his knees, rose to a crouch and discovered a pair of snapshots hanging on the rock wall above two sets of personal effects.

He recognized Hosteen Silver's photo first. Beneath it, on the floor of the cave, were his foster father's favorite jeans—an old pair with worn knees and a paint stain—and his bolo tie.

He focused the beam of the flashlight on the other photo. It was a photo showing Angelina in a wedding dress standing beside a man in a suit. That suit appeared to have been folded and placed below the photo, along with a gold wedding band.

Hearing a muted sound, he turned his head to see Kim crouched at the entrance.

"What is this place, a memorial?" Kim whispered, coming up beside him.

"Of a sort, I guess," he answered in a quiet voice. As he looked into the darkness, he spotted a small flicker of light, like that from a cigarette lighter, followed by the soft glow of a newly lit candle.

The jar candle was on a large wooden box and beside it was Angelina, sitting on a low, three-legged stool. She was holding a shiny steel pistol in a shaky hand, the barrel aimed right at them. "You shouldn't have followed me here. This is my place—and theirs. We can be together here."

For a moment Rick had no words. Then he saw the basketball-size propane bottle beside the box, only a few feet from Angelina.

"You must miss them terribly," Kim said, backing away slightly.

"They never really loved me, but here we're together."

"Angelina, put the pistol down and come outside with us," Rick said. "More violence isn't going to solve anything."

"Don't worry. We won't suffer. We'll all disappear in a big ball of light. I can't miss." She shifted, aiming the pistol at the valve on top of the propane bottle.

The woman was clearly not in her right mind. One shot would destroy the valve, the propane would escape and the candle would ignite the gas, blowing them to bits.

"It's time for me to join my men. This wasn't supposed to include you, too, but Hosteen Silver will appreciate the company."

Seeing her finger tighten around the trigger, Rick grabbed

Kim's hand and yanked her to the ground. The pistol went off with an ear-shattering blast. The metal propane tank passed over their heads like a low-flying jet, bounced off the roof of the cave and disappeared out the opening.

Rick turned and saw Angelina on her side, staring at the candle, extinguished by the rush of air and gas. Dust began to shower down, followed by rocks and big chunks of sandstone.

"Out! Everything's coming down," he yelled, wrapping his arm around Kim and pulling her out of the cave.

They leaped out headfirst and slid down the steep slope several feet before he finally managed to grab a ledge with his free hand and stop their slide.

A faint scream somewhere above them was followed by a loud crash as the cave collapsed under the weight of the cliff above. The earth shook and clouds of dust shot out. Big chunks of rock came tumbling down.

Rick pulled Kim to his side, shielding her with his body as loose earth, plant debris and sandstone chunks pelted them.

They waited, heads buried beneath their arms until the earth stopped shaking. An enormous slab of sandstone directly overhead was teetering back and forth.

"Let's move!"

They half slid, half crawled to the bottom, scrambling to their feet just as there was a final, enormous thud. The sandstone slab tipped, crashed onto the steep slope, then slid halfway down before coming to a stop in a cloud of dust.

Kim couldn't stop shaking. "I thought we were done for," she said, her voice breaking.

Rick pulled her into his arms. "Me, too, and all the time we were stuck there, all I could think of was how much time I'd wasted."

He cupped her face in his hands and kissed her. "I love you, Kim. Marry me."

"Yes!"

They heard footsteps and broke apart to find his brothers standing there.

Daniel laughed. "Jeez, guy, you're covered in dust and dirt, weeds and stickers in your hair—basically you look like a pistol-packing lizard that just crawled out of an ant bed. Where's the romance? Couldn't you have waited for wine and roses, or at least gotten down on one knee?"

"We'll do the rest later, but I'm not wasting one more minute," Rick replied, kissing her again.

"Quit goofing off, slacker," Preston yelled from farther down. "We've still got work to do here."

"Hey, don't ruin the moment," Daniel yelled back.

Rick looked down at Kim, then pointed. "Look at Copper Canyon, off in the distance. No matter what happens, it continues to stand. That's the way it'll be with us."

"I know," she said and kissed him. "Some things were just meant to be."

Epilogue

A week had passed, and with all the major questions answered now, there was no reason not to resume their personal lives again.

Rick had wanted to keep their wedding simple, with only a justice of the peace, his brothers and their families present, including Kim's uncle Frank. The event, scheduled to begin in forty-five minutes, would be the first held at Copper Canyon.

While the women got ready in the next room, Rick stared at Hosteen Silver's journal. With all of them present, they'd read it at first light that morning.

"That's an amazingly detailed history of all the sacred objects he used for each Sing," Rick said. "It's a very special kind of family history."

"None of us will become medicine men, but this kind of knowledge should be preserved," Kyle said.

"Let's keep it safe and secure for the next generation," Preston suggested. "Think of the journal as Hosteen Silver's legacy."

"I like that," Paul said with a nod. "Who's to say one of our children won't become a medicine man or woman?"

Daniel's phone buzzed, signaling a text message. "It's the justice of the peace. He's running ahead of schedule."

Paul went down the hall and knocked on the closed door. "The judge is going to be early. Fifteen minutes. You ladies okay with that?"

A moment later Kim came out and Rick moved to where she stood. "You look beautiful."

She looked down at her dark silk slacks and lacy cream blouse. "I'm ready," she said, running her fingers through her hair.

"It's not too late to change your mind if you want a fancier wedding."

"No. This place made you the man you are, and everyone who counts in our lives is here, including my new family. I couldn't ask for more. It's perfect."

Excitement was thick in the air as they gathered outside. It was truly an Indian summer at the moment. The October sun was high in the sky, it was almost seventy degrees and today the canyon was unusually silent. It was almost as if it were holding its breath.

A gentle breeze blew past them as they stood beside the tallest pine, a tiny blue feather from a piñon jay floated by. She caught it in her hand. "Look! How beautiful!"

Rick looked down at it, amazed. "Hosteen Silver had one he carried in his medicine pouch. It's a symbol of peace and happiness—a powerful omen."

"You told me once that the good in him is part of Universal Harmony, so in a way, he's here with you today."

"I think so, too," Rick murmured, lifting her hand to his lips and kissing it gently.

The justice of the peace arrived. Climbing down from his oversize pickup, he joined the gathering. "We all here? Everyone ready?"

Seeing Rick nod, he opened a small book and began. "Dearly beloved…"

Memories were made one day at a time, and as Rick looked at his bride, he knew today was just the beginning.

* * * * *

"I'm sorry this happened to you."

His voice was gentle. Almost a whisper. And even though Rosalie figured that being in his arms was a very bad idea, she just didn't have the strength to push him away.

Austin made a soft shushing sound and eased her deeper into his arms. Until she was pressed against him. Even with the tears and her heart shattering, she felt his body. Heard the quick rhythm of his breath.

Just as when she had spotted him at the table with his bedroom hair and eye-catching jeans, the trickle of heat went through her. A bad kind of heat that she didn't want to feel for him. But felt anyway.

Rosalie pulled in her breath, taking in his scent with it, and suddenly everything that happened couldn't compete with what she knew they were both feeling right at this moment.

KIDNAPPING IN KENDALL COUNTY

BY
DELORES FOSSEN

Published in Great Britain 2014
by Mills & Boon, an imprint of Harlequin (UK) Limited,
Eton House, 18-24 Paradise Road, Richmond, Surrey, TW9 1SR

© 2014 Delores Fossen

ISBN: 978-0-263-91379-8

46-1214

Harlequin (UK) Limited's policy is to use papers that are natural, renewable and recyclable products and made from wood grown in sustainable forests. The logging and manufacturing processes conform to the legal environmental regulations of the country of origin.

Printed and bound in Spain
by CPI, Barcelona

USA TODAY bestselling author **Delores Fossen** has sold over fifty novels with millions of copies of her books in print worldwide. She's received the Booksellers' Best Award and the RT Reviewers' Choice Award, and was a finalist for a prestigious RITA® Award. In addition, she's had nearly a hundred short stories and articles published in national magazines. You can contact the author through her webpage at www.dfossen.net.

Chapter One

Rosalie McKinnon tightened her grip on the Beretta that she'd stolen and stepped out of the house and onto the narrow back porch. She stayed in the shadows, away from the milky kitchen light that was stabbing through the darkness.

There was only a thin lip of an overhang on the roof, so after just a few steps, the December rain spat at her. Not sleet exactly, but close enough. Rosalie didn't know if she was shivering from the fear or the cold. It didn't matter. Shivering wasn't going to stop her.

Nothing would.

Tonight, she would get answers. Even if she had to shoot *him*.

She made it down the slick, uneven limestone steps and into the sprawling backyard. She paused just a couple of seconds to make sure no one in the house had noticed that she'd left. With all the decongestants and antihistamines she had managed to slip into the guard's coffee, maybe he'd be out long enough so he wouldn't realize that she was missing.

If not…

Well, best not to go there.

Even though she had stolen the guard's gun after he'd

passed out, there were other armed guards on the grounds. If they discovered her, she'd be dead within seconds. Especially if they figured out what she was doing. They were no doubt capable of killing.

That also applied to the man she had to see.

Maybe, just maybe, he'd be sleeping, too, so she could get the jump on him. It was the only chance she had of making this plan work.

Hurrying now, Rosalie crossed the bare winter grass to a much smaller house at the back of the barn. Once, it'd probably been a guest cottage when the ranch was a real working operation. Now there was no livestock around, no hint of the life that'd once gone on here other than a tractor and hay baler that had been left to rust away. These days, the place was a glorified prison for the babies being processed for black market adoptions.

Since it made her sick to her stomach to think of that, Rosalie pushed the thought aside and tested the doorknob on the cottage.

Unlocked.

A big mistake on his part.

Rosalie opened the door and stepped inside. All dark and toasty warm. It smelled of too-strong coffee and the fast-food burgers that'd been brought in for their dinner.

The only light in the room of the cottage came from the kitchen in the main house, where she'd just been. It cut like slivers down the tiny front windows that were streaked with rain.

It took a couple of moments for Rosalie's eyes to adjust, and in the shadowy silhouettes, she saw a desk, a sofa and the small bed against the wall. There were two interior doors, both closed, and from what she'd learned from the guard's idle chatter, one was a bathroom. The other, a bedroom that was being used as a storage closet.

But it was the man on the bed who grabbed her full attention.

He was on his side, facing away from her. No cover on him, and he appeared to be wearing the same jeans and shirt he'd had on when she had spotted him earlier in the yard.

The guard had called him *boss*.

She'd yet to see him up close, but Rosalie had gotten another glimpse of him from the upstairs window of the main house. His dark brown Stetson had covered most of his face, but she'd watched to see where he would go. And he hadn't gone far—just to the cottage. All in all, it wasn't the worst place to confront a monster because he was alone here, away from the guards who would protect him.

Keeping the Beretta by her side, she walked closer, her heart thudding with each soft step. She had to remind herself to breathe. And to keep a clear head. Her instincts were to shoot, or run, but neither of those things would get her what she needed.

Too bad she wasn't a cop like her siblings. They would have no doubt handled this much better.

But then they would have never gotten into this place.

Not with their cops' eyes and attitudes. Plus, they'd all been tied up with other leads and other investigations. Important ones. Her mother was about to stand trial for first-degree murder, and while finding the baby was critical, so was the trial since her mother was facing the death penalty.

That's why she'd come up with her own plan several months ago while she was staying at her family's ranch.

A plan that'd started with finding any info to get her inside this place or any other place that would possibly lead her to her daughter.

Rosalie leaned over and jammed the gun to the back of the man's head. "I want answers," she managed to say even though her throat clamped shut. Her voice had hardly any sound.

He moved, just a fraction. "Darlin'," he drawled.

Her shoulders snapped back, and it was that split second of shock that caused her breath and body to freeze.

The man reached out, lightning-fast, snagged her by the right hand and stripped her of the Beretta. In the same motion, he pulled her down onto the bed with him and rolled on top of her, pinning her beneath him.

That unfroze her.

Her heart jolted, throbbing in her ears, and Rosalie started to fight back. She couldn't just let this man kill her.

"Play along," he growled, his voice no longer a drawl but rather a whisper. "There's a camera."

She'd already brought up her knee to ram any part of him that she could reach, but she stopped. Stared at him. Well, she stared at what she could see of him, anyway.

"Rosalie," he muttered.

Mercy. How did he know her real name? She was using a fake ID with the name Mary Williams. If he was onto her, why hadn't he already told the guards?

"Who are you?" she tried to ask, but he put his hand over her mouth.

"I figured you'd drop by," he said. No longer a whisper, and the cocky drawl had returned. "I saw you eyeing me earlier from the window."

She had. She'd *eyed* him and committed everything she could see about him to memory from his sandy-brown hair to lanky build. He normally wore a shoulder holster, and judging from the bulge in the back of his coat, he had another gun tucked in the back waistband of his jeans.

And the keys.

Three of them.

They jangled from a metal ring hooked to his belt loop.

Rosalie believed one was for the truck she'd seen him driving, but one of the others was for the room inside the main house where she'd gotten a glimpse of computers and files. The room was always locked, and there was a camera mounted on the doorjamb, but she needed his keys to get a look at those files.

She glanced around, to try to see if there was indeed a camera here, but the room was too dark.

"Who are you?" she asked, shoving his hand from her mouth.

He pulled back, stared down at her, though she still couldn't clearly see his face. "You don't know?" But he didn't wait for an answer. He mumbled some really bad profanity, and his grip tightened on her wrists. "Why the hell are you here, anyway?"

He didn't shout it, but she had no trouble hearing the anger in his voice. Or maybe not anger, but something.

What was going on? She couldn't see enough of his face to recognize him, and that raspy whispered voice wasn't enough of a clue. He could be friend or foe, but clearly he fell into the latter category since he was the boss here.

So, what was her next move?

She hadn't thought beyond getting answers and then trying to escape, but clearly she hadn't expected this. Whatever *this* was.

"Did you come here to kill me?" he demanded, still whispering.

"If necessary."

Except a dead man couldn't tell her what she needed to know. But she would have pulled the trigger if it'd come down to it. Unfortunately, she no longer had a gun as a bargaining tool. She had only shaky hands. Shaky body, too, and her heart just kept pounding.

The moments crawled by. Him, still staring at her and obviously waiting for an explanation. The only sounds were the rain pinging against the window and their rough breaths.

"Pretend," he finally snapped.

Rosalie didn't get a chance to ask what the heck that meant before his mouth went to her neck. He nuzzled it, as if kissing her, but he was still mumbling profanity, and his jaw muscles were way too tight for this to be a real kissing session.

So, what was this? Some kind of act for the person on the other end of the camera? If so, why was he trying to cover for her?

"I'm not leaving without answers," Rosalie whispered. "And I want these babies safely out of here and back where they belong."

"Pretend we're having sex or you might not be leaving at all. You'll be dead. And so will I."

That was the only warning she got before the pretense went into full swing. He kneed her legs apart, yanking off her green scrub pants. He didn't touch her panties, thank goodness, and he threw the covers over them.

He fumbled between them, pretending to unzip his jeans before the fake thrusting started.

"If necessary?" he said, repeating her response to his

question of *Did you come here to kill me?* "If you're not here for revenge, then why did you come?"

Revenge, yes, she wanted that. And justice. But more than those things, she just wanted answers.

It was impossible to think with everything going on. The sex was fake, but it was still a man's body shoving against her. And then there was the fear. Obviously, this man knew her. Knew she was as phony as the sex they were having. So, why hadn't he shouted out for the guard?

Why hadn't he killed her?

After all, he had her gun and his.

"I'm looking for my baby," she said. Her mouth trembled. And she felt her heart breaking all over again.

He stopped moving, met her gaze. For a few seconds, anyway. Then, he let out a loud groan, the sound of a man who'd just reached a climax, and he collapsed against her.

"You had a child," he said. Not a question exactly but more like something a person would say when trying to piece things together.

She nodded. Bad idea. It caused her mouth to brush against his neck, and because his sex was still aligned with hers, she felt a stirring.

Yes, this was pretend, but his body was obviously having a hard time remembering that.

"I gave birth to a baby girl nearly a year ago." Eleven months. Six days. Heck, she knew the hours and minutes.

"Nearly a year ago," he repeated. "She was your fiancé's baby?"

Again, not a question that she'd expected. Rosalie nodded and tried to tamp down the massive lump in her throat. Her eyes burned with tears that she couldn't cry. Tears wouldn't help her baby now.

"Sadie…that's what I named my daughter. She was born eight and a half months after my fiancé was murdered."

The memories of that day came. Of his shooting. That horrible flood of images that just didn't stop. So senseless. Her fiancé, Special Agent Eli Wells, had died because of a botched investigation, and Rosalie had wanted to die right along with him.

And then she'd learned she was pregnant.

The baby had saved her. Because she'd put all her love and emotions into surviving, into the pregnancy, so she could have the child of the man she'd loved.

"Someone stole Sadie from the hospital just a few hours after she was born," Rosalie added, "and I've been looking for her ever since."

His breath was thicker now, practically gusting. "She wouldn't be here. They only bring newborns here, and they've only used this place for a couple of months."

Yes, she knew that from the guard's ramblings before he'd actually dozed off from the meds that she had slipped him. "I thought there would be records on the computer in a locked room of the house."

"There are. But only for the babies being held at this location. You're sure the black market ring took your daughter?"

"No." And it hurt to admit that. She wasn't sure of anything, but she'd exhausted her leads and had gone with this different angle. "A criminal informant said there might be information here."

There was a lot more to it than that, but Rosalie didn't want to rehash everything it'd taken to bring her to this point. All the lies, the payoffs and the bogus identity she'd had to create.

"Why haven't you killed me?" she came out and asked. "And how do you know who I am?"

Again, he took his time, looking down at her as if trying to figure out what was going on. Rosalie was doing the same thing to him.

"What criminal informant did you use?" he asked, obviously dodging the questions.

Of all the things that were up in the air here, that didn't seem very important. "A guy from San Antonio. Lefty Markham."

He groaned, cursed and rolled off her and to his side. But he immediately pulled her against him. Face-to-face. Like a couple having some pillow talk after a round of sex.

"He's your stepbrother's CI," he whispered. "Why the hell didn't you bring Seth in on this?"

Seth Calder, not just her stepbrother but also an FBI agent. So, not only did this man know who she was, but he also knew details about her life that he shouldn't know.

"Because Seth's checking out another lead over in El Paso. The CI said the baby-holding area here at the ranch wouldn't be here much longer."

"It won't be. The plan is to move tomorrow."

Oh, mercy. So soon. "I need to see those records. Please help me. *Please.*"

Yes, she was begging but she would resort to a lot more than that to learn where her baby had been taken.

"I'm Austin Duran," he said.

His voice was so soft, barely audible, but it slammed through her as if he'd yelled it.

"Oh, God," she said a lot louder than a whisper.

"Yeah." He moved away from her so they were no longer touching.

The name was as familiar to her as her own. But not

in a good way. It was a name she'd cursed. A bogeyman who'd robbed her of her hopes and dreams.

The man who'd killed Eli.

Not in the eyes of the law, though, and it certainly hadn't been labeled murder. But Rosalie knew that Austin Duran was the FBI agent who had botched the investigation that'd led to Eli's murder.

"Yeah," he repeated. There was a lot of emotion hanging on that one word. The pain. The memories.

Everything Rosalie was feeling.

"You thought I'd come here to kill you," she mumbled. "You thought I was avenging Eli's death."

He didn't confirm that. Didn't need to.

"I didn't get a good look at your face." And that's why she hadn't instantly recognized him. Strange that she hadn't sensed that he had been so close, because she'd spent all these months hating him.

And Rosalie would use that hate.

In fact, it could be better than a gun.

"You're here undercover?" she asked.

He nodded. "I'm looking for…someone." ·

She didn't care about that. Didn't care about anything right now but her daughter. That included choking back her hatred for this man and making this work for Sadie and the other babies who were being held inside so they could be sold like cattle.

"You owe me," she insisted. "For Eli's death. And you're going to help me find his missing baby."

Austin didn't jump to do just that. He lay there, silent as death, and Rosalie was about to repeat her demand when she heard the sound.

Something she definitely didn't want to hear.

Footsteps.

Those steps were the only warning they got before there was another sound. The door flew open, and Austin scrambled in front of her.

But it was too late.

Two armed guards hurried into the cottage, and both pointed assault rifles at them.

Chapter Two

Austin had already spent the past twenty minutes or so cursing fate. And cursing Rosalie's untimely arrival in the cottage. It wouldn't do any good, but now he cursed the guards and those rifles trained on him.

"What the hell do you two want?" Austin growled, and he made a show of zipping up his jeans.

Austin didn't know the guys' names. Over the past week since he'd been undercover at the ranch, the flow of guards had stayed steady, none of them remaining in place for more than forty-eight hours. But it didn't matter what they called themselves. Austin just needed to get them out of there.

"Well?" Austin added in his worst snarl. He made sure he sounded like the person in charge.

He wasn't.

Heck, he didn't even know who had that particular title of being in charge or who exactly was watching him on the camera. However, it was pretty clear that someone had gotten suspicious of Rosalie's visit. The mock sex hadn't fooled them, and if Austin didn't do something fast to diffuse the situation, it could go from bad to worse.

The pair of guards exchanged glances as if trying to

figure out what to do, but the guy on the right had a communicator in his ear, so he was no doubt receiving instructions.

"Why is she here?" The goon on the right tipped his head to Rosalie.

Austin gave him as cocky and flat of a look as he could manage. "Why do you think?"

"She's supposed to be inside," he snapped.

"The babies are asleep," Rosalie volunteered as if that explained everything.

It didn't, of course.

There were two newborns inside, along with a nanny and the guard. Since Rosalie had no doubt been hired as a nurse, she should have been inside and nowhere near Austin's quarters.

"I'll be going," Rosalie mumbled. She fished around on the floor for her scrub pants and pulled them on. She also pushed her long blond hair from her face.

Austin noticed that both her voice and hands were shaking, but hopefully the guards would think that was a reaction from being caught in the act of a lover's tryst. And nothing else.

Soon, if they got out of this, he'd need to convince Rosalie to leave so he could get on with his investigation.

This was a *bad* place for her to be.

She started for the door, but the men blocked her path. And they didn't lower those rifles. "You two know each other?" one of them asked.

"We do now." Austin shot her a sly smile. "But I'm ready for her to leave. Gotta get some sleep."

And he waited.

The guards still didn't move, though he could hear some chatter on the one guard's earpiece. Austin wished he could snap his fingers and make the real boss appear so they could settle this man-to-man, but so far he didn't have even a description of the person responsible for so much pain.

"Walk her back to the house," one of the guards finally said to Austin. "Make sure she stays put."

Austin tried not to look or sound too relieved, but he was. Rosalie and he had just dodged a bullet or two.

For now, anyway.

The real boss obviously didn't trust him, or the goons wouldn't have been sent in to see what was going on. Maybe that meant Rosalie and he would be placed under a more careful watch. However, she wouldn't be reined in like that.

Nope.

There'd be no deterring Rosalie from looking for her stolen baby. Austin knew how she felt, but he also knew that her persistence would get her killed the hard way. He couldn't let that happen.

She was right about one thing. He did owe her.

But that was a debt he could never repay.

Still, maybe he could do something to bring his late partner's baby back to her mother's arms.

The guards stepped back. Finally. And as soon as they were out of the doorway, Austin grabbed his shoulder holster and coat from the peg near the door. He still had his backup weapon in the holster in the back waistband of his jeans, but if this little walk to the house went wrong, he wanted all the firepower he could get.

"Come on," Austin told Rosalie and got her moving.

He picked up her Beretta, as well. Or rather, the guard's Beretta. Austin wasn't sure he wanted to know how Rosalie had gotten it from the man.

She glanced back at the guards, who were now making their way to the barn. Not an ordinary one, either. It had become a modified command post and living quarters to house the guards and all sorts of people who'd been coming and going. Austin had sneaked some photos and jotted down license plate numbers, but he was a long way from piecing this together.

"Why didn't my brother know the FBI had undercover agents working the black market adoptions here?" Rosalie whispered.

"Because the FBI doesn't know I'm here."

Her mouth dropped open, and she looked ready to accuse him of something, but she must have remembered that she'd sneaked in here, too. Of course, he had the training to carry out undercover work.

Rosalie didn't.

But she obviously had some kind of contacts to get her in this place. Austin sure had. Well, one contact, anyway. A former FBI agent who'd helped him create the bogus background and references so Austin would look "legit" to someone running a criminal operation. It had worked, and he'd been hired as head of security at this particular site.

Austin purposely kept their steps slow to give them time to talk, and he looped his arm around her waist so they'd look like the lovers they were pretending to be.

"Who hired you for this job?" he asked.

Rosalie shook her head. "I made all the arrangements through the criminal informant. He said word on the street was the operation was looking for nannies and nurses. I'm an RN. So I had a fake ID made. Created fake work and a computer bio, too."

Austin tried not to groan. Lefty Markham was a piece of slime who'd sell his mother for a quarter.

"The job interview, if you can call it that, was done over the phone," she added. "Along with transportation arrangements. This morning, a truck arrived at an abandoned gas station just off the interstate to pick me up, and the driver made me put on a hood so I couldn't see where he was taking me."

That was standard practice for this operation. So, the fake bio and ID must have fooled the person in charge of hiring her. Still, that didn't mean anyone trusted her.

Nor him.

The camera proved that, and Austin was well aware that he was constantly being watched. Even now.

"You said your daughter was taken eleven months ago?" Austin whispered. He kept them walking at a slow pace toward the house.

Rosalie nodded. "Why? Do you know something about her?"

She sounded hopeful, but Austin would have to crush those hopes right off. "No. I'm here looking for my nephew. He's a newborn, and someone kidnapped him."

Rosalie pulled in a hard breath, and even though it was dark, he thought he might have seen some sympathy in her eyes. "So we can find them both."

"No." He stopped, turned her so she could see that this wasn't up for negotiation. "I'll find them, and you're getting the heck out of here. I don't care how. Pretend you're sick or something. I just want you off the grounds tonight."

She was shaking her head before he even finished. "I can't leave. I have to find my baby." Her voice broke, and he saw the tears shine in her eyes.

Austin huffed. "Look, I know you have no reason to trust me, but you won't be doing your baby any good by getting yourself killed. These men are dangerous, Rosalie, and they'll do whatever it takes to keep this operation secret and profitable."

He could tell by the little sound she made that he hadn't convinced her, so Austin would have to do more than talk. "Then I'll make the arrangements," he added. "But one way or another, you're leaving tonight."

Before she could respond, or argue, the back door to the house creaked open, and the guard staggered onto the porch. Unlike the other two, Austin knew this one. Walter Ludwig. Not very bright but trigger happy.

A bad combination.

Walter had a rifle in his right hand and aimed his left index finger at Rosalie. "She drugged me and stole my gun." And even though he was still staggering, the man pointed the rifle at her.

Austin stepped between them, held up his hands in a calm-down gesture. "Everything's okay," he lied. "It was all just a misunderstanding."

Not the best excuse, but Austin didn't want to say too much. Every word now could be risky.

"She drugged me," the guard repeated, and he came down the steps, closer to where they stood. "And now she's gonna pay for that. Get out of the way, boss."

"Not happening. Just put down the rifle, Walter, and we'll talk about this."

"Don't wanna talk." His words were slurred, and he had to lean against the porch post to steady himself. "I just want her dead real quick."

Austin cursed under his breath. He had to figure out a way to diffuse this now, or else the other two guards would hear the raised voices and come running. They were already suspicious of Rosalie and him. Which meant the pair just might encourage Walter to commit murder.

"Move away from her!" Walter growled, and despite his unsteady footing, he came off the porch. Charging right toward them.

Austin pushed Rosalie to the side so he could latch on to the rifle and turn it away from her. Walter's finger was on the trigger. Poised and ready to fire.

"If you shoot, a bullet could ricochet and hurt one of the babies," Austin tried again.

His attempt at logic didn't work. Walter was in a rage. Every muscle in his body primed to fight, and it was obvious he wasn't going to listen to reason.

"I'm gonna kill her!" Walter snarled, and when he tried to bring up the rifle to do just that, Austin knew he had no choice.

He bashed the Beretta against the side of Walter's head. It wasn't a hard enough hit to kill the man, but it caused him to drop like a bag of rocks to the ground.

"What's going on?" someone asked, and a moment later, the nanny, Janice Aiken, looked out from the kitchen door. She gasped, pressing her fingers to her mouth.

But that wasn't the only voice that Austin heard.

The barn door opened, and he knew it wouldn't be long before both guards came out to see what was wrong. This had plenty of potential to end in the worst possible way.

"What should we do?" Janice asked. "I'll help."

"She's on our side," Austin explained to Rosalie.

Well, maybe.

He didn't have time for details and especially didn't have time to make sure that he trusted Janice. So far, it appeared the nanny was ready to put an end to the black market baby operation, but he wasn't a hundred percent sure of that. He definitely hadn't counted on trusting her this soon. But one thing he did know: the babies were worth a lot of money, so even if Janice was in on the scheme, she would indeed protect them.

For now, that had to be enough.

Austin turned to Rosalie, took out one of the keys and handed it to her. "It's for the truck. Use it in case something goes wrong. For now, go inside and help Janice get the babies ready to move."

Rosalie gave a shaky nod and hurried into the house with the nanny. They'd barely gotten the back door closed when Austin reeled around and faced the pair of guards who were storming toward them.

"What the hell happened?" one of them demanded.

"Personal dispute. Walter here wanted to sample my lady friend, and I didn't want to share."

Walter moaned, twisting on the soggy ground. "She drugged me."

And despite the moans, that accusation came through crystal clear.

Austin smirked at the man. "I think Walter just had a little too much to drink."

Yeah, it wasn't much of an explanation, but Austin didn't think he could say or do anything at this point that would convince the guards that this was nothing that concerned them.

The guard on the right glanced at Walter. Then, Austin. And finally at the house. "Get the woman out here now so we can talk to her."

That put a hard knot in Austin's stomach. "And then what? You kill her and leave us without a nurse? What happens if one of the babies gets sick, huh?"

The man lifted his shoulder, took aim at Austin. "Nurses are replaceable. And so are you. Drop your weapons."

Oh, man. He really hadn't wanted it to come down

to this because the guards likely knew some critical information that would help him find his nephew. And Rosalie's baby. That wouldn't happen if he had to kill all three of them.

Or if they managed to kill him first.

Austin adjusted the grip on his gun so he'd be ready in case the bullets started. He'd have to shoot the one on the right first, dive to the side and hope he got lucky enough to take out the second before the guy got off a shot.

Risky at best.

But his only option now.

Austin brought up his hand, ready to fire, but it was already too late.

The guard pulled the trigger.

Chapter Three

Rosalie and the nanny barreled up the stairs toward the nursery, but the sound of the blast stopped Rosalie in her tracks.

Oh, mercy.

Had the guards killed Austin?

It didn't matter that he was essentially her enemy. She didn't want him shot, especially since he'd been trying to cover for her.

Rosalie hurried into the nursery, running past Janice to get to the window. She braced herself to see a dead Austin lying on the ground, but the only person she saw was Walter. He was crawling back toward the porch. No sign of Austin or the two other guards.

"What's happened?" the nanny asked, and she scooped one of the sleeping newborns into her arms.

Rosalie shook her head just as she heard another shot. It was so loud that it seemed to shake the entire room.

She managed to get a glimpse of Austin. He was still armed, but he was pinned down near some shrubs on the side of the house. The guards had taken up cover behind what was left of the tractor and hay baler.

"We need to get out of here," Janice reminded her.

Yes, they did. But Rosalie watched as Austin had to

scramble away from yet another shot. He was doing this
to give them a chance to escape, but it could turn into a
suicide mission for him.

"Let's go," Janice pressed. She put both of the tiny babies in a single carrier seat and looped the handle over
her left arm.

"Is there another gun in the house?" Rosalie asked.

Janice's head jerked up. "There's one on the top of
fridge. It's in the way back, so it's hard to see and reach.
But you can't be thinking of helping him."

Yes, that's exactly what she was thinking. Rosalie
wasn't sure she wanted to trust this woman with the truth
about what she was really doing there, but the bottom
line was that Austin might be her best bet in finding her
daughter. Because it was personal for him, too, since he
was on a mission to find his nephew.

Plus, there was the part about his owing her for Eli's
death.

It wasn't exactly fair to play the guilt card, but she
was many steps past being desperate. She'd do *anything*
to find Sadie.

"Here," Rosalie said and pressed the truck keys into
the nanny's right hand. Too bad she didn't have a phone
to give her, as well, but the guards had taken those from
them. "The truck's out front, away from the gunfire. Get
the babies out of here."

"But what about you? The boss said we should leave,"
Janice reminded her.

Rosalie ignored that and got Janice moving. Thankfully, the sound of more shots caused the woman to hurry,
and they made their way down the stairs and to the front
of the house.

"Drive toward the interstate," Rosalie instructed. "And stop at the first police or fire station you see."

Janice gave a shaky nod and one last look before she raced out the door and to the truck. Rosalie didn't wait to watch her leave. She figured the moment the guards heard the roar of the engine that they'd try to stop the nanny from fleeing with the babies.

That couldn't happen.

Rosalie hadn't been able to protect her own child from being taken, but she could do something about these two. She went to the kitchen, slapped off the lights and stood on her tiptoes so she could search the top of the fridge.

She found the gun.

It didn't take long, just a few seconds, before she heard the truck start. The guards heard it, too, and one of them lifted his head, ready to bolt toward the vehicle.

Austin stopped him.

He fired a shot, sending the man back behind the tractor. But he didn't stay put. The guard and his partner started firing. Nonstop.

All the bullets were aimed at Austin.

Walter kept crawling, coming closer to the house, and Rosalie saw him lift his rifle toward Austin. She wasn't sure Austin would be able even to see the man, and it was a risk she couldn't take.

Rosalie didn't think beyond giving the babies the best possible chance at escape. She opened the kitchen door, and the fridge, as well, so she could use it for cover once she fired.

Walter spotted her right away and pointed the gun at her. However, she pointed her gun right back at him.

And she got off the first shot.

She hadn't aimed for any particular part of him, but

the bullet slammed into either his chest or his shoulder, causing him to drop back to the ground.

God, had she just killed a man?

As horrible as that thought was, it would be worse if Walter had managed to shoot Austin, Janice or the babies.

The other guards cursed at her, and both fired into the house. Even over the sound of those shots and her own heartbeat crashing in her ears, she heard Austin.

"Get down!" he yelled.

Rosalie didn't do that. She fired another shot at the guards. Austin did the same, and it kept the men pinned down long enough that they weren't able to stop Janice from escaping. Rosalie caught just a glimpse of the truck taillights as the nanny sped away.

The relief flooded through her.

And the fear.

What if the guards had already managed to call someone to get them out there to the road? And what if they managed to stop the truck? She doubted they would hurt the babies. There was too much money to be made from them.

But they'd kill Janice.

"You're both gonna die!" one of the guards shouted.

The threat had no sooner left his mouth when Austin fired again. Two shots. One for each guard. And both men dropped to the ground.

Everything seemed to freeze. The cold rain. The echo of those shots. The lifeless guards. Everything except Austin. With his gun still pointed at the guards, he jumped onto the porch and went straight toward her.

"Whoever's on the other end of the cameras will send someone after us," Austin warned her. "We have to move fast."

Rosalie knew he was right, but like the rain and the

guards, she felt frozen. Austin helped with that, too. He took her by the arm and ran out of the house with her. Not toward the driveway, where Janice had just driven away. But rather toward another barn that looked ready to collapse under the weight of an old, sagging roof.

"Firing at those guards was stupid," Austin snarled. "You could have been killed."

She wanted to argue, wanted to remind him that he could have been killed, as well, but Austin kept her moving. Running. And when he threw open the barn door, she saw the other truck.

"Where's the nanny?" he asked, shoving her inside the vehicle.

"I told her to drive to a police or fire station."

If he approved of that, he didn't say. Instead, he hot-wired the truck, fast, the engine roaring to life, and he slammed on the accelerator. The back tires skidded on the wet, slippery ground, but Austin quickly gained control.

"I'll need to drop you off somewhere." He spared her a glance before those lawman's eyes kept watch around them again. No doubt for anyone following them. "I have something I need to do."

"Something involving this baby farm?"

He didn't answer her right away. "Yeah."

There was a lot of emotion in that one-word response. Rosalie didn't know Austin that well, but she'd been engaged to an FBI agent. Was the sister of one. She knew the personal risks they were willing to take.

"Your cover's been blown," she reminded him.

Well, it had been if any of those guards had survived or if the people behind those cameras had been able to figure out what was going on. Heaven knew who was already on the way out to intercept them.

Austin just shook his head. "I have something important to do. Keep watch," he added, his voice clipped now.

She did. Rosalie kept her gun ready, but that didn't stop the feeling that Austin was withholding something she needed to know.

"There's a safe house about ten miles from here," he explained. "I'll drop you off there and call someone to come and get you. Seth can put you in protective custody."

Because she would now be a target. Rosalie didn't welcome that, but she'd known it was a risk before she'd ever started this.

"Where are you going?" she pressed.

Austin mumbled something she didn't catch. Cursed. Then, he shook his head. "There's a second place. Not too far away. Once I have you safe, I can go there."

It took a moment for that to sink in. "You mean another baby farm?"

"Yeah. It's a lot bigger than this one. Maybe even the command center for the entire operation."

Mercy. This was exactly what she'd been looking for. Despite the ordeal of the shooting and the breakneck speed that Austin was driving, Rosalie could feel a glimmer of hope.

"I haven't been able to get onto the grounds of this second house to access the records," he continued, "but I know there are babies being held for processing. If the guards heard about what just happened here, they'll shut down that place and move the babies."

Austin's gaze slashed to hers for just a second. "My nephew could be there."

"And my daughter. Or at least the records to show me where she was taken. I have—"

"I can't take you with me. It's too dangerous."

Rosalie heard the words, and she knew they were true. But that didn't matter. "I'm going with you. You can't stop me."

That brought on some more profanity. "It's dangerous," he repeated.

"Do you really think I care about that now or that I want you to care about it?" Despite the high speed, she scooted closer to him, so he could hopefully see the determination in her eyes. "Put yourself in my place."

Her voice broke. And the blasted tears came. Tears that wouldn't do Sadie any good, so Rosalie tried to choke them back.

"I have to find my daughter," she managed to say. "And you'd just be wasting time taking me to the safe house. The guards could be moving the babies and records right now. If that happens, we might never find them."

Again, no immediate answer. He just volleyed glances among the road, their surroundings and her, but Rosalie saw the exact moment that he realized she was right.

"You'll stay in the truck," he snapped. "And don't make me regret this."

Rosalie didn't say anything. Didn't want to utter a word that would make him change his mind. She only wanted to get to the house and see if her daughter was there.

Or any babies for that matter.

Yes, Sadie was her priority, but she couldn't bear the thought of any child or parent going through this.

Austin took the next turn off the road. Then, another. Thankfully, he seemed to know exactly where he was going. That would save time, but would it get them there fast enough?

Rosalie remembered the communicator that one of the guards had been wearing when they'd stormed into the cottage and found Austin and her in bed. If the guard had been wearing that during the attack, then someone would have already been alerted to a problem. The people behind this would soon link that problem back to Austin and her.

And Janice.

Rosalie added a quick prayer that the nanny had already made it to safety with the babies. Too bad she didn't have a way to contact Janice, but maybe they could do that soon.

"Thank you," she whispered to Austin.

"Don't," he snapped like a warning. "Because I'm not doing either of us any favors here." He paused and, even in the dim light from the dash, she saw his jaw muscles stir. "They've killed people, Rosalie. And they'll kill again."

That reminder caused her heartbeat to kick up a significant notch, and she thought there was even more that Austin had to say. But he didn't say it.

He just kept driving.

The rain was coming down harder now, the wipers slashing at the fat drops, but it was still hard to see. It got even harder when Austin turned off his headlights and slowed down. Using just the parking lights to guide them, he turned onto another road, drove about a quarter of a mile and then brought the truck to a stop.

He cursed.

"What's wrong?" she asked, but Rosalie was afraid to hear the answer.

"There should be vehicles." Austin got his gun ready, opened the door a fraction and looked around them. He killed the parking lights. Inched closer.

Once her eyes adjusted to the darkness, she saw the silhouette of what appeared to be a large metal barn. Austin was right—no vehicles. No lights, either. The place looked deserted.

He reached over, his hand brushing her leg, and he grabbed a flashlight from the glove compartment. He flicked it on and turned it toward the ground.

That set off another round of profanity.

"There are plenty of tire tracks that have dug into the muddy road," he relayed. "We must have just missed them."

No! It felt as if someone had just clamped a fist around her heart, and Rosalie tried to choke back a sob.

"Maybe they left records." She hoped so, anyway.

Austin inched the truck closer to the building while he kept the flashlight aimed at the ground. He turned it off only when they reached the front of the barn.

The double sliding metal doors were wide-open, and it was pitch-dark inside. If anyone was lurking in there ready to attack, Rosalie couldn't see them.

"Get down," Austin ordered.

She did. Rosalie got onto the floor as Austin drove right into the building.

"Empty," he mumbled.

But then he hit the brakes.

Rosalie lifted her head to try to see what had captured his attention. It appeared to be a white piece of paper nailed to one of the walls.

Austin turned on the flashlight, pointed it toward the paper, and she saw the words scrawled there.

You're a dead man, John Mercer.

"John Mercer," Austin repeated. "That's the name I've been using at the baby farm."

That hardly had time to register in her head when she heard the slight hissing sound.

"Hold on!" Austin shouted. He threw the truck into reverse and slammed his foot on the accelerator.

Just as the wall of fire shot up in front of them.

Chapter Four

Austin held his breath and prayed that he'd get Rosalie away from the building in time.

The truck bolted through the doors, and the moment they were outside, Austin spun the steering wheel to get them on the road. He hit the gas again and got them moving.

Not a second too soon.

Behind them, the building burst into a fireball.

Obviously, someone had put a hefty amount of accelerant inside, and it'd worked. It wouldn't take long for anything left inside to be destroyed.

Hell.

These goons were trying to cover their tracks, and in doing so they might have erased the very information that he needed to find his nephew.

"Call 911," he told Rosalie, tossing her his phone. Austin kept watch around them to make sure they weren't about to be ambushed. The narrow road was lined with trees on both sides, and that meant plenty of places for the shooters to hide. "Tell them we need the fire department and the locals out here. I want this entire area sealed off."

Austin wasn't sure how she managed it because her hands were shaking so hard, but Rosalie made the call.

Maybe, just maybe, there might be something left to recover.

"I have to find out if Janice made it to someplace safe,"
Rosalie said the moment she finished the 911 call. "Oh,
God," she added in a mumble. "What if the local county
cops are in on this?"

"Don't borrow trouble," Austin reminded her.

He took his phone, scrolled through the numbers, located the number of his partner at the FBI, and gave the
cell back to Rosalie. "Text him. Tell him to BOLO Janice Aiken and that she's driving a black truck registered
to my undercover alias, John Mercer." Austin rattled off
the license plate. "I want him to call me the minute he
finds her."

"BOLO," she repeated while she wrote the text. "Be
on the lookout."

She'd obviously picked up some cop jargon from Eli or
maybe her stepbrother Seth. Austin figured Seth wasn't
going to like Rosalie's rogue investigation, and Rosalie
wasn't going to like it when Austin called her stepbrother
so that Seth could force her to back off. Since she wouldn't
listen to him, he had no choice about doing that.

"These baby thieves know you've betrayed them,"
Rosalie said after she finished the text.

Yeah, they did. The note proved that.

You're a dead man, John Mercer.

And while the idiots behind the baby farms probably
didn't know his real identity, it wouldn't be long before
they figured out he was FBI. After all, they had countless
images of him from those surveillance cameras.

Of Rosalie, too.

"You shouldn't have come here," he insisted. Obviously, he was repeating himself, but Austin hoped she realized just how much danger she was in.

"You came," she pointed out.

Austin tossed her a scowl. The only thing he knew about Rosalie was what Eli had told him. That she was the quiet, shy type who was downright squeamish about his job as a federal agent.

Well, she'd clearly changed *a lot*.

This was no quiet, shy woman next to him. Or maybe Rosalie had just managed to put her squeamishness aside so she could find her daughter. Still, that wouldn't happen if she got herself killed.

"What do we do now?" she asked. "What if there's no evidence to recover from that building or the baby farm?"

Austin slowed as he approached the junction that would take him back to a main road. "I continue the investigation, and you go home."

She huffed and would have no doubt argued with him about that if the movement hadn't grabbed their attention.

Austin was almost at a full stop at the intersection when someone darted out in front of the truck. He automatically pushed Rosalie down onto the seat, and in the same motion, he took aim at the man.

"Don't shoot!" the man yelled. He had his hands in the air but almost immediately dropped one to his arm. Thanks to the headlights, Austin could see blood on the sleeve of his jacket. "They tried to kill me."

Austin had a fast debate with himself. He could just drive off and call for someone to come and get the guy. After all, despite that injury, this man could be part of this baby farm operation.

And that's why Austin lost that mental debate.

Because if he was indeed part of the operation, then

that meant he had answers, and Austin wouldn't get those answers if he allowed him to disappear. Or die.

"Stay down," Austin warned Rosalie.

Did she listen?

No, of course not.

She lifted her head, and Austin nudged her right back down before he lowered his window.

"I need help," the man insisted, walking toward the truck.

"Don't come any closer," Austin warned him, and he took aim at him. "Who are you?"

"Sonny Buckland. I'm a P.I. from Austin."

"Send another text to Sawyer Ryland, my partner at the FBI," Austin told Rosalie. "Have him run this guy's name and ask him to hurry." While she did that, Austin pinned his attention to the man. "Open the sides of your jacket so I can see if you're armed."

"I'm not," he insisted, and he winced when he pulled back the side with the blood. "They took my gun when they found me snooping around the place."

"They?"

"Three armed guards. Big guys. The only reason I managed to escape is because they got a call from someone who told them to get out fast. I ran. That's when one of them shot me."

That meshed with what Austin figured had happened. The person monitoring the cameras at the baby farm had likely made the call to let the guards at this place know there'd been a breach in security.

"How do you know I don't work for those guards?" Austin came right out and asked.

"If you did, you would have already killed me."

True. But that didn't mean Austin would blindly trust

this guy. The guards could have left him behind with orders to finish off anyone who got near the place.

Sonny clamped his hand over his injured arm and fired nervy glances all around them. "Stating the obvious here, but it's not safe to hang around. We need to get out of here."

Austin nodded. "You're not going anywhere with us until you convince me you're not working for the baby snatchers."

"I'm not working for them!" Sonny practically yelled. Then, he groaned, a mixture of pain and frustration. "A client hired me to find his missing pregnant friend. I followed some leads that I got from a criminal informant, and it led me to this place."

Rosalie made a soft sound of agreement, and even though Sonny's story meshed with hers about getting the info from a CI, Austin shot them both scowls for inserting themselves into a dangerous investigation. Yeah, he'd done the same thing. And not with authorization, either. But he was a trained agent. Neither of them was.

Of course, Sonny could still be a threat.

"Did you learn who was behind this operation?" Rosalie asked the man. "Did you find any records or anything that could help us locate some missing babies?"

Sonny huffed and made more of those uneasy glances around. He looked on the verge of trying again to press Austin to get him out of there, but maybe he realized the fastest way for that to happen was to give them any info he had.

"I did learn something," Sonny said. Then, paused. "I think a piece of scum named Trevor Yancy is responsible for at least some of the baby kidnappings."

Rosalie sucked in her breath, and her hand went to

her mouth. Austin tried to rein in any response, but just like that, his thoughts jerked him back to a bad place, a bad time.

Eli's murder.

Rosalie was no doubt doing the same thing. Because the man Eli and he had been investigating for gunrunning and a whole host of crimes was none other than Trevor Yancy.

"You know Yancy," Sonny said. Not a question, either.

Obviously Austin hadn't done a good job of hiding his reaction. No surprise there. Austin was responsible for the way that investigation had turned out, and it had turned out in the worst possible way.

With Eli shot dead by an unknown assailant.

And Yancy a free man.

If Yancy was indeed involved with the baby farms, then the question was why? Was it just another illegal venture on his part, or was there something even more sinister going on here? Something to do with Rosalie and him?

"What makes you think Yancy's connected to this?" Austin demanded.

Sonny shook his head. "I'll tell you once we're out of here. These men will kill us all if they come back."

Austin couldn't dispute that, and despite his need for the truth, he could no longer keep Rosalie at the center of this possible danger. He was already responsible for Eli's death. Best not to add hers to the nightmares that he stood no chance of ever forgetting.

With a firm grip on his gun, Austin opened his truck door, but before he could get out, Rosalie caught his arm. "You're not going out there."

For a split second Austin was taken aback by her concern. Her touch, too. But just as quickly as she'd touched him, she pulled away her hand. He realized then that her concern wasn't aimed at him but rather their situation. If he got shot, her chances of getting out of there and finding her daughter would decrease big-time.

"I'm only going to frisk him," Austin told her.

He stepped from the truck and did just that. Sonny cooperated, lifting his hands away from his body and wincing in the process.

"No gun, like I said," Sonny explained. "But I've lost some blood."

Yes, he had, and that meant Austin's first stop had to be a hospital, and the nearest one was back in the ranching town of Silver Creek. He could leave Rosalie there, as well, since he knew the sheriff and deputies. He doubted Rosalie would like that, but Austin didn't intend to give her a choice.

"You can ride in the back of the truck." Austin motioned for Sonny to hop in, and the man did. It was freezing cold and wouldn't be a pleasant ride, especially considering his injury, but Austin couldn't risk allowing him in the cab of the truck with Rosalie and him.

"Keep an eye on him," Austin said to her when he got back in.

He checked the road to make sure no one was out there waiting for them, and when Austin didn't see anyone, he got them out of there fast.

"Trevor Yancy," Rosalie mumbled. She turned in the seat so she could nail her attention to Sonny. "Has his name come up in your investigation of the baby farms?"

"No." Austin didn't have to think about that, either. A lot of names had popped up. Potential suspects and kidnap victims. But if he'd seen anything about Yancy related to this, he would have definitely remembered.

"Is it possible…?" Rosalie's breath hitched, and even though they weren't touching, Austin could practically feel her muscles tensing. "Would Yancy have kidnapped my daughter and your nephew because Eli and you had been investigating him?"

Anything was possible when it came to a snake like Yancy.

Anything.

And since that wasn't likely to make Rosalie's breath stop hitching, Austin didn't spell it out for her. Still, this could be the lead that Austin had been searching for. He reached for his phone to have someone bring in Yancy for questioning, but it dinged before he could do that.

"It's a text from FBI Agent Ryland," Rosalie relayed. She still had hold of his phone and stared down at the screen. "He said there's a Sonny Buckland who's a P.I., and he's attached a photo of him." She held it out for Austin to glance at.

The photo was definitely of the same man who was now riding in the bed of the truck. At least Sonny hadn't lied about his identity, but that didn't mean Austin was anywhere close to trusting him.

"Sonny has no criminal record," Rosalie continued to read. She paused though and cleared her throat. "And your partner wants to know what the heck is going on, except he used a lot more profanity than I just did. He also wants you to call him *now*."

She showed him that part of the text, too, though Austin didn't have to see it to know that Sawyer had likely figured out that Austin wasn't on vacation as he'd claimed. Nope. He was on an unauthorized undercover investigation that had just gone to hell in a handbasket.

"I'll call him as soon as I've dropped off both Sonny

and you," Austin said more to himself. Rosalie obviously heard it, though.

"I want to go with you to question Yancy or anyone else connected to this," she insisted.

"Yeah, I bet you do, but it's not going to happen. No way will I put you in danger like that."

"I'm already in danger!" she practically shouted, but the fit of temper disappeared as quickly as it'd come. "I need to find my daughter. Eli's daughter," she added, probably because she figured it would touch every raw nerve in his body and soften him up.

He couldn't let it work on him.

His phone vibrated, indicating he had an incoming call, and he saw Sawyer's name on the screen. His partner had obviously meant that part about Austin calling him back now.

Bracing himself for questions he wasn't ready to answer, Austin took his phone, issued another "Keep watch" to Rosalie and answered the call. He didn't put it on speaker, and that was probably the reason Rosalie scooted across the seat—so she could hear.

"Well?" Sawyer said the moment Austin answered.

"I was looking for my missing nephew," Austin settled for saying.

"Yes, and our boss already figured that out. He's not happy, Austin, and he wants you back from your *vacation*."

"I'll be back soon." He hoped. "For now, I just need your help. I'm en route to the Silver Creek hospital to drop off an injured P.I. who's either a witness or a person of interest in some assorted felonies. I'll be there in about five minutes. Can you make some calls and arrange for him to be guarded?"

Sawyer didn't answer for several snail-crawling moments. "Sure."

"I also need you to have someone secure two crime scenes on the farm road that runs directly east of the town of Silver Creek," Austin added. "Both were baby farms and are owned by a dummy corporation, Real Estate Investments. There's not much left of them, and there are possible explosives planted around the grounds."

"I'll get someone out there right away," Sawyer assured him. Another pause. "You had a BOLO on a woman driving a black truck registered to your alias?"

"Yeah—"

"A deputy here in Silver Creek just phoned it in. They found her." Sawyer paused again. "It's not good news, Austin. The woman's dead."

Chapter Five

Rosalie's heart went to her knees. She couldn't stop the brutal thoughts and images from going through her head. Images of Janice's frantic escape from the baby farm and the ordeal that had led up to it.

At the time Rosalie had believed that escape was the woman's best chance of surviving.

Obviously, she'd been wrong.

"Oh, God." Rosalie grabbed the phone from Austin and put it on speaker. "What about the babies? Janice had two newborns with her."

"Who is this?" Agent Ryland snapped.

Austin mumbled some profanity and made the final turn toward the hospital. "She's Rosalie McKinnon."

Agent Ryland repeated her name. "She was engaged to Eli." Even though Rosalie didn't know Agent Ryland, the man obviously knew her since it wasn't a question.

"And she's also Seth Calder's stepsister," Austin added. "I ran into her while I was undercover." He glanced at her, as if he might add more, but then shook his head. "Now, what about the babies?"

"Both are fine. According to the deputy, Janice drove to the sheriff's office, but she was already injured when she got there. She'd been shot."

Rosalie's heart just kept dropping. She was beyond thankful that the babies were okay, but it was terrifying to think of Janice being pursued by these monsters while she was trying to get the newborns to safety.

"The babies are being taken to the hospital," Agent Ryland continued. "Just as a precaution. There's not a scratch on them. And, of course, child protective services will be brought in. Will the woman's killer try to come after the babies?" he came right out and asked.

Rosalie already knew the answer and dreaded hearing it.

"Possibly," Austin said without hesitation.

"I'll get right on it," Ryland answered, also without hesitation, and he ended the call.

"This is all my fault," she whispered.

Austin made a yeah, right sound. "The fault lies with the person who set up the baby farm."

True, but if she hadn't put Janice in a position where she had to escape, the woman might be alive. "If I'd stayed with her and the babies, this might not have happened."

"Yes, it would have, and you'd be dead, too. Those guards wouldn't have wanted any witnesses to get away."

And since both Austin and she were just that—witnesses—then, yes, the men would have tried to shoot her, too. But at least if she'd been there, she might have been able to stop it and Janice might be alive.

Austin drove into the hospital parking lot and came to a stop directly in front of the E.R. doors. Sonny climbed out, not easily, and while still clutching his injured arm, he headed inside.

"Stay close to me," Austin warned her, and as he'd done while they were on the road, he kept watch around them.

The rain had stopped, but the wind took a swipe at her.

She was already shivering from the spent adrenaline, and the bitter cold only made it worse.

The moment the E.R. staff saw Sonny, they rushed forward and whisked him away to one of the examination rooms. A security guard wearing a uniform trailed along behind them.

Rosalie looked around, hoping to see the babies and whoever was guarding them, but the E.R. was empty except for a woman sitting at the intake desk.

"I'll need to get some information from you about the patient," the woman said.

But Austin waved her off. "Nothing much we can tell you. We just gave him a ride here."

That wasn't the whole truth, of course, but Austin probably didn't want to get into any details of the investigation with someone who wasn't law enforcement.

"I'll check on the babies," Austin said when Rosalie continued to look around.

He took out his phone, stepped to the far side of the room, but before he could make a call his phone rang. He groaned and showed her the name on the screen.

Seth.

Now it was Rosalie's turn to groan. Agent Ryland had likely called Seth.

"Let me talk to my sister," Seth ordered. Even without the call being on speaker, she had no trouble hearing him.

"I'm fine," Rosalie jumped to say to her brother when Austin handed her the phone.

"You're not fine if you were in the middle of an undercover investigation. Have you lost your mind?"

Probably. Hard to have a sound mind with her baby kidnapped. "I don't expect you to understand why I did what I did."

"Oh, I understand it all right. I want to find my niece as much as you do, but I don't want my sister dead in the process. Put Austin back on the phone," he ordered, sounding very much like the hardheaded brother that he was.

"How the hell did she manage to get inside an undercover operation, and exactly how close did she come to dying?" Again her brother's voice was so loud that Rosalie didn't need the speaker function to hear him.

Austin's gaze met hers, and she silently pleaded with him not to tell the truth. It was best if she broke the details to Seth after he calmed down. Whenever the heck that might be.

"Rosalie's okay. She was just in the wrong place at the wrong time," Austin said, but he shot her a glare. No doubt because he wasn't happy about the lie or her involvement in any of this.

"From what I'm hearing, you were both at the wrong place. You do know your boss is ticked off about this?"

"Yeah, I heard," Austin mumbled. "Can't be helped."

"We got a lead on the missing babies," Rosalie volunteered since she doubted Austin wanted to continue to listen to this scolding any more than she did.

She moved closer to the phone, and in doing so, her cheek brushed against Austin's. The slight contact stunned her, as if it'd been more than just an accidental touch, and she eased away from him.

Austin's gaze stayed on her, and he cleared his throat. Obviously, he wasn't any more comfortable touching her than she was touching him.

Except it hadn't been just discomfort on her part.

Rosalie felt that trickle of heat. The kind of man-to-woman heat that she couldn't possibly feel when it came to Austin, so she quickly shoved it aside and hoped it didn't come back.

"Trevor Yancy's name came up in connection with the baby farms," Austin told Seth.

"Hell," Seth mumbled.

And that was Rosalie's reaction, too.

Well, it was after she managed to force that *trickle* to take a hike. It was easier to do now that Yancy was in the forefront of her thoughts.

Yancy and his hired gun could be the people responsible for the attack that had left Eli dead, and she wanted the man to have no further connection to her and her family. However, Yancy might have the ultimate connection if he'd been the one to kidnap Sadie.

"I'll deal with Yancy," Austin continued. "And I'll drive Rosalie home as soon as someone arrives to take over for me here at the hospital."

"Don't take her home yet." Seth cursed, groaned, cursed again. "I'm tied up with a case here in El Paso, so I'm asking you to do me a favor. Protect her. Make sure these goons don't come after her. And, Rosalie, don't you dare say you can take care of yourself."

Since that's exactly what she'd been about to say, Rosalie just stayed quiet and aimed her own glare at the phone. She loved Seth, and he'd been more of a real brother to her than her own three blood-kin ones had been, but she couldn't stop looking for her precious baby.

No amount of warnings from anyone, including Seth or Austin, would stop her.

"Sawyer said these goons killed a woman," Seth went on, talking to Austin now. "And if so, they could come after Rosalie."

That made her feel a little light-headed. She'd considered that, of course, but what she hadn't realized was that if Austin took her to her family's ranch, that she could put all of them in danger, too. Her pregnant sister, Rayanne, was there. Her father, as well, along with her oldest brother's wife and toddler son. She didn't want them caught up in the middle of this dangerous situation.

"I'll get Rosalie to a safe house," Austin assured him, and before either one could give her a say in the matter, they ended the call.

She had to make Austin understand that she wasn't going into hiding. "I don't want to go to a safe house. I want to find Sadie."

But she was talking to the air because Austin's attention was no longer on her. It was on the lanky dark-haired man who came through the E.R. doors. Rosalie immediately spotted the silver badge clipped to his belt and figured he was carrying a weapon beneath his buckskin coat.

"Agent Duran?" he said, heading their way. "I'm Deputy Gage Ryland. I'm here to guard the man you brought in."

"Ryland," Austin repeated. "You're Sawyer's cousin?"

The deputy nodded, the corner of his mouth lifting a little. "Around here, just about every Ryland has got a badge." The half smile quickly faded. "Tell me about this guy I'll be guarding."

Austin showed the deputy the photo that Sawyer had sent him on his phone. "His name is Sonny Buckland, a P.I. I found him near a baby farm that I'm investigating."

His mouth tightened. "You think he killed the woman with the babies?"

"No." But then Austin huffed and shrugged. "He was with us when that particular shooting happened, but I can't rule out that he's not part of it in some way. In fact, he could have been the one to give the order to have her shot."

The deputy nodded. "Then, I won't let him out of my sight. We need to catch the SOB who put a bullet in the woman and endangered those babies."

Rosalie couldn't agree more. "How are the babies? Where are they?"

He tipped his head toward a hall off the E.R. "We brought them in through a side entrance. Two other deputies are with them and will escort them to Child Protective Services when the social workers arrive."

That made her breathe a little easier, but her heart was still slamming against her chest.

"My brother's the sheriff," Deputy Ryland continued, "and he's on his way to what's left of the baby farm sites. We'll have a CSI team out there, and the FBI's been called in."

With all that, they might find something.

Correction: they *had* to find something.

"What exactly happened to Janice? How did she die?" she asked. Part of Rosalie didn't want to know the details, especially since she felt responsible, but the other part of her had to know.

"She was shot," the deputy explained. "It appears the bullet went in through the back window of the truck she was driving, and it struck her in the side of the neck. It's a miracle she managed to get away from her attacker. A miracle, too, that the babies weren't hurt."

Just hearing that spelled out caused her knees to buckle, and if Austin hadn't caught her, Rosalie was afraid she would have fallen. It wasn't just *these* babies who caused her reaction. Though they were the immediate concern. But if the monster behind this had put these two babies at such horrible risk, then her daughter was in the same danger.

Mercy, it hurt too much to think about that. And she'd tried to keep the bad thought aside. Impossible to do that now that she'd dealt with those guards face-to-face. Rosalie knew what they were capable of and how far they'd go to keep their operation under wraps.

Deputy Ryland must have noticed the alarm on her face and probably in every inch of her body because he grumbled something about checking on Sonny, and he stepped away, no doubt so Austin could tend to her.

"Come on," Austin said, taking her by the arm. "I'll get you to that safe house."

Rosalie wanted to stay put, to learn as much as she could from whatever else Sonny might tell them. However, even she couldn't deny that she was shaken to the core and needed a few hours to regroup.

After that, she'd have to get away from Austin.

Protect her, Seth had told him, and it didn't matter about the bad blood between Austin and her. She figured Austin had no plans to let her out of his sight.

Well, temporarily, anyway.

He'd likely put her in some other agent's protective custody so that he could get on with finding his nephew and putting an end to the baby farms. He'd want to exclude her while doing that.

But that wasn't going to happen.

"How far is this safe house?" she asked.

"Not far. But we'll have to drive around first to make sure we aren't being followed. And it's not a place we want to use for long. It's best if I make arrangements for another place outside the county."

That would put her even farther away from the baby farm. From Janice's killers, too. But it wasn't a trade-off Rosalie wanted since she needed to find answers about

Sadie, and sadly, those killers might have those answers. Once they were at this interim safe house, she would somehow have to convince Austin to stay in the area.

That wouldn't be an easy task.

Austin paused when they reached the E.R. doors and looked out. There were no other vehicles near his truck, just the same ones that had been in the parking lot when they'd arrived. Still, he hurried, and the moment he had her inside, he drove away.

"You okay?" he asked.

"No." Rosalie didn't even try to lie, especially since she was still shaking.

He made a soft sound of agreement. "I'm sorry. I know the shooting must bring back memories of Eli."

"Everything brings back those memories," she mumbled.

"Yes." And that's all he said for several moments. "I know saying I'm sorry won't help, but I am sorry."

Rosalie heard the words. Every one of them. But she couldn't respond. She'd been raised to be polite. To not do anything intentionally to hurt a person's feelings, but there was no way she could let him off the hook.

Eli was dead.

And Austin was partly to blame.

There were probably a lot of details of the investigation she didn't know, but Seth had given her the big picture. Austin and Eli had been undercover investigating an illegal weapons ring, and when a hired gun of the operation had tried to flee, Austin had gone after him.

And in doing so, Austin had essentially blown their covers.

As a result, Eli had been gunned down a few seconds later by a second hired thug, who then disappeared along with his partner whom Eli had been chasing. All of this had happened just weeks before Eli and she had planned to walk down the aisle. Rosalie hadn't even had a chance to tell Eli that he was going to be a father since she'd learned the news herself only that morning.

As horrible as all those memories were, they gave her something to focus on. Something other than Janice's murder and the danger to all those babies.

Probably because she was still shivering, Austin cranked up the heat and took the road out of town. He didn't go far, less than a mile, before he turned around and went in the opposite direction.

"See anything?" he asked.

Rosalie was about to say no, but she caught something out of the corner of her eye. A vehicle was parked on a side road. No headlights, and it didn't pull out and follow them. However, because of the events of the night, it put her on edge.

"Yeah, I saw it," Austin said, following her gaze to the side mirror. "It could be a spotter, to try to figure out which direction we're going."

And that meant it could be someone connected to the baby farms. "Too bad we just can't stop and question the person inside."

"Not with you in the truck." Austin continued to glance at the vehicle while he turned back toward town. "I'll try another road."

The words had hardly left his mouth when the vehicle pulled out onto the road, following them.

"Get down in the seat," Austin warned her.

Rosalie slid down, but she stayed high enough so she could watch from the side mirror.

Austin handed her his phone. "Call Sawyer. Tell him

there's been a change of plans, that I'm taking you to the Silver Creek sheriff's office instead so they can guard you there."

She hated being pawned off, but her mere presence was stopping Austin from going after the person in the vehicle. Rosalie hoped once he dropped her off that Austin would go in pursuit with plenty of backup.

Before she could press Sawyer's number, the phone rang, and she saw a familiar name on the screen.

Deputy Gage Ryland.

Mercy. She prayed something hadn't happened to the babies. Rosalie pushed the answer button so hard that she nearly broke the phone, and she put the call on speaker.

"Are the babies okay?" she jumped to ask.

"Fine," Deputy Ryland answered. "That's not why I'm calling. Is Agent Duran there?"

"I'm here, but I've got someone tailing me. I'm heading to the sheriff's office now."

"Make a detour to the hospital, and I'll have someone take care of the tail."

Austin and she exchanged an uneasy glance. There'd been nothing urgent in the deputy's voice when she'd met him at the hospital, but there was definitely some urgency now.

"I'm with the injured P.I. you brought in," Gage continued, "and I think you should get back down to the hospital fast. We've got a *big* problem."

Chapter Six

That was definitely not what Austin wanted to hear Deputy Gage Ryland say.

We've got a big problem.

Austin already had enough of those. A dead woman. Two destroyed crime scenes. And a whole mess of loose ends he needed to be working on.

Including taking Rosalie to a safe house.

"What's going on?" Austin asked Gage.

"A guy just showed up at the hospital, and he demanded to see the P.I., Sonny Buckland. I told him it'd have to wait, that he was still being stitched up, but before I could send him on his merry way, Sonny came out of the examining room. Armed. He snatched the security guard's gun and aimed it at the guy. Sonny's holding him at gunpoint now."

Of all the problems that Austin had imagined, that wasn't one of them.

Austin shook his head. "And who exactly is the visitor?"

"Trevor Yancy."

Even in the darkness, Austin could see the surprise dart through Rosalie's eyes.

The concern, too.

"I wouldn't have called you," Gage went on, "but this Yancy idiot is egging Sonny on, along with demanding to see Rosalie and you. I'd really rather resolve this without bullets."

So would Austin, especially since the babies might still be nearby.

"I'm on the way," Austin assured Gage, and he turned and headed in the direction of Main Street.

"I want to go with you," Rosalie insisted. "It'll only waste time if you drop me off at the sheriff's office first. And besides, it sounds as if the sheriff and his deputies already have their hands full."

Austin couldn't dispute any of that, but there was another angle to this. "You've already been put in enough danger tonight."

She took hold of his arm, forcing him to make brief eye contact. It was just a glance, but Austin could see the determination written all over her face.

"Trevor might have kidnapped my daughter," she reminded him. "And your nephew. If he did, I want to see his reaction when you ask him about it."

"You're not getting a chance to see his reaction or anything else." Then, Austin huffed. "Sonny's armed, and I don't want you caught in the middle of whatever beef these two morons have against each other."

And it was that beef that Austin was especially eager to learn more about. Sonny had said he'd suspected that Yancy had played a part in at least some of the baby kidnappings, so that might explain why the P.I. would want to hold Yancy at gunpoint.

But why wouldn't Sonny just have Gage arrest Yancy?

Something more was going on here, and Austin intended to get to the bottom of it.

Apparently with Rosalie in tow.

Even if he dropped her off at the sheriff's office, there were no guarantees that she'd stay put. Or that she'd be any safer there than she would be with him. She wasn't under arrest, though he was sure he could come up with some kind of charges to force her to stay put or declare her a material witness. Still, it would take time to do that, and time wasn't something that was on his side right now.

If Sonny managed to shoot and kill Yancy, then Austin might never learn the truth about the stolen babies.

Cursing his situation and this whole blasted mess, Austin drove toward the hospital.

"Thank you again," Rosalie said when she obviously realized where they were going. She also released a long breath, one that sounded as if she'd been holding it for a while.

Austin darn sure didn't say *You're welcome* because he figured there were too many things that could go wrong with this situation.

Especially since both Sonny and Yancy were suspects.

Even if Gage hadn't told him about the trouble going on, Austin would have known something was wrong the moment that he pulled to a stop by the E.R. Several medics and nurses were outside, huddled together against the bitter cold, and they were out there because Gage had almost certainly evacuated the immediate area.

Austin didn't have a badge to flash. It was too risky to carry one while undercover, but no one questioned him when he identified himself as a federal agent and went back into the E.R. He spotted Gage immediately, his gun drawn, and every part of his body on alert.

"Stay here," Austin warned Rosalie, and with his own gun drawn, he went into the hall to join Gage.

There, in the examining room, he saw the tall, heavily muscled man with blond hair.

Yancy.

He was backed into a corner. Literally. He had his hands lifted in the air. Sonny was in the opposite corner, the examining bed between them, and he did indeed have a gun pointed right at Yancy.

Despite the raised hands, Yancy looked calm, wearing an expression more suited for a social visit than a crime in progress. However, Sonny's face was beaded with sweat, and the fresh stitches on his arm weren't even bandaged. Judging from the way the supplies and equipment had been scattered around the room, the medical staff had left in a hurry.

It'd been over a year and a half since Austin had seen Yancy, but the man hadn't changed much. He still wore a pricey suit that probably cost more than Austin made in a month, and he still had that cocky expression that Austin wished he could knock off his face.

Despite the fancy clothes, Yancy was nothing but a rich punk.

"Austin," Yancy greeted, and the corner of his mouth lifted into a dry smile. "How kind of you to come to this little get-together."

Austin ignored his sarcasm and the man himself and instead turned to Sonny. "Put down that gun now, and then you can tell me what the hell this nonsense is all about."

"It's about *him,*" Sonny snarled with his gaze still staked to Yancy. Sonny's hand was shaking, and he was grimacing as if in pain. Not good. Since his shaking finger was also on the trigger. "Yancy came here to set me up."

Austin glanced at Rosalie to make sure she was staying put. She was. "Set you up how?" he asked Sonny.

But Sonny didn't jump to answer, and Yancy's renewed smile made Austin even more uneasy.

"I used to work for Yancy," Sonny finally said. "I was his top security man, and when I discovered some things that didn't mesh, he fired me."

Yancy dismissed that with a carefree shrug. "He violated my privacy by poking his nose where it didn't belong. And he found nothing illegal. Only some personal emails that he misinterpreted."

"Oh, I found something all right," Sonny argued. His gaze slashed to Austin. "But the emails disappeared. That's why I went to the baby farm, looking for proof, and I'm sure it was Yancy who gave the order to have me shot because I was close to finding out that he'd kidnapped all those kids."

Austin heard Rosalie make a sound of surprise. She obviously hadn't missed what Sonny had just said, and almost immediately Austin heard her footsteps, heading straight toward them.

Oh, man.

Austin didn't even bother to tell her to stay back. She wouldn't. Not when she thought she could learn something about her missing baby.

However, he did try to keep himself between her and the gun Sonny was holding. Sonny didn't seem to want to hurt Rosalie, but Austin wouldn't take the risk of a stray bullet coming her way.

"All lies," Yancy said without a shred of guilt in his voice.

"All truth!" Sonny practically yelled.

"Settle down," Austin warned him, and both Gage and

he moved closer to Sonny in case they had to go after that gun Sonny was still holding.

"Did you kidnap my daughter?" Rosalie came out and asked Yancy despite his denial just moments earlier.

"Of course not. If I were looking for some way to get back at your late fiancé and Austin for their witch hunt of an investigation, I would have gone after them, not your little girl."

His tone was so placating that Rosalie took a step toward him, as if she might try to force the info from him, but Austin hooked his arm around her and held her back.

Since he figured Yancy would just continue to deny any wrongdoing, Austin went with a different approach. "If you're innocent, why come here to the hospital?" he asked Yancy. "And how the heck did you even know you'd find your former employee here?"

Another shrug from Yancy. "I had my people watching Sonny. A precaution since he'd threatened to get even with me. They followed him to the place that he's calling a baby farm. My men had no idea what it was, of course—"

"You're lying," Sonny snapped. "You knew exactly what it was because the address was in one of those emails I found."

"Ah, the emails that don't exist." Yancy made things a thousand times worse by adding a smile.

Sonny would have gone after him, too, if Austin hadn't stopped him. Thankfully, Gage moved in to protect Rosalie so that Austin could concentrate on diffusing this dangerous situation. He took full advantage of Sonny's pain and shaky hand to knock the gun away from him. Sonny tried to go after it again, but Austin pinned him against the wall.

"You know the deputy here has to arrest you," Austin

reminded Sonny. "So, don't do anything else stupid to make it worse."

That last part seemed to do the trick because Sonny stilled. Well, his body did, anyway, but he glared first at Yancy and then at Austin. "You're arresting the wrong man. You should be putting that snake behind bars." And he tipped his head to Yancy.

"I'll gladly arrest him, too, if you have any proof that he's connected to the baby farms."

"No proof," Yancy insisted. "And there won't be because I haven't done anything wrong. Well, not recently, anyway. And nothing that I'd confess to doing."

Yancy smirked again.

Mercy, maybe Austin should have let Sonny hang on to that gun. That wasn't exactly a legal brand of justice, but justice might be served in the end if somebody wiped that smirk off Yancy's face.

"If your men followed Sonny as you said," Rosalie continued, talking to Yancy, "then they likely know who killed the woman who escaped."

For the first time since this whole conversation had started, Yancy looked a little bewildered. Of course, that could be faked.

"They didn't see anyone get killed," Yancy insisted. "If they had, they would have reported it to me, and I would have called the cops like any responsible citizen."

"Right," Austin mumbled, slinging some of that attitude right back at Yancy.

"Right," the man repeated. "Make me out to be the bad guy here if you want, but you'll want to press Sonny for more info about the lie he just told about those emails. I'm sure you've already considered he said that to cover his own butt, that he's the one who's involved with the baby farm. It would explain why he was really out there tonight."

Sonny made a sound of outrage. "I was out there looking for proof of your connection," he repeated.

"And you found nothing." Yancy gave him a flat look before turning his attention back to Austin. "I've been doing some digging of my own because I figured Sonny would try to frame me."

"What'd you find?" Austin demanded when Yancy didn't continue.

"You'll want to check on a past acquaintance of Sonny's. A woman named Vickie Cravens."

Sonny cursed. "Don't you dare drag her into this."

Now Yancy lost some of that cool composure. His eyes narrowed, and his teeth came together for a moment. "You started this game by dragging me into it. If you play with fire, then don't expect to stay alive for very long."

"Who's Vickie Cravens?" Rosalie asked.

"Sonny's former lover," Yancy supplied. He put back on the coat that he'd been holding. "She's worked as a nanny from time to time, and I suspect she's working for the baby farms. Maybe even helping him run them."

"She wouldn't have done anything like this," Sonny insisted.

While buttoning his coat, Yancy started out of the room. "Do your job," he said to Austin. "And you'll find Vickie isn't as innocent as Sonny would like her to be." His mouth bent into another of those nails-on-a-chalkboard smiles before he strolled away.

"Vickie's innocent," Sonny muttered. He no longer looked like the man who'd just challenged Yancy with a gun. He sank down onto the edge of the examining table. "It's Yancy who's behind this."

Austin got right in Sonny's face. "And if he is, I'll be the one to find the evidence. No more grabbing guns from guards—"

"I thought he came here to kill me. I needed that gun to defend myself."

Sonny sounded convincing enough, but Austin's mood was well past the stage of just being bad, so he didn't give him any benefit of the doubt.

"Just stay away from this investigation," he warned Sonny. Austin glanced at Rosalie. "You, too. You're not going to try to question Vickie Cravens."

She stared at him, and he could see not just the weariness in her eyes but also the frustration. Vickie could have info about Rosalie's missing baby, but if so, it was info Austin would get without her.

"You can finish up here?" Austin asked Gage.

Gage nodded. "I gotta arrest him for wielding that gun, but if I don't have anything else to charge him with, then I figure he'll be out by morning after he makes bail."

It was a reminder that if Sonny was indeed guilty of the baby kidnappings, then Austin had to find something fast to keep him behind bars. Of course, *fast* couldn't start to happen until he got Rosalie to a safe house.

Austin thanked Gage and got Rosalie moving toward the exit. Even if this incident hadn't just happened, he would have still made sure it was safe to step outside, but he took a second and third look since Yancy might still be out there. Or the person who'd tried to follow them.

"You okay?" he asked Rosalie when she pulled in a long breath.

"No." Since she didn't look steady on her feet, Austin looped his arm around her waist. Her gaze fired to his as if she might object over the close contact, but she only gave a weary sigh.

"Yeah," he mumbled. He knew exactly what that meant. The danger had created a strange partnership that neither of them had seen coming.

Austin was about to hurry them to his truck when his phone rang, and he saw Sawyer's name on the screen. Maybe, just maybe, his partner had found out something so Austin could make an arrest.

"Please tell me you have good news," Austin greeted Sawyer, and he eased Rosalie away from the doors and back into the waiting room.

"Nowhere near it," Sawyer answered.

Austin groaned. "What went wrong now?"

"You did. Just heard something that you're not gonna like. Trevor Yancy sent a boatload of proof about your unauthorized investigation to the deputy director."

Oh, hell. "I'll be there ASAP to clear things up."

"I think it'll take more than talking to do that," Sawyer added. "Because the boss wants your badge *now*."

Chapter Seven

Rosalie stared at the sterile white ceiling of the safe house. Again. She'd been doing a lot of that since Austin and she had arrived about eight hours earlier. Hard to sleep in a strange bed with so many things unsettled both in her mind and with her botched investigation.

Now she had to deal with the danger.

And the fear that she wasn't any closer to finding Sadie than she had been nearly a year ago when someone had kidnapped her.

It was morning now, the sun creating slivers of light through the blinds, but she didn't get up. She didn't have enough energy to force herself to move. Plus, she didn't hear Austin stirring, something that she would have been able to do in the small two-bedroom house.

The place was literally in the middle of a pasture, miles from town. No traffic, no other sounds, so that earlier she'd had no trouble hearing Austin make multiple calls and pace over the bare hardwood floors.

He was just as troubled as she was.

Maybe more, if that were possible. Because from what she'd heard, he hadn't managed to keep his badge. Still, he'd brought her to the safe house and had kept her in his unofficial protective custody.

For now, anyway.

He was probably eager to give that particular duty to someone else so he could continue with the investigation and soothe things over with his boss. Losing his badge would cut him to the core.

That got her moving from the bed. She had to make arrangements for her own security and work out how to continue the investigation while still staying safe. She'd gotten so close before those monsters had destroyed the evidence and killed Janice, and she needed to find another way to get close again.

Maybe Vickie Cravens was the key.

Austin had already made a call about the woman. One of many calls he'd made on the drive to the safe house, and since he was no longer officially an FBI agent, he hadn't been able to request an FBI background check on her.

Still, Sawyer had run one, and he'd gotten Vickie's phone number and address for Austin, but she hadn't answered when Austin had tried to contact her. Austin had left her a message to call him, that he could help her. Rosalie had memorized the number and would try to call Vickie herself as soon as she was someplace safe.

If a safe place existed, that is.

Since she didn't want to go to her family's ranch and bring the danger there, she had to bite the bullet and call her brother Seth. Yes, he'd likely chew her out again for her undercover attempt, but it was better than the alternative of begging Austin to let her tag along with him.

Not that Austin would let her, anyway.

In his eyes, she was the worst kind of trouble and could interfere with his own investigation.

Heck, he probably even blamed her for losing his badge. After all, if she hadn't gone to that baby farm and essentially blown his cover, he might have been able to find the evidence to stop this operation in its tracks. She seriously doubted his boss would have fired him if he'd managed to unravel one of the highest-profile cases in the state.

Rosalie used the small adjoining bathroom to wash up, and she changed into jeans and a gray sweater that she found in the closet. Obviously, things left by the FBI since there were a variety of sizes and clothing items, and it made her wonder how many other women had stayed here while trying to outrun danger.

She, on the other hand, wouldn't try to outrun it if it meant finding Sadie.

Rosalie kept her footsteps light so that she wouldn't wake up Austin but then really wasn't surprised to find him already at the kitchen table, sipping coffee and reading something on his laptop.

He looked about as rested as Rosalie felt—which wasn't very rested at all. His hair was mussed and too long to be regulation length. There probably hadn't been many opportunities for a haircut while he'd been under-cover. Like her, he'd changed his clothes and was wearing jeans and a black T-shirt that hugged his chest in all the right places.

She mentally groaned.

No way should she have noticed something like that. And that was yet another good reason to put some distance between them.

"What's wrong?" Austin asked.

Obviously, he'd seen something alarming in her expression. Rosalie was glad he wasn't a mind reader because there was no way she wanted him to know that momentary lapse she'd just had about him.

"Any news?" she asked, helping herself to some coffee while also avoiding his question.

He nodded. "All bad. Want to hear it, anyway?"

Now Rosalie groaned for real, and since she figured she might need to sit for this, she sank down at the table across from him.

"Sonny's already out of jail," he started. "And Yancy doesn't want charges pressed against Sonny. Of course, Gage can still charge him with reckless endangerment, but since Sonny doesn't have a record, I doubt he'll get any jail time."

Rosalie shook her head. "Why wouldn't Yancy want charges pressed against Sonny? Sonny pulled a gun on him."

"Who knows? Maybe because he wants Sonny out of there. That way, if something else goes wrong, Yancy can say that Sonny did it." Austin paused. "And maybe it'd be the truth. Just because he was shot, it doesn't mean I trust Sonny. In fact, that wound could have been self-inflicted so we would trust him. He could have done it so he could figure out how much we learned about the baby farms."

Hearing that aloud sent a chill through her, but she'd had the same reaction to Yancy. It sickened her to think a monster like that might have been the one to take Sadie.

"Still no answer from Vickie Cravens," Austin went on, obviously continuing with that bad news. "Sawyer had a local cop go to her place to do a welfare check, but she wasn't home. There's also no sign of the person who tried to follow us last night or the guards who escaped from the second baby farm."

Maybe because they were all long gone. Both a relief and a scary thought. If they had fled, then they wouldn't be around to try to kill Austin and her. But if they were gone, so was any info they could have given her about who was behind the operation.

"I guess the CSI didn't find anything at the two baby farm sites?" she asked.

"Nothing. They'll keep looking, of course."

Yes, but she was betting the guards had destroyed anything that could prove helpful. "This isn't just a cottage industry," she said, thinking out loud. "The person doing this has money and is well-organized."

"Maybe well-hidden, too." Austin cursed, shoved his hand through his hair and stood. Pacing, again. "I figure this is a pyramid operation. One top dog with lots of sites. Each site operates independently of the others, so if one goes down, it doesn't take the others down with it."

Rosalie swallowed hard. "Then it might be impossible to find the person who took the babies."

"Hard, yes. Impossible, no. I'm not giving up on finding my nephew."

"Even though it cost you your badge?" she asked.

A muscle flickered in his jaw. "I won't stop, no matter what the cost." He sat in the chair next to her and stared straight into her eyes. "But you'll have to. You can't put yourself in the line of fire like this."

Rosalie considered just lying. Telling him what he wanted to hear, that she'd go home and wait for someone else to find her baby. But she was tired of waiting. She'd been the good girl too long, listening to various lawmen who had told her to let them do their jobs.

Well, they hadn't done their jobs.

They hadn't found Sadie.

"I can't stop," she told him. "But it's not your problem."

"To hell it's not. I can't let you go out there and get yourself killed."

"It's not your responsibly to keep me safe."

The flat look he gave her said differently.

Oh, no. They weren't about to go there with this conversation.

"You don't owe me because of Eli," she insisted.

"That wasn't what you said at the baby farm," he reminded her.

"I was desperate, and I blackmailed you, but now I'm letting you off the hook. Besides, you've got enough on your plate." She paused. "How much work will it take you just to get your badge back?"

Austin turned, ready to bolt out of the chair, and she saw the pain this was causing him.

"For what it's worth, I'm sorry," she added. "Eli always said you were married to the badge."

"Yeah." And a moment later, Austin repeated it. "The only thing I've ever wanted to be was an FBI agent. But my sister is blood. So is her son. I have to get Nathan back home before Christmas."

Rosalie nodded, swallowed the lump in her throat because that was her wish, too, for her own baby. "When was Nathan kidnapped?"

"Right after he was born nearly four months ago. My sister had a C-section, and she had some problems with blood loss right afterward. She nearly died, so no one got around to taking pictures of the baby. He was stolen just a few hours later. Someone had tampered with the security cameras and jammed the tracking chip used in the hospital bracelets."

Oh, God. His story brought her own painful memories to the surface. Not that they were ever far from her mind.

At least she had a photo of Sadie, but her sweet baby had been taken much the same way. A very precise, or-

ganized crime since the tracking chip in Sadie's bracelet had been jammed, as well, by placing several Wi-Fi
scramblers throughout the hospital. If that hadn't been
done, the chip in the bracelet would have triggered the
security alarm when the kidnapper stepped outside the
hospital with her. As it was, it'd taken the kidnapper less
than five minutes to get in and out.

It sickened her to think of how many times that same
crime had been committed since the start of these baby
farms.

"If you don't know what your nephew looks like, then
how will you know if you find him?" Rosalie asked.

Austin seemed to be in such deep thought that it took
him a moment to answer her. "According to the nurse who
assisted with the delivery, Nathan has a large strawberry-
shaped birthmark on his left leg."

That would help, but only if they got a close look at
the baby.

"I'm guessing your sister already put this info out there,
in case someone adopted a baby with a birthmark like
that?" Rosalie pressed.

"Of course." He stared at her. "And no one came forward. I think that probably means that the person who
adopted him or bought him knew they were doing something illegal."

Yes. She'd come to the same conclusion. "We don't
even know how many babies are missing. From everything I've learned about this operation, they kidnap ille-
gals and homeless girls and force them into surrogacy.
They kidnap pregnant women, too, and they steal babies."

"And they murder the women," Austin reminded her.
His gaze came to hers again. "That's why you have to

back away from this. You can't be a mother to Sadie if you're dead."

Rosalie cursed the blasted tears that watered her eyes. She'd cried an ocean of tears over this, and the crying jags only drained her. They didn't help. And that's why she tried to blink them back.

As she did most other times, she failed.

Austin cursed again, clearly not any happier about the tears than she was, and Rosalie figured it was a good time to go back into the bedroom and get control of herself. She didn't make it far.

Still cursing, Austin reached out, snagged her by the shoulder and hauled her to him. He wasn't gentle. Not at first, anyway. Rosalie could practically feel the frustration in the corded muscles of his arms. But then his grip around her relaxed.

"I'm sorry this happened to you." His voice was gentle, too. Almost a whisper. And even though Rosalie figured that being in his arms was a very bad idea, she just didn't have the strength to push him away.

Austin made a soft shh-ing sound and eased her deeper into his arms. Until she was pressed against him. Even with the tears and her heart shattering, she felt his body. Heard the quick rhythm of his breath.

Felt it, too.

When his chest rose against her breasts.

Just as when she had spotted him at the table with his bedroom hair and eye-catching jeans, the trickle of heat went through her. A bad kind of heat that she didn't want to feel for him. But did, anyway.

Rosalie pulled in her breath, taking in his scent with it, and she got a feeling of a different sort. Her heart raced, slamming against him.

And he noticed, all right.

Heck, maybe she was giving off some kind of weird vibe because Austin pulled back, his gaze meeting hers. His left eyebrow lifted a fraction. Rosalie figured what he was silently asking—was she actually attracted to him?— but it was a question she had zero intentions of answering.

His grip melted off her, and Rosalie stepped back, but his gaze stayed on her mouth. She was well aware of this because her attention stayed on his eyes.

Bedroom eyes, too.

Oh, mercy.

She was in trouble here.

"You've been under a lot of stress," Austin mumbled, as if that explained everything going on between them right now.

Yes, it was a nightmarish time for her, but Rosalie doubted stress could cause this warmth that she was feeling in just about every part of her body. Still, she nodded, accepting the out he'd just given her. She needed to take that *out* a little further though and get the heck out of there and away from Austin.

"You plan to call Seth now?" Austin asked.

Had he read her mind about that, too?

Of course, maybe it hadn't taken any mind-reading powers. She didn't exactly have a lot of options here.

Rosalie nodded and was about to ask if she could use his phone, but it buzzed before she could do that. Since they'd had only bad news all morning, she tried to brace herself for more but prayed for a better outcome.

"It's Vickie," Austin said, glancing at the screen, and he hit the button to put the call on speaker.

"Agent Duran?" the woman immediately said, but she didn't wait for him to answer. "I need to talk to you *now.* Get here to my place as fast as you can. And hurry. They're coming to kill us."

Vickie hung up but not before Rosalie heard a sound on the other end of the line that sliced right through her.

A crying baby.

Chapter Eight

"You don't have time to ditch me," Rosalie repeated. "We have to get to Vickie and stop her and that baby from being hurt."

She'd been saying variations of that same thing during the entire half-hour drive from the safe house to Vickie's house. Austin figured she was right, but still he couldn't risk taking Rosalie into yet another dangerous situation.

That's why he'd called for backup from the San Antonio cops.

Once Austin arrived at Vickie's place, he could hand Rosalie off to the officers and then find out what the heck was going on. Maybe it wasn't too late to help Vickie and get her and the baby out of harm's way.

Of course, *They're coming to kill us* wasn't the kind of thing someone said unless the person was already in harm's way. If he couldn't get to her in time, maybe SAPD could.

Austin pushed the accelerator as hard as it was safe to do, speeding toward Vickie's house on the outskirts of San Antonio. He also kept watch around them in case the gunmen were using this as some kind of ruse to draw Rosalie and him out into the open again. Rosalie kept watch, as well, her gaze firing all around them while she kept a white-knuckle grip on the armrest.

"The baby could be Sadie," she mumbled.

Yeah, she'd been repeating a version of that, too, since Vickie's call.

"Don't get your hopes up," he said, doing some repeating of his own. There were likely dozens of babies connected to this operation, and the odds were slim that it was Rosalie's daughter.

"Hope is all I have."

Her voice was small and shaky. Barely a whisper. However, Austin heard every drop of the raw emotion in it, and he knew it was going to be a bear to keep her out of this situation. He understood her need to see if this was Sadie, but at the moment he had an even greater need to keep her safe. Then, he could rescue Vickie and the crying baby.

His phone buzzed, and without taking his attention off the road, Austin answered it.

"I'm Detective Hernandez, SAPD," the man said. "We're at Vickie Cravens's house now, but she's not here."

Rosalie made a sharp sound of concern, mimicking the way that Austin felt. "She could be hiding inside." Austin hoped. Hiding and unharmed.

"We looked," the detective explained. "Her back door was wide-open so I went in and checked every room. She's not here."

Austin hated he had to ask his next question. "Any sign of foul play?" And he held his breath, waiting for the answer.

"Not really, but her purse and car are here, and there's a can of baby formula opened on the kitchen counter. Looks like she left in a hurry."

Or was taken in a hurry. Austin wasn't sure where

Vickie had been when she'd made that frantic call to him. It was possible she'd been somewhere else and heading to her house and that's why she'd told him to go there. If she'd seen any signs that it wasn't safe to go inside, she could have escaped. Or maybe the escape had happened after the danger was right on her. Either way, he refused to believe, yet, that the worst had happened.

"Maybe she has two vehicles," Austin suggested. "And she could have used the second one to get away."

"She only has one car registered to her," Detective Hernandez explained. "The houses out here are pretty far apart, but we'll canvass the area and talk to her neighbors. She might be with one of them or may have borrowed a car."

Maybe. But as determined as these baby farm guards were, Austin had to admit to himself that they would have already gone after her no matter where she'd tried to flee.

If Vickie had told the truth, that is.

After everything that Rosalie and he had been through in the past twenty-four hours, Austin wasn't about to trust anyone completely. However, he had to do whatever it took to get the baby to safety.

"I'll be there in about five minutes," Austin told the detective.

"Vickie could have gotten away," Rosalie concluded when Austin ended the call. "She seemed to have had some kind of warning, a long enough one to call you."

Yeah. She'd said they were coming to kill her, not that they were already there. Since they'd had enough bad news, Austin decided to hold on to that as a positive sign. Even if Vickie had had only a couple of minutes' head start, it might have been enough for her to escape and hide from her would-be attackers.

But where the heck was she now?

Following the instructions on his GPS, Austin took the final turn toward Vickie's house. Technically, it was inside the city limits, but it was still fairly rural with the thick trees and narrow road leading to the pastoral-sounding neighborhood of Eden Waters.

He was about to repeat his warning to Rosalie that she couldn't be part of this. The warning died on his lips, however, when he saw the auburn-haired woman. She was partly concealed behind a winter-bare oak tree, and she had something clutched in her arms.

"Vickie," Rosalie and he said in unison.

Austin hit his brakes, pulling his truck to the side of the road, and drew his gun. He also had to catch hold of Rosalie's arm to keep her from bolting.

"She looks terrified," Rosalie insisted.

"And looks can be deceiving," Austin insisted right back. "Plus, this could be some kind of a trap."

But if it was, then it was a darn good one. The woman's gaze met his, and even from the twenty-yard or so distance that separated them, Austin was pretty sure he could see the fear in her eyes.

"We have to protect that baby." Rosalie shook off his grip, and she would have no doubt bolted again if Austin hadn't stopped her.

"Wait here," he ordered, and he made sure that's exactly what it was. *An order.* Austin handed Rosalie his phone. "Call Detective Hernandez and tell him where we are. I want him here now so he can guard you."

Of course, Austin would still have to keep an eye on Rosalie to make sure she stayed put and that the guards didn't use this opportunity to sneak up on them.

"There's a gun in the glove compartment," he added

and gave Rosalie one last glare of warning before he opened his truck door. "I'm Agent Duran," he called out to the woman.

As with the fear he'd seen earlier, he thought maybe now there was some relief. Still clutching the bundle in her arms, she started running toward them. "I'm Vickie Cravens."

"Get down," Austin told Rosalie.

He didn't look back to make sure she did it. He kept his attention nailed to the woman and the area around her. Vickie was doing the same, her gaze darting all around as she made her way to him.

"We have to get out of here," Vickie insisted. "I got a call, and they're on the way."

"Who's on the way?" Austin demanded, and he moved in front of her to block her from getting into the truck.

Vickie's breath was gusting, and she frantically shook her head. "No time to explain now."

Austin would have argued that, but the sound stopped him cold. The baby cried, squirming beneath the blanket, and he knew that he couldn't just stand there and wait for something else bad to happen.

He cursed the fact that Rosalie was in the truck. Cursed also because he had put her right back in the middle of possible danger. He hoped it didn't turn out to be the same kind of mistake he'd made with Eli.

Austin checked as best he could to make sure Vickie wasn't armed, and he helped her onto the seat between Rosalie and him. Thankfully, Rosalie had taken the .38 out of the glove compartment, but Austin prayed neither of them had to use a weapon, especially not in such close quarters.

He spotted the cop car coming up behind them. Hernandez, no doubt. "Call him," Austin said to Rosalie. "Tell him to follow us."

Though her hands were still shaking, Rosalie managed to do that.

"We can't go to SAPD," Vickie quickly said, fumbling to put on her seat belt. "I'm not sure I can trust them. I'm not sure I can trust *you*," she added, volleying glances at both Rosalie and him.

"Then why'd you return my call and ask for help?" Austin pressed.

Vickie choked back a hoarse sob. "Because someone said I could trust you. A friend."

"Sonny?" Rosalie asked. She leaned closer to Vickie, obviously trying to get a look at the baby in the blanket.

"No. Not Sonny. Someone who works as a criminal informant." Vickie didn't hesitate, either. "Why, does Sonny have something to do with this?"

The question was right for someone who was innocent. Her seemingly surprised reaction, too, but again, Austin knew this sort of thing could be faked.

Still, it was best to get answers someplace safer.

He drove off, heading toward Sweetwater Springs. Rosalie wasn't going to like the fact he was taking her back home, but one of her brothers was the sheriff there, and Austin wanted some help that didn't involve the FBI.

"I need to know if the baby is my daughter," Rosalie said.

"No." Again, Vickie didn't hesitate, but she did look puzzled by the question. "It's a boy. Why? Did someone take your baby?"

She nodded, swallowed hard. "Do you know anything about a missing baby girl? She'd be eleven months old." Rosalie took hold of the woman's arm, turning her so that Vickie was facing her. "Do you know where my daughter is?"

"No. I'm sorry. I didn't see any records, not for your baby or anyone else. I just got a few emails and phone calls. Mostly from the fake adoption agency and then a few from the couple who was supposed to adopt this baby."

That was a start. Records weren't the only thing that could help Rosalie and him. Once they had the name of the person responsible, then they could force him or her to talk.

Of course, Vickie could be that person.

And it could be his nephew she had in her arms.

Austin couldn't see much of the child because of the way Vickie had him clutched against her, but he could see the baby's wispy brown hair. Maybe the color of his nephew's hair. He just didn't know.

Heck, he didn't even know if this baby was four months old, the right age for his sister's missing son.

"Why do you have this child?" Austin demanded.

Vickie gave another hoarse sob. "I didn't know the operation was illegal. I swear, I didn't. I just needed a job, and I'd done work as a nanny. That's why I wasn't suspicious when this nanny agency contacted me out of the blue and asked if I'd take a temporary position to care for a newborn."

"I want the name of the agency and the person who contacted you," Austin insisted.

"It's fake. I figured that out when I got suspicious and tried to call them, but the number wasn't working. Neither was the email they'd used to contact me. I was only supposed to keep the baby for a couple of days, until his adoptive parents picked him up, but the days turned to weeks. Someone from the agency kept calling, saying it wouldn't be much longer."

So, something had obviously gone wrong. But if this baby was connected to the pair of now-destroyed baby farms, then why hadn't the person in charge come and taken the child? A healthy baby boy would have fetched a good price for a black market adoption.

"I still want the name of the agency. The adoptive parents' names, too," Austin continued. Though those were probably fake, as well, if the agency had been. "You'll also give me a detailed statement of everything that went on from the moment this agency contacted you."

Vickie nodded, moaned softly. At least Austin thought she'd moaned, but he realized Rosalie had made that sound. She was staring down at the baby, but he could see the pain all over her face. This wasn't her child. Her baby was still out there somewhere, and it was shattering her heart.

Just as it was doing to Austin's own sister.

"I called Sonny," Vickie went on before Austin could ask more about the baby in her arms. "I told him something suspicious was going on. He said he'd check things out for me."

"Is that why he was at the baby farm?" Rosalie asked.

Vickie's eyes widened. "A baby farm? God, how many babies were taken?"

"We're not sure," Austin answered. It was the truth, but he also didn't want to give Vickie too many details. Even if she was innocent, she might warn Sonny. Or she might even be connected to Yancy. "When did you call Sonny?"

"Last night."

If that was true, then Sonny had found the place darn fast. Either that meant Sonny had gotten lucky or he'd known where to look. The uneasy glance Rosalie gave him let Austin know that she'd come to the same conclusion. Soon, very soon, he needed to question Sonny again because the man hadn't been the one to bring up Vickie's name back at the hospital.

Yancy had.

Maybe Sonny hadn't wanted to implicate Vickie in this, and that could have been the very reason Yancy had told Austin about the woman. Either way, Sonny might be able to give them answers.

"How old is that baby?" Austin asked. It was hard to do with his thoughts scattered in a dozen different directions, but he tried to keep watch around them. Tried to keep his emotions in check, too.

"Four months. I've had him with me since he was just a couple of days old."

The age was right, after all. Austin had to force himself to release the breath he was holding. He also had to tamp down the hope he felt rising in his chest.

Rosalie reached over and eased back the side of the blanket. "Does he have any kind of birthmark?" The baby was wearing a blue one-piece suit so it was hard to see much of him.

Vickie nodded. "It's red. The shape of a strawberry."

Hell.

Because he had no choice, Austin hit the brakes and pulled off onto the shoulder. He reached for the baby, to see if the birthmark was in the right spot, but his hand felt rough and tight. Too rough to be touching a baby.

Thankfully, Rosalie did it for him.

The little boy had fallen asleep, but Rosalie gently opened the snaps and pushed the fabric away from his left leg.

It was there.

In the exact spot where his sister had said it would be.

"He's my nephew," Austin heard himself say, though he wasn't sure how he managed to speak. There was a huge lump in his throat now, and the muscles in his chest were too tight for him to breathe.

"I can drive," Rosalie suggested.

Obviously, she'd noticed this had hit him like a heavyweight's punch. So many emotions, including sheer relief, all coming at him at once. He'd done what he had promised his sister—he'd found Nathan.

Austin shook his head. "No, I can do this." He didn't want them out in the open any longer. "I can call my sister once we're in Sweetwater Springs."

Then, he could also start the process of having the baby tested so they'd have definitive proof.

Still, Austin felt the proof in his gut.

This was his missing nephew.

He got the truck moving again, trying not to hurry, but that's exactly what he wanted to do.

"Sweetwater Springs?" Vickie questioned. "We can't go there. I can't trust the sheriff."

Rosalie pulled back her shoulders. "You mean Cooper McKinnon?"

Vickie frantically nodded again. "He's the son of the people involved in this. I looked him up on the internet, and I know he's their son."

The color drained from Rosalie's face. "What are you talking about?"

"It was their name on the agency paperwork," Vickie insisted. "Roy and Jewell McKinnon. They're the ones who arranged to adopt this baby."

Oh, no. Austin definitely didn't like the sound of that.

"That can't be right," Rosalie insisted, and she kept repeating it.

Austin wanted to reach over and try to reassure her that this could all be some kind of misunderstanding, that there was no way her parents or brother could be involved in this, but he saw the blur of motion just ahead.

A large SUV pulled directly out in front of them.

And it stopped right in the middle of the road.

Austin had to slam on his brakes. Not good since the roads were slick, and he went into a skid. He did a quick check of his rearview mirror to make sure Hernandez was still following them. He was. But the cop appeared to be fighting to keep control of his patrol car, too.

"Hold on," Austin warned them, praying that they didn't have a collision. The baby wasn't even in a car seat and could be hurt in just a fender bender.

Pumping the brakes and steering into the skid, Austin managed to stop the truck. Barely in time. But he didn't have time to do anything else.

Because two men jumped from the SUV.

They were armed, wearing ski masks, and both men aimed guns right at them.

"Get down!" But Austin didn't wait for Rosalie and Vickie to do that. He pushed them down on the seat and got ready to return fire.

"Oh, God," Rosalie whispered. "I think it's the guards from the second baby farm."

Yeah. But it didn't matter who they were. There was no way Austin would let them get their hands on Rosalie or his nephew.

Hernandez managed to stop just inches behind the truck. Austin opened his door, still using it for cover, got out and trained his own gun on the men. Hernandez did the same.

"All we want is the nanny," one of the masked guys snarled. His voice sounded firm enough, but he was volleying nervous glances between Austin and the detective. So was his partner. They probably hadn't expected to encounter two lawmen.

"Don't let them take me," Vickie begged.

Austin had no intention of letting that happen, but what he didn't want was a gunfight with Rosalie and the baby caught in the middle.

"Put down your guns," Austin warned the men.

Again, the pair gave each other uneasy looks, and that upped Austin's own concern. He hoped like the devil that he could trust the lawman behind him. If not, Rosalie, Vickie and he were in a lot of trouble.

"If you don't give us the nanny," one of the men said, "we start shooting."

The nanny. But not the baby. "Why do they want only you?" Austin asked Vickie.

"I don't know. Maybe because I learned about the fake adoption agency."

Maybe. Or maybe this was all a ploy to make Vickie look innocent.

Either way, Austin prayed those men didn't pull their triggers, but just in case they did, he readied himself for the worst. One of the men backed up as if he might jump into the SUV and leave. Not the best solution, but it could be the only way to stop a gunfight.

But that didn't happen.

The idiot pulled the trigger, the shot blasting through the air and landing in the front bumper of the truck.

Austin cursed and did what he'd hoped he wouldn't

have to do—he returned fire. So did Detective Hernandez, and Austin heard him calling for backup. He also heard the baby's cries. The gunshot had woken him up.

Both masked men hurried behind their SUV. Both shooting into the truck. Austin wanted nothing more than to take them out, but he couldn't stay where he was. He had no choice but to jump back into his truck so he wouldn't be gunned down. Staying alive was the only way he could protect Rosalie and the others.

"I don't want them to hurt the baby," Vickie said. "I'll go with them."

Even though the adrenaline was spiking through him and he was concentrating on the attack, that set off alarms inside Austin's head. Maybe Vickie was just being protective of the baby, but he had to wonder if she wanted to go with them because she was part of their operation.

But if so, then why had she called Austin?

Again, it could have been to throw suspicion off herself. Maybe she knew that Yancy had brought up her name and that it made her a person of interest. Sonny could have even told her about Yancy's allegation.

"You'll stay put," Austin insisted, and he put the truck in gear and tried to maneuver around the SUV.

Hard to do with the SUV taking up most of the road.

It also didn't help that the cruiser was right behind him. That didn't give Austin much room to move. He threw the truck into Reverse, backing up as much as he could so he could drive onto the shoulder.

Rosalie levered herself up, placing her body in front of the baby. Protecting his nephew. He hated that she was forced to do that, but there wasn't an alternative. They had to protect the little boy. Those bullets could come through the engine and into the cab of the truck. And as an adult, she stood a better chance of surviving an injury like that.

The shoulder of the road was nothing more than gravel and ice, and the truck tires on the passenger's side wobbled, threatening to send them straight into the ditch. That couldn't happen because then they'd be sitting ducks.

The gunmen were still behind cover of their SUV. Still shooting. But they were aiming for the tires now. At least they weren't shooting at them, but it was still a dangerous situation. Plus, the gunmen were moving, adjusting their positions so that they could get a better shot at stopping them.

Austin cursed. He hadn't come this far to rescue his nephew only to have the gunmen snatch him away again. And despite their insistence that they only wanted Vickie, Austin figured the plan was to get both her and the baby back while they eliminated Rosalie, him and the cop.

Behind him, Hernandez jumped into his cruiser, backing up just enough to give Austin some room to maneuver. Still, the tires shimmied over the slick surface, and he couldn't get enough traction.

The bullets kept coming, and he felt one slam into the front tire on the driver's side. That's when Austin knew he couldn't wait any longer.

"Hold on," he warned Rosalie and Vickie, and he hit the button to disable the air bags. He couldn't risk having them deploy and hurting the baby. A split second later, he floored the accelerator.

The front end of the truck bashed into the SUV and sent it crashing into the gunmen. It knocked them both to the ground. But only temporarily. They came up ready to fire.

Austin pressed hard on the gas again. The truck fishtailed, and the partially deflated front tire didn't help matters. He had to wrestle with the steering wheel to keep the vehicle on the road.

Behind him, he saw the detective doing the same. Trying to get the heck out of there. Maybe it wouldn't be long before backup arrived, and the gunmen could be arrested.

But not by Austin.

He couldn't risk the lives of the people inside his truck. However, this was definitely a score he intended to settle later.

Austin cleared the SUV, pushed hard on the accelerator and drove away, the bullets still coming at them.

Chapter Nine

"You should go home and let me handle this," Rosalie's brother Seth insisted—again.

He was using that overly protective brother tone that Rosalie both loved and hated.

At the moment, she felt more of the latter.

Rosalie totally understood his concern. After all, it had been only a few hours since Austin and she had been caught in that gunfight, but attacks like that wouldn't stop unless she found answers about who those men were behind the masks.

"I want to hear what Mom has to say," Rosalie insisted right back—again.

If her mother knew anything about the baby farms or Austin's nephew, then Rosalie wanted to hear it from Jewell's own lips.

And find out why her mother hadn't volunteered it to her sooner.

That's why Rosalie had insisted on coming to the jail to have this chat with her mother.

Of course, Vickie could be and likely was lying about her parents' involvement. Or worse. Vickie could be the culprit behind the baby farms, and the attack could have been orchestrated to make her seem innocent. That's why the FBI was questioning her.

Not Austin, though.

His boss had refused to let him have any part of that when they'd shown up at the FBI building shortly after the latest attack. Probably a good thing, too, since he had a much happier task of reuniting his sister with her son. The reunion wouldn't be an official one until the DNA test results were back, but Rosalie knew with all her heart that the child was indeed back where he belonged.

It was bittersweet for her.

On the one hand it gave her hope that she'd be reunited with her own baby, but the waiting was crushing her like deadweight.

Seth checked the latest text that popped onto his phone screen, glanced around, no doubt wondering what was taking so long. Rosalie and he hadn't had an appointment for this jail visit, and according to the warden, their mother was tied up with some kind of statement with her lawyer. Rosalie didn't care how long the wait would be. She wasn't budging.

"Anything on the investigation?" she asked when Seth's attention went back to the text. "Have they found those gunmen who got away?"

Seth shook his head to both questions, and even though he didn't make a sound, she could feel his frustration. Mixed with her own, the visiting room at the county jail was heavy with it and all the other emotions coursing through her.

"Vickie refused protective custody," Seth added a moment later.

"Why?" After the attack, Rosalie couldn't imagine the woman doing that. Unless Vickie truly had nothing to fear from the gunmen, that is. But if Vickie had been the person in control of the baby farms, she should have at least accepted protective custody so she wouldn't appear guilty.

"Vickie says she doesn't trust cops," Seth explained. "But I also get the feeling that she plans to do some investigating of her own. Maybe you can tell her what a really dumb idea that'd be."

She gave him an obligatory smirk.

Seth gave her one in return, and he was better at smirking than she was. "After you talk to Mom, you'll go back to the ranch."

Rosalie didn't look at him because he would see in her eyes that she had no intention of doing that. Or of giving up on the search for her baby. She just kept her attention on the glass where she hoped her mother would soon appear.

"Are you ever going to tell me how you got involved in this mess?" Seth asked.

"I would, but you won't like it, and right now, we both have enough to deal with."

That earned her a glare that she could see in the reflection of the glass. It earned her some profanity, too. "Did you do anything illegal?"

Rosalie lifted her shoulder. "I used your home computer to find the criminal informant who helped me get the job at the baby farm."

"*My* computer," he flatly repeated. "The one I didn't password protect because I didn't think my sister would go snooping on it?"

"Yes, that computer," Rosalie mumbled. The one he kept in the ranch guesthouse that they shared.

Oh, that made his glare even worse. "And let me

guess—the reason you asked me to give you shooting lessons about two months ago was because of this?"

Since it was true, Rosalie settled for another shoulder lift. "I needed two things to start my plan to find Sadie. A way into the baby farm operation and a way to defend myself if something went wrong."

And things had indeed gone wrong.

Seth would have no doubt given her another scowling reminder about that, followed by another lecture, if his phone hadn't buzzed. When he glanced at the name on the screen, it instantly brought him to his feet.

"I have to take this, and it might be a long conversation," he said, shielding the phone screen from her before he stepped outside the room.

She hadn't seen the caller's name, but maybe because Seth was about to learn yet something else that she wouldn't want to hear. This way, he could try to shelter her, something he'd been doing since this nightmare had started eleven months ago. But sheltering wasn't going to help. Only finding Sadie and the truth would do that.

Rosalie stared at the glass, trying to tamp down the wild thoughts that kept zinging through her head. And she kept going back to one huge question. If her parents had had some part in this, why hadn't they told her?

Certainly not because they were behind the baby farms.

No, she was sure of that.

Until recently, Rosalie and her father, Roy, had been estranged for over twenty years—since her mother had left the ranch under a cloud of suspicion about an affair and rumors of murdering her lover. A murder accusation that had put Jewell behind bars while she waited for a murder trial. But her mother was innocent of the crime. Innocent of the baby farms, too.

Still, Rosalie couldn't get Vickie's accusation to quit eating away at her.

The visiting room door eased open, and Rosalie braced herself for Seth's return with more bad news. But it wasn't her brother who stepped in.

It was Austin.

Her heart went straight to her throat. "Did something go wrong?" And just like that, so many bad possibilities came to mind. "Did someone kidnap your nephew again? Did they find the men who attacked us?"

"No to all of it." He shook his head, seemed a little surprised by her questions. "My nephew's fine and with my sister at our family's ranch." Austin showed her the photo on his phone. A woman smiling through her happy tears as she clutched her baby in her arms.

The relief came as quickly as the dread and fear, and before she even realized she was going to do it, Rosalie threw her arms around him. That obviously surprised him, too, judging from the way his muscles tensed.

Then quickly relaxed.

That caused Rosalie to tense, as well, because they shouldn't feel this comfortable in each other's arms. Even if she did. And worse, not just comfortable.

But safe.

Austin kept his hand on her waist even after she came to her senses and eased away from him.

"Sorry," she said. "But when I saw you, I thought the worst."

Austin flexed his eyebrows, and the corner of his mouth lifted. "That's not usually the reaction I'm aiming for." But he quickly shook his head. "I can understand it in your case, though."

That half smile sent another trickle of heat through

her, but Rosalie decided to blame it on the fact that he hadn't come to deliver bad news. It'd been a while since she'd heard anything good, and a baby reunited with his mother definitely qualified as good.

"What about Detective Hernandez?" she pressed. "Is he all right?"

"Fine. A little shaken up, of course. SAPD is out looking for the men who shot at us. The plates on their SUV were fake, though, so that's a dead end."

Rosalie had already expected that. The men had come there to attack them. Maybe to kidnap Vickie and the baby, too. Unless they were idiots, they wouldn't have used a vehicle that could be traced back to them. That was also the reason they'd worn masks—to conceal their identities.

"But why did you come?" she asked.

No more half smile, but he did give another flex of his eyebrows. "To help you find your daughter."

The old wounds and bad blood instantly made her suspicious. "I've already told you that you don't owe me anything."

Now his gaze came to hers.

Oh, no.

She saw it then. That same blasted trickle of heat that she felt in her own body. Rosalie muttered some profanity.

"It's not just *that*," Austin corrected. Thankfully, he didn't clarify what he meant. "Well, not totally that, anyway. I'm already familiar with the investigation. And I have some time on my hands since I'm on a thirty-day suspension." He took her by the shoulders when she looked away. "I *need* to help you."

No doubt to relieve the guilt over Eli's death. But that wasn't the only source of guilt in the room. This unwanted attraction made her feel as if she were cheating on Eli even though he'd been dead well over a year and a half. Being around Austin wasn't likely to ease the heat or the guilt, either.

And that's why it was best if they parted ways.

She heard the footsteps. Again, not Seth. These came from the other side of the building, and a moment later, Rosalie spotted the guard ushering her mother into the visiting area.

"Rosalie, I'm sorry I kept you waiting," Jewell said, her voice as thin and weak as she appeared. The orange prison jumpsuit swallowed her and washed out her color even more than it already was. "My lawyer had some good news. A witness has come forward who might be able to clear my name. I don't know all the details yet, but we should know more soon."

It was news Rosalie hadn't expected, but it was indeed welcome. She was about to press for the identity of the witness, but Jewell spoke before she could.

"Something's wrong," she said, looking first at Rosalie and then at Austin.

"Maybe," Rosalie settled for saying. She tipped her head to Austin. "Do you remember Agent Duran?"

"Of course. Eli's former partner. How are you, Austin?" If there was any hint that her mother blamed Austin for Eli's death, it certainly wasn't in her voice. She was warm and welcoming, as if greeting him at her home rather than the county jail.

"I'm fine. Thank you."

"Good." Jewell gave them both another looking over. "I suspect I owe you a thanks for taking care of my daughter. I don't know the details, but judging from your expressions and the fact that the guard said Seth is here, too, you've had a *difficult* morning." She paused. "And you think I can help in some way?"

"I was, uh, doing some investigating," Rosalie started. "I ran into Austin, and we met a woman. Vickie Cravens."

The name hung in the air for several moments, and Jewell shook her head. "You think I know her?"

"She said you did." Rosalie had to clear her throat to continue. "She's a nanny and claimed Roy and you were going to adopt a baby that she was keeping."

"Oh." Jewell pulled in a quick breath.

Sweet heaven. Her mother certainly wasn't denying it.

"The baby was my nephew," Austin added. "Were you aware of that?"

"No, absolutely not." Jewell pressed her hand to her throat as if to steady herself. "But Roy and I have been working together to find Sadie since she was first kidnapped."

"What do you mean?" This was the first Rosalie was hearing about that. "Working together?"

Jewell nodded. "You were heartbroken, crushed, and I knew I had to do something to get Sadie back. Roy has contacts in law enforcement, so I called him. After that, we met a few times to discuss what to do."

"You okay?" Austin whispered to her, and it took Rosalie a moment to realize she had gone board-stiff. Austin slipped his hand over hers, and this time Rosalie didn't move away from him.

"There's a lot of bad blood between my parents," she mumbled. So much, in fact, that she figured Roy was the last man on earth who'd help her mother.

"Roy and I split up twenty-three years ago," Jewell explained. "It's a long story."

Not really. Rosalie could summarize it in just one

sentence. "Roy believed my mother had an affair, and amid rumors that she'd murdered her lover, Roy kicked her, me and my sister off the family ranch."

Even now, that was still an open wound for her, and it was the reason she still hadn't been able to call Roy her father. Painful baggage indeed, though she was trying to get past it. Only because she had more immediate matters to handle—finding her baby and stopping her mother from being wrongfully convicted of murder.

"After the rumors of the murder, Roy and I decided to divorce," Jewell corrected. "And I took my twin daughters with me. Rosalie and her sister were young, barely six years old. But our boys were older and could speak for themselves. They wanted to stay with their father, so Roy raised them."

Unlike Rosalie, there was no bitterness in Jewell's tone or body language, but Rosalie figured it had to be there somewhere under all that calm composure. Despite the rose-colored spin her mother had just put on things, Rosalie believed that Roy had demanded that she leave.

"Five months or so after Sadie was taken," Jewell continued, "Roy and I were worried when the cops and FBI weren't finding anything. So, we put out the word through some shady sources that we were looking to buy a baby. One that we hoped to use to help heal Rosalie's heart."

"That wouldn't have happened," Rosalie jumped to say.

"I know," her mother assured her. "But we thought saying that might convince the person behind the black market adoptions. And it did, I guess. Weeks later, someone finally called Roy using a voice scrambler, and whoever it was used a prepaid cell that couldn't be traced. The person said someone would contact Roy when they had a baby for us."

Rosalie hadn't suspected any of this. Of course, she'd been so involved with her own search and her own pain that she wasn't looking for clues that her mother had been doing the same thing.

With Roy's help, no less.

Rosalie remembered something else and shook her head. "But Vickie knew your names. She said you were to adopt Austin's nephew. Why did you ask for a boy if you were looking for Sadie?"

"We didn't ask for a specific baby. If we had, we would have asked for a baby Sadie's own age, but we thought that would make them believe we were only searching for our granddaughter. Instead, we said we wanted to adopt a child. Any child." Her mother stopped again, gathered her breath. "Roy paid them twenty-five thousand through a wire transfer to an offshore account with the agreement that they'd get another twenty-five grand once we had the baby."

Fifty thousand. That was the going rate for one of these babies? It sickened Rosalie to think of these monsters selling babies for cash. There was no price tag she could put on her precious daughter.

"Finally, Roy and I got a call that a baby boy was ready for adoption, and that we could have him within a week," her mother went on. "We were told to wait and that we'd get instructions about the pickup and how to make the final payment. After I was arrested, the person didn't contact us again."

Her mother's arrest had happened nearly four months ago. Right about the time that Austin's nephew had been kidnapped.

Maybe the arrest had scared off the baby broker?

That had to be it because these baby sellers wouldn't

have cared if the arrest made Jewell an unsuitable mother. However, they might have thought Roy would be under some kind of police surveillance.

Austin added some profanity under his breath and gave Jewell a hard stare. "I can't believe Seth would have let you do something like that. It was dangerous. The person behind this could have killed both of you."

"Seth didn't know. *Doesn't* know," Jewell corrected, her cheeks flushing a little. "I'd like to keep it that way, especially since the deal didn't go through. And if it had, we would have gladly brought in Seth, Cooper and anyone else to catch these monsters. We would have done anything to rescue not only that child but any others we might have found."

Rosalie and Austin exchanged another glance, and she saw the questions in his eyes. If Yancy was indeed behind the baby farms, then he could have targeted Austin's nephew to give to Roy and Jewell. A way to dig the knife in even deeper to punish Austin for the investigation that had nearly landed Yancy in jail.

But if so, it was risky, too, since Yancy must have suspected that her parents would have just turned the baby over to the authorities. Of course, Yancy would have still gotten the fifty grand. He was a rich man, but he probably wouldn't have turned down the cash, and besides he could have had plans just to kidnap the baby boy again. Or scam another set of prospective parents into paying for a baby they'd never get.

"Roy and I didn't tell anyone what we'd done," Jewell went on, "because we thought someone might be monitoring our phone calls. Or at least keeping an eye on us. They likely wanted to make sure what we were doing wasn't some kind of a setup. If we'd told you or Seth, we were afraid it would have blown the deal."

Instead, her mother's arrest had blown it.

The door opened, and Seth walked back in. With one sweeping glance, he took in the whole room, no doubt noticing Jewell's troubled expression.

And the way Austin was holding Rosalie's hand.

"Bad news?" Austin asked, getting to his feet so he could face Seth.

Seth shook his head. "We found something. We might finally have some proof of the person who set up the baby farm."

Chapter Ten

Sonny.

Austin hated that the man's name kept popping up in all the wrong places. Here Sonny had been out of jail only a few hours on the gun charges, but this was a new reason to bring him right back in. Austin had read through the financial report and saw the same red flags that Seth had.

Something wasn't right on several levels.

For one thing Sonny had two offshore accounts—not exactly standard practice for a run-of-the-mill P.I. Then, there were the cash transfers and withdrawals from his Texas bank. Not enough to trigger an investigation. Just enough to keep him under the radar of the authorities.

Or at least it would have been enough if he hadn't become a person of interest in the baby farms investigation.

"It all seems, well, almost too obvious," Rosalie said, studying the financial report from over Austin's shoulder. "I mean, if Sonny's behind the baby farms, why would he leave this kind of evidence out there for someone to find?"

Austin made a sound of agreement. "But then, Sonny's done plenty of *too obvious.* Like being at the second site of the baby farm and pulling a gun on Yancy at the hospital. All of that makes him look guilty."

And in doing so, it also made him look innocent and as if he'd been set up. Either by Yancy or someone else.

Rosalie must have come to the same conclusion because she huffed and sank back in the chair next to him. Her brother Cooper, the sheriff of Sweetwater Springs, had been generous enough to let them use his private office to go through the financials while they waited for Sonny to arrive for questioning.

Yet something else that was generous.

If Cooper hadn't allowed Austin and Seth to question Sonny at the sheriff's office, then it would have had to be moved to the FBI building in San Antonio. Where Austin wouldn't have been allowed even to witness the interview much less take part in it.

"I owe your brother Cooper," Austin mumbled.

Rosalie made another sound, not one of agreement this time. "I was surprised that he allowed it. Cooper isn't exactly on good terms with Seth, my sister and me."

Austin didn't have to ask why. They'd been raised by their mother. Cooper and his brothers, by their father. After twenty-something years of estrangement, that was a huge rift to mend.

"So, why then did Cooper let us come here?" Austin asked.

She shrugged, glanced away when Austin tried to make eye contact with her. "I think he feels sorry for me. Like you do," she added.

Austin did feel sorry for her, but sadly, it wasn't the only thing he was feeling for her. Ditto for the guilt. Every time he looked at her—like now—he got that jolt of a reminder that Rosalie was a darn attractive woman.

The jolt was put on hold fast when the door flew open

and Seth poked in his head. "Sonny's on his way. Should be here in the next ten minutes or so, and he's bringing his attorney."

"He should," Austin agreed. "If Sonny doesn't have a solid explanation for what's in that financial report, then he could end up in jail again."

Even though this was just an interview for the man, the stakes were sky-high. Not only for Sonny but for all of them. Because Sonny might surprise them all and confess to everything.

Seth shrugged. "I don't care who I have to arrest as long as Rosalie stays safe. After the interview, you'll take her back to the ranch."

"Of course," Austin said as at the same time Rosalie argued, "I can get myself back to the ranch."

"Those guards from the baby farm are still out there," Austin quickly reminded her.

She didn't continue to argue, but Austin could still see the uneasiness that she felt about being around him. Seth mumbled a thanks and left, shutting the door behind him.

Austin figured this was a subject that he should just let die, but he couldn't seem to make himself shut up. "When you look at me, do you think of Eli?"

Rosalie didn't jump to answer. In fact, she turned away from him, her gaze going to the window.

"I'm sorry," he added. "If I could change that, I would. You don't know how many times I've wished that I'd been the one to die that night."

Still no verbal response, but she swallowed hard. "I used to want that. But in a perfect world, you both would have lived, and Yancy or whoever else was responsible for that attack would have been arrested."

Austin had to mentally replay that, and he took her by the arm and eased her around to face him. "You mean that?"

She nodded, swallowed hard again. "And when I look at you, I don't think of Eli. That's the problem."

He replayed that, too, and even if he hadn't been looking her straight in the eyes, he still would have realized what she meant.

Rosalie was talking about this attraction between them. He'd felt it, of course. And like her had fought it like crazy. Because it didn't make sense. Even if he could dismiss the bad blood that'd been between them, they were still in the middle of a dangerous investigation. Hardly the time to start lusting after someone.

"For what it's worth," Austin said, "it's a problem for me, too."

Since that only revved up the concern in her eyes, Austin wanted to put his arms around her. To tell her that everything would be okay. But with the fire and energy zinging between them, that wasn't a good idea.

Did that stop him?

No.

When it came to Rosalie, he just didn't seem to have a lick of sense. He tugged her closer, fully expecting her to hold her ground and keep her distance.

She didn't.

Rosalie landed in his arms as if it were the most natural thing in the world. It felt as if she belonged there, too, and it didn't help cool down the heat.

"This is a mistake," he heard himself say.

It was. That didn't stop him. Austin lowered his head and put his mouth on hers.

He'd braced himself for the guilt and all the other feelings he'd expected. However, those didn't come. He was too wrapped up in the avalanche of sensations. The softness of her lips. Her taste.

That silky little moan that purred in her throat.

All those things slammed through him, and just like that, he was starved for her and had to have more. Austin slid his hand around the back of her neck, deepening the kiss and pulling her closer and closer to him.

Mercy, she tasted good.

Felt even better.

Rosalie did her own share of deepening. She lifted her hands, first one and then the other, sliding them around his neck and completing the body-to-body contact between them.

Not good in a bad way.

He could feel her breasts. Could feel her heart thudding against his chest. And, of course, he could feel the need brewing. It wasn't something he'd ever expected from her.

Or from himself.

But here it was. Strong, hot and getting hotter with each passing second.

Austin forced himself to back away. Not easy. The majority of his body yelled at him to go right back for more, but he wanted to give her a chance to catch her breath and rethink this mistake they were making.

He saw the surprise in her mist-gray eyes, but the heat was there in abundance, as well.

"You can slap me if it'll help," he offered. Austin hoped his god-awful attempt at levity would ease the sudden tension between them.

It didn't.

"I don't think anything will help." She groaned and stepped away from him. "This shouldn't be happening."

All Austin could do was nod in agreement. "If I could stop it, I would, but the truth is, I've always been attracted to you."

He expected her to laugh or give him the slap that she'd said wouldn't help, but Rosalie just stared at him. Then, she nodded.

"You knew that?" he asked.

Another tentative nod. "But I also knew you wouldn't act on it because of Eli, because he was your partner and friend."

Well, heck.

All this time he'd thought he had done a decent job of covering up his feelings for her. Apparently, he sucked as much at that as he did at resisting her now.

"I can't promise you that I won't kiss you again," Austin confessed.

Rosalie stared at him as if she might try to convince him otherwise, but the door flew open again, and Seth looked in at them. They stepped away from each other as if they'd been caught doing something wrong. Not far from the truth.

And Seth noticed all right.

Maybe because Rosalie's breathing still hadn't leveled, her mouth was slightly swollen from the kissing and their faces were no doubt flushed.

Seth didn't have to tell them that Sonny was there because Austin immediately heard the man's voice. And not just Sonny's, either, but another voice that he hadn't expected to hear.

"Yancy came with him?" Austin automatically stepped in front of Rosalie.

"Yeah," Seth verified. "Sonny said he's got proof that

it's really Yancy behind the baby farms, and he wanted him at the sheriff's office so all of us could hear it."

Austin groaned. If there was indeed proof, then he would welcome it, but he didn't want to go another round with these two bozos. Not with Rosalie so close, anyway.

"I can handle this if you'd like," Seth offered.

This time Rosalie and Austin answered in unison, and they were clearly on the same page. "No," they said.

Even though Austin would have preferred Rosalie to stay out of this, he wouldn't try to force her to do that. Not that he could have, anyway. She would do anything to find her daughter. Including facing down the man who might have been responsible for Eli's death.

Austin stepped out ahead of Seth and aimed glares at both Yancy and Sonny while the sheriff and his deputy were frisking the men for weapons. "If either of you draws a gun," Austin warned both Sonny and Yancy, "I'll be the one to shoot first, and I'll put you in the cemetery, not the hospital. You both got that?"

Sonny gave a crisp nod, but Yancy only chuckled. "Same ol' Agent Duran. Always was too high-strung for me. Same with this one." He hitched his thumb to Sonny. "And now he's here to accuse me once again of something I didn't do. Brought his ambulance-chasing lawyer with him, too."

"I'm Patrick Donald," the lawyer said. He was young, probably barely out of law school, and looked more like a linebacker than a lawyer, which meant he likely doubled as Sonny's muscle or bodyguard.

Since this could easily launch into a full-scale argument, Austin motioned for the men to follow Seth, Rosalie and him to the interview room. He'd start with them together at first. An unofficial chat since he couldn't conduct an official one. Then, Yancy and Sonny could be separated so that Seth could take actual statements.

Or if they got very lucky, confessions.

Austin would like nothing more than to have these two locked up so the attacks against Rosalie would stop and she could be reunited with Sadie.

Sonny moved slowly, clutching his arm. No doubt because of the gunshot wound. Austin wasn't about to have any sympathy for the man though because Sonny could have gotten that injury while operating the baby farm. Of course, Austin might change his mind about that sympathy if Sonny came through on giving them info they could actually use.

"Before you give us this proof about Yancy's guilt," Austin started, looking at Sonny, "explain your own *guilt.*"

He stepped into the room with the men but didn't go far, mainly so he could keep Rosalie in the doorway in case something went wrong. Yes, they'd been searched for weapons, but that didn't mean they couldn't have somehow sneaked one in.

"You mean the financials you have on my client," the lawyer volunteered. He fumbled with the papers that he pulled from a folder he was holding. "The offshore holdings are bogus. My client had nothing to do with those."

"You can prove that?" Seth asked, maneuvering around his sister to join Austin shoulder to shoulder.

Seth had probably made that adjustment in his position for the same reason that Austin had—to try to shield Rosalie. But it didn't work. She came right in next to her brother and Austin.

"I can prove it with time," the lawyer insisted. "But my client shouldn't have to go to such measures. He's innocent, and someone is obviously setting him up." Donald's gaze shifted to Yancy, where his accusing glare landed.

"There you go again," Yancy griped. "Trying to put the blame on me, like always."

Austin cut Yancy off with a quick slicing motion of his hand and kept his attention pinned to Sonny. One battle at a time, and he was nowhere near done with Sonny.

"What about the deposits and withdrawals in your U.S. account? Did someone fake those, too?" Austin asked.

"No," Donald said, speaking for his client. "Those were legitimate expenditures and deposits for my client's P.I. business, and you can contact his accountant if you have specific questions."

"Oh, we'll contact him all right," Austin assured him, and he hoped it sounded like the threat that it was. If there was any dirt to find on Sonny, he intended to find it.

"Did you take my daughter?" Rosalie asked, obviously aiming the question at Sonny.

"No," Sonny immediately answered. His lawyer caught on to his arms, no doubt to stop him from saying anything else, but Sonny just shook off the man's grip. "But I'm pretty sure Yancy did."

Sonny reached inside his coat, and the gesture prompted both Seth and Austin to draw their guns. Yancy laughed again, but Sonny lifted his hands.

"I was just taking out the proof you'll need to put this piece of slime behind bars," Sonny insisted.

Austin gave him the go-ahead nod, but neither he nor Seth put away their firearms until he saw that it was indeed just an envelope that Sonny took from his inside coat pocket. Sonny opened it, took out three photos and spread them on the metal table in front of him.

All three pictures were grainy, as if taken from a long-range camera lens, but Austin had no trouble recognizing the place.

It was the baby farm where Rosalie and he had been.

"No!" Yancy practically shouted, and he reached as if to snatch up the photos, but Seth blocked him from doing that.

Both Austin and Rosalie moved closer for a better look at what had prompted Yancy's reaction. It didn't take Austin long to figure it out.

Yancy was in all three of the photos.

"It was a setup," Yancy snarled. "I thought I was meeting a business associate there who was interested in buying the property from me. Now I see that was a ruse to get so-called proof of my involvement in this mess."

Rosalie and Austin exchanged glances. "You own the baby farm?" she asked Yancy.

Yancy opened his mouth, closed it, and he stuffed his hands in his pockets. "One of my corporations owns the land and rents it out," he finally said, as if choosing his words carefully. "I own dozens of properties. So many I don't even know where they all are."

"You own dummy corporations," Austin argued. "And there's no honest reason for that. Plenty of dishonest ones, though."

Yancy's smug look returned. "I don't like mixing apples and oranges, especially since my last divorce. Lost a boatload of money to that witch, so the corporations help me keep things, well, organized."

And it kept assets hidden so that he couldn't be readily identified for criminal activities.

"Who rented the baby farm?" Rosalie demanded. But she didn't just demand it. She stepped around Austin, went straight for Yancy and got right in his face.

Yancy met her stare. "I don't know."

"He's lying." Sonny got to his feet and jabbed his index finger at the pictures. "He was there. He knows what's going on because he's the one behind it."

"I'm not behind it. That's the truth," Yancy added when Seth, Austin and she groaned. A muscle flickered in his jaw. "I'm not the only one who structures their business with corporations."

"What the heck does that mean?" Austin snapped.

"It means my people didn't do a thorough job of checking out the person who rented that ranch property for the baby farm. Or checking out the person who set me up for those photos. The names are all fake, part of a dummy corporation."

"Convenient," Austin mumbled, and he cursed.

Rosalie looked as if she wanted to curse, too. Or cry. This had to feel like another blow to her heart. Yet another stone wall in the investigation. Still, they might be able to chip at this wall and figure out what was behind it.

"You'll give us everything you know about your own corporations," Austin told Yancy. "Including the one you claim set you up."

Austin expected Yancy to argue since the FBI could use that info to uncover criminal activity, but after several snail-crawling moments, the man finally nodded. "I'll have my lawyer deliver anything that might apply here to the sheriff's office."

Now it was Sonny who cursed. "Anything he gives you will be fake. All lies."

"You mean like those photos?" Yancy fired back. "Seems like you're doing way too much finger-pointing, Sonny-boy. If you ask me, you're acting like a guilty man with all these wild accusations."

That set off another round of arguing, and Austin moved Rosalie out of the middle. Seth took over, issuing both men threats if they didn't settle down. He also motioned for Austin to get Rosalie out of there. Austin was about to do just that when his phone buzzed.

"It's Vickie," Austin whispered to Rosalie after glancing down at the screen. Since there was no way he wanted Yancy or Sonny to hear the conversation, he took Rosalie into the hall and shut the door.

"Are you okay?" Austin greeted Vickie when he answered. He hoped those baby farm guards hadn't come after her, though it was a possibility since Vickie had refused protective custody.

"I'm scared." That fear came through loud and clear in her voice. "I remembered something about your nephew and the man who brought him to me."

"What?" Austin asked. Rosalie obviously heard what the woman said because she pulled in her breath, waiting.

"Something important," Vickie said. "But I can't get into it over the phone. We need to meet because I have something to show you."

Chapter Eleven

While she paced, Rosalie listened for Austin's phone, willing it to ring.

Something that she'd been doing for the past hour.

It shouldn't be hard to hear the ringing sound because the guest cottage at the ranch wasn't large, since it was just two small bedrooms, a bath, a living room and kitchen. Not nearly enough space to put much distance between Austin and her.

Unfortunately, though, it'd been just enough for her not to hear all of his phone conversations. And he'd had plenty of those. For each one, Austin had spoken in hushed tones, never putting the calls on speaker, probably in the hopes of not disturbing her.

It hadn't worked.

Nothing would at this point except finding her baby and putting an end to the danger.

Since Austin was sleeping on the sofa in the living room, Rosalie wasn't pacing in there but rather in the kitchen, and she figured the pacing wouldn't end until the phone rang. It was only six in the morning, and since Vickie hadn't given them a specific time when she would call to arrange a meeting, it didn't necessarily mean there was reason for alarm yet.

Still, Rosalie was just that—alarmed.

She wanted the woman to call so they could meet her and see whatever it was she wanted to show them. And she wanted Vickie to do that before anything else went wrong. Whoever was behind the baby farm would likely attack Vickie and anyone else who tried to shed light on the illegal adoptions. Unless Vickie was setting up this meeting so that Austin and she could be silenced. Since that was a possibility, it'd mean they would have to take plenty more precautions.

Including emotional precautions on her part.

Especially since the reason for her emotional precautions was only a few feet away. Rosalie kept her footsteps as light as she could and paced closer to the living room so she could get another glimpse of the cowboy on the couch.

And even while sleeping, Austin was definitely still a cowboy.

He had his black Stetson slung over his face, and he was still wearing his jeans and boots. The sofa was too short for him, so his feet were propped up on the armrest. He looked ready to jump right into action.

Well, except for that unbuttoned shirt.

Rosalie didn't want to notice his chest, but she did, anyway. That chest looked as if he knew his way around a gym, but she suspected it'd come from working hard on his family's ranch. It was definitely a body that got her attention.

She touched her fingertips to her mouth, remembering the kiss that shouldn't have happened. She hadn't even tried to resist him but instead had stayed there in Austin's arms while he stirred the heat inside her.

The heat was still stirring.

And that unbuttoned shirt sure didn't help.

She silently groaned, forced herself to look away. Soon, very soon, after they'd dealt with Vickie's possible news, Rosalie would have to figure out a way to make Austin understand that this wasn't his fight. She appreciated his help, but being close to him like this just wasn't a good idea.

Because she was falling for him.

That caused her to mumble some profanity, and she turned to go back into the kitchen.

"You don't have to leave. I'm awake," Austin said, without taking the Stetson from his face.

Even though he couldn't actually see her, he might have figured out that she'd been gawking at him. That wouldn't help with the attraction, either, so Rosalie came up with a quick excuse. "I was just making sure that Vickie hadn't called."

"She hasn't." Austin added a groggy-sounding sigh and sat up. With his shirt still open. He tossed his Stetson on the coffee table and scrubbed his hand over his face.

"You should have taken Seth's bed," Rosalie commented. "He didn't make it in last night."

Of course, Austin already knew that. He'd taken a shower about five hours earlier before crashing on the couch, and he would have no doubt heard if Seth had come in since her brother would have had to walk right past him. Rosalie wasn't sure what'd kept Seth, but he was likely working on this investigation and had crashed at his office. Something he did more often than not.

"Should you try to call Vickie?" she asked.

"I did, about two hours ago. The call went straight to voice mail."

Oh, mercy. She prayed that meant nothing had gone

wrong with Vickie, but with everything else going on, that was a strong possibility.

"You do know that you can't go to any meeting that Vickie sets up?" Austin asked. Except it wasn't exactly a question. More like a statement of fact.

"I need to go," she insisted. "I need to find out what she wants to show us."

Austin was shaking his head before she even finished. "I can't put you in that kind of danger again. Seth will go with me, and I'll wear a wire so you can hear what's going on. But you'll stay here at the ranch. Your brother Colt told me that the ranch hands are all armed, and that he'll make sure to be here when Seth and I are gone."

This was the first she was hearing of any of this. "Did you talk to Colt about this when we were at the sheriff's office yesterday?"

"No. About two hours ago. I called him. He's already set up some extra security and has ranch hands on patrol so that no one tries to use the fence to get onto the ranch."

So, he'd gotten even less sleep than she'd originally thought. And during his sleepless time, he'd managed to come up with a plan with her brother to exclude her from talking with Vickie.

Rosalie didn't like that, and she was ready to voice that displeasure when he stood, stretching and giving her an even better peek at the chest that she shouldn't be peeking at. She forced herself to look away. But not before Austin got a glimpse of her face.

"This is about that kiss, isn't it?" Austin mumbled, but he didn't wait for her to confirm it. He strolled toward her, finally doing something about that unbuttoned shirt. "I should apologize."

Rosalie found herself dumbfounded again. It probably

wasn't a good idea for them to be discussing the attraction, but when Austin reached her, he slid his hand around the back of her neck and pulled her to him for a brief but scalding-hot kiss.

"I should apologize for that, too." He made a sound as if he liked what he'd tasted, and his gaze landed on the coffeepot. "Thank God, caffeine."

He helped himself to a full mug while Rosalie stood there with what she was sure was a gobsmacked look on her face. He gulped some of the coffee down with his attention still on her.

"You hate me," he concluded.

"I hate myself," she countered. But then had to shake her head. "I'm just confused."

"About your feelings or me?"

She had to think about that a moment. "Both. You know we shouldn't be feeling these things, right?"

"Yeah, but I also know that wanting the attraction to stop doesn't work." He paused, had more coffee. "After we find Sadie and you get on with your life, maybe then you'll be able to forgive me."

"I have forgiven you. That's the problem. I've forgiven you, but I can't forgive myself for feeling this…guilt."

He nodded. "Part of me died that night, too, with Eli. But I'm not sure that's what he would have wanted."

It wasn't. Rosalie knew that in her heart, but she just couldn't let go. And that's why she stepped back when Austin reached for her again.

She got just a glimpse of the troubled look on his face before his phone rang. He hurried, grabbing it so fast that he nearly knocked it off the table.

"It's Vickie," he let her know as he answered it, and this time he put the call on speaker.

"Sorry that I didn't answer my phone, but I've been on the move since we talked," the woman immediately said. "Someone was following me when I tried to go back to the motel where I was staying."

Rosalie could hear the fear in her voice. Or rather Vickie *sounded* afraid. After everything they'd been through, Rosalie wasn't about to take that at face value. Vickie could be playing some kind of sick game with them.

"When and where are we meeting?" Austin demanded.

"I'm at the McKinnon ranch. Well, near it, anyway. I'm on the road just outside a closed cattle gate. If you open it, I can drive in and we can talk now."

Austin cursed. "You shouldn't have come here. That's too risky for you and Rosalie. Meet me at the sheriff's office in town."

"No. I told you I don't trust the cops. I'm not going there."

"You can trust the sheriff," Rosalie insisted. "He's my brother."

Now it was Vickie who cursed. "I don't care who he is. If you want the information I have, then open the cattle gate right now. If not, I disappear, and you'll never see what I have or me again."

Sweet heaven. Rosalie could practically feel the debate going on inside Austin because she, too, was having the same reaction.

She wanted to trust Vickie, but it was a huge risk to allow her onto the ranch. After all, she could still be working for the person behind the baby farm or could be the culprit and had come there to kill them. To permanently silence them in case they'd learned anything while undercover.

"I'll come to you," Austin finally said. "But first tell me what you have. I want to make sure it's worth risking my neck."

"Oh, it's worth the risk, all right. But it'll cost you. I need money to get away from here, and I figure the McKinnons have plenty of it."

Blackmail. That turned Rosalie's stomach, but if she were in Vickie's shoes, she might be forced to consider doing the same thing.

"How much do you want?" Rosalie asked.

"Ten grand."

Rosalie didn't know the financial workings of the ranch, but she knew it was very successful, and it was highly likely that there was at least that much or more in the safe in Roy's office.

"I'll call the main house," Rosalie whispered to Austin, but he caught on to her hand to stop her.

"I'm not just walking down to you, carrying ten grand," Austin said to Vickie. "You need to tell me what you have."

Silence. For a long time. So long that Rosalie's heartbeat started to throb in her ears. If the woman refused and just drove away, the information might be lost. Still, there was Austin's safety to consider. Rosalie definitely didn't want him out there if this could turn into another attack.

"Well?" Austin prompted.

"The man who brought me your nephew called himself Jack Smith," Vickie finally said. "There was a woman with him, dressed in white scrubs like a nurse. Anyway, the baby had some kind of seeds on his blanket."

"Seeds?" Austin and Rosalie asked in unison. That certainly wasn't something Rosalie expected Vickie to say.

"I mean the baby was clean and everything except for

those seeds. I asked about them. More like casual conversation, you know, and the woman said they'd picked up the baby at the grain mill about ten miles from where I lived. Smith shushed her right up, and told me that the birth mother had hidden the pregnancy from her parents, and that she met them there at the mill so her folks wouldn't find out that she'd given birth."

"And you believed Smith?" Austin pressed.

"I did at the time. I didn't think anything more about it until after this mess with the baby farm broke loose. Then, I began to think it might be a ruse of some kind. I mean, why would the birth mother choose to meet them in a grain mill?"

"You mean the old abandoned one on the other side of town?" Rosalie had only vague memories of the silo that jutted up in an overgrown field.

"That's the one," Vickie verified. "It's exactly ten miles from me just like the woman said, and there's not another one in the area. I went over there last night, looking for answers."

"You did what?" Austin cursed again.

"I didn't go alone. I took a couple of friends with me. They were armed, but the guns weren't needed. Nobody was there. Just some boxes with files in them." Vickie paused. "The files are connected to the baby farm."

"Files," Austin snapped, not sounding at all happy about this. "You contaminated a scene that could be critical to this investigation."

"I found proof of the person who got Rosalie McKinnon's daughter," Vickie insisted. "And if you want it, it'll cost you ten grand. I'll be waiting at the end of the road."

"Meet me at the sheriff's office," Austin argued, but

he was talking to himself because Vickie had already ended the call.

Austin jabbed the button to return the call. No answer. It went straight to voice mail.

"I'll see about getting the money," Rosalie said, hurrying to the landline in the kitchen.

She considered calling her sister, who was still staying in the main house with her fiancé, but Rayanne was pregnant, and Rosalie didn't want her anywhere near Vickie or the danger. Her brother Cooper was at his own house, which was about a quarter of a mile away. Not far, but it would eat up precious moments if he was the one she involved in this. Ditto for her other brother Tucker.

That left her younger brother, Colt, and her father.

Rosalie pressed in the number, not sure which she would get, and it was Colt who answered on the first ring.

"What the hell's going on?" Colt immediately said. "The ranch hands just called, and there's a woman parked right in front of the gate—"

"I need ten thousand in cash," Rosalie interrupted. "The woman says she has information about my daughter."

Rosalie took a deep breath, praying that whatever files Vickie had would do just that—help her find Sadie—and that it would all happen without anyone else getting hurt.

"I'll be right there," Colt assured her before she could tell him that she'd pay him back as soon as she could get to the bank.

Like Vickie, Colt quickly ended the call, and Rosalie hurried back to the front of the cottage to see what was going on. Austin was already outside on the porch, his gun drawn and his attention on the small black car at the end of the road.

"Stay back," he warned her.

Rosalie did, but it was hard to do that with possible answers this close. It seemed to take an eternity, but she realized it was less than five minutes before Colt emerged from the main house and headed toward them. He, too, was carrying a gun and a thick plastic bag.

Austin turned around, snagged her gaze and slipped his cell into his shirt pocket. "Wait here, and I mean it. Don't you even think about going out there with me. Call me, and I'll leave my phone on so you can hear what's going on."

She nodded, her breath hitching a little when he idly brushed a kiss on her mouth and headed out, Colt falling in step right along beside him. As Austin had instructed, she called him, but he didn't speak when he answered the call. Probably because he wanted to keep his attention on the woman who stepped from the car.

It was Vickie all right.

The woman had a large cardboard box that she set on the ground next to the fence, and she took out a manila folder from it.

"I want the money," Vickie said when Austin and Colt approached her. "Then, you'll get the files."

"Show me that folder first," Austin countered.

Because his back was to her, Rosalie couldn't see Austin's expression, but it must have been adamant enough for Vickie to rethink her demand. She handed him the folder.

Colt kept his gun trained on the woman while he volleyed glances at both Austin and the folder he opened. Time seemed to stop. Not her heart, though. It was slamming against her chest so hard that it hurt her ribs.

"Give her the cash," Austin finally said. He glanced

back over his shoulder at Rosalie. "Judging from the birthday, this could be Sadie's file."

Rosalie sucked in her breath so hard that she nearly got choked. "And?" was all she managed to say.

She heard Austin's hard breath, too, but it was Vickie who answered. "Tell Rosalie that it has the name of the person who bought her daughter."

Chapter Twelve

Austin wished like the devil that he could stop Rosalie from going with him for this visit, but he knew he didn't stand a chance of making her stay at her family's ranch. One way or another she would confront the man whose name had been in the file that Vickie had given them.

Trevor Yancy.

Austin shouldn't have been surprised to see Yancy's name on those papers claiming he was the one who'd *bought* Sadie. After all, the man was a serious suspect in the baby farm investigation and a multitude of other felonies. However, just the fact that it was Yancy meant that Rosalie wasn't going to settle for anyone but her confronting him.

He couldn't blame her.

But Austin darn sure could do whatever it took to protect her.

That's why he was driving her to Yancy's estate in San Antonio while her brother Colt followed them in his truck. In addition, Austin had called SAPD and asked them to send out a patrol car to keep an eye on the estate, to make sure Yancy didn't try to run. Maybe, just maybe, Yancy would confess to everything, turn over a perfectly healthy Sadie to Rosalie and then Colt could arrest the piece of slime.

Austin only hoped Rosalie and he could keep their own tempers in check during this little chat.

He had a lot of dangerous energy brewing inside him, and that anger was headed right toward Yancy. The man had likely caused Eli's death, and now he might have been the one to kidnap Rosalie's daughter.

If Yancy had done that, he was going to pay hard.

"Hurry," she insisted.

Rosalie kept her attention on the phone, and pressed Redial yet again. As with the other half dozen times that she'd tried to call Yancy on both his cell and home phones, the man didn't answer. Maybe because he didn't take calls this early or maybe because Vickie or someone else had given him a heads-up that Rosalie and the law were on the way. Of course, Austin wasn't sure why Vickie would do something like that since she'd been the one to give them the file, but with all the insanity that'd gone on, anything was possible.

"If Yancy's not home, we'll find him," Austin promised her, and it was a promise he would keep no matter what it took. Too bad though that he couldn't keep it after he had Rosalie tucked safely away. He hadn't stopped her from going to the estate, but if this turned into an all-out search, he wanted her far away from any path that Yancy and his hired thugs might take.

"I want to hear what he has to say about those adoption papers," Rosalie mumbled.

"So do I. But if he does actually answer your call, it's best not to ask him if he has Sadie. We wouldn't want to spook him and have him run with her."

"I doubt he can be spooked. He's arrogant and certain that he's above the law. He's not."

No, he wasn't. "But until we have Yancy in our sights, it's best if you keep the adoption questions general. Don't ask specifically about Sadie. Agreed?"

He could tell she wanted to argue with him about that, but she finally nodded.

Her grip tightened even more on the phone until Austin thought it might shatter. Heck, she might shatter, too. Not with tears this time, but he could feel the rage boiling inside her just as it was with him.

"You have to remember that Vickie or someone else could have faked that paperwork," Austin reminded her.

The anger flashed in her eyes as if she might argue about that, as well, but then a rough groan left her mouth. "I know. Vickie could be lying to cover her own guilt."

Yeah, and that's the reason Austin had called Rosalie's brother, the sheriff, so he could escort Vickie into town for questioning. Vickie hadn't liked that one bit, but Austin didn't care. She'd possibly destroyed evidence by going to that grain mill.

And maybe worse.

"Maybe Vickie pretended to go to the grain mill to cover up any DNA evidence that might be there. *Her* DNA," Austin clarified.

Rosalie made a sound of agreement. "But if she's guilty, why didn't she stay hidden away? She's the one who contacted us about your nephew. Vickie could have just stayed in hiding or given the baby to someone else so that she wouldn't be caught with him."

Unfortunately, Austin could see that from another angle. "She could have heard that I'd been working undercover to find Nathan and thought she'd better cut her losses. By giving him to us, she might have hoped to get the heat off her and put it on someone else."

"And she could have used the files to set up Yancy," Rosalie finished for him a moment later. "That would explain why she didn't just blow up the grain mill." Her eyes narrowed. "That doesn't mean Yancy's innocent, though."

No, it didn't. But with all the finger-pointing that Sonny, Vickie and Yancy were doing at each other, it was hard to home in on the guilty party.

Rosalie tried Yancy's number again. Same result. No answer. She checked the estimated time of arrival on the GPS. Yet something else she'd been doing since they started this drive from the McKinnon ranch. They were still a half hour out, and that likely felt like an eternity to her.

It did to Austin, too.

It also didn't help that they were in the middle of a long stretch of rural property.

He'd taken the back roads to get there as fast as possible, but it meant Rosalie, Colt and he were at risk for another attack. The rural road would be a good place for it. Of course, the gunmen could have come after them on the highway, too. No place would be truly safe until the men were found and put in jail along with their boss.

And maybe their boss was Yancy.

"If Yancy has Sadie—"

"Don't go there," he insisted.

Austin hooked his arm around her and dragged her as close to him as the seat belt would allow. It wasn't exactly a hug to comfort her, but it was the best he could do. He definitely didn't want her to think about why Yancy would have purchased her child.

Because nothing good came to mind.

There was no acceptable reason for a weasel like Yancy to buy a baby.

That sent a new round of rage through him. If Yancy had done anything to Sadie, then no way would Austin be able to keep his temper in check. He would aim every bit of his venom at the man.

"I'm trying Yancy's cell again." Rosalie pressed Redial again, and Austin was about to tell her that she should just wait until they got to his place. But this time, she didn't get his voice mail.

Yancy answered.

"It's early," Yancy snarled. "What in Sam Hill do you want at this hour?"

Probably because she was so shocked that he'd actually picked up, it took Rosalie a moment to find her voice. Or maybe she was remembering all the things that Austin had warned her that she shouldn't say to him.

"What do you really know about the baby farms?" she asked.

Yancy cursed. "Not this again. I'm getting sick and tired of these—"

"Did you try to adopt a baby?" Rosalie snapped.

Austin held his breath, wondering if it might not be a good idea, after all, to go ahead and try to spook Yancy. The SAPD patrol was hopefully already in place at his house so they could stop the man from fleeing. And if Yancy did indeed run, it would just confirm his guilt.

"Who the devil told you that?" Yancy asked.

"Just answer the question," Austin insisted, using his lawman's tone that no doubt set Yancy's teeth on edge. "Did you have anything to do with trying to adopt a baby?"

"Yeah," Yancy finally said after mumbling plenty of

profanity. "About a year ago, but I didn't go through with it. The only reason I wanted a kid was to keep my wife happy so she wouldn't divorce me and take a fortune. She decided to leave me, anyway, so I canceled the adoption."

Rosalie glanced at Austin to see if he was buying this, but he had to shrug. It sounded exactly like something Yancy would do, and Yancy had been through a bitter divorce. From what Austin remembered, there'd been no prenup, and Yancy's ex-wife had gotten millions from his estate.

Still, that didn't mean Yancy hadn't taken Rosalie's daughter.

"You have any proof that you backed out of the deal?" Rosalie asked.

A few long moments crawled by. "You got proof that I didn't?"

"Yes, I think we do."

Yancy's next round of profanity was significantly worse. "I told you I had no part in that business with the baby farms, and if you've got something that says different, then it's a lie just like the ones Sonny-boy was spewing."

"You're sure?" Austin pressed, causing Yancy's profanity to continue.

"Damn straight. And ask yourself this little question. Why would an operation like this keep records lying around for someone to find? They wouldn't. So, anything you find or will find has been manufactured to make somebody look guilty. And in this case, that manufacturing has been aimed at me."

Yancy had a point, but it was a point all three suspects could make. There was situational evidence to suggest that all of them had motive and opportunity to pull off an operation like this. Sonny and Yancy had the means with their bank accounts, and Austin was sure if he dug harder, that he'd find Vickie had those same means.

"If you're telling the truth," Rosalie said, obviously ignoring his question, "then you won't mind if we search your house."

"Heck, yeah, I mind—"

Yancy continued to talk, but Austin tuned him out. That's because he saw the large SUV coming down the road toward them, and it looked like the vehicle their attackers had used. Not a good time for this to happen since Austin was approaching a bridge where there'd be no place to maneuver.

He moved his hand over his gun and was about to call Colt to alert him, but the SUV swerved directly into their lane.

And it came right at them.

ROSALIE HAD HER attention focused on Yancy's rant so it took her a moment to realize that something was wrong.

Oh, God.

It was happening again. They were in danger.

"Hold on!" Austin shouted a split second before he jerked the steering wheel to the right. If he hadn't done that, the SUV would have crashed right into them.

Instead, their front bumper bashed into the concrete guardrail on the narrow bridge. Her body jolted forward only to be slammed back again when the air bags deployed and hit her right in the face.

She couldn't see, but mercy, she could feel. The impact knocked the breath right out of her. Thankfully, though, Austin seemed to be able to react. He quickly batted down the deflating air bag on his side because the truck was still moving. And Rosalie got a glimpse of where they were headed.

Straight down the bank and into the creek.

Austin fought the steering wheel, and he hit the brakes. But it was already too late. Rosalie put up her hands to brace herself for the impact.

She didn't have to wait long.

It seemed only a blink of an eye before the truck plowed right into the water. The impact gave her body another jolt, knocking her off balance. Before she could even get the door open, icy water started pouring into the cab.

"Colt's behind us," Austin mumbled.

Maybe he said that so she wouldn't panic and would remember that they had backup. However, her brother could be under attack, as well.

Rosalie frantically tried to open the door, and her heart skipped a beat when it didn't budge. Neither did Austin's, but he slammed his shoulder against it until it gave way, and he pried it the rest of the way open with his hands.

"Come on," he said, keeping his gun and phone above the water that was rushing in.

He caught on to her wrist and pulled her closer toward him. However, he didn't get out. Austin looked up at the SUV, probably to make sure they weren't about to be gunned down when they exited the vehicle.

"They're still out there on the bridge," Austin told her. "Keep low and move fast."

That didn't help steady her heart, and she was already shaking so hard that Rosalie was afraid she wouldn't be able to move. Austin made sure she did, though. With the water inside the truck already chest high and getting deeper, he pulled her into the creek.

The water wasn't over their heads, but it was freezing,

and the cold blasted through her. Her teeth started to chatter and she was shaking. Still, Austin kept her moving. Not toward the gunmen and Colt but toward the bank on the opposite side of the creek.

Her heartbeat was so loud in her ears, and with the water raging around them, it took Rosalie a moment to realize some of what she was hearing were gunshots.

Sweet heaven.

Not again.

They were under attack and literally out in the open. Plus, her brother was no doubt being shot at, too. Hopefully, Colt had managed to stay safe and could return fire.

Somehow, Austin was able to keep his gun and phone out of the water while he also kept her moving. Her heart was pounding even harder, her breath barely there by the time they made it to the bank. It was a mixture of dead grass, icy mud and rocks, and they crawled toward one of the large boulders. With her wet clothes weighing her down, each inch was a challenge.

The moment that Austin got her behind the boulder, he turned and fired at the people shooting at them. Rosalie got a glimpse of the men then. Both had taken cover behind their SUV. One had his weapon aimed at them. The other had his aimed in the direction of Colt's truck. She didn't see her brother, but she heard the sound of the gunshots coming from his direction.

Thank God.

Maybe Colt would be able to capture at least one of the men so that Austin and she could finally get some answers as to what was going on. However, she wasn't sure it was a coincidence that they'd been attacked so close to Yancy's house.

Was Yancy trying to kill them so she wouldn't find her daughter?

That only made her anger and resolve stronger, and Rosalie wished she'd managed to hang on to a gun so that she could help Austin and Colt return fire.

"Backup's on the way!" Colt shouted to them.

Rosalie didn't know if that was a bluff or if Colt had actually managed to make a call with all the chaos going on around them. Either way, it stopped the men from shooting, and she saw one of them motion toward the other.

The pair hurried to get back inside their SUV.

Oh, mercy. "They can't get away," Rosalie whispered. Even though she didn't want more bullets coming toward them or Colt, she also didn't want them to escape. Obviously, neither did Austin.

Cursing, he levered himself up, took aim and fired a shot at the man getting behind the steering wheel. His first shot missed.

His second didn't.

Rosalie saw the man's shoulder snap back, and he howled in pain. However, it didn't stop him. He jumped into the driver's seat and slammed the door shut. His partner did the same on the other side of the SUV.

Both Colt and Austin didn't stop shooting. Austin came out from behind the boulder, and standing, he fired directly at the driver again. The bullet tore into the glass, shattering it.

Just as the driver jammed on the accelerator.

Even if he was hurt and bleeding, he was still managing to get away.

The SUV flew past Colt's truck, barely missing her brother.

"Come on," Austin said, pulling Rosalie to her feet.

She wasn't sure how he managed to move so fast as they hurried back into the creek and toward the bank. While still keeping watch around them, Colt barreled down the slick incline to help them. The moment they made it back out of the water, the three of them raced toward his truck.

"Are you hurt?" Colt asked.

Austin gave her a quick once-over and shook his head. "Hurry," he told Colt. "We have to find those gunmen."

Colt didn't waste another second. He gunned the engine, and they went in pursuit.

Chapter Thirteen

Austin looked at the purple bruise on Rosalie's cheek and cursed again. He had no idea when she'd gotten it, but it'd probably happened when they'd plunged into the creek.

Where they could have died.

He was responsible for that. He should have done everything to stop her from going to Yancy's estate, should have forced her to let him protect her. But he hadn't, and she'd paid another high price for it.

"I must look pretty bad, huh?" Rosalie mumbled.

She had another sip of the hot tea that one of the Sweetwater Springs deputies had fixed for her. In addition to the tea sipping, she was also pacing back and forth in front of the doorway of the sheriff's office.

Since she was still shivering a little from the adrenaline crash, the hot tea obviously wasn't doing its job. Ditto for the change of dry clothes that her brother had brought for both Austin and her from the ranch. Of course, tea and dry clothes weren't nearly enough to erase the nightmarish memories from this latest attack.

Or erase the fact that their attackers had gotten away again.

The men were out there, no doubt ready to come after

them the first chance they got. It was up to Austin to make sure another chance was the last thing they got.

"You look fine," Austin assured her.

She made a *yeah, right* sound and paused her pacing so she could glance out into the squad room. The place was cluttered with cops, two of them her own brothers. Her other brother, Tucker, a Texas Ranger, was also there. All of them were on the phone. All trying to track down those gunmen and deal with the Yancy situation.

Obviously, no one had made any headway or they would have come into the sheriff's office, where Rosalie and Austin were waiting for news.

Any news.

But especially news that concerned the search warrant they'd managed to get for Yancy's place. With luck, there'd soon be a team of cops and FBI agents, including Seth, streaming through the house and grounds to look for any shred of evidence.

With even better luck, they'd find Sadie.

Of course, Yancy's place wasn't the only lead they had. Austin was sure he'd wounded one of their attackers. Colt had possibly wounded the other. It meant the men would have to get medical attention, and maybe they'd do that at a hospital where their injuries would be reported. Then, once they had the gunmen in custody, it would make it easier to find out who'd hired them.

Austin hoped so, anyway.

Sooner or later they had to catch a break that didn't end in them nearly being killed.

"I don't know if I can stand around here waiting much longer," Rosalie said, gripping the cup of tea so hard that her knuckles were turning white.

Yeah, he felt the same way, and yet Austin knew there was little more that they could do. Well, other than take Rosalie back to her family's ranch.

Something she'd repeatedly refused.

Austin couldn't blame her.

Since she couldn't be at Yancy's house while it was being searched, the sheriff's office was the next best place. At least they'd be there when Yancy was brought in, and there was no doubt about it—the man would be brought in for questioning.

As a minimum, Yancy had to answer questions about the files that Vickie had given them. Of course, he'd lie about them, but with the photos from Sonny and now the files, that might be enough to make an arrest. Being tossed behind bars might get Yancy to bargain with them, and he could just open up about Sadie and anything that he might actually know about her.

Eleven months was a long time to hold a child, and that meant there might be records for payment of nannies and baby supplies. Well, there would be if Yancy hadn't simply given her away to someone. But maybe there'd be something in his house about that, too. Yes, Yancy was careful, always covering his tracks, but maybe he'd gotten sloppy about this.

"I wish you'd see a medic," Austin tried again when he gave that angry-looking bruise another glance. Perhaps this time, she would actually agree.

But Rosalie only shook her head and touched her fingers to the wound on her face that kept snagging his attention. "It's not bad. I'm okay."

"You're not okay. You're still shaking." Austin stood,

went to her and pried the cup from her hands so he could set it on the desk.

"It's not a good time for you to hold me," Rosalie protested.

That was yet something else they could agree on, but it didn't stop Austin from pulling her into his arms because she looked as if she needed it.

Heck, who was he kidding?

He needed it, too. Needed to feel her next to him. Needed the way she sort of melted against him. He got it all right. But it came at a high cost—it only made him need her more. And it broke down even more of those barriers that she kept putting up between them.

Rosalie eased back, just a little, meeting him eye to eye. That wasn't a happy expression on her face. "We keep getting closer and closer."

Austin figured his expression wasn't happy, either. "I want you," he settled for saying. "So yeah, we're getting closer."

Rosalie stared at him a long time, as if trying to figure out a way to dismiss what he'd just admitted, but then she huffed. Her breath from that huff was still on his mouth when she kissed him. She didn't settle for a peck but instead turned it into the kind of kiss that he knew they should be avoiding.

Oh, man.

He was just plain brainless when it came to Rosalie, and Austin proved that by kissing her right back. The timing sucked. Same for the location. But did that stop him?

Nope.

He kept it up until both of them were in serious need of some air. Or maybe a bed.

"I'm not sure I'm ready for this," she said, her mouth

still way too close to his. "And it could be that I'm just using this right now, using *you,* to get my mind off Sadie."

Since it was the equivalent of a *no,* that got him backing away. Or rather it would have if Rosalie hadn't caught on to the front of his shirt to anchor him in place.

"But I don't think I can stop myself, either," Rosalie added. "And maybe I'm not using you at all. Maybe I just…want you."

Since that was pretty much the equivalent of a big green light, Austin went after her again, and he could have stood there kissing her for hours if he hadn't heard the footsteps headed in their direction. He broke away from her just as Colt stepped into the doorway.

Rosalie's brother wasn't an idiot, and his lifted eyebrow let Austin know that he knew what was going on. But that raised eyebrow lasted only a second before Colt motioned for them to follow him.

"The team's out at Yancy's place," Colt explained as they made their way to a desk in the corner of the squad room. "Yancy's not there, but the team entered the premises, and one of the SAPD officers is recording the search. Thought you'd like to watch on the computer."

That was a massive understatement, and Rosalie practically ran to the laptop centered on the desk. Sure enough, it was the front door of Yancy's place. Austin had been there at least a half dozen times when questioning the man about various investigations, including the one leading up to Eli's murder.

The officer filming the search walked into the massive marble foyer, where a maid was waiting and glaring. Obviously, she wasn't pleased about this intrusion, but she didn't try to stop them.

"The maid said no one else was home," Colt explained.

"What about a baby?" Rosalie asked.

Colt shook his head. "It was the first thing Seth asked her, and she claims a baby's never lived at the estate, and she's worked there for ten years."

Austin could practically feel the disappointment ripple through her. And the relief.

"The maid's on Yancy's payroll," Austin reminded her. "Judging from her expression, she's loyal to him, which means she'd lie to protect him."

Yeah, that was bittersweet, too, because if the woman was indeed lying, they might find Sadie today. In Yancy's house. But it would mean the monster had had Rosalie's precious baby all this time. Since that only caused Austin's blood to boil, he tried to push the possibility aside. Best to wait and see how this all panned out.

Best-case scenario was for the cops to find Sadie's file and for Rosalie to learn that her baby had been adopted by a loving family. Illegally adopted, that is. Then, Rosalie could petition for the baby's return once she'd done the DNA tests. It wouldn't be a simple process, but this search could give them a start.

The cop with the camera moved past the maid and into the adjoining living room, where another officer was going through a cluttered bookshelf. Austin watched as the cameraman made his way to the side of the house and to Yancy's office.

"There's Seth," Rosalie mumbled when her brother came into view. The camera was filming him while he was at Yancy's desk going through the drawers.

Rosalie automatically reached for her phone, no doubt to call her brother, but then she groaned when she realized that she'd lost it in the creek. Instead, she snatched up the one on the desk, pressed in his number, and a moment later Austin saw Seth answer the call.

"Seth—" Rosalie said.

"We haven't found anything," Seth immediately interrupted, glancing up at the camera as if to make eye contact with his sister.

"Where's Yancy?" Austin asked, and he pressed the button to put the call on speaker.

"There was no sign of him when we arrived. The maid says he's away on business, but she could be lying. We've got the airports covered and a BOLO on his vehicles."

Rosalie shook her head. "Yancy might be on the run."

But something wasn't right about that. Yancy wasn't a runner. He'd come close to arrest many times and had always relied on his team of high-priced lawyers to keep his butt out of jail.

Maybe this was something his lawyers couldn't fix.

Like his guilt over running a baby farm. The baby farm could net him murder charges along with other assorted felonies.

There was some chatter outside Yancy's office, and Seth got up to check it out. Thankfully, the officer with the camera followed Rosalie's brother out into the hall and to the bottom of a massive curved staircase.

"You need to get a look at this," a uniformed cop told Seth.

"It's not what you think," the maid shouted, following right along behind them as they hurried up the stairs.

Oh, man. What the heck had they found?

Since Rosalie suddenly didn't look too steady on her feet, Austin slipped his arm around her waist. They didn't have to wait long to see what was happening.

The camera soon picked up the officer standing outside a room at the far end of the hall. Beside him, Rosalie pulled in her breath, and they watched together. The officer in the doorway stepped aside so that Seth and the cameraman could get a look.

"Oh, God," Rosalie said, her hand flying to her mouth. Austin repeated it.

Because it was a nursery. And not just any old nursery. This one was drenched in pink. The walls, the bed, the toys.

Everything for a baby girl.

"It's not what you think!" the maid repeated, and she tried to shoulder Seth and the cameraman aside. That didn't work. And the glare that Seth gave her could have frozen Hades a couple of times over.

"Where's the baby?" Seth demanded.

The maid frantically shook her head. "There's no baby. Never was. Mrs. Yancy had this room set up because they planned to adopt a baby, but the adoption didn't go through because they got a divorce."

That meshed with what Yancy had told them, but Austin wasn't about to believe Yancy or his maid. Apparently, neither was Seth. He went into the room, looking around for what seemed an eternity.

"It doesn't look as if the crib or the room has been used," he finally said after a heavy sigh. "Rosalie, I don't think Sadie was here."

Again, Austin could see the conflict of emotions on her face, and it was a good thing he was holding on to her because she practically sagged against him.

"Just in case, I'll have the CSI team process the room," Seth continued. "We might find something. Might find something on his computers, too, because I'm confiscating all of them along with the files in his office."

Good. Maybe Yancy had left something incriminating behind. Austin could hope so, anyway. The minutes were just ticking away, and if they hoped to have Sadie home by Christmas, then…

Austin mentally stopped.

Home.

Not his home, either, but Rosalie's. It would be an incredible reunion, one that he would do whatever it took to make sure it happened. But after that, Rosalie and Sadie would be out of his life. Without the danger, there'd be no excuse for him to stay around. Yes, the attraction was there between Rosalie and him.

But there was also the doubt.

Maybe once she had Sadie, the doubt would be more than enough for Rosalie to tell him to take a hike. That sure didn't settle well in his stomach or any other part of him.

"Is something wrong?" he heard Rosalie ask, and it took Austin a moment to realize she was talking to him and that there was a concerned look on her face.

Great. He didn't want to add to her troubles, so he shook his head. "Just thinking."

And wondering how stupid he had to be to fall for a woman who wasn't ready to fall again. Especially not for him. The bad memories would always be there, and he wasn't sure the bad ones would ever outshine the good ones.

"We got a visitor," one of the officers told Seth. That got Austin's attention back where it belonged. On the search going on at Yancy's estate.

The cameraman continued to get footage of every nook and cranny of the nursery, but Seth stepped out of the room and out of camera range.

"Sonny's here," Seth told them, and he motioned for the cameraman to film what could easily turn into another encounter. Sonny seemed to bring trouble with him wherever he went.

It wasn't long before Austin heard the man's thundering voice. "Where the hell is he?" Sonny demanded.

Sonny was coming up the hall toward Seth and moving a lot easier than he had the last time Austin had seen him, but he was just as riled as he had been when he'd pulled a gun on Yancy at the hospital.

"I have no idea. I was hoping you could tell me where Yancy is," Seth countered.

"Well, I can't," Sonny snapped, but he held up an envelope for Seth. "But he's trying to set me up again."

"Funny, Yancy keeps saying the same thing about you." Seth took the envelope that Sonny practically slapped into his hand.

The camera angle was bad and Austin couldn't see what Seth took from the envelope, but it appeared to be photos.

Seth studied them for several long moments, and the cameraman finally moved in on the image.

A baby.

"Who is this?" Seth demanded.

"Read the memo." Sonny rifled through the eight-by-ten black-and-white photos to what appeared to be a single paragraph.

Seth did read it. Too bad Austin couldn't do the same, but whatever was on the page caused Seth to pull back his shoulders. "Where the hell did you get this?" His gaze snapped to Sonny.

"Someone broke into my office and put it in one of

my files. I'm sure they did that for you to find so you'd arrest me."

A soft gasp left Rosalie's mouth. "Is it Sadie?" But she didn't wait for Seth or Sonny to answer. "Let me see the photos. Hold them up to the camera."

Austin hadn't seen a photo of Sadie, but he could tell from Rosalie's reaction that this was indeed her baby. It was a snapshot of a newborn baby sleeping in a carried seat.

Rosalie moved as if to bolt to the door. No doubt to go see the photos for herself, but Austin stopped her.

"Don't come here," Seth warned her. Even though he couldn't see his sister, he must have known what her reaction would be.

Every muscle in her body was tight now, but she cursed and stayed put. "Show me the rest of the photos."

Seth did after he, too, mumbled some profanity. The next picture was also of Sadie in the arms of a woman. The camera was on the baby, not the person holding her, so Austin could see the little girl's blond hair and a round baby face.

"Who's that woman with her?" Rosalie demanded, and Seth repeated the question to Sonny.

"I don't know." No shout from Sonny this time. He scrubbed his hand over his face and appeared to be in as much shock over this as they were. "Like I said, someone planted the photos in my office. But I'm guessing that she's a nanny."

Probably, and she appeared to be taking good care of the baby. That was something at least. But Austin wanted more—the woman's identity and where the picture was taken.

Maybe Seth could get those answers from Sonny.

Seth went to the next photo. No newborn this time, but Austin was pretty sure it was Sadie. The little girl was about four or five months old, lying in a crib and smiling from ear to ear, kicking her arms and legs as she looked up at the person who'd taken her picture.

Austin tightened his grip on Rosalie when she wobbled again. She finally sank into the chair, her attention nailed to the laptop screen and her trembling fingers pressed to her mouth.

"That next picture's been photoshopped," Sonny insisted. "It had to have been."

Rosalie moved closer to the screen, but Seth turned away so that he got a look at the photo first. No doubt so he could try to shelter his sister in case it was something he didn't want her to see.

Seth cursed. It wasn't mumbled this time, either.

"Show it to me!" Rosalie demanded just as Sonny repeated, "It's a fake."

"I'll have the lab check and make sure it's real," Seth told her. "It has a date stamp on it that says it was taken three days ago." He finally held the photo up for Rosalie to see.

She gasped.

The photo was of a little girl, blond curls haloing around her head. She was smiling in this snapshot, too, and looking up at the woman who was lovingly holding her in her arms.

And that woman was Vickie.

Chapter Fourteen

Everything inside her felt as if she was spinning out of control, but Rosalie tried to hang on to her sanity. Especially since Seth, Austin and even Sonny had reminded her that the photos could have been doctored.

Still, that was her baby in the pictures. Rosalie was sure of it.

She sat at the kitchen table and studied the copies of the photos that Seth had faxed to the ranch guesthouse. Probably a ploy to make sure she stayed put with Austin while the cops looked for Vickie and Yancy. It was working.

For now.

But with this pressure cooker of emotions building inside her, she couldn't spend days or even hours waiting for answers from two people who had seemingly disappeared.

Austin was on the phone, pacing the guest cottage living room, but he also kept his eye on her. Something he'd been doing a lot since they'd arrived about an hour earlier. Like Seth, Austin was afraid she'd go stark raving mad and run out the door.

The probability for that was fairly high.

She ran her fingertips over the photo that according to the time-date stamp been taken only days earlier. Rosalie touched the image of her baby's hair. Her face. There were so many features that she recognized. The shape of Sadie's face was like her own. Ditto for the hair. Rosalie had seen photos of herself as a child, and her own hair was exactly like the cloud of curls.

But that was Eli's smile.

It broke her heart and warmed her all at the same time. A part of him had lived on. Too bad Rosalie hadn't been able to experience it firsthand.

God, she'd missed so much.

Eleven months was a lifetime to be apart from her child.

Rosalie's heart was broken over that. And the pain crushed her chest so that it felt as if someone had put her entire body in a vise. Squeezing and choking her until the panic attack started to crawl through her again.

Rosalie threw back the chair, got up and headed for the door. She needed some fresh air. Needed to run. To scream. To do something to stop the torture. A panic attack wouldn't do anyone any good, and it would only cause Austin and Seth to worry about her even more.

If that was possible.

"The guards from the baby farm," Austin reminded her. He stepped in front of her just as she opened the door. "If you go outside, they could use long-range rifles to shoot at you."

He locked the door, set the security system, eased his arm around her and tried to maneuver her into the living room. But Rosalie held her ground. She couldn't sit down a moment longer.

"Give me some good news," she begged. "Please."

Judging from the length of time it took him to answer, he was clearly having trouble coming up with something. "The photos are top priority for the lab, so we should know within an hour or two if they're fake."

"They're not fake." Then, she shook her head. "The baby is real. It's Sadie. *My* baby. But it's possible that Vickie's image was doctored in."

Or not.

It sickened her even more to think of Vickie having had Sadie all this time. Of course, there were worse alternatives.

Like Yancy or Sonny.

Of the three, Vickie seemed the safest choice, but if she'd lied so easily to their faces, then heaven knew what she was capable of doing to a baby.

"The cops and the FBI are working this hard," Austin reminded her. "And Seth will make sure there are no delays." No doubt a second attempt to give her some more good news.

Yes, it was good, but it didn't seem nearly enough. Though it would never happen, she wanted every law enforcement agency in the state on this.

"You should sit back down," he said.

This time when he urged her into the living room, she went, but she stopped first to grab the photos. She dropped them on the coffee table so she could look at them when they sat on the sofa.

"Someone has her," Rosalie mumbled. "Seth and the others have to find out who that is."

"They will. They're looking for Vickie and Yancy right now," Austin assured her. "And Seth will call the moment he finds out anything. If the lab can identify where the photos of Sadie were taken, then we can get a search warrant."

Yes, her mind knew that, but that didn't make this situation more bearable.

"You don't have to keep yourself together for my sake,"

Austin added. "If you need to lose it, then go ahead. Scream, curse, kick, do whatever will help."

"Kick?" she questioned.

The corner of his mouth lifted a little. "I was hoping you'd go for one of the other choices, but my shins are ready if you need to kick something."

"If I thought for one minute it'd help, I might try it." She paused, and though she hadn't intended for her gaze to go in that direction, she eyed the front of his jeans. "Just not your shins, though."

He feigned a wince. "Okay, but please don't aim *there*."

Rosalie didn't laugh, but it did ease the tension a bit. Something she hadn't thought possible just moments earlier. Leave it to Austin to work some magic and lighten her mood.

"Sit," he suggested. "Breathe." His voice was smoky deep now, like a smooth shot of whiskey. It was void of all the raw emotion they'd been through in the past couple of days.

Rosalie didn't sit, but his suggestion caused her to calm down enough so that she could study the photos again. Yes, she'd already studied them until her eyes were burning, but this time she noticed something obvious that she'd missed.

There wasn't much background in the shots of Sadie, but in all three cases, it appeared to be the same room. Not a dingy holding cell, either, but rather a cheerful-looking nursery. Exactly the kind of room she'd set up for her baby at her house in Kendall County.

"Maybe the person who adopted her didn't know she'd been stolen," Rosalie said. Maybe this person holding her baby wasn't the monster she was making the individual out to be but rather a loving parent who'd desperately wanted a child.

That thought helped. Some.

So did the way that Austin pulled her deeper into the curve of his arm. Yet something else that was smooth and comforting. It was dangerous for her to get so close to him right now, but Rosalie didn't care. Austin understood what she was going through.

He understood *her*.

And right now, the curve of his arm felt like the right place to be. Sadly, this was more than just a comforting gesture, though. His arms were a place where she could shut out these painful memories and find comfort of a different nature.

She turned to face him. Also dangerous. But she wanted to kiss him. Wanted to feel something other than this dark storm that had hemmed her in like a straitjacket.

And she felt *something* all right.

One touch of his mouth to hers, and she got a quick reminder of why this wasn't a very good idea. The dark storm vanished, but in its place came a storm of a different kind. A fiery-hot one that threatened to burn them alive.

A sound of surprise rumbled deep in his throat. Rosalie heard the question there, too.

Is this a good idea?

It wasn't.

But that didn't stop her.

She slid her hand around the back of his neck, bringing him closer so she could lose herself in the kiss. Lose herself in his touch. In Austin.

He automatically adjusted, turning, so he could gather her in his arms and deepen the kiss.

Yes!

This was the fire that she wanted. *Needed.* And Rosalie would have done her own share of kiss-deepening if Austin hadn't pulled back.

Their breaths were already gusting, and she could feel the urgency in her body. Still, he held her back from him, his gaze meeting hers.

"Think this through. Be sure it's what you want," Austin said, obviously giving her an out.

Rosalie did think about it. Well, as best as she could, considering the kiss had done its job of clouding her thoughts and common sense. Or maybe Austin alone was responsible. Either way, she didn't have to think long.

Even if she regretted it, she was going to be with him.

And Rosalie let Austin know that by pulling him back to her.

AUSTIN DIDN'T FEEL any hesitation from Rosalie. Just the opposite. But he had to wonder—was this about him, or did she just need him for a distraction?

He didn't know the answer. Wasn't sure that Rosalie did, either, but it didn't take long for that thought to fly right out of his head.

The kiss pulled him right in.

Still, he couldn't deny that he wanted Rosalie more than his next breath. She clearly wanted him, too, and even though he should stop, he didn't.

Austin figured since he was about to jump right into a Texas-size mistake that he might as well make the most of it. Something that neither of them would ever forget. He slipped his hand around the back of her neck, dragged her closer and kissed her the way he'd been wanting to kiss her for days.

With nothing held back.

Her taste slid right through him like fire, and he brought her closer and closer until they weren't just plastered against each other, they were maneuvering to get themselves even closer. That wasn't possible though with their clothes still on.

So Austin did something about that, too.

He slipped his hand beneath her top, unhooking the front clasp on her bra, and her right breast spilled into his hand. One touch, and he knew he had to have more. He shoved up her top and moved his kisses lower to her nipples.

Rosalie made a sound of pleasure, urging him closer all the while she fought with the buttons on his shirt. Soon she was touching his chest. Her hands on his bare skin. And coupled with the kisses, that only made him burn hotter.

Since her top kept slipping back down, Austin rid her of it, taking off her outer shirt and the tank top beneath it. Now he could kiss her without the barrier of her clothes, and it had exactly the effect he'd expected—it left both of them wanting a whole lot more, and he quickly figured out that this foreplay wasn't going to last nearly long enough.

"The bedroom," she managed to say.

Austin hadn't even thought to move this elsewhere, but it was a good idea in case Seth or someone else came into the cottage. So he scooped her up, and while the kisses raged on, he made his way to her bed. Talk about no finesse, but the moment her back touched the mattress, she pulled him down with her.

Everything sped up ever more. She tugged at his clothes. He tugged at hers. They sucked at it because they continued the maddening kisses, but he finally managed to strip off her jeans, dragging her panties off with them.

Oh, man.

The site of her naked robbed him of what little breath he had, and it drove home the realization that this wasn't going to last nearly as long as he wanted.

"Jeans," she said, her voice all silk and whispers. "Hurry."

Rosalie shoved down his zipper, touching him in the wrong place. Or rather the right one if he hadn't already been rock-hard and raring to go. He helped her with his jeans but mainly so he could get the condom from his wallet. Best not to make things worse by having unprotected sex.

Obviously, he wasn't moving fast enough for her because Rosalie tried to help with the condom.

Really not a good idea.

Especially since she kept repeating "hurry," and her touch was taking him many steps past the crazy stage. With that *hurry* repeating through his head, Austin eased into her.

And froze.

The sensations were too good. Too perfect. And even though his body was urging him on to hurry and finish this, to find the release for this need, he also paused just so he could savor the moment.

Rosalie looked up at him, her breath gusting. Her eyes wide. Her gaze focused solely on him. She opened her mouth, slowly, as if she might repeat that one word that'd driven them here to the bed.

But this time it wasn't *hurry* that she whispered.

It was his name.

Austin.

He held his breath, wondering if she had come to her senses and wanted to put an end to this. But, no. She pulled him back down, her mouth on his, for a kiss that fired his blood and his heart at the same time.

"Austin," she repeated in that same silky tone that she'd said *hurry*.

But hurrying wasn't necessary. That look, the sound of his name. The kiss. And being this close to her. All of that pinpointed until he had no choice but to move inside her.

Rosalie moved, too, going right into the rhythm of the strokes that would finally get them what they wanted.

Release.

Austin managed to snag her gaze at the moment that she climaxed. Her eyes were unfocused. Her breath wild. But he caught on to her chin and held the eye contact so he could watch her go over.

"Austin," she repeated.

No more hurry-up tone. Just Rosalie saying his name, just her urging him to join her as she fell.

So, that's what Austin did.

Chapter Fifteen

Rosalie braced herself for the slam of guilt that she was certain would come. Especially after that incredible climax with Austin.

But no guilt.

And, of course, that made her feel guilty.

Part of her—the logical, sane part—had known that this was coming. Austin and she had been skirting around this attraction for two days now, and with all the adrenaline and energy, it had to bubble over and send them straight to bed.

Which is exactly what it'd done.

They were both single. Both dealing with the same emotions from someone trying to kill them. The same search for the truth about her daughter and the baby farms. It was only natural that she would be lying beneath him and enjoying some nice little aftershocks of the climax. There was nothing wrong with it.

But the other part of her—the crazy, guilt-ridden part—also knew they'd landed in bed for all the wrong reasons.

Well, one wrong reason, anyway.

They shouldn't have carried things this far until they'd worked out their feelings for each other. She wasn't the sort who slept with a guy and then walked away, and she had to brace herself for a broken heart.

Because he might indeed do just that—walk away.

Austin, too, had to be dealing with the guilt of sleeping with his late partner's fiancée.

Or not, she amended, when he lifted his head, located her mouth and kissed her until Rosalie could have sworn she saw little gold stars. Of course, maybe that was just because the kiss went on for so long that she wasn't getting any oxygen to her brain.

Either way, it was an amazing kiss to top off what'd been an equally amazing experience.

"You said my name," Austin said, giving her that lazy smile that made her toes curl.

Yes, many times if she remembered correctly. "It seemed the right thing to say."

Rosalie smiled, too, hoping to keep the moment light. She wanted to hold on to this feeling just a little bit longer. Austin gave her another smile for a moment, too, but she could also see the worries in the shades of all that blue in his eyes.

"I don't want you to cry about this, about anything that has to do with us," Austin added as if choosing his words carefully. Which he probably was. He also likely figured that the ship had sailed on telling her not to feel guilty.

"No tears," she promised, but Rosalie wasn't sure it was a promise she could even keep.

Especially if Austin left.

That feeling came at her again. The one that made her feel as if someone had clamped on to her heart. She'd already lost so much, but the thought of losing Austin, too, just seemed, well, unbearable.

"I'll give you a minute." Austin dropped another of

those mind-numbing kisses on her mouth and got off the bed to head to the bathroom.

Since she was suddenly aware that she was stark naked on the bed, Rosalie got up too and gathered her clothes that had been strewn over the room.

"No tears," Austin repeated, calling out to her from the bathroom.

Even if she had been on the verge of crying, it wouldn't have happened. Not after a butt-naked Austin stepped into the doorway.

Oh, mercy.

Why did just seeing him cause her to go all hot again? Maybe because he had a perfect body to go along with his other good attributes. Or maybe because she just couldn't seem to get enough of him.

"You're blushing," he pointed out.

"Because I'm gawking at you and wishing I could have you all over again."

Rosalie hadn't exactly intended to blurt that out, but she did like the way it caused the corner of Austin's mouth to lift into a sexy smile. He walked to her, that smile still on his face, and he reached for her. But reaching was as far as he got because his phone rang.

Just like that, Rosalie snapped out of her heated trance. The call could be about the investigation.

Or about Sadie.

Austin snatched his phone from his jeans pocket and started to dress while he took the call. What he didn't do was put it on speaker. Maybe because he was going to try to buffer any bad news they got.

But buffering wouldn't work.

"Who is this?" Austin asked the caller.

Rosalie hurried to him, as close as she could get so she could figure out what was going on.

The voice was mechanical, like one of those scramblers that kidnappers used.

Oh, God.

This had to be the person behind the baby farm. The person who might have Sadie.

Rosalie practically ripped the phone from Austin's hand and jabbed the speaker button.

"Are you two still listening?" the person asked.

"We're here," Austin answered. "Now, who are you and what the hell do you want?"

"I think I'll be the one to ask the questions," the person answered. The smugness came through even with the scrambler, and Rosalie wished she could reach through the phone lines and force this monster to give Sadie back to her.

"I need you to get the files and computers that were confiscated from Yancy's place," the caller continued. "Not just the flash drives, either, but the laptops in case anything is on the hard drives. Have someone bring them to you, then I'll tell you where I need you and Rosalie McKinnon to deliver them. Only the two of you. If you bring anyone else, the deal is off."

Austin and she exchanged glances. Yancy's things? Did that mean it was Yancy himself calling, or was this just another way to set him up? With everything that'd happened, neither option would surprise Rosalie.

"And why would I bring you Yancy's files and computers?" Austin demanded.

"Oh, didn't I mention that already? Must have slipped my mind." The smugness went up a notch. "We're working out a deal here, Agent Duran. You give me the items you took from Yancy's house—all of the items—and I'll give you something that you want real bad."

"What?" Austin snapped.

The silence crawled on until her stomach was clenched into a knot.

"I'll give you Rosalie's daughter, of course," the caller finally said. "She's here with me now."

And Rosalie heard something that sent her heart straight to her knees. It was a baby's voice, repeating a single word.

"Mama."

Chapter Sixteen

"I don't want you to do this," Austin said to Rosalie for the umpteenth time.

He figured he could say it a thousand times more and she still wouldn't listen.

The bad part about that?

Austin didn't blame her one bit. If that was his little girl out there, he wouldn't keep away, either. Still, he wanted Rosalie to stay safe, and delivering a "ransom" to a baby snatcher wasn't a good way to stay safe.

Especially since this particular ransom was fake.

The FBI hadn't gone along with the notion of removing what could be critical evidence in a multiple-felonies investigation, so Austin and Seth had come up with what they hoped would be enough to fool the kidnapper. They'd copied some of Yancy's business emails and such and made duplicates of some of the files.

Maybe it would be enough to get Sadie.

If this snake really had her, that is.

Austin wasn't even sure an eleven-month-old baby was capable of saying "Mama" or that it was proof that the baby was indeed Sadie. However, the simple repeated syllable had been more than enough to convince Rosalie that she was going through with this stupid plan.

At least now they had a drop point. The kidnapper had phoned again two hours after the first call and had demanded that Rosalie and Austin meet him at the site of the now-abandoned baby farm where Rosalie and he had worked undercover. It was remote, and there were plenty of places to hide.

Too many.

And that's why Rosalie's brothers Colt and Cooper had gone ahead of them to scope out the place from a distance. If the kidnapper had brought gunmen—and he or she almost certainly had—then Austin wanted to know what they were up against before they ever stepped foot on the place. Better yet, Austin wanted the hired guns eliminated so he could deal with this moron baby snatcher face-to-face.

Too bad the cops hadn't managed to locate Yancy or Vickie.

Austin would have liked to have tails on both of them. Or just have thrown them both in jail. However, they did have a tail on Sonny, and Austin was getting text updates on the man. So far Sonny had gone into his room at the Sweetwater Springs hotel, and he hadn't come out. Maybe Sonny would stay there so they'd have one less suspect to worry about.

Of course, that didn't mean that Sonny hadn't hired gunmen to launch another attack. Or set up a ruse that could get Rosalie and him out into the open.

Like this one.

"No," Rosalie said when Seth tried to talk to her. "I'm going."

Seth was one of the most hardheaded people Austin had ever met, but he'd clearly met his match with Rosalie.

Seth's jaw tightened, and his *do-something* gaze slashed to Austin.

Austin just gave a heavy sigh and shook his head. "She'll wait in the vehicle when we make the drop, and Colt, Cooper and you will stay out of sight so you can protect her."

That was the compromise Austin had finally made with Rosalie. After a heated *discussion*. She'd wait in a bullet-resistant car that the FBI used for dangerous undercover assignments. Seth would follow them to make sure they weren't attacked from behind. And Colt and Cooper would provide backup after they'd made the site as safe as possible.

Nothing about the plan was ideal, and it'd take a miracle to pull it off. Still, it was the best possible plan under the worst possible circumstances.

Austin's phone buzzed, and he saw a text from Colt.

No one appears to be around. Will keep looking to make sure.

That was good. Except that Austin remembered those explosives and fires that'd been rigged at the second facility. It'd be hard for Colt and Cooper to check for that without putting themselves directly in harm's way, so that meant Austin had to keep watch for anything that could blow them all to smithereens.

Yeah, this was no piece-of-cake assignment.

Austin fired off a text to Colt. "Anything on infrared?"

Rosalie's brother had brought equipment that would detect the body heat of anyone nearby. It wouldn't give them the caller's identity, but it would be able to tell them how many hired guns they were up against.

"Nothing," Colt answered.

That was both good and bad. It meant gunmen weren't nearby. Well, unless they were using some kind of heat-shielding camouflage. Of course, there'd be no need for gunmen and camouflage if the plan was just to blow them up, and the infrared wouldn't detect any explosives.

"It's time," Rosalie said, glancing at the clock.

Her hands were shaking.

Heck, she was shaking, and she couldn't seem to make herself stand still. She'd been pacing, fidgeting and trembling head to toe since the phone call from the kidnapper. Austin didn't expect any of those nerves to get better in the next hour or so.

"We need to leave," Rosalie added.

It's was only a twenty-minute drive to the site, and the drop-off time was forty-five minutes, but Austin understood her urgency to get out the door. Too bad that each moment outside put them in even greater danger. Of course, with their luck, the attacker could somehow launch explosives at the cottage if they stayed put.

"I'll drive slow," Austin said to Seth, knowing that Seth would do the same.

All of them were anxious to see if the kidnapper did indeed have Sadie, but it wasn't a good idea for them to stand around outside at the abandoned baby farm, waiting for this guy to show up. He or she could hurl explosives at them there, too, after getting the info from Rosalie and him.

Austin hurried her out to the car that he'd had Seth park directly outside the back door. Thanks to Seth, the fake files and computers were already on the backseat. They'd made a show of putting them there, too. Seth had brought in the fakes from the FBI office, so if anyone was watching the ranch, then maybe the stuff would appear to be the real deal.

It was nearly dark and bitterly cold. The wind was gusting, and Austin felt the flecks of sleet spit at him.

Great.

Now the weather was working against them. The roads would be slick, adding yet another level of danger to this already dangerous situation.

"I'm not stupid," Rosalie said when he pulled away from the ranch. "I know this is likely a trap, but I also know that in the past eleven months, this is the closest I've come to finding my baby."

Austin slid his hand over hers. It was about the only thing he could do to try to comfort her, and it wasn't much of a gesture. At least he didn't think it was much until her fingers closed around his for a quick squeeze.

It definitely gave him some comfort, anyway.

He glanced behind them to make sure Seth was following. He was, and he was keeping a safe distance so that it wouldn't readily appear that he was following them.

Of course, the kidnapper would be looking for something like that, and since the snake had been adamant about Rosalie and Austin coming alone, then he or she would be looking for any sign that they hadn't followed the rules and had brought backup.

Seth would have to drop way behind them when they approached the baby farm. And that was yet another part about this plan that Austin didn't like.

"Those photos are of Sadie," Rosalie continued several minutes later. "That means someone associated with this has her."

It did. But it didn't mean that person was going to hand

Sadie over to them. Or that the person demanding the ransom was also the one who'd taken those photos.

Austin kept that to himself.

"If it isn't Yancy who's doing this," she went on, "then it's someone who wants to make him look guilty." Rosalie paused. "I'm hoping it's Yancy so we can put him behind bars for the rest of his life."

Yeah, Austin was hoping that, too, but maybe Vickie would be a less formidable foe. Except that Vickie could have hired just as much firepower as either Sonny or Yancy.

His phone buzzed. No text this time but an incoming call, and the caller's name and number were blocked.

"The kidnapper." And Austin hit the answer button and put it on speaker.

"I see that you're on the way," the caller greeted them. "Lose Agent Calder though before you get here."

Austin mumbled some profanity. "You had the ranch under surveillance?"

"Of course. There's a lot at stake here."

There was. And that's why Rosalie's brothers had used binoculars to check if there was someone watching, but they hadn't spotted anyone. Still, that didn't mean the kidnapper hadn't managed to get a camera close enough to monitor their every move and could have been doing that for days. With all the ranch hands and workers on the sprawling McKinnon ranch, it wouldn't have been that hard to do.

"I'm guessing the sheriff and deputy are at the baby farm checking things out," the caller went on. He didn't wait for Austin to respond. "Good. They can stay there, and once you tell Agent Calder to take a hike, you can deliver those goods that the two of you put on the backseat of the car. How much trouble did the FBI give you about getting the stuff?"

"Plenty." And Austin hoped that meant that the kidnapper believed the evidence was real. "You said the drop-off was the baby farm," he snapped.

And while the location sucked, Austin figured any alternative would suck even more.

"There's been a change of plans," the kidnapper said. It was that same smug tone that he'd used with his earlier calls. "Call Agent Calder now. Tell him to turn around and go back to the ranch."

"Why? So it'll be easier to kill us?" Austin came right out and asked.

"No. Because I don't want to make it easier for you to kill me. Especially since I'm holding the kid and all."

Rosalie sucked in a hard breath. "Don't you dare hurt my baby!"

"Wouldn't dream of it. She's my ticket to that evidence. Oh, and by the way, she's cute and sleeping like a baby for now. Keep it that way by following the rules. Ditch Calder and within five minutes, you'll have your kid."

Austin knew there was no way Rosalie could simply dismiss that as a lie. There was too much hope in her eyes to believe that she couldn't soon have her baby in her arms.

"Where are you?" Austin demanded of the kidnapper, but he was talking to himself because the caller had already hung up.

Cursing, Austin hit the end call button and glanced in the rearview mirror at Seth's car. Then, he glanced at Rosalie.

"We have to do it," she insisted. "We have to tell Seth to stop."

Austin had a quick debate with himself, but he knew there was only one solution here.

And it was a bad one.

"Call Colt and Cooper first to give them our location. Then, call Seth," he finally said. "Tell him to pull off the side of the road until the kidnapper contacts us about the exchange."

Rosalie gave a shaky nod and made the calls in the order he'd told her. Cooper and Colt gave her a quick okay. Seth argued, of course, but he would do as they asked.

Austin hoped.

And while he was hoping, he added that maybe there was some way he'd be able to get Rosalie out of this alive while also rescuing Sadie.

Behind him, he saw Seth pulled to the side as they'd requested, but Rosalie's brother was also voicing his disapproval of the change in plans. However, Seth didn't get a chance to voice it for long because another call came in on Austin's phone.

"It's the kidnapper again," Rosalie said, quickly ending the conversation with her brother. As before, the screen showed that the caller ID had been blocked.

Austin automatically slid his hand over the gun in his shoulder holster. "What now?" Austin asked the moment Rosalie answered the call.

But the kidnapper didn't jump to answer. The moments crawled by, and if Austin hadn't heard the guy breathing, he would have thought no one was on the line.

"All right," the kidnapper finally said. He was still using the voice scrambler that made him sound like a cartoon character. "Agent Calder is far enough away so you can take the turn just ahead."

The windshield wipers were smearing the sleet on the

windshield, so it took Austin a moment to see the road. Except it was more of a dirt-and-gravel path than an actual road. He eased on the brakes so he wouldn't go into a skid, and he made the turn.

Also slowly.

He turned on his high beams, hoping it would give him a better look of their surroundings. There were plenty of trees and shrubs. No houses. But just ahead he spotted a dark-colored SUV parked in the center of the path.

Rosalie took the gun from the glove compartment.

"Yeah, that's me," the kidnapper said. "Drive closer."

Austin didn't. He came to a full stop then and there.

"Rosalie stays in the car while you and I make the exchange," Austin insisted.

Again, the guy took his time answering. Maybe because he or she figured it would put them even more on edge. Austin wasn't sure it was possible to do that since every nerve and muscle in his body was on full alert.

"Suit yourself," the kidnapper finally said.

Austin hadn't thought it possible, but that indeed made him even more concerned. He'd expected an argument.

One that Austin was sure he would lose.

So, was this some kind of trap to get him out of the car so Rosalie could be kidnapped?

Or worse?

But if this bozo just planned to kill them, why hadn't he just started shooting? Maybe because the kidnapper suspected the car was bullet-resistant? Either way, there was nothing about this setup that Austin liked, and it just kept getting worse.

"I'll put the laptops and files on the side of the road where I'm parked," Austin said, trying a different angle. "Once that's done, you come and get it."

"Oh, I don't think that would be a good idea," the kidnapper answered. "It's the weather, you see. Wouldn't be good for the baby to be out for too long on a winter night like this. No. I'm thinking a better solution would be for you to drive closer. Less time outside for the kid."

But closer meant Rosalie and he would be easier targets.

"You haven't asked for proof that I've got the baby," the kidnapper added. "Well, here it is."

Austin didn't have to wait long this time. Only a few seconds. Before the interior light came on in the kidnapper's SUV. The light stabbed through the sleet and darkness, and even though Austin was parked a good thirty feet away, he had no trouble seeing the figures inside.

Two adults, both wearing dark clothes and ski masks.

And one of the masked adults was holding up a baby.

"Sadie," Rosalie said on a rise of breath, and she threw open the door.

Chapter Seventeen

Rosalie didn't even manage to get her foot out the door before Austin latched on to her shoulder and hauled her back into the car.

"I have to get to Sadie," she blurted out.

She heard the panic in her own voice. Felt it in every inch of her body, but she couldn't make herself stop. Everything inside her was screaming for her to get to her baby.

"You can't help Sadie if you're dead." Austin dragged her even closer to him and got right in her face. "Don't give them a reason to pull their triggers, not with the baby between them and you."

Sweet heaven.

She hadn't even considered that, but she did now. The threat of her own death didn't frighten her, but she couldn't bear the thought of doing anything to hurt Sadie. And if she stepped out there, those men might indeed try to shoot her because they thought she was some kind of loose end that needed to be tied up permanently.

Rosalie's gaze snapped back to the SUV ahead of them. The interior light went out, and she could no longer see the men or the baby. That didn't help with the panic and the nerves. At least if she could see Sadie, she would know that her little girl was all right.

Well, as all right as a baby could be while being held by kidnappers.

"Give her to me," Rosalie sobbed, knowing it wouldn't do any good. These monsters were using her precious baby as a bargaining chip. They didn't care that it was tearing her apart.

"Oh, you'll get her all right," one of the kidnappers said. "Just have Agent Duran drive closer and put the evidence in the covered plastic bin by our SUV. The sooner he does that, the sooner you'll get the kid."

And with that, he ended the call.

Rosalie couldn't think—her mind was a whirl of emotions and thoughts. She was about to ask Austin what they should do, but before she could say a word, he took the phone and texted Seth to give him their location and told her brother to approach on foot. Probably so the sound of his car engine wouldn't be detected. On foot though Seth might not get there soon enough to help them rescue Sadie, and he would be out in the open, possibly an easy target.

"We have to stall them," Austin said, easing the car close to the SUV. Not quickly. He inched along at a snail's pace. "We have to give Colt, Cooper and Seth time to get into place."

It made sense, but it also meant it would take even longer before she could get to her baby.

Austin kept driving, the car bobbing along on the uneven surface of the road, and he came to a stop a good ten yards from the SUV and a green plastic bin. He waited, glancing at the phone. Probably waiting to see if the kidnapper would order him to go even closer.

But no call came in.

"Stay put," Austin warned her, and he held eye contact

with her again. Even in the dim light, she could see the warning he was giving her—*Don't go out there*.

Rosalie nodded.

"And keep watch all around us," Austin added. He put the car in Park, turned off the engine and the headlights. "I don't want anyone sneaking up on us."

She nodded again, and Rosalie lowered the window just a fraction so that she'd hopefully be able to hear anyone approaching their car.

Austin kept his gun in his right hand, and he stepped from the car, volleying his attention all around them, especially at the SUV where they were holding Sadie. He opened the back door and took out the first of the three laptops. Not quickly, either. He took his time getting a grip and moving it out of the vehicle and into the bin on the side of the gravel road.

His phone buzzed again. "It's the kidnapper," she relayed to Austin and hit the call button to put it on speaker.

"Hurry up for Pete's sake," the man snarled. "We don't have all night. You got two minutes to get that stuff out of the car, or we're driving off with the kid."

"No!" Rosalie practically shouted.

The kidnapper hung up but not before she saw something else in the interior of the SUV. The illumination from his phone was just enough that she could make out someone else in the backseat.

"There are three of them," she whispered to Austin.

Mercy, that didn't help with the panic. She was an okay shot, but the extra person meant that Austin and she were outgunned. Rosalie prayed that her brothers made it there soon. Maybe their sheer presence would be enough to get the kidnapper to surrender.

She could hope, anyway.

Austin picked up the pace of moving the equipment while Rosalie kept her attention nailed to the kidnapper's SUV. Not that there was anything to see. But those seconds were ticking by. She wasn't sure if the man had been bluffing when he said they'd drive away, but it was a risk she couldn't take.

With the window down and the back door open, it didn't take long for the bitter cold to seep inside their own vehicle. The sleet was cutting like razors through the lights of the high beams, and the howling winter wind slapped at the tree branches, creating too much noise for her to hear much of anything.

The moment Austin finished moving the last of the laptops, his phone buzzed again, and when she answered it, Rosalie did hear the kidnapper's scrambled voice.

"It's too late," the voice said. That was it. The only warning she got before she heard the roar of the SUV's engine. The driver spun the car around, the tires digging into the soft ground on the side of the road.

What the heck was he doing?

But Rosalie soon got an answer to that when the driver hit the accelerator.

"No!" Rosalie shouted.

If the kidnappers even heard her, it didn't do any good.

Because the SUV sped away.

AUSTIN'S HEART SLAMMED against his chest. No. This couldn't be happening. Not when they were this close to getting Sadie from the kidnappers.

"Hurry!" Rosalie called out to him.

He did exactly that. Austin jumped back behind the wheel of the car and took off in pursuit.

Right now, every second was precious. He had no idea

how long this particular ranch trail was, but he couldn't let the kidnappers make it out to a main road. If that happened, well, he couldn't go there.

"Why are they leaving?" Rosalie asked in between repeating for him to hurry.

"Maybe something spooked them." Like Seth, Cooper or Colt though Austin hadn't seen any signs of them. Austin pushed the accelerator hard. Going much faster than he should on the narrow, icy path. Still, it wasn't as if he had a lot of options here. He had to follow that SUV.

"Put on your seat belt," Austin warned Rosalie, "and stay down."

She did the first but not the second. Probably because she couldn't stop herself from watching the road ahead. She was also whispering a prayer.

They certainly needed a prayer or two.

Things were already bad, and there were plenty of things that could get even worse tonight. At least they were all alive. For now.

He had to maneuver the car through some tight curves on the uneven surface, and the trees and shrubs were so close to the path that they scraped like fingernails against the side of the car. The unnerving sound sure didn't help steady his breathing or heartbeat.

"If they're leaving the files and laptops behind," Rosalie said, "then maybe they didn't really want them in the first place."

Austin had already come to that conclusion. Not that he'd ever thought this was about the evidence. But he went back to his original idea. That maybe all of this had been staged to convince them that Yancy was behind this.

Or maybe Yancy believed by making himself look guilty that it would in turn make him appear innocent.

A weird reverse psychology and exactly the sort of thing that Yancy would do to play with their heads.

Either way, this could have been a ruse to throw Rosalie and him off track. However, that didn't answer the question about the baby.

"You're sure it was Sadie in the SUV?" he asked while he fought the steering wheel to stay on the road.

"I'm sure." She didn't hesitate, either.

That was enough verification for Austin. He never discounted gut feelings, even when a gut feeling could be leading them right smack dab into the middle of danger.

He took another sharp curve and immediately had to hit the brakes. The SUV was there, parked, not on the road this time but about twenty yards away in the center of a small clearing. The headlights were off, ditto for the interior light, and it was hard to tell if anyone was inside.

Austin hoped like the devil that they hadn't ditched the vehicle and used another trail to get out. If so, it'd be darn hard to find them since he wouldn't even have a description of a secondary vehicle.

"Don't get out," Austin reminded Rosalie, and this time she stayed put. Both of them stared at the SUV, waiting, while keeping watch around them. "Maybe the kidnapper will call soon."

But soon didn't happen.

The seconds dragged on, giving Rosalie and him plenty of time to think of all the bad things that could happen in the next couple of minutes.

"If they've already left, we need to know," Rosalie finally said.

Yeah. And the longer they waited, the farther away the kidnappers could get. If they were indeed fleeing, that is. If not, well, that was a chance Austin was about to have to take.

"Wait here, and I mean it," he repeated, taking his phone from her and shoving it into his pocket. Then he gave her a quick kiss. "There's a burner cell in the glove compartment. Use it to call Seth if anything goes wrong."

She took hold of his arm when he reached for the door. "Was that a goodbye kiss?"

"I hope not."

"Well, it felt like one." Her breath broke, and Rosalie leaned toward him and returned the kiss. "Swear to me that it won't be a goodbye."

Even though time definitely wasn't on their side right now, he took a moment to make eye contact with her. "I promise," Austin said.

At best, it was wishful thinking.

At worse, an out-and-out lie because it was a promise he had no control over keeping. Once he stepped out there, he was essentially a sitting duck with at least three hired guns in the area.

Still, he stepped out. And Austin kept his gun ready. It was impossible to stay behind cover, but he used the trees, skirting around them to make his way to the SUV. Eventually, though, he would have to step out into that clearing and hope that Seth and the others would soon arrive for backup.

"Are you there?" Austin called out to whoever might be in that SUV.

No answer.

He glanced back at the car to make sure Rosalie was staying put. She was, thank God. And he hurried even closer to the SUV and ducked behind a scraggly mesquite.

Not much cover, but if the kidnappers had wanted to shoot him, they'd already had ample opportunity.

"I left the files and laptops on the road," Austin went on while he inched closer.

The windows on the SUV were heavily tinted, and there wasn't even a moon for him to see shadows inside. However, if Rosalie was right, there were three of them. Plus, the baby. And the baby meant despite his having his gun ready, that the last thing he'd be doing was firing shots.

Maybe the kidnappers were on the same page.

Austin pulled in a long breath and stepped out from the tree. He didn't charge forward. Best not to look as if he were on the attack. However, he was still a good five yards from the SUV when he heard something he didn't want to hear.

Movement near the car.

He shifted in that direction, hoping that he didn't see Rosalie hurrying toward him.

But he saw something much worse.

She was out of the car all right, and someone was behind her.

That someone had a gun pointed at Rosalie's head.

Chapter Eighteen

Rosalie heard the sound behind her a split second too late. She felt someone hook an arm around her neck. Before she could even react or shout out a warning to Austin, the person snapped her back and pressed a gun to her temple.

"Move and you die," he growled in a whisper right against her ear.

And there was no mistaking that it was a *he.* The person wasn't using a voice scrambler, and the hard muscles of his chest pressed against her back.

"Rosalie!" Austin called out, and while using the trees for cover again, he started to race toward her.

"Wouldn't do that if I were you," the man said, taking aim at Austin and then cursing him when he apparently didn't have a clean shot. "Could be bad for her health."

Without the scrambler, Rosalie had no trouble recognizing the voice.

It was Sonny.

All of the events of the past eleven months started to whirl through Rosalie's head. Was this the monster responsible for taking her daughter, or was Sonny just a hired thug? She desperately wanted to know the answers, but more than that, she wanted Austin and her baby safe.

"The cops were watching you," she said to Sonny. "You were in your hotel room."

"Was," he corrected. "I slipped out the back."

Not good. The other cops in Sweetwater Springs didn't know he was here.

With his gun aimed, Austin ducked behind a tree about ten yards away. "Let her go," he ordered.

"Can't do that. She's coming with me for now." Even though she couldn't see Sonny, she felt him move slightly, maybe glancing around. "I might let her go as soon as I have the situation with her brother contained."

Oh, God. Seth. They weren't going after him, too. She prayed Seth would be able to stay safe.

"What does her brother have to do with this?" Austin asked.

"I figure he's nearby. Or he soon will be. Too soon for me to get out of here with both him and you on my tail. Rosalie can help with that."

Sonny was taking her hostage. To use her as a human shield so he could try to stop or even kill Seth and Austin.

It was well below freezing, and her teeth started to chatter. She was shaking, her breath seemingly frozen in her lungs. Still, she had to focus on what had to be done here. And what had to be done was getting her hands on Sadie.

"Where's my baby?" Rosalie asked.

"She's nearby, too. You'll get to see her soon enough. All you have to do is cooperate and come with me. I'll take you both somewhere so you can live out a long, happy life."

She desperately wanted to believe him, but it was hard to believe a man with a gun at her head.

Austin leaned out, shook his head. "You have no intentions of letting either Rosalie or me walk away from this."

Sonny lifted his shoulder. Definitely not a denial. But then, Sonny probably figured that Austin and she knew way too much to let them go. They didn't. Well, other than knowing that Sonny was almost certainly part of the baby farms.

"Did you shoot yourself so you'd look innocent?" Austin asked. Rosalie realized he'd moved closer.

"No, one of my employees accidentally did that when we were trying to clear out of the second baby farm. But I thought it was a nice touch. It got me in the back of your truck that night, didn't it?"

Yes, it had, and on that entire drive to the hospital they'd been riding with a coldhearted monster.

"Why did you take my baby?" she asked, not in a whisper, either. She was hoping for the sound of her voice to cover any sounds that Austin might make. Also, it might give her brother a warning that something was wrong.

Again, Sonny looked around. "When I was working for Yancy, his wife asked me to help with an adoption. She wanted a kid, and I'd heard about an operation that dealt in black market babies. I decided to start one of my own. Two of them, in fact. But thanks to you two, I had to blow up one of the places."

So, Sonny was the one who'd set up the baby farms. Or at least the two near Silver Creek.

"Yancy wanted Rosalie's baby?" Austin asked. Again, he'd moved.

"No, that idiot had no idea what was going on. I targeted Rosalie's baby so if things went wrong, then Yancy would be the patsy, and the proof of it would be that he was the one who had the kid."

Rosalie had to clamp her teeth over her bottom lip to stop herself from screaming. "But you tried to kill Yancy at the hospital."

"Another nice touch, huh? Wasn't really trying to kill him, but after that, it put Yancy at the top of your list of suspects, didn't it?"

It had, and Austin's and her distrust and hatred for Yancy had made it even easier to suspect him. Of course, Sonny had been a suspect, too. For all the good it'd done them. Here they were with Sonny calling the shots.

For now.

Maybe Austin or even Seth could soon do something about that. Maybe she could, as well. If she managed to drop down, then perhaps that would give Austin a clean shot. Of course, if she failed, both of them could die.

"And you continued the ruse of setting up Yancy by having us bring his files and computers," Rosalie concluded. She wanted to learn all she could in case they needed it to put this monster behind bars. Of course, for that to happen, they needed to get that gun out of his hands.

"Yep," Sonny readily admitted. "I used Yancy's computer to set up the baby farms. There are hidden files on them. Nothing that Yancy would have found, but I figured the FBI wouldn't have any trouble. Also figured you'd bring me fake computers. No way would the FBI let something like that out of their hands."

Sonny was right about that, too. So, that meant this was all designed to lure Austin and her out so they could be killed. And now, she might get Seth killed, too, unless Austin could get close enough and at the right angle to stop Sonny.

"Who has my baby?" she asked Sonny.

"She's safe and with one of my employees. Don't worry. She's been well taken care of all these months."

Rosalie felt Sonny's muscles go stiff.

"Agent Duran, you need to stay put," he growled, "or Rosalie dies before seeing her kid. You wouldn't want that, would you?"

The thought of seeing her baby even for a few moments caused her heart to soar. But the feeling didn't last long. Rosalie didn't want Sonny to kill her in front of Sadie. Her baby was too young to know what was going on, but still the nightmare might stay with her for the rest of her life.

"Did someone adopt Sadie?" she asked, and Rosalie prayed that she could live with the answer. "Did Yancy's ex-wife get her?"

"No." Sonny looked around again. "After Yancy's marriage went south, I decided to sell the kid to another buyer, but that deal fell through. Then, things heated up with the baby farm investigation, and I figured it best if I kept the kid in case something went wrong. And it did."

"There's no reason to hold on to her now," Rosalie insisted, though she knew nothing that she said to him would do any good. He'd committed so many criminal acts that she figured his heart was untouchable.

"Yeah, there is. As long as I have her, your badge-carrying family will back off."

Sweet heaven. He planned to keep using Sadie. Not that she'd expected anything less, but it turned her blood to ice to hear it spelled out.

"Where's Yancy?" Austin called out. He seemed close. Maybe close enough to do something.

"In hiding." Sonny chuckled, clearly amused about that. "All the evidence will point to him looking very guilty, and he's trying to cover his butt. He'll surface soon enough, I'm sure, and the FBI can arrest him."

Yes, with evidence that Sonny had faked. She wanted Yancy behind bars, but not like this.

"What about Vickie?" Rosalie asked. "Was it really her in the photo, and does she have my baby?"

"Nope to both. I was telling the truth when I said she was innocent in all of this. The photo was just to get you looking in her direction and to muddy the waters. She's great in the sack but not very bright. I wouldn't have trusted her to be a real part of this. Look how she ran when just a little thing went wrong."

That little thing involved Austin's nephew.

That created a new surge of rage inside her. Sonny was playing a dangerous game with innocent lives. Without thinking, she drew back her elbow and rammed it into Sonny's stomach. In the same motion, she dropped to the ground, hoping that Austin had a shot.

Cursing, Austin leaned out and fired.

But so did Sonny.

The shots blasted through the air.

Austin ducked behind the tree, barely dodging Sonny's shot, but Austin's own shot missed, too.

He cursed.

This was exactly what Austin had been trying to prevent. Rosalie being caught in the middle of gunfire. Worse, Sonny dropped down, too, trying to grab hold of Rosalie again, and in doing so it took out any chance that Austin had of a second shot.

Austin raced toward them, trying to position himself between Rosalie and Sonny, but it was already too late for that. Sonny managed to keep hold of her, and he slung her between them.

Using her as a human shield.

Since Sonny didn't have complete control of his gun, Austin went after the man's hand so that he couldn't aim it at Rosalie. That cost him big-time because Sonny punched him, hard. So hard that Austin could have sworn something in his head exploded, and for a few crucial seconds, it robbed him of his breath.

That didn't stop Austin.

He went after Sonny again, and this time managed to land a punch of his own.

Rosalie twisted and squirmed, trying to get out of the fray, but Austin couldn't help her because he had his hands full with Sonny.

"Back away from him!" someone shouted.

Austin got just a glimpse of a muscle-bound man hurrying from the SUV. Great. One of Sonny's hired guns, no doubt. He didn't need this, and Austin slammed his gun against Sonny's head so he could put an end to this before the goon made it to them.

The bash to the head caused Sonny to fall back. But the man didn't stay down. He reached out, latched on to Rosalie's hair and pulled her back in front of him. He put his gun to her head again.

Hell. That wasn't the way Austin had wanted this to play out.

Austin scrambled behind one of the trees so that Sonny wouldn't gun him down. He couldn't save Rosalie if Sonny killed him.

"Let's try this one more time," Sonny snarled. "Move and she dies real fast."

Sonny's breath was ragged, and his face was bleeding. Austin figured he looked about the same. Thankfully, the only bright spot in all of this was that Rosalie didn't seem to be hurt.

Austin needed to do something fast to keep it that way.

"I was trying to do her a favor by letting her see the kid," Sonny added, glancing around him again.

"I doubt that," Austin argued. "You're not the do-a-favor type. I'm guessing you want Rosalie alive so you can draw Seth out. I'm also guessing that you're afraid Seth won't let this go once Rosalie disappears."

Sonny smiled. "Can't leave a bulldog like Calder out there. While I'm at it, those other three brothers of hers will have to go, as well. Yancy'll get the death penalty for all of their deaths. Yours, too."

Rosalie made a sound, anger mixed with fear, and Austin shook his head, a warning for her not to throw another elbow. This time, Sonny might just pull the trigger.

"You had a chance to kill us the night we picked you up in my truck," Austin reminded him.

"That would've been too soon. Had to figure out first what you two knew and if you'd told anyone anything that could lead back to me. Had to keep you close. And now that I've figured it out, you both know way too much to keep drawing breath."

"We didn't have a confirmation of who owned the baby farms," Austin insisted. "Not until tonight."

"Yeah, but you would have figured it out soon enough. Agent Calder's not the only bulldog in these woods. You would have kept coming until you got to the truth, and that truth would have put me behind bars."

If Austin had his way, it would do more than that. Sonny would get the death penalty because Austin knew

for a fact that some of the birth mothers had been murdered at the baby farm.

"You okay, boss?" the thug asked, coming even closer.

"Yeah." Sonny spit out a mouthful of blood. "Stay close
but check on Hutchins. He should have been here by now."

Austin didn't know the man. The name hadn't come
up in the investigation, but he guessed this was another
hired gun.

One who'd been sent to find Seth.

Maybe Seth, Cooper and Colt would be able to evade
this Hutchins and the second goon. Austin needed that
to happen because he intended to do whatever it took to
get Rosalie out of this.

And he saw his chance when the hired gun walked
away to go after Seth.

"Don't do anything stupid," Sonny said, probably because he knew that Austin was about to do something. "I
have another *helper* in the SUV. This one has some long-
range shooting skills, and since I'm not too concerned
now about keeping Rosalie alive much longer, my man
will pull the trigger."

Austin made a split-second glance behind him, but as
before he couldn't see inside the SUV. With all the schem-
ing that Sonny had done, though, it wouldn't surprise him
if several hired guns were in there.

There was a sound to his left, maybe footsteps. Maybe
Seth. However, before Austin could even look in that direction, he heard another sound.

The SUV door opening.

Hell. He didn't need another guy with a gun getting
in on this. But it wasn't a man. It was a gray-haired
woman, and she was clutching what appeared to be a
baby in a blanket.

"You said the baby wouldn't be in danger!" the woman shouted. With that, she turned and ran straight for the woods.

A man jumped out from the SUV. The rifleman, no doubt, and he volleyed glances between his boss and the woman.

"Go after her!" Sonny shouted. "And when you find her, kill her and bring me the kid."

Chapter Nineteen

"No!" Rosalie shouted, and she would have tried to go after the woman if Sonny hadn't yanked her back by her hair.

Pain shot through her, but it was nothing compared with the pain stabbing through her heart. The woman had Sadie, Rosalie was sure of it, and if the hired gun found her as Sonny had ordered, Sadie might be hurt, too.

And even if the woman managed to get away, it was possible that Rosalie would never see her baby again.

That couldn't happen.

This had to end tonight so she could be reunited with Sadie.

"I have to see her," Rosalie tried again, and she fought, squirmed and did whatever she could to try to break loose of Sonny's grip.

"Let her go," Austin ordered, stepping out from cover and putting him in the direct line of fire.

Sonny immediately turned his gun on Austin. And fired. Thank God Austin got out of the way in time.

"Sonny!" someone shouted before he could take aim at Austin again. Whoever it was, the person sounded as if he was running straight toward them.

"Hutchins," Sonny mumbled.

One of his hired guns. The one who was supposed to be out there hunting down Seth. She'd hoped her brother had managed to take care of him, but apparently not.

Did that mean Hutchins had managed to kill Seth?

Rosalie choked back a gasp and the tears. None of that would help her now. Only escaping would do that, and then she could get the baby and find Seth.

Her gaze connected with Austin when he looked out from the tree. Too bad they weren't mind readers because if they could work together, they might be able to come up with a plan that wouldn't get them both killed.

Austin had been right about one thing. If Rosalie died, it could have devastating consequences for Sadie. Either Austin or she had to stay alive to make sure Sadie lived.

Mercy, though, it hurt to think of losing Austin.

He didn't deserve this. He'd made her fight his own, and he was out here because of her. Because he cared for her.

Rosalie's feelings went a lot deeper than that.

She was in love with him.

And it was the worst time possible for her to realize that. Maybe she would get a chance to tell him.

"It's me. Don't shoot," Hutchins warned Sonny, and several moments later, the man reached them. He had a bulky build and was wearing a black ski mask that he'd partially lifted up on his face.

"We got a big problem, boss," Hutchins said. "Leon's dead. I found him just up the road. Somebody had snapped his neck."

"Hell." And Sonny repeated it. "I sent him to check on you. Where the devil is Calder?"

Hutchins shook his head. "I don't know. Don't know

about the other two lawmen, either. If they're out there, they're keeping quiet."

That caused Sonny to spew another round of raw profanity. "Find them. Kill them."

The death order had barely left Sonny's mouth when there was a sound that Rosalie didn't want to hear.

A gunshot.

Even if it was one of her brothers doing the shooting, she didn't want the bullets fired around the baby. She also didn't want Seth, Cooper or Colt hurt, but she knew it was possible that the shot had been aimed at any one of them.

While he kept a firm grip on her hair, Sonny pulled her behind a tree and moved a small communicator on his coat collar so that it was closer to his mouth. "Hendricks?" he said into the piece.

Nothing.

Rosalie wasn't sure, but she was guessing this was the goon who'd gone after the nanny.

"Hendricks?" Sonny repeated not just into the communicator, but he shouted out the man's name.

"Won't do any good to yell for him," someone yelled. "I just put a bullet in him."

Yancy.

What the heck was he doing here? Rosalie couldn't see him, but judging from the sound of his voice, he was in the woods where she'd last seen the nanny and baby.

Oh, God. Had Yancy done something to them?

"What the hell do you want, Yancy?" Sonny snarled.

"Figured that'd be kinda obvious. I'm here because you're trying to set me up. Not gonna happen. I didn't have anything to do with those kidnapped brats."

Rosalie didn't know where to aim her anger, but she was actually glad that Yancy had eliminated the man going after the nanny. One hired gun down, but she had no idea how many others there were.

Plus, now they had to contend with Yancy. Even though he appeared to be there to stop Sonny, she didn't trust him. He could try a reversal of Sonny's plan and kill them all, setting it up so that Sonny looked guilty.

"This isn't your fight," Sonny yelled back to Yancy. "Leave now, and you won't get hurt."

"Well, you see, I'm thinking this is my fight." Yancy sounded like his usual cocky self. "Now, I don't care a rat's butt if Rosalie and Austin get killed in the process, but, Sonny-boy, you're about to meet your unholy maker."

That was the only warning they got before Yancy started shooting.

AUSTIN LAUNCHED HIMSELF at Rosalie to pull her to the ground so he could get her out of the path of Yancy's shots.

But Sonny beat him to her.

Sonny scrambled behind one of the trees and dragged Rosalie with him. Why, Austin didn't know. Sonny had plans to kill Rosalie and him, anyway, but maybe he didn't want his enemy to get that *privilege*.

Yancy's shots slammed into the tree that Sonny and Hutchins were using for cover with Rosalie. However, Yancy also sent a few Austin's way. Since Yancy had already killed the hired gun who'd gone after the nanny, or so he'd claimed, then it was clear he didn't intend to leave any witnesses behind.

Austin stayed low and looked around, hoping to catch a glimpse of Seth, Cooper or Colt. If they were out there—and he was pretty sure they were since someone had broken the other thug's neck—then they were keeping well hidden. Austin hoped they were close enough in case he needed backup for what he was about to do.

And what he was about to do was get Rosalie the heck out of there.

That was the first step, and then they had to go after the nanny. Unless there was another vehicle nearby, then it meant the woman was out in the freezing-cold woods with a baby. Plus, there was the likelihood that Sonny had other hired guns out there. Ones who'd worked the baby farm for him.

In other words, goons who would do anything, including murder.

Another of Yancy's bullets slammed into the tree just above Austin's head. Since the man wasn't taking time to reload, he'd obviously come with multiple weapons. Still, he'd eventually run out of ammo unless he, too, had brought significant backup with him.

A strong possibility.

Sonny and his man were doing their own share of returning fire, and while they were occupied with Yancy's attack, Austin inched his way toward Rosalie. She had her head down, thank God, but she was also looking in his direction. Obviously waiting for him to put his plan of escape into motion.

Except the plan was a thin one.

Basically, Austin intended to grab Rosalie, head to the bullet-resistant car and, once he had backup in place, the search for the nanny and the baby could begin.

"Move back," Austin mouthed to her, hoping that Rosalie could understand what he was saying.

Hutchins understood it all right. The hired gun pivoted, turning his weapon on Austin.

The shots came fast.

So fast that it took Austin a moment to realize that Hutchins hadn't been the one to pull the trigger.

The shot had come from Yancy.

And the bullet hit Hutchins squarely in the chest. Obviously a kill shot because Hutchins crumpled to the ground without making a sound.

"You're gonna pay for that!" Sonny shouted. He came out from the tree, his gun already aimed at Yancy, and started firing.

Nonstop.

Austin took advantage of the moment and hurried to Rosalie. He hooked his arm around her waist to get her moving just as he heard a too-familiar sound. One of the bullets slamming into someone. He made a quick glance over his shoulder.

That someone was Yancy.

The man made a guttural sound of raw pain, falling. His gun dropped right along with him.

Sonny didn't waste a moment savoring his victory of killing an old foe. He whirled around, turning his gun on Austin and Rosalie. They scrambled behind a boulder in the nick of time.

Another shot came their way. Then another. Sonny took cover behind the tree again, protecting himself and keeping them pinned down at the same time.

Since his heartbeat was already crashing in his ears, it took Austin a moment to hear something else. And this time it was a welcome sound.

Sirens.

Lots of them.

Rosalie's brothers had come through with plenty of backup. But would the cops arrive in time? Sonny's shots were coming way too close.

Since Austin was covering Rosalie's body with his, he could feel her knotted muscles. Could hear her ragged breathing. She'd come way too close to dying—again—and there was still time for Sonny to try to get off one more deadly shot.

That's what Austin had to prevent.

"I love you," she said.

At least that's what Austin thought she said. But he had to be wrong about that.

Didn't he?

Like the earlier kiss, maybe this was her way of saying goodbye, but he sure as hell wasn't ready to say goodbye to her.

"Rosalie? Austin?" someone called out.

Seth.

He sounded close enough to help Austin put an end to this.

"Over here," Austin shouted back just as he levered himself up a little and fired a shot at Sonny.

Sonny jumped back behind cover and sent another shot Austin's way. Austin braced himself for another hail of bullets. Sonny's last-ditch attempt to take them out before he turned his killing efforts on Seth.

But that didn't happen.

"This isn't over," Sonny said, adding some vicious profanity.

And he took off running.

Since Rosalie was flat on the ground, at first she didn't understand why Austin practically jumped off her. And then she lifted her head and saw what was happening.

No!

Sonny was getting away, and worse, he was running in

the same direction as the woman with the baby. If Sonny caught up with them, he might carry through on his death order, and the baby could be hurt in the process.

"We have to stop him," Rosalie insisted.

Even though Austin tried to take her by the arm and stop her, she threw off his grip and instead got him moving after Sonny.

"There might be other gunmen out there," Austin reminded her.

The thought of it spiked her heart even more, but she couldn't let Sonny take this fight to Sadie. Thankfully, Austin must have understood that because he finally gave up struggling with her and moved ahead of her so he could quicken the pace.

"We're here!" Austin shouted over his shoulder.

Rosalie glanced back and saw Seth running after them. Good.

They might need an extra gun or two before this was over. Also the sirens were close now, probably right on the road where Austin had left the car. If there were any of Sonny's goons on that side of the clearing, Cooper and Colt could take care of them.

Austin didn't wait for Seth to catch up. He kept her moving until they reached a thick clump of trees, and he pulled her behind them with him.

"Sonny could be waiting somewhere to ambush us," Austin whispered.

That put her heart right back in her throat. It was exactly the sort of thing that scum like Sonny would do. Still, they couldn't just stand there and wait because if his plans weren't to ambush them, then he was escaping.

That couldn't happen.

If he got away, the danger would just continue, and

worse, she might never get Sadie back. If Sonny managed to get his hands on Sadie again, he would no doubt make sure Rosalie never found her.

Austin and she waited, the wind and the sleet swiping at them. Mercy, it was so cold, and her baby was out there in this with a killer on her trail.

"Any sign of Sonny?" Seth asked when he hurried into the trees with them.

Austin had to shake his head. All of them were breathing through their mouths now. All of them on edge and primed for a fight.

"We can't wait any longer," she insisted, figuring she would get an argument from at least one of them.

She didn't.

Austin motioned for Seth to go to the left, and he motioned for her to follow him to the right. They fanned out, looking and listening for any sign of Sonny or another of his hired guns.

Both Austin and Seth turned on their phones and used the light to have a look at the ground. Rosalie didn't see anything, but Austin must have because he gestured at Seth again, and they took off, heading deeper into the woods.

Rosalie tried to pick through all the sounds. The bitter wind, their footsteps crunching onto the icy ground and her own heartbeat. She hoped to hear something that would help them find Sadie.

But there was nothing.

They just continued to work their way through the clutter of trees and shrubs while Austin followed some kind of tracks that she couldn't even see.

"It'll be okay," Austin whispered to her.

It took her a moment to realize the reason he said that

was because she had a death grip on his shoulder. Rosalie eased back her fingers a little, but there was nothing she could do to ease the tension in her body.

Or forget what she'd said to Austin earlier.

I love you.

Judging from the look he'd given her, he'd been just as surprised by it as she had been.

But it was true.

It had taken their near deaths for her to come to that realization, and the timing couldn't have been worse. When this was over and Sadie and everyone else was safe, Rosalie needed to make sure that her saying "I love you" didn't mean anything.

Well, nothing except that she meant it and would probably get her heart broken.

Austin hadn't given her even a hint that he was ready for a relationship. Yes, they'd had sex, but again, that'd happened after yet another nightmare attack. She didn't want that to have been the reason he'd landed in bed with her, but she had to accept that it had played a big part in it.

And that his feelings weren't the same as hers.

Soon, after she had her baby in her arms, she could work that all out. If Austin wanted to work it out, that is. It was entirely possible that once Sadie was safe and Sonny was behind bars, that Austin would leave and go back to his own life.

That didn't help soothe her thoughts any.

Of course, there was nothing about this situation that was *soothing*. They were literally on a life-and-death run to save her baby, and if they didn't get lucky, it was a race they might lose.

They kept moving, the air so cold that she thought

maybe her breath had frozen. Austin finally stopped, lifted his hand and pointed toward a pair of oaks just ahead.

Seth nodded.

Rosalie didn't immediately see what had captured their attention. Not until she caught a glimpse of the movement. It looked to be the sleeve of a man's coat.

Maybe Sonny's.

She expected Seth and Austin to move closer to try to capture him. But they didn't. They stayed put, their gazes firing all around them.

And she soon figured out why.

The rush of movement came from their right. A blur of motion.

Sonny.

He ducked behind some shrubs but not before Rosalie saw that he wasn't wearing a coat. That meant he'd likely planted his coat as some kind of trap to lure them out. Thank God Austin and Seth hadn't fallen for it because her instincts had been to go after it and find Sonny.

"Get all the way down on the ground," Austin whispered to her.

It was an effort with her tight, frozen muscles. The moment Rosalie managed to do as he'd said, Austin took off.

Sweet heaven.

She hadn't expected that and didn't want him running right into the path of Sonny's gun.

There were footsteps to her left, and while her brother stayed low, Seth made his way to her. He hovered over her, waiting. Rosalie waited, too, and each second seemed to take an eternity. It sickened her to think of Austin out there, trying to finish this fight, but there was no other choice. She wondered if he knew just how thankful—and terrified—she was that he was willing to risk everything.

"What the hell?" Sonny snarled.

She lifted her head just enough to see Austin launch himself at the man. He'd obviously circled around Sonny and sneaked up on him. Now they were in the middle of another fight.

"Stay here," Seth told her, and he raced toward Austin and Sonny.

There was no way she could stay put, but Rosalie did keep cover behind the trees as she made her way toward Seth and Austin. She certainly didn't want to get close enough to Sonny to let him grab her and use her as a human shield again.

However, she saw something that caused the skin to crawl on the back of her neck.

Sonny had his gun aimed right at Austin.

"No!" she screamed, and she bolted toward them.

Maybe Sonny hadn't expected her to be so close. Or for her scream to be so loud. Either way, he glanced over at her.

It was just a split second.

But it was enough of a distraction for Austin to knock the gun from Sonny's hand. He didn't stop there. Austin shoved him onto the ground and put his own gun right against Sonny's throat.

"Give me a reason to pull this trigger," Austin said, his voice dripping with the emotion of the nightmare that this monster had put them through.

Rosalie walked even closer despite Seth's attempts to stay between her and Sonny. But she wanted to get a look at Sonny's face.

And she did.

He was smiling.

If Seth hadn't caught on to her, Rosalie would have

gone after Sonny to punch him. Or at least she would have tried to do that. How dare this SOB smile after what he'd done to them and so many other families.

"You didn't win," Sonny said, staring at her.

That sent an even icier chill through her. "What do you mean?" she asked at the same time that Austin said, "Ignore him. He'll say anything to get to you because he knows he'll be spending the rest of his life behind bars."

"Yeah," Sonny readily agreed. Still smiling. "But even behind bars, I still win."

Austin hauled Sonny to his feet and used the plastic cuffs that Seth handed him to restrain the man. "How do you figure that?" Austin asked.

"Easy. The woman who had the baby? The nanny," Sonny clarified. "She has orders, and I know for a fact she'll carry them out, especially after what she saw tonight. She'll be afraid for the baby, and she would have headed to the other car that we left just up the trail."

Rosalie put her hand on her chest because it felt as if her heart might beat out of her chest. "What do you mean?" she repeated. "Where is she?"

Sonny's smile stretched across his face. "The nanny is leaving the country as we speak, and she's been given the money and the resources to disappear for good." His smile turned to a taunting laugh. "You'll never see your daughter again."

Chapter Twenty

Austin wanted to believe Sonny was lying about the nanny disappearing with Rosalie's baby. After all, Sonny hadn't told the truth about much else. But this was exactly the kind of stunt a man like him would pull.

The nanny wouldn't be around to testify against him.

And there'd be no absolute proof that he'd ever had Sadie kidnapped. Unless there was some kind of DNA evidence in the car, that is, but Austin was betting Sonny had made sure there wasn't.

"Where's the nanny?" Austin demanded.

Sonny just kept on smiling. A bad mistake. Because Austin didn't even try to hang on to his temper. He punched Sonny in the face. Sonny's head flopped back, and even with the blood spreading across his mouth and teeth, he managed to keep that damn smile.

"Please," Rosalie begged, and Austin could hear every bit of the agony in her voice.

Agony that was clearly giving Sonny pleasure. Since he'd been captured and was about to spend the rest of his life in jail, he wanted Rosalie to have that same life sentence.

"Give me some time alone with him," Seth said. Unlike his sister, there was only one emotion in his voice.

Rage.

Seth would likely beat Sonny within an inch of his life. Austin wanted to do that himself, but time was precious right now, and he didn't want to spend that time trying to get answers from this piece of slime.

"The airport," Austin said. "If she's leaving the country, that's where she'll go. And Sweetwater Springs has a small airport that's only about ten miles away."

That finally got the smile off Sonny's face. Austin hoped that meant he'd hit pay dirt. Of course, he could be doing that to taunt them, to get their hopes up.

Seth took out his phone. "I'll call the airport and see if there are any flights about to leave. If so, I'll have them stop the plane from taking off."

Rosalie shook her head. "But what if she goes somewhere other than Sweetwater Springs?"

"I'll call Colt and have him help," Seth explained. "Cooper and he are out here in the woods looking for the nanny and any other thugs this idiot might have brought with him. If they both start making calls, then we should be able to stop her from getting away."

Good. Austin wanted all the help they could get.

"Go to the local airport," Seth insisted. "If the nanny's not there, if she's headed to San Antonio instead, we'll stop her."

Austin didn't hesitate to take Seth up on his offer. Neither did Rosalie. They started running back toward the car. It seemed to take an eternity to get there, but the second they were inside, Austin started the engine and got them moving.

He hadn't thought it possible, but the roads seemed even slicker than before. Maybe that would work for them.

"The nanny cared about the baby," Austin reminded

Rosalie. "She wouldn't have run if she hadn't. And that means she'll take care driving on these roads."

It could slow the woman down just enough for Austin to catch up with her. Of course, there was another obstacle once they had the nanny and the baby.

What if the little girl wasn't Sadie?

Austin wasn't sure Rosalie would be able to handle that. Wasn't sure he could, either. He didn't know Sadie. Had never held her in his arms the way Rosalie had, but it would crush him to have her disappear.

He didn't want to think about what it would do to Rosalie.

"Seth should have called by now," she mumbled.

She sounded on the verge of panicking, and he couldn't blame her. The stakes were sky-high right now, and with the road conditions, they were still about eight minutes out from the airport.

"Back in the woods, you told me that you loved me," he said.

Yeah, the timing sucked for this particular conversation, but it might stop them both from losing their minds. Or maybe it would just add to it, he amended when he saw the flash of surprise in Rosalie's eyes.

"You didn't mean it," he concluded. "I get it. Adrenaline. Heat-of-the-moment kind of thing—"

"I meant it."

Oh.

That gave him a jolt of emotions. All good ones. Despite the hell they'd just been through, he found himself smiling. Judging from Rosalie's expression, that didn't help settle her nerves.

"It doesn't make things better," Rosalie continued before he could gather his thoughts and answer her. "Nor easier. Just the opposite—it complicates things. And for the record, I don't expect you to return the feelings. In fact, I'm not sure I want you to."

Well, that caused his smile to go south. Austin shook his head, sure he was missing something that should be obvious.

"You don't want me to love you?" he came right out and asked.

She huffed.

Yep, this clearly fell into the obvious category, and he was too thickheaded to figure it out. He was about to ask her to spell things out for him, but his phone rang, and he saw Seth's name on the screen when he took it from his pocket. So that he could keep both hands on the steering wheel, Austin put the call on speaker and gave the phone to Rosalie.

"Please tell me you're close to the airport," Seth snapped.

"About three or four minutes out. Why?" And judging from the sense of urgency in Seth's voice, Austin was afraid he wasn't going to like the answer.

"Because there's a small plane about to take off, and I believe the nanny and baby are on it."

"Oh, God," Rosalie mumbled. "Were you able to stop it?"

"Yeah, but there might be another problem. There's a lone air traffic controller running the place this time of night, and he just radioed for the pilot to abort takeoff. That doesn't mean the nanny won't just get off the plane, get back in the car and head elsewhere."

Rosalie repeated that *Oh, God.*

"I'm hurrying," Austin assured Seth. He ended the

call so he could focus on getting them to the airport in one piece.

The sleet kept coming at them, pelting the windshield and making it hard to see. It didn't help that Rosalie's breath was gusting now, much as it'd been when she was facing down a killer like Sonny.

Of course, these stakes were even higher now.

She could lose her baby forever.

Austin took the turn to the airport. Too fast. But thankfully, he didn't go into a skid. He managed to keep the car on the road, heading straight toward the small metal hangar that sat just off the runway. The moment he pulled in front of it, he saw the plane.

Thank heaven.

It hadn't taken off, but the engine was still running. If necessary, he'd drive the car in front of the plane to stop it from taking off.

"There," Rosalie said, pointing to the side of the hangar.

Austin looked in that direction and spotted an SUV, similar to the one that Sonny had used to get to the woods. There was white steam coming from the exhaust pipe, which meant that engine, too, was on.

Before Austin could bring his car to a full stop, Rosalie bolted out, making a beeline toward the SUV.

"Wait!" Austin called out to her, but just as he'd expected, she didn't listen. Too bad because Sonny could have a hired gun waiting in there.

Or worse.

Maybe the nanny wasn't even here at the airport with the baby. Maybe this was another of Sonny's tricks to lure them to a spot where they could be gunned down. It wouldn't get him off the hook with the felony charges, but Sonny might take pleasure in their suffering.

Austin threw the car into Park, drew his gun and got out so he could hurry after Rosalie. However, before he could get to her, she yanked open the SUV door on the driver's side.

And she froze.

Austin could have sworn his heart froze, too, because he was terrified that she was looking down the barrel of a killer's gun. He got his own gun ready and took aim the moment that he came to a stop.

But it was no killer staring back at them.

It was the woman they'd seen in the woods. Midfifties with gray hair and a thin build. She was alone. Well, maybe. She certainly wasn't holding the baby, and there was no thug in the seat next to her.

That put a knot in Austin's gut.

Until he glanced in the back and saw the infant seat. It was facing the rear of the SUV, and he couldn't tell if it was empty or not, but he'd soon remedy that. Austin threw open the rear door.

And there she was.

A beautiful sleeping baby.

She was snuggled into thick blankets, and because the car's heater was on high, she didn't appear to be cold.

"Don't hurt her," the woman insisted, and she jumped from the car to try to push Austin away. He held his ground, but she just kept on pushing despite the fact he outsized her and was armed.

"He won't hurt her," Rosalie said. "We're here to save her."

She eased onto the backseat next to the baby. With her fingers trembling, she reached out and touched the baby's hand. Rosalie's breath hitched in her throat, and the tears came. Austin wanted to go to her, to hold her, to share what he hoped was about to be a happy reunion, but he had some business to settle first.

"Who are you?" the woman demanded.

"Austin Duran, and this is Rosalie McKinnon. Now, who the heck are you?" He used his FBI tone even though he wasn't sure it was necessary. The woman seemed to be trying to protect the baby, and her size didn't make her much of a threat.

"Laura Keels," she said, and her wary gaze went from him to Rosalie. Austin expected her to try to stop Rosalie from touching the baby, but she didn't. "Did you say your name was McKinnon?" she asked.

Rosalie nodded, but she didn't take her attention off the baby. She eased the baby from the seat and took her into her arms.

"McKinnon," the nanny said once more, and she turned to grab something from the car.

Austin didn't let that happen. He caught on to her and put her against the door the way he would any criminal suspect.

"I don't have a gun," she insisted. "But I do need to show you something. It's in my wallet in the diaper bag on the passenger's seat."

There was indeed a diaper bag on the seat, and while he didn't see a weapon, he had no intentions of letting her get to her wallet to show them anything. Not yet, anyway.

"I need answers. Why were you working for a man like Sonny?" Austin asked.

She frantically shook her head. "I didn't know he was violent. I didn't know he'd done anything wrong. Please tell me he's under arrest."

"He is."

It was hard to tell if Laura was telling the truth, so he motioned for her to continue.

"I'm a nanny. I've been one for over thirty years, and when Sonny contacted a former employer and offered me a job, I took it. He brought me the baby eleven months ago, and I've had her ever since. I've cared for her just as I would all the babies I've loved and raised over the years."

"And you didn't wonder if the baby had been kidnapped or stolen?" Austin snapped.

Rosalie kept the baby cuddled in her arms, but she looked up at Laura, obviously waiting for the answer to that.

"Of course not," Laura insisted. "Sonny said the baby's father was a drug lord. A very dangerous man. And that the baby's mother had gone into hiding and that she'd be back to claim the child when it was safe."

Austin huffed. "You believed that?"

"I didn't have any reason not to." Laura paused, her own tears now streaming down her cheeks. "Not until tonight. Not until I saw what a violent man Sonny really was. He said we were only going to see the baby's mother. I didn't know there'd be guns and shooting."

"Did Sonny hurt the baby?" Rosalie asked. "Did he touch her?"

Laura's eyes widened. "No. God, no. I would have never let that happen. I cared for her, kept her safe until she could be reunited with her mother."

Rosalie swallowed hard. "I believe I am her mother."

He braced himself for Laura to deny that. But she didn't. She looked at him again. "I need to get something out of my wallet. It's something you need to see."

Austin kept his gun on her and finally nodded. Laura

didn't make any fast moves, probably because he didn't seem too friendly, and once she'd taken the wallet from the diaper bag, Laura pulled out what appeared to be a small strip of plastic.

Thanks to the interior lights of the car, he saw that it was the kind of bracelet that hospitals put on newborns. It was pink and there was something written on it.

McKinnon Baby Girl.

"Room 112," he read from the bracelet along with the date.

Sadie's birthday.

Rosalie's breath shattered, and the sound she made— relief mixed with joy—caused the baby to stir.

"It's Sadie," Rosalie managed to say. She pressed a flurry of kisses on the baby's face. "That's the date she was born, and that's the room I was in at the hospital. She's mine. She's really mine."

Yeah. They would need to do a DNA test, of course, but it would only verify what they already knew. That this was Rosalie's daughter.

Just as a mom would do with a newborn, Rosalie eased back the blanket, checking for fingers and toes. They were all there, and Sadie looked like a perfectly healthy child.

"I took care of her," Laura repeated. "She's a good baby, but I always knew that she needed her mom and dad. You'll take good care of her, too."

It wasn't a question, but Austin nodded. No doubt about it. He would take care of her and Rosalie.

If Rosalie let him, that is.

He clearly had some things to work out with her, especially that part about her not wanting him to love her. Austin still wasn't sure how to get around that.

His phone rang. It was Seth, again. And Austin realized he should have already called him with an update since Seth would be worried about his sister. The reunion had obviously distracted him.

"Rosalie's fine," Austin said the moment he answered. "We found the nanny in time." And he had to clear away the lump in his throat when he saw the way that Rosalie was looking at her daughter. "The baby is Sadie."

Seth made a sharp sound of relief. "You're sure?"

"Yeah, we have proof."

Another sound of relief. "How's Rosalie handling that?"

"About the way you'd think." Her face was practically glowing from the love that was there. "The nanny's still here, and I'm hoping once you're finished booking Sonny that you can take her statement."

"Colt and Cooper can deal with this sack of slime," Seth insisted. "Oh, and I just got off the phone with headquarters. You'll get the collar for Sonny so you'll be getting your badge back. My advice is to take a day or two, though."

That wasn't even on Austin's radar right now, but he was sure later he'd appreciate that. Especially since working out of the San Antonio office would keep him close to Rosalie.

And he'd definitely take that time off, maybe more than a day or two.

"I'm on the way to have that chat with the nanny," Seth said, and with that, he hung up.

Good. Austin was glad that Seth would help tying up the loose ends because he had something of his own that he had to finish. He started with Laura.

"I need to check you for weapons," he said, figuring he wouldn't find any. And he didn't. Nor did the woman object to the search. When he was done, he tipped his head to the hangar.

"Wait in there. Agent Calder from the FBI will be here soon to ask you some questions."

She shook her head again, and new tears sprang up. "I swear I didn't know I was doing anything wrong."

"That's what you need to tell Agent Calder. He'll take your statement, and if you know anything that can add to our case against Sonny, then tell him that, too."

Though more wouldn't be necessary. Sonny had confessed to so many felonies that he'd be locked away for life. As a minimum. But if they could also pin Janice's murder on him, then he might get the death penalty.

Laura gave a shaky nod, started toward the hangar but then looked into the car at Rosalie. "Can I kiss her goodbye?" Laura asked.

He could see Rosalie think about it, probably because she wasn't ready to give up another moment with her baby, but she finally motioned for Laura to come closer. The nanny leaned down and kissed the top of Sadie's head.

"She doesn't like peas but loves country music," Laura added to Rosalie. "If she gets fussy at night, just put on George Strait. That'll soothe her right down. Oh, she can crawl anywhere, fast, and I think she might be walking by the new year."

Rosalie hung on to each word. Precious little bits of information for things that'd she wanted to know about her baby.

"I think that's everything, but if you got any questions, I'll give Agent Calder my number so you know how to get in touch with me."

Rosalie nodded.

"Be a good girl for your mama," Laura said softly to the baby.

Sadie smiled. "Mama."

That put some fresh tears in Rosalie's eyes, too.

"I taught her to say that," Laura explained, "because I figured one day you'd finally get to see her, and you'd want to hear her say it to you."

Rosalie's breath fluttered. "I do. Thank you for taking such good care of her."

The women's gazes met, and Laura brushed a kiss on Rosalie's cheek, as well, before she started toward the hangar. The moment she was away from them, Austin got into the car with Rosalie and Sadie and closed the door. Not because he thought Laura was a threat but because he wanted to keep Sadie warm.

Sadie turned and looked at him. Studying him, actually, as if trying to figure out who he was. At least she didn't seem frightened of him.

"I'm Austin," he said, though it seemed silly to introduce himself to a baby.

Still, Sadie must have liked it because she smiled at him, and he could have sworn that his heart doubled in size. Man, how was it possible to love someone this much after just one look at her?

Rosalie looked at him, smiled, too, and kissed Sadie's fingers when the baby touched Rosalie's mouth. "Thank you for helping me find her."

You're welcome was the standard response, but Rosalie and he were well past that.

He hoped.

"You said you didn't want me to love you," Austin reminded her.

Surprise flashed through Rosalie's eyes, and she fumbled with whatever she was trying to say to him.

Austin decided to help her along with that fumbling. "I think you meant you didn't want me to feel obligated. And I don't. It wasn't obligation, the danger or the spent adrenaline that had me taking you to bed."

Everything stilled, as if the earth itself was holding its breath and waiting for him to finish. Rosalie was certainly waiting, and her mouth had dropped open a little. Sadie was touching his chin. All in all, it was a perfect moment to say what he wanted to say.

"Rosalie, I took you to bed because I'm in love with you."

There it was, all out in the open.

Well, almost.

"And I want you to marry me so that you, Sadie and I can be a family," Austin added.

Rosalie kept staring at him, her mouth still open.

Sadie playfully pinched his nose.

Then, Rosalie's breath swooshed out, and she moved so fast to kiss him that Austin didn't even see it coming. But he sure as heck felt it. That kiss did a lot more than just warm him from head to toe. It gave him the answer he wanted. Still, Austin needed to hear the words.

"Will you marry me?" he repeated with his mouth still against Rosalie's.

She kissed him, but he could feel her smiling while she did it. "I love you with all my heart, so my answer is yes. Yes. Yes. I'll marry you."

He would have been happy with just one yes, but he did like her enthusiasm.

Apparently, so did Sadie, because she clapped her hands.

It was yet another perfect moment. Austin was betting there'd be plenty more times just like this one.

A lifetime of them, in fact.

He gathered Rosalie and Sadie into his arms and was ready to start that new life with both of them.

* * * * *

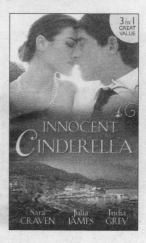